D1258556

TAKE
BUDAPEST!

TAKE BUDAPEST!

THE STRUGGLE FOR HUNGARY, AUTUMN 1944

KAMEN NEVENKIN

First published 2012

by Spellmount, an imprint of The History Press
The Mill, Brimscombe Port
Stroud, Gloucestershire, GL5 2QG
www.thehistorypress.co.uk

© Kamen Nevenkin, 2012

British Library Cataloguing in Publication Data.
A catalogue record for this book is available from the British
Library.

ISBN 978 0 7524 6631 6

Typesetting and origination by The History Press
Printed in Great Britain

CONTENTS

ACKNOWLEDGEMENTS

I offer my grateful thanks to the following: Alexey Filippenkov, Alexey Isaev, Artyom Astafiev (Russia); David Glantz (USA); Dénes Bernád (Hungary); Didier Laugier (France); Jan-Hendrik Wendler (Germany); Kaloyan Matev (Bulgaria); László Némedi (Hungary); Markus Reisner (Austria); Michael Wood (United Kingdom); Mikhail Filippenkov (Russia); Mirko Bayerl (Sweden); Orlin Nevenkin (Bulgaria and Belguim); Paweł Sembrat (Poland); Rashit Musin (Russia); Ron Klages (USA) who passed away in 2007; Shingo Hikino (Japan); Stefano di Giusto (Italy and Belgium); Thomas Peters, Tom Houlihan (USA).

FOREWORD

Few military operations conducted during the Soviet-German War 1941–1945 had more varied dimensions and significance than the Red Army's offensive in Hungary, which began in October 1944, and the ensuing siege of Hungary's capital, Budapest, on the Danube river. Militarily, this offensive, together with the siege of Budapest and German counteractions designed to restore its fortunes in the Danube basin, represented the culminating stage of offensive operations the Soviet Army began in August 1944 to drive Axis forces from the entire Balkans region. Politically, the offensive was a Soviet attempt to continue the dissolution of Hitler's Axis alliance by driving Hungary from the war. Economically, the offensive began a five-month-long struggle for possession of Budapest and the nearby vital oilfields of the Lake Balaton region, which provided much of the fuel for the panzers and aircraft of Hitler's Army and Luftwaffe. Underscoring the significance of this and other operations in Hungary and Austria, in early February 1945 Stalin's Red Army would shift the focal point of its strategic offensive operations away from the approaches to Berlin and towards western Hungary and Vienna in the heart of the strategically vital Danube basin.

Kamen Nevenkin's new book examines one aspect of this five-month struggle, specifically, the Red Army's attempts to reach and seize Budapest by a coup de main in late October and early November 1944. After accurately detailing both Hitler's and Stalin's fixation on Budapest, as well as their respective strategies for seizing or retaining the region, Nevenkin provides a riveting narrative of the ensuing combat during the Red Army's initial drive to capture the city. He exploits a wide range of newly available Russian archival materials and long-existing but only weakly exploited German unit records, juxtaposed against a host of old and new memoirs by commanders and private soldiers alike, to track the course of the offensive during late October and early November from both the German and the Soviet perspectives. Unlike previous accounts, where known German formations fought against ghostlike Russian masses, this study brings alive the actions of specific forces on specific days and the successes and frustrations experienced by each side and their commanders and soldiers.

This is operational military history at its best, where commanders lead identifiable forces, successfully or unsuccessfully, on a recognisable battlefield of villages, towns, and open spaces. On this battlefield, as always, the customary fog of war rules, replete with examples of successes, failures, surprises, and inevitable human frustration. This lively narrative is backed up by clear and understandable maps so necessary to dispel the fog and explain to the reader what actually happened and why.

This reader hopes that this volume is only the first of many intended to lift the veil on all of the operations conducted in the Budapest region from their beginning to their end in March 1945.

David M. Glantz
Carlisle, Pennsylvania

[Before retiring from the US Army in December 1993, Colonel David M. Glantz served for over 30 years in various field artillery, intelligence, teaching, and research assignments in Europe and Vietnam, taught at the United States Military Academy, the Combat Studies Institute and Army War College. He founded and directed the US Army's Foreign (Soviet) Military Studies Office. He has written or co-authored more than 60 books as well as hundreds of articles on Soviet military strategy, intelligence, and deception and the history of the Red Army, Soviet military history, and World War II.]

1

LIKE CLAUSEWITZ; ALMOST

1

Hitler had always shared the view of Clausewitz that 'war is a continuation of politics by different means.' During the war he repeatedly maintained the primacy of political over military considerations in the formulation of his strategic plans. This became especially evident in the last year of the war when the Führer began increasingly to concentrate his armoured reserves in certain regions in order to achieve given political objectives. In late 1944 there were two such areas: Hungary and the Ardennes. Even though these battlefields were geographically distant, in Hitler's mind they were tightly bounded to each other by one thing: oil.

Hitler still believed that his forces might be able to stand fast for a long time if they could deliver a heavy blow in the West before the end of the year. One such successful offensive, he hoped, would cause a split among the Allies and force London and Washington to seek a separate peace with Germany. In turn, this would allow the Third Reich to concentrate its efforts exclusively on the Eastern Front. The Führer also hoped that a successful outcome of the attack in the Ardennes would buy more time for the armament industry to produce enough of the new advanced weapons – heavy tanks, jet aircraft, diesel-electric submarines, V2 ballistic missiles – and to complete the development programs of other 'wonder weapons', such as the nuclear bomb.

That autumn the bad weather was producing rain, fog and low-lying clouds that grounded the mighty Allied Air Force and caused supply problems for Eisenhower's forces. The front line, which now was running along the prewar German border, was far shorter than it had been on the eve of the Normandy landing. This was advantageous for the Germans: it eased supply difficulties, increased manoeuvrability, made them less vulnerable to enemy air attacks and less dependent on radio communications (and therefore decreased the impact of Ultra interceptions). It seemed to Hitler that fate itself had sent him this grey autumn and that a favourable opportunity had come at last to realise his plans for a major offensive.

The planning began in mid-September and on 8 October Colonel-General Jodl, the Chief of Staff of the High Command of the Armed Forces (OKW), presented a draft plan for the attack to be mounted in the end of November.[1] A mighty force of 32 divisions (including 12 panzer and panzer-grenadier) would strike through the Ardennes towards Antwerp, capturing Brussels in the process. The effect of this would be to entrap and destroy all of the Allied forces operating in the Low Countries. It was clear that the American lines would be breached, but the rapid exploitation of the initial success depended heavily on the available fuel stocks.[2] And they were scarce. So scarce that the German commanders had to rely on captured fuel dumps to fulfil the planned objectives.

The Third Reich was fuel starved and the signs were everywhere. In the West the daily allowance of gasoline dropped to about 5 tons per division; in the Balkans the retreating Army Groups F and E could hardly count on any deliveries of fuel for the first fortnight of November and drastic economy measures were imposed; in Italy some panzer units were getting 7 per cent or less of their authorised gasoline allocation; on the Eastern Front the stocks of aviation spirit were at so low a level that the Luftwaffe could no longer provide adequate air support to the ground forces; the Kriegsmarine could maintain the U-Boat warfare at its present level only at the expense of the allocations of diesel fuel to the surface warships.[3]

The training of the reserves was also deeply affected. The practical exercises in the SS-panzer divisions of *Oberstgruppenführer* Sepp Dietrich's 6 Panzer-Army, which was destined to be the principal strike force for the impending offensive in the West, were severely hampered by the fuel shortages; there was virtually no fuel for tactical training or for the training of the drivers.[4] The same applied to the Luftwaffe and Kriegsmarine, where the training hours of the pilots and crews were reduced.[5] The lack of fuel could be sensed even more tangibly in the everyday life of Nazi Germany: road and water transport almost ceased, the production of war material, industrial and agricultural goods declined and even paramilitary organisations, such as *Organisation Todt* and *Reichsarbeitsdienst* (RAD), functioned with great difficulty. Still worse, although fighter aircraft production had reached its climax in September 1944 (3031 single-engine fighters were delivered),[6] the Air Fleet 'Reich' was less and less capable of defending the towns and factories, because there wasn't enough fuel. The pilots showed courage and self-sacrifice, but were unable to appear in any significant strength to cause any serious damage to the Allied bomber armadas.

2

Only a few months earlier the fuel situation had been quite comfortable for the Germans. Then the oil supplies of the Third Reich had been coming from two different sources: imports and crude or/and finished petroleum products and gasoline produced by the powerful German chemical industry through synthesis of coal, air and water as raw materials. The natural oil obtained from the oilfields in Romania (Ploieşti), Hungary (Nagykanizsa), Austria (Zisterdorf), Lower Saxony (Harz region) and Galicia (Drogobycz), together with production from the synthetic oil industry, guaranteed that the Wehrmacht could still operate efficiently despite the increasing pressure on all fronts. Everything changed in the spring of 1944 when the Axis chemical and oil industries were selected as a top priority target by the Allied Bomber Command and from the beginning of April 1944 were hit hard. During the summer the production of the chemical works decreased considerably, while the normal functioning of the Ploieşti installations literally ceased and by the time the Soviets seized the area at the end of August, the Romanian oilfields had only a symbolic significance and were making little practical contribution to the Nazi war effort.

The effect of the bombing raids was cumulative. During an interrogation held shortly after the war, Albert Speer, the Hitler's Minister of armaments, confessed:

> The shortage of liquid fuel first made itself felt in the aviation categories. The stocks of Romanian natural oil in Germany enabled the manufacture of both motor spirit and diesel fuels to be continued for several months further.
>
> In considering this question account must be taken of the OKW reserve and at the same time of the reduction in the quantities in circulation.

In the Luftwaffe the shortage of liquid fuel became insupportable from September 1944 onwards, as from that date the allocation was cut down to 30,000 tons a month, whereas the monthly requirements amounted to between 160,000 and 180,000 tons. So far as the Army was concerned, the shortage of liquid fuel, which in this case was also due to supply difficulties, first became catastrophic at the time of the winter offensive of 16 December 1944...[7]

Speer did his best to show the Führer the implications of the catastrophe. On 30 August he sent the following top-secret report to Hitler:

My Führer,

The last air attacks have again hit the most important chemical works heavily. Thereby the three hydrogenation plants, Leuna, Breux and Poelitz, although only recently in commission again, have been brought to a complete standstill for some weeks.

As the home defence against enemy air attacks promises no appreciably greater results in September as against August, chemical (oil) production in September must now be considerably decreased.

Nevertheless, no effort will be spared to restore the hydrogenation plants so that past production, at least, can be made possible in a short time.

The effect of these new raids on the entire chemical industry are extraordinary, as severe shortages will occur not only in liquid fuels but also in various other important fields of chemistry ...

With these results the enemy has hit the chemical industry so heavily that only by abnormal changes in the conditions is there any hope for the retention of the bases for powder and explosives (Methanol), Buna (Methanol and nitrogen for explosives and agriculture). At the same time the loss in carburettor and diesel fuels is so widespread that even the severest measures will not be able to prevent bad effects on the mobility of the troops at the front.

The possibility of moving troops at the front will therefore be so restricted that planned operations in October will no longer be able to take place. With this fuel situation offensive moves will be impossible.

The flow necessary for the supply of the troops and the home country will therefore be paralysed in the late autumn of this year, since substitute fuels, such as producer gas, are also inadequate to provide the essential help in all sectors ...

If the attacks on the chemical industry continue in the same strength and with the same precision in September as in August, the output of the chemical industry will drop still further and the last stocks will be consumed.

This means that those materials which are necessary for the continuation of modern war will be lacking in the most important fields.[8]

Another report followed shortly afterwards. Even though it was dealing with several important issues, like the shortages of metal-containing ores, it once again was focused predominantly on the fuel situation. Speer guaranteed that if adequate air cover was provided, the following quantities would be delivered to the Wehrmacht every month from October onwards:

aviation fuel	100,000 tons
J2 fuel for jet aircraft	15,000 tons
carburettor fuel	95,000 tons
diesel fuel	68,000 tons
heating fuel	80,000 tons

But what is most important for us in the document in question is that, perhaps for the first time, the importance of the Hungarian oilfields was underlined; according to Speer, the Magyar state could deliver 75,000 tons of crude oil every month.[9] The Ploieşti area had just been lost and from that moment on 'the Hungarian oilfields' would become for Hitler a magic talisman against which no one could argue. Before long the Nagykanizsa oil region would lose its simple geographical meaning and turn into a spell that could work miracles.

In September the Wehrmacht finally managed to stabilise the battlefronts in the East, Italy and the West; Hitler's most urgent problem now became how to safeguard the rapidly decreasing stocks of fuel. There were further air raids on the chemical plants and for some time the output ceased completely. Nevertheless, it was the Allies who gave the Führer a breathing space. In spite of the orders of the Combined Chiefs of Staff, during September and October only 10 per cent of the bomb tonnage was dropped over oil targets compared with more than 25 per cent in July and August.[10] This allowed Speer to rebuild the oil installations and to increase production. In November it amounted roughly to 96,000 tons, which was only one third of what had been produced in April but it was a major improvement that allowed Hitler, by imposing strict economies, to conserve his stocks and to postpone the crisis for a short while. Very welcome assistance was provided by the bad weather, which that autumn arrived unexpectedly early and gave the oil installations in the Eastern Germany and Czechoslovakia air cover that was beyond the capabilities of the Luftwaffe.[11] Stabilisation of the frontlines was of course a blessing. In the summer the Wehrmacht had needed more than 300,000 tons of motor fuel and aviation spirit per month; in October, when warfare shifted predominantly to static defence, only about 97,000 tons were consumed.[12]

Speer's September report expressed a little bit more optimism than in the previous month. On 5 October he submitted a document to Hitler where once again the importance of the Hungarian oil region was emphasised:

My Führer,

After the last attacks on the hydrogenation plants and refineries repair of those works is still found to be possible in a relatively short time as the number of men employed on this work has been increased.

If no new attacks take place we may count in October on the following quantities, which include the fuel gained from the German and Hungarian mineral oil production:

Aviation fuel (September production: 9400 tons)	64,000 tons
Carburettor fuel (September: 48,400 tons)	60,600 tons
Diesel fuel (September: 77,300 tons)	100,300 tons

… The troops will forego fighter support, which cannot give them essential relief nowadays, if they know that in this way their fuel basis is secured and that munition supplies will not cease owing to lack of powder and explosives.

Front officers in the West, whose supplies of weapons, tanks and munition have improved during the last fortnight, know only one concern and question: Will it be possible to supply the fuel for future operations or will the air attacks of the enemy prevent this? …[13]

The output of the Hungarian oilfields at Nagykanizsa gradually increased and reached its wartime peak in 1943, when 837,710 tons were produced.[14] However, already in the next year, due to the natural run-down of the available oil, the accelerated wear and tear on machinery, the decrease in productivity and last but not least, by Allied bombing, the production started to decline. During the spring and the summer of 1944 the Magyar oil installations and refineries, as well those in Austria, became one of the priority targets of the Allied Air Forces. This approach proved to be effective; of the seven big refineries producing a yearly 1,025,000 tons of oil, five were almost completely out of commission by November 1944.[15] By the end of September the Bomber Command considered its work done and in October the Allied Intelligence reported the following:

> Austria: Only a small quantity of crude oil has been processed during the month. Repairs to several refineries are being pressed forward; two of them may be ready to resume operations shortly.
> Hungary: All the refineries are out of operation or in Russian hands.[16]

In October and November the Allied bombers made no attacks on oil targets outside the Ruhr-Rhineland area and this definitely had given respite to Hitler and further increased the worth of the Nagykanizsa and Zisterdorf oilfields in his eyes. We may judge the importance of the Hungarian oil for the Nazi war machine from the following words from Speer during his post-war interrogation:

> It proved possible to maintain a minimum production of motor spirit and diesel oil right up to the end of the war because the supply of crude, including that from the Hungarian oil fields, was sufficient to produce 60,000 tons of each type of fuel per month.[17]

But for the Führer the value of the Hungarian plain was not limited to the oilfields only. The Székesfehérvár region was the German industry's primary supplier of bauxite, a heterogeneous, naturally occurring material from which aluminum is produced. The Úrkút mine, just west of Veszprém, was the Third Reich's last remaining source of manganese, a key component in iron and steel making. Magyar industry, of which the major plants were grouped in the northern and northwestern parts of the country, as well in and around Budapest, was closely bound to Germany. But Hungary has long been an agricultural country and its importance as a food exporter was well known to the Führer; in 1944 alone 50,000 tons of meat were 'sold' by Budapest to its 'partner'.[18] In the autumn of 1944 Hungary was Germany's last significant European ally and as such granted protection to the southern lands of the Reich in general and in particular to the 'Vienna gate', the Austrian armament industry and the Zisterdorf oilfields.

3

Hitler had recognised the geopolitical importance of Hungary long ago. During a visit Horthy paid to the Wolfschanze HQ in East Prussia, the Führer made the following prophetic statement to the Magyar regent: 'The war would be lost should the Russians overrun the Hungarian plants.'[19] It is no wonder that when he learned about the intentions of Budapest to leave the war, Hitler ordered his troops to occupy Hungary and in March 1944 forced Horthy to appoint a collaborationist government under the 'narrow-minded' Lieutenant-General Döme Sztójay, a long-serving ambassador to Berlin. But the new Hungarian cabinet only nominally governed the country; the Austrian-born Führer was traditionally suspicious[20] towards the Hungarians and, in order to impose full control over his ally, appointed a staff of his own trusted men.

SS-*Standartenführer* Dr Edmund Veesenmayer, a former high-school teacher from Bavaria, became the actual ruler of the state (his official position was 'Minister 1st Class and Plenipotentiary of the Reich in Hungary'). He was 'amongst the best-trained of the party diplomats, an extremely cunning man and, being a Nazi, a worshipper of Hitler and rabidly anti-Semitic. Otherwise he had an excellent bearing and a quick mind.'[21] The other 'key players' were SS-*Obergruppenführer* Dr Otto Winkelmann, a chief of the Police and SS in Hungary (*Höherer SS und Polizeiführer* or HSSPf in short), SS-*Sturmbannführer* Dr Wilhelm Höttl, the head of SD in Hungary, *SS-Standartenführer* Dr Hans Geschke, the chief of the Gestapo in Hungary, SS-*Obergruppenführer* Karl Pfeffer-Wildenbruch, the commander of the Waffen-SS in Hungary (*Befehlshaber der Waffen-SS Ungarn* and the notorious SS-Obersturmbannführer Adolf Eichmann, the chief of the Gestapo's Jewish section. All of them were members of the HSSPf's staff under Winkelmann, who was the direct and personal representative in Hungary of Himmler himself. Furthermore, the members of the HSSPf's staff acted as Himmler's principal liaison officers with the command authorities of the Wehrmacht in Hungary.

Miklós Horthy.

The Gestapo took over the functions of the police and began its bloody activities immediately after the occupation. A number of politicians, statesmen, officers, journalists, academics and other prominent anti-Nazi Hungarians were arrested and sent to the concentration camps. With the help of the leading fascist organisation – Szálasi's Arrow Cross Party – and the Hungarian Gendarmerie, as well as the approval of sections of the Magyar population, massive persecutions of Jews were carried out. Within two months they escalated to deportations of the latter to the extermination camps in Poland and the Reich. Under the supervision of Eichmann, over 450,000 people (in fact almost all of the provincial Jews) were sent to the camps by the beginning of July and of these less than 120,000 survived the war.

The Magyar economy was harnessed to the Axis war effort. A German economic 'expert', a certain Bunzler, remained in Hungary with a large staff. The Jewish-owned plants were taken over by the SS while the others were put under strict German control. 'Internal politics and economic life in Hungary were at the complete mercy of a hopeless war and the German terror, not to mention the unfortunate regime of Sztójay and company,' wrote Géza Lakatos, the last premier-minister of Horthy's era. 'Robbery and looting were the order of the day and the Sztójay government actively helped the systematic plundering of the country's crops and livestock for export to Germany.'[22]

In spite of the efforts of the new regime, the decrease in the Hungarian industrial production, which had been steadily declining since the autumn of the previous year, could not be reversed. The equipment in the plants and factories began to wear out and even the most ruthless exploitation of natural resources could not increase output. The German takeover of 19 March 1944 worsened the economic situation. The costs of the occupation were transferred

Above: These SS-troops of the 22 SS-Cavalry Division stand in the garden of the Royal Palace in Buda after the successful Arrow Cross putsch of 15 October 1944. (Charles Trang)

Left: A Hungarian soldier and an SS-cavalryman have a talk in the aftermath of the Arrow Cross coup near one of the King Tigers of Heavy-Panzer-Battalion 503, Budapest, 16 October 1944. (Charles Trang)

to the Hungarian budget. Mobilisation of the *Honvédség*, the mass deportations of the Jews and sabotage of production by resistance groups, plus the Allied bombing raids, all accelerated the disintegration of the economy.

For Hitler, however, it was still very much worthwhile. During the night conference of 31 July/1 August in *Wolfsschanze*, while discussing the situation in Southeast Europe, he stated:

> Nevertheless, we must meet certain safeguards. The most critical safeguard is and will remain the initial securing of the Hungarian area – the only possible substitute for the sources of food that we lose otherwise, and also a source of many raw materials: bauxite, manganese and so on. But above all for transport purposes – the pre-requisite for the Southeast. Securing the Hungarian area is of essential importance to us – so important that we can't overestimate it at all. We first must think about what in terms of new troop arrangements we can either bring in or build up there, to be able at any time, if necessary, to anticipate or prevent a Hungarian coup d'etat against Herr Horthy.[23]

The mounting crisis in all the European theatres during the summer of 1944 eventually forced Hitler to face the truth that some areas, such as the Balkans, could not be held. That is why in August he asked Speer to analyse how long the war would last if the Third Reich evacuated Finland, Norway, Italy and the Balkans and fall back into the so-called 'minimum economic region'. In the south/southeast, the border of this 'region' was to run along the Alps, the river Sava in Serbia and the river Tisza in Hungary.[24]

In September the final verdict on Hitler's 'minimum economic region' was ready. In many respects this report would map out the German strategy for the rest of the war, which makes it worth summarising:

1) The following areas are considered of critical importance for the industry of the Reich:
a) Southern Norway – 50 per cent of the total supply of Molybdenum and the most significant proportion of ferrosilicon
   Western Slovakia and Hungary/Budapest – major production sites for aircraft assembly and weapon manufacturing factories
b) Hungary – 90 per cent of Bauxite supply
c) Minette area in Lorraine – 22 per cent of steel production

2) The production capacity of the Reich and the following areas:
   Italy (south of the Alps, east of Trieste)
   Croatia (the Sava line)
   Hungary (the Tisza line)
a) Mineral oil – from October to December 1944 for Wehrmacht (including the Hungarian production), monthly
   Aviation fuel – 100,000 tons
   Carburettor fuel – 95,000 tons
   J2 for jet fighters – 15,000 tons
   Diesel fuel – 68,000 tons
   Heating oil – 80,000 tons
b) Bauxite – Aluminium stocks will be exhausted in the fourth quarter of 1944. The aluminium supplies depend on the supplies of bauxite.
   Western Hungary: monthly 75,000 tons = 13,000 tons aluminum content
   In the spring of 1945 in the Upper Danube: 15,000 tons = 2200 tons aluminum content
   Demands of Luftwaffe: 23,000 tons per month

The demand for the fourth quarter of 1944 could be met. In 1945 the output will be reduced by 25 per cent, which will make itself felt in 1946.

c)   Chrome – (85 per cent of the output – for steel-refining)
The main source: New Bulgaria. Stocks in the Reich, 1.9.1944: 33,000 tons.
Monthly demand: 3900 tons, reducible to 3200 tons. Available quantities: for 10 months.
The chrome-dependent military production will phase out in early 1946.

d)   Antimony (alloys of lead) – 70 per cent for accumulators for tanks and submarines, the rest – in the cable manufacturing, ammunition and chemical industry
23 per cent of the output – from Serbia.
Stocks in the Reich, 1.8.1944: 2200 tons.
Monthly delivery from Western Slovakia and Hungary: 150 tons.
Monthly consumption: 400 tons. Estimated availability: 3 years.
Antimony demand 3 months after the cessation of the production of submarine batteries.

e)   Molybdenum –75 per cent for steel-strengthening, 25 per cent for electrical engineering, fuel synthesis and chemical industry.
Stocks in the Reich, 1.7.1944: 400 tons.
Monthly consumption: 74 tons. Total supply from the Balkans and Southern Norway: 76 tons. After the loss of these sources the total monthly supply will be reduced to 21 tons. Reduction of the monthly consumption down to 65 tons is possible. Available quantities: for 9 months. If replaced with tungsten: 13 months. The molybdenum-dependent production will phase out in April 1946.

f)   Nickel Stockpiles, 1.8.1944: 8900 tons. Supply after the loss of Finland and Southern Norway: 200 tons per month. Production in the Reich could be increased to 400 tons per month by December 1945. Full coverage of the needs until the end of 1945, after that only 50 per cent of this quantity could be ensured. One has to take into account that from mid-1946 onwards nickel-dependent production will be reduced by half.

g)   Zinc stockpiles, 1.8.1944: 195,000 tons. Monthly supply: 23,000 tons. Available quantities: for 41 months. Shortages of zinc will occur in the industry by July-August 1948.

h)   Copper stockpiles: 365,000 tons for 27 months.

i)   Lead stockpiles, 1.8.1944: 204,000 tons. Monthly supply: 13,200 tons (excluding the Balkans). Monthly consumption: 18,000 tons. Available quantities: for 42 months (until the spring of 1948).

j)   Ferrosilicon (for steel-strengthening). Total monthly supply: 9735 tons (including 3200 tons from Norway, 335 tons from Sweden and 2,200 tons from Italy). Stockpiles: 14,100 tons. Monthly consumption: 7200 tons. Available quantities (less Norway, Sweden and Italy): for 4½ months.
Alternative: conversion of the carbide ovens in the Reich from the production of Ferrosilicon; required saving of production of 3000 tons of nitrogen per month.

k)   Manganese ore (for steel-strengthening). The production of 2.6 million tons of crude steel monthly requires 7000 tons of manganese ore. These are delivered from

Germany   1155 tons
Slovakia   1750 tons
Hungary   1150 tons

            4055 tons

The difference of 3000 tons could be met till the end of 1946 from the manganese stocks of 86,800 tons. After the loss of Hungary and Slovakia the manganese supplies will last until the end of 1945. The production will start suffering from the lack of manganese by July 1945.

i) Sulphur (dependent on the production of Norway). Stockpiles: 40,000 tons. Monthly consumption: 16,000 tons.

 In 1944 the chemical plants of the Reich will keep producing 7–8000 tons monthly, by the end of 1945 there will be 16,000 tons of sulphur already produced.[25]

By the time the report was completed, the Third Reich had lost the Romanian oil, the Finnish nickel and molybdenum, the French bauxite, the Swedish iron ore and the Balkan chromium and manganese, but Speer estimated that the loss of the peripheral European territories, especially the Balkans, would not immediately paralyse the German war economy. The most serious effects were foreseen in food supplies; the minimum required by the working population would not be ensured in the long run. Regarding industry, Speer's experts estimated that Germany could hold out until early 1946, although not much longer, but only assuming the absence of Allied air raids.[26]

Some of Speer's estimates were based on bizarre calculations. He concluded, for instance, that the copper stocks were satisfactory, but the 450,000-ton stock of copper included 'copper registered but not yet mobilised', e.g. church bells.[27] On the other hand, it had been estimated that bauxite stocks would be exhausted earlier than copper. The situation with so-called special steels was disastrous. Because of the scarcity of steel-alloy metals, the alloy content of armour and gun shells was to be reduced. The production of carbide-core ammunition almost ceased. 'If the present production of special steels is continued, chrome supplies will be exhausted by 1 January 1945,' Speer concluded.[28]

By mid-October the Soviets were about to cross the 'border' of the 'minimum economic region' and their final victory seemed to be close. They did not yet know that the Führer already had made his mind up; Hungary would be the place where he would make his last stand. And Hungary would become the centre of his universe, his last hope for survival, his curse and obsession.

2

AN EXEMPLARY ARRANGEMENT OF LARGE ISSUES

1

Every dictator has his fears and Joseph Stalin was no exception. In the late 1920s, he was afraid that he might lose out in the power struggle with the other 'old Bolsheviks' of Lenin's immediate circle. In the 1930s he worried that opposition to his policies was growing. In the late 1930s, he thought the military was planning a coup against him. But after the victory at Stalingrad Stalin was at least no longer afraid of losing the war; it was evident to everybody that the downfall of the Reich was just a matter of time. From that moment on, only one thing haunted Stalin's waking thoughts and dreams: that his allies, and Churchill in particular, would land somewhere in the Balkans, advance straight to the north and steal a large piece of Europe from him. This scenario never left him for a minute.

These fears were not without foundation. At the Tehran conference in November 1943 an agreement was reached that the Allied offensive of 1944 would take place in Northern France and nowhere else and all plans for a landing in the Balkans or bringing Turkey into the war were rejected. Thus Churchill was kept away from the Soviet southern flank. Nevertheless, in the months that followed the British Premier continued to toy with the idea of reaching Central Europe before Stalin via Austria and the Balkans. Even in September 1944, when the Red Army had already reached the Carpathian basin, Churchill still believed that his idea was realisable:

> I was very anxious to forestall the Russians in certain areas of Central Europe. The Hungarians, for instance, had expressed their intention of resisting the Soviet advance, but would surrender to a British force if it could arrive in time. If the Germans either evacuated Italy or retired to the Alps I much desired that Alexander[1] should be enabled to make his amphibious thrust across the Adriatic, seize and occupy the Istrian peninsula, and try to reach Vienna before the Russians.[2]

This is especially evident in the British plans outlined by Field-Marshal Alan Brooke at the Quebec conference (12–16 September 1944). During the first meeting of the Combined Chiefs of Staff at noon on 12 September, Brooke said the he thought that the troops of Army Group C might fail in their retreat to the Alps and be annihilated in the Po plain. In that case, and if the Germans also withdrew from the Balkans, the way to the so-called 'Ljubljana gap' might be open, and from there to Vienna, which could be reached during the winter.[3] The Americans did not object in principle to the British proposal and were willing to leave their landing craft in the Mediterranean. On 13 September Churchill commented with satisfaction that 'the idea of our going to Vienna, if the war lasts long enough and if other people do not get there first, is fully accepted here.'[4]

By 16 September the Combined Chiefs of Staff had completed their final report to the British Prime Minister and the American President and it was read during the final day of the conference. Their recommendations about the Italian theatre were as follows:

1.   No major units should be withdrawn from Italy
2.   The American 5th Army should remain in Italy for the time being
3.   The assault shipping should be retained 'at present' for use in the Istrian peninsula.[5]

After the reading of the document Churchill thanked Admiral King for 'promising to lend us his landing craft for an attack on the Istrian peninsula'. In turn, King emphasised that the assault ships would also be needed for a landing in Burma and 'we must therefore make up our minds about invading Istria by 15 October.'[6]

True to their obligations as Allies, on 19 September Churchill and Roosevelt sent a joint message to Stalin. They did not even make an attempt to mask their real intentions:

We have arrived at the following decisions as to military operations in our conference at Quebec just concluded:

Our present operations in Italy will result in either: (A) The forces of Kesselring[7] will be routed, in which event it should be possible to undertake a rapid regrouping and a pursuit toward the Ljubljana Gap; or (B) Kesselring will succeed in effecting an orderly retreat, in which event we may have to be content this year with the clearing of the plains of Lombardy.

The progress of the battle will determine our future action. Plans are being prepared for an amphibious operation to be carried out, if the situation so demands, on the Istrian peninsula.[8]

In the same spirit of frank diplomatic communication, on 22 September the Allied Mediterranean Command, which was quartered in Caserta, near Naples, refused any armistice negotiations with Horthy's envoys. Hungary was now within the Soviet zone of military operations, so the Magyar Regent was told to treat with the person he deeply distrusted: Joseph Stalin. The elderly Admiral, who had been hoping to surrender honourably to the Western Allies, now had no other choice but to send a mission to Moscow.

The above moves were, as a matter of fact, a clear message to the Kremlin: 'We give you Hungary and, possibly, Yugoslavia, but we won't let you take Austria and enter Bavaria. If you have any other objectives in mind, let's talk.'

Stalin took this frankness as a clear warning. He used the visit of Marshal Tito, the leader of the Yugoslavian communist partisans, in Moscow (21–28 September 1944) to reach a conclusion about the conduct of the joint operations against the German troops in the Balkans. Yugoslavia, however, was an official member of the Anti-Nazi coalition and therefore the status of the Soviet troops had to be determined before the beginning of the offensive. That is why on 26 September Moscow informed London and Washington about the forthcoming entry of the Red Army into Yugoslavian territory and emphasised the fact that it would be done following a request by the Soviets to the Yugoslavian command for permission and its purpose would be to bring more troops to the Hungarian battlefield.[9]

With this move the sly Stalin effectively countered the ambitions of his Western partners to forestall him in 'certain areas'. He set a political trap; from that moment on every Allied country intending to enter or cross Yugoslavian territory would feel obligated to ask Tito for permission. Stalin's latest trick was soon broadcast all over the world: on 29 September the Soviet news agency TASS announced that the 'National Committee of Liberation of Yugoslavia and the Command of the Yugoslavian Peoples Liberation Army' had 'agreed to fulfil the request of the Soviet Command' for a 'temporary entry permit' for 'that Yugoslavian territory which borders with Hungary' and that the Soviet troops would leave Yugoslavia once the 'operational tasks' were completed.[10]

2

The rapid progress of the Soviet drive through the Balkans raised more acutely the problem of coordination and separation of responsibilities in Southeast Europe between Moscow and the Western Allies. The question was posed for the first time by London in the spring of 1944 because no official demarcation line had been set in Teheran. In June Roosevelt recognised a provisional demarcation line between the Allies and the Soviets for a period of three months. But by the end of the Quebec conference that period had elapsed and now Churchill was more anxious to discuss these problems in person with Stalin. On his initiative a meeting was arranged in Moscow, which was scheduled to start on 9 October.[11] En route to Moscow Churchill landed in Naples on 8 October and attended a meeting of the Mediterranean Command to discuss how the Italian deadlock could be broken.

In spite of the fact that in Italy the advance of Alexander's multinational 15th Army Group was almost brought to a halt by ammunition shortages and lack of reinforcements, the British planners were still full of optimism that the changing situation in the Balkans offered consider-able opportunities for a quick victory. There seemed to be two possible ways by which this could be done: amphibious attack on the Istria peninsula, including Trieste, or landing south of Fiume and advance to the north towards Trieste.[12]

Since neither of the options stood out as preferable, General Wilson, the Supreme Allied Commander of the Mediterranean Theatre, was asked to examine in more detail the particular implications of the amphibious attacks and to prepare a report to the Combined Chiefs of Staffs as soon as possible. The report was ready on 10 October, but its conclusions were quite discouraging; it turned out that a sea-borne attack on Istria in 1944 would be impossible. Still worse, Wilson emphasised, the Allied efforts in Italy now seemed unlikely to contribute in the near future to the overall campaign in the West.[13]

3

Even though the prospects on the southern wing of the Eastern Front looked bright, at the end of September 1944 Stalin was still concerned about Churchill's next move. The dic-tator was highly suspicious of the attitude of his Allies in the region, be they the British or the Yugoslav communists. 'He trusted nothing but what he held in his fist, and everyone beyond the control of his police was a potential enemy,' wrote Milovan Djilas, a member of the Yugoslav communist mission to Moscow in 1944, after the war.[14] Stalin knew that in the course of the summer of 1944 Churchill several times had tested Tito's willingness to support an eventual landing in Istria and each time the reply was evasive. Therefore it is no wonder that during their meeting in Moscow in late September 1944 Stalin pressed Tito for a definitive answer about his attitude if the British really did force a landing in Yugoslavia. 'The Yugoslavs will fight,' Tito promised.[15]

As the meeting with the British leader drew near, Stalin's nervousness grew. He viewed Churchill's diplomatic overtures simply as an attempt to defeat him in the great game of global politics and Churchill himself as 'the kind of man who will pick your pocket for a kopeck if you don't watch him.'[16] Stalin planned to make Central Europe completely his own and needed to hold the trump cards. The conquest of the Hungarian kingdom could become such a card. The peace negotiations with Horthy's representatives were about to lead to a repetition of the Romanian 'scenario', but nothing was certain yet. Colonel-General Sergei Shtemenko, then head of the Operations Department of the General Staff, recalls the emotional state of the 'Father of the Peoples' on the eve of the summit:

> Antonov[17] was assigned to prepare the report on the situation at the front, which as usual was drawn up in the Operations Department of the General Staff ... On the eve of the first day of talks,[18] the Supreme Commander sent for the report so that he could look it over ... Stalin was alone. Without asking any questions, he greeted me, took the report, and went into his office. He filled his pipe, started puffing at it, and sat down at his desk quite unhurriedly ...
>
> I sat down not far away, ready to answer questions; but Stalin proceeded to correct the report, snuffling and grunting as he did so, without asking any questions.
>
> When he had almost reached the end, the Supreme Commander indicated a passage in the text with his red pencil, and said, 'Right here, Comrade Shtemenko, we'll describe our plans a bit more forcefully than in the draft report. We'll say that we'll strive to reach the German border sooner, and for that purpose we'll first smash Hungary. Our main interest will lie here, in Hungary ...'[19]

Of course, Stalin did not intend to prevail through strategic arguments alone. Miklós Horthy, the elderly Magyar Regent, could also be a great asset. Horthy had already begun to consider strategies for surrendering to the Allies in the summer of 1944. He clearly demonstrated his willingness to leave the sinking ship by stopping the deportations of the Hungarian Jews to the death camps (in July) and by dismissing Sztójay's pro-Nazi government (in late August). The next logical step was to send truce envoys to the enemy camp, first to Bari and then to Moscow.

The Magyar peace delegation arrived in Moscow on 1 October. By the time of the above-mentioned meeting of Stalin with the leadership of the General Staff, the negotiations were already in full swing. Soviet hopes that the 'Romanian scenario' could be repeated were high, and Stalin and his entourage expected that before long the Red Army would be standing at the gates of Vienna, ready to pour into Bavaria.

4

In Hungary there was one man who had been initiated into Stalin's plans. His name was Marshal Semyon Timoshenko, the *Stavka* representative for the 2nd and 4th Ukrainian Fronts and in reality supreme warlord of the southern wing of the Red Army. The 49-year-old shaven-headed Ukrainian was a friend and supporter of Stalin for over 25 years and this special relationship ensured rapid advance in his military career.

Timoshenko was brave, merciless and fully devoted to the communist cause. As a field commander he was not successful; he was incompetent and unable to handle military complexities. Having previously held positions as a front commander, in the spring of 1943 he was relieved of front-line duty and since then had been used as Stalin's plenipotentiary on various sectors of the Eastern front.

Stalin was well aware of Timoshenko's limited military skills; on the eve of the German invasion he characterised him as 'a fine person with a big head, but with a brain the size of a fig'.[20] Nevertheless, he respected him for his boundless fidelity. It was definitely this that led to Timishenko's last wartime assignment: in May 1944 the Marshal was appointed Stavka representative[21] for the 2nd and 3rd Ukrainian Fronts.[22] In other words, he was chosen to lead the Soviet conquest of Southern Germany.

Left: Marshal Semyon Timoshenko, the *Stavka* representative with the 2nd and the 4th Ukrainian Fronts.

Below: The Battle of Debrecen (6–28 October 1944), as discussed in Chapters 2 and 4.

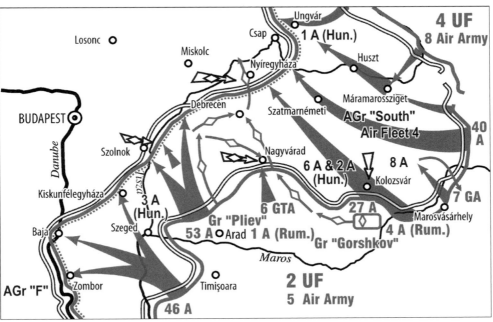

During the first week of October Timoshenko summoned the commanders of the 2nd and 4th Ukrainian Front to discuss future actions in Hungary in view of the upcoming visit of Churchill to Moscow. Special attention was given to Budapest itself. After the speeches of the front commanders, the member of the military council of 4th Ukrainian Front General Mekhlis and the chief of staff of the 4th Ukrainian, General Korzhenevich, who commented on the conduct of operations, Timoshenko summarised the meeting and formulated the conclusions:

> We shall bypass Budapest to the north and the south, aiming minimal forces for direct assault. As far as I know, forthcoming negotiations of comrades Stalin and Molotov with Churchill and Eden in Moscow will demand a prompt decision on the Hungarian question, therefore we can't count on long preparations for the operation.[23]

5

The ambitious Soviet offensive that was intended to solve once and for all the 'Hungarian question' began on 6 October. Marshal Malinovsky, the commander of the 2nd Ukrainian Front, was aiming to cut the rear communications of the Axis troops defending the Carpathians (Army Group South) and destroy them before they could withdraw to the western bank of the river Tisza. The town of Debrecen, the largest traffic junction in that part of the country, was to fall into the hands of the Red Army by 9 October.

From the very beginning, however, the Debrecen Operation did not go as planned. At Nagyvárad the powerful mobile formations unleashed by Malinovsky ran into a determined enemy defence and their advance stalled. On the other hand, on the left flank General Shlemin's 46th Army made very good progress and during the night of 10/11 October seized

A battery of Soviet 76mm ZiS-3 guns towed by lend-lease trucks across the Tisza, autumn 1944. (The Photo Archive of the Ministry of Defence of Bulgaria)

Romanian infantry cross the Tisza via a pontoon bridge, autumn 1944. (The Photo Archive of the Ministry of Defence of Bulgaria)

Szeged. Now the Soviets were in possession of an important bridgehead on the western bank of the Tisza, which would allow them to launch an attack on Budapest from the south.

Shlemin's troops were just entering Szeged when Horthy declared that he had accepted the demands of the anti-Nazi coalition and preliminary conditions for an armistice had been worked out at the Moscow peace talks.[24] The Hungarians asked that the advance of the Soviet forces on the Budapest axis be held in order to give time for more Hungarian units to concentrate in the vicinity of the capital to counteract any action by the German Army. Stalin agreed and the General Staff issued the necessary instructions. At 16:25 MT[25] on 11 October the 2nd Ukrainian Front ordered the 46th Army and its right flank neighbour, the 53rd Army, to hold the already secured bridgeheads over Tisza and switch over to the defensive.[26]

In accordance with the agreement with Horthy, the Stavka[27] sent Malinovsky in person to Szeged for talks with representatives of the Hungarian government on the details of the preliminary conditions of the armistice. Much to Malinovsky's surprise, the Magyar delegation was led by a colonel (Lóránd Utasi) unprepared to discuss any matters of consequence. The Soviet Marshal tried to obtain more information about the disposition of the Axis forces as well why the Hungarian troops had not withdrawn from the Tisza defensive line, but did not get a sensible reply. Finally he dictated his terms[28] to the Hungarian leadership and Utasi returned to Budapest.

On 13 October Malinovsky submitted to the Stavka his plans for the next stage of the Debrecen Operation. In essence, while the main body of the Front would attack towards Debrecen with the objective of speeding up the drive of the 4th Ukrainian Front into the Hungarian Plain and entrapping the Axis forces retreating from Transylvania, the 46th and 53rd Armies would hold their defensive positions along the Tisza, waiting for a favourable opportunity to advance on Budapest from the south. He made no allusion to possible cooperation with the Hungarians or an eventual attack on Budapest.[29]

A Soviet rifle battalion of the 37th Rifle Corps moves down a Szeged street, probably on 12 October 1944. (The Photo Archive of the Ministry of Defence of Bulgaria)

Malinovsky also submitted a report to the Supreme Commander about the unsatisfactory course of the talks with the Magyars. When Stalin received it, he instructed Antonov to prepare a note to the head of the Hungarian peace delegation and dictated the text. The note in question, which was signed at 19:25 on 14 October, was in fact nothing but an ultimatum; the Soviets castigated the Magyar government because it 'had chosen not to fulfil' the pre-armistice conditions and demanded that within 48 hours of receipt of the note all connections with the Germans had to be broken off, the Germans themselves had to be attacked immediately and the Hungarian Army had to withdraw from Romania, Yugoslavia and Czechoslovakia.[30]

Horthy received the Soviet note on the fateful morning of 15 October along with other troubling news. Nevertheless, he dared to take action and by mid-day announced publicly that Hungary had broken her alliance with Nazi Germany. The proclamation was broadcast and repeated many times in several languages. The country was immediately thrown into a state of anarchy, but the situation did not develop beyond that point. Malinovsky and Timoshenko waited and waited, but the magical gate to Budapest did not open. When the news of Szálasi's coup reached the Soviets, Stalin decided to act immediately and ordered the 46th Army to mount an attack on Budapest.[31] But it was already too late: by that time the Regent's residence had been taken by force and Skorzeny's SS-paratroopers and the Arrow-Cross militiamen were looting the offices in the palace, the route to the capital had been barred for the Soviets and the reign of fascist terror, bloody and ruthless, had begun.

The failure of the Hungarian about-face brought uncertainty and confusion not only in the Hungary itself, but amongst the leading Soviet military strategists too. All previous plans were now useless because Horthy was no longer part of the game. In the days that followed Szálasi's coup d'etat the HQs of the fronts were overwhelmed with contradictory messages and no one was able to draw a correct picture of the situation. There was still a hope that the *Honvédség*, the Hungarian army, would follow the call of the 76-year-old regent and turn its weapons against the Germans. But even though a considerable number of soldiers deserted, the three Magyar field armies neither changed sides nor disintegrated and continued to fight shoulder to shoulder with the Wehrmacht against the Soviet onslaught.

A characteristic event deserves to be mentioned in order to illustrate how unrealistic were those hopes of the Soviet command. General Béla Miklós, the commander of 1 Army, was not at his headquarters at Huszt when Horthy announced the armistice and heard the proclamation of the Regent over the radio. He immediately issued an order to his army to cease hostilities with the Soviets and attack the Germans. Nobody followed it, because his troops, meanwhile, had received a rescinding order from the Chief of the General Staff, General Vörös. Upon his return to Huszt, Miklós learned about this countermanding order and now he was well aware that he would be obliged to withdraw his own order. Shortly afterwards he was directed to appear at the headquarters of Colonel-General Gotthard Heinrici, the commander of the German 1 Panzer-Army and his immediate superior, the next day, 16 October. Miklós, suspicious of arrest, defected through the frontline with one of his officers to the Soviets who escorted him to the HQ of the 4th Ukrainian Front, where he arrived on the morning of 17 October.[32]

His interrogation was led by the notorious Lev Mekhlis (the chief political officer of the 4th Ukrainian Front). During it Miklós told the Soviets that he had defected on Horthy's command and now, because of the arrest of the Regent, he was the Supreme Commander of *Honvédség*. Moreover, such was the wish of Horthy himself, Miklós told the interrogators. Later on, he had a phone conversation with an unknown member of the Hungarian peace delegation in Moscow. In the course of it he repeatedly demonstrated confidence that soon 1 and 2 Armies would obey his orders to turn against the Germans and announced that he would issue instructions for immediate action by radio. Miklós's side of the conversation was recorded by the Hungarian writer and communist Béla Illes, translated and sent by Mekhlis to Stalin.[33] Indeed, soon the General spoke on the radio and asked the commanding officers of his Army immediately (no later than 06:00 MT on 19 October) to order their units to change sides. Few followed his instructions.[34] At Timoshenko's suggestion, shortly afterwards ten Hungarian officer POWs were sent through the frontline with Miklós's order. Timoshenko, the front command and the General Staff patiently waited to see what effect the order would produce, but to no avail. On 21 October Miklós once again spoke on the radio to the Hungarian soldiers calling them to defect to the Soviets. This time more men responded to his appeal by leaving their units, but many were driven by the desire to return to their homes, not to join the Soviets.[35]

In the last ten days of October all hopes that the *Honvédség* could become an ally vanished. Everywhere the Hungarians continued to fight side by side with the Germans and an armistice was not to be expected. On 23 October the General Staff reported to Stalin that Miklós's order had not produced a sufficient effect on the Magyars.[36] The reaction of the dictator was brisk and on the evening of the next day a special directive was signed and sent to Timoshenko, 2nd and 4th Ukrainian Fronts:

> In view of the fact that the Hungarian forces have not ceased hostilities against our forces and are continuing to maintain a common front with the Germans, the Stavka of the Supreme Command orders that on the field of battle you must act toward the Hungarian troops just as you would toward the German ones, without differentiating between them, you must inform all of the troops of the front of this.[37]

6

The meeting in Moscow between Stalin and Churchill took place against a backdrop of mounting victory for the Red Army in Transylvania and in the Balkans and coincided with the signing of the armistice with Horthy. It is no wonder that the Hungarian question featured strongly in the discussions. Already, at the first meeting with Stalin on 9 October, the British Premier proposed the carving up of southeast Europe into joint British-Soviet spheres of influence and outlined on half a sheet of paper the division. Regarding Hungary (and Yugoslavia) Churchill suggesteded the Soviets and Britain go halves. Churchill recalled how the deal was closed:

> I pushed this across to Stalin who had by then heard the translation. There was a slight pause. Then he took his blue pencil and made a large tick upon it, and passed it back to us. It was all settled in no more time than it takes to set down.[38]

It was not 'all settled' yet. Stalin was not satisfied with his influence in Yugoslavia and especially in Hungary. Molotov and Eden turned the evening session of 10 October into a political auction. The Soviet foreign minister demanded a 10 per cent increase in Yugoslavia and a larger share in Hungary. This led to some Soviet concessions with regard to Bulgaria and a declaration that Moscow was largely uninterested in Greece. Finally, the balance sheet between the two ministers was 'signed off'. On the next day an agreement was reached that the British would keep 'their' 50 per cent in Yugoslavia while Soviets would get 80 per cent in Hungary and Bulgaria.[39]

The British Prime Minister hastened to explain the percentage deal with the Soviet dictator to the War Cabinet and on 12 October sent a report to his colleagues in London. 'They are taking great interest in Hungary, which they mentioned, erroneously, was their neighbour.'[40]

The evening session of 14 October was devoted to the military situation. Both leaders and their staffs sat down to discuss the state of the affairs in Europe and Far East. Field Marshal Brooke was the first who took the floor and presented the Allied operations in Western Europe. After hearing Churchill's and Stalin's remarks, he moved to the next topic, the Mediterranean theatre:

> In Northern Italy the Germans will retreat either through the Brenner Pass, or through the Ljubljana Gap … The Allies have prepared a sea landing on the Istrian peninsula. The moment is approaching when the armies of the Allies will meet the Russians.

To this Stalin replied: 'The Soviet command doesn't intend to move far to the west in Yugoslavia. The Soviet command counts on the Allied armies meeting the Red Army in Austria.'[41]

The American General Deane covered the situation in the Pacific. After him the floor was given to General Antonov who read the previously prepared report. During the briefing Brooke and Churchill pressed him with questions about Soviet intentions and when asked about the immediate objectives of the Red Army, the Deputy Chief of the Soviet General Staff answered:

> The Soviet troops are faced with two primary tasks: conclusion of the operations in the Baltic region and knocking Hungary out of the war. When these operations are completed, the Soviet troops will be faced with the task of invading Germany. How it will be possible to invade Germany in many respects will depend on the results of the operations the Soviet troops are conducting now. Anyway, it is possible to tell that the successful conclusion of the operations in Hungary will open one more line of approach to Germany, which favourably differs [from others] because the Germans don't have prepared lines of defence there.[42]

On 16 October Roosevelt rejected the request of the British Prime Minister for three fresh divisions for the Italian front and thus put an end to Churchill's hopes of launching a speedy landing in Istria and subsequent push through the 'Ljubljana gap' towards Vienna.[43] The American President had been backed up by the British General Staff; on 14 October the London planners, after examining the theatres, concluded that it would not be possible to launch a 'major offensive' in Italy before January 1945.[44] In spite of this cold shower, Churchill held his nerve like an experienced poker player and kept gambling with his host. On 17 October at the final meeting with Stalin, the Prime Minister, who had just learned about Horthy's abdication, expressed his hopes that the Allied armies in Italy would reach the 'Ljubljana gap' 'as fast as possible'. Had he done this intentionally? Was he bluffing? Or with his fascination with the 'Ljubljana gap' was this just wishful thinking? No one knows. But the Kremlin dictator, who was still unaware of the negative standpoint of the Joint Planners on the continuing of the operations in the Apennines, instantly felt tricked; the crafty Englishman was trying to steal Eastern Austria from him!

Austria played an important role in the Soviet plans for driving into the Third Reich from the south. The country offered one very attractive feature: the so-called 'Vienna gate', a narrow gorge at the Austrian capital where the Danube flows between the Alps and the Western Carpathians. Through this 'gate', the Stavka believed, the Red Army could advance deep into Bavaria and strike Nazi Germany in its very heart. Alongside the strictly military challenges, there was another obstacle of a purely political nature: the country had not been divided yet between the future victors.

The division of Austria, which was not discussed in Moscow, promised to be very difficult. Earlier Soviet military plans (if any) are not known, whilst those of the British were straightforward: to march 'at once' into Austria should Germany suddenly collapse. The question was first raised in August 1944, when London proposed the dividing of the country into three 'horizontal' occupation zones: British, American and Soviet. But when this was submitted to the Soviets, they made a counterproposal: Austria should be divided east-west. By the time of the Moscow conference, the negotiations were still in their early stages; both parties were very sensitive about their future spheres of interest simply because their next military efforts were still undefined.[45]

Churchill's words shook Stalin. Shtemenko's memoir makes it clear that the Soviet dictator had smelt a rat:

> As he was leaving Moscow, Churchill expressed satisfaction with the talks, and reacted in his own way to the insertion Stalin had made in Antonov's report as to aiming the main thrusts of the Soviet Armed Forces toward Hungary. The British Prime Minister expressed the hope that the Anglo-American forces would reach the Ljubljana Gap in Yugoslavia in the shortest possible time. Naturally, the thought that what Churchill had said had been carefully weighed in advance. His remark could only signify an intention to break into the centre of Europe through Ljubljana, going around the southern end of the Alps, and to reach Hungary and Austria before the Soviet forces did. Once again we could sniff the 'Balkan variant', served up with a different sauce. Needless to say, the Supreme Commander noticed this immediately.[46]

Churchill's farewell words (coupled with the failed Magyar about-face) forced Stalin to face the reality that the time for diplomacy had ended. The time of brute force and military supremacy had come.

7

Despite the refusal of the American President to divert three divisions to Italy and the discouraging report of General Wilson, neither the British Prime Minister nor the Mediterranean Command were keen to give up their hopes of breaking through to Vienna before the beginning of winter. On 21 October Churchill, on his way back from Moscow, chaired a meeting held in Naples. It turned out that there were still good prospects for success; the three American divisions would not be forthcoming, but most of the assault vessels were still on hand. Field-Marshal Alexander announced his readiness to start withdrawing frontline divisions immediately after the capture of Bologna. In view of the situation in Yugoslavia, Wilson proposed an 'economical attack': these divisions should be landed on the Dalmatian coast instead in Istria, and due to the smaller size of the amphibious shipping, the initial assault should be carried out by only one division.[47]

Churchill liked the suggestions, but many details had yet to be examined and Wilson was asked once again to prepare a report to the Combined Chief of Staff and a plan for a landing on the Dalmatian coast with the objective of seizing Fiume and cutting the rear communications of Army Group C. Furthermore, Wilson was advised to draw attention to the 'favourable developments' in the Balkans and the need to take advantage of them by launching the attack.[48]

The report was ready on 24 October and it buried Churchill's hopes of forestalling Stalin in southern Central Europe; Wilson stated that the advance could begin in the first week of February at the earliest. Furthermore, it found no strong support with London authorities, just the contrary. Of course, Churchill was furious. After the percentage deal with Stalin he not only intended to protect the undisputed parts of Europe from the Red Army, but to shield the eastern Italian provinces from Tito's territorial demands. The Prime Minister did not hide his disappointment and on 30 October he sent the following minute to General Hastings Ismay, the Deputy Secretary to the War Cabinet:

> One of the absurd things in all the plans which are submitted by A.F.H.Q.[49] [Mediterranean], is the idea that if they move in February they will be in time to effect anything. In the three months which they say must elapse before they are capable of movement, the whole of Yugoslavia will be cleared of the Germans, who will either have been overwhelmed or made their escape to the north. Very likely this will take place in six weeks. The Yugoslavs will then occupy Trieste, Fiume and other towns which they claim. So what will be the need of an expedition and all the landing-craft, and so on?
>
> The days of those slow-moving, heavy-footed methods are over, but we still cling to them with disastrous results.[50]

8

Churchill's farewell words definitely had left Stalin puzzled, but not for long. The repeated hints of the British Prime Minister that the Allied thrust through the 'Ljubljana gap' was impending did not fall on deaf ears. Rght from the outset relations between the Soviet Union and the Western Allies were characterised by permanent mutual distrust. 'Additional' information was garnered through the wide network of spies operating on both sides of the Atlantic. While the British delegation was returning home, undercover agents of the Kremlin were preparing their final reports about the future course of Allied operations.

The meeting in Naples had not begun when an NKGB agent informed Moscow that no Allied large-scale offensive would take place in Italy during the upcoming weeks and months. The report arrived on 20 October 1944:

> Already during the preparation for the Allied landings in southern France, Churchill and the Commander of British troops in the Mediterranean basin, General Wilson, stubbornly tried to convince Roosevelt and the Joint Chiefs of Staff of the US forces to abandon the operation. Instead, they proposed the troops intended to participate in this operation be used for a

landing in the Trieste area and further progress in Austria in order to be there (as well as in the Balkans) before the Red Army.

Roosevelt, in principle, categorically refused to make any changes in the plans. In early October 1944, in a personal telegram to Roosevelt, Churchill brought up the question of the need to make some corrections in the intended plan for sending in US reinforcements to the European theatre of operations. Roosevelt has replied that both he and the chiefs of staffs of the US armed forces couldn't agree with Churchill's proposal to send to Italy the US troops that had been intended for France. Roosevelt has said that during the impending winter Kesselring's army wouldn't be defeated anyway. Moreover, the Germans would be able to keep their front in Italy intact, even if they would be forced to pull out 4–5 divisions and transfer them, for example, to the Western Front. On the other hand, Eisenhower was actively preparing a breakthrough of the German front and, in connection with this, the American first echelon forces, which had been badly mauled in the previous battles, should be replaced. This exchange could be made possible only if the troops sent to Europe were placed at his disposal and not transferred to Italy. At the same time, Roosevelt has insisted that the Russian advance in the Balkans and Austria would likely have a far bigger effect militarily on the Germans in Italy than all Allied activities on the Italian front.

Until recently the British government still hoped that the Allied forces under the command of General Wilson would arrive in Austria before the Red Army and it was hoped that General Wilson immediately would declare himself a military governor-general of the country with all the ensuing consequences. The British Foreign Ministry has prepared in advance a proclamation by Wilson to all Austrians on behalf of all Allied nations, which the British Foreign Office intended to bring to the attention of the Soviet and American governments.

The successes of the Red Army in the Balkans forced the British to abandon that intention. On 14 October the British Foreign Office informed its ambassador to the United States that, in all likelihood, the Russians would arrive in Austria first, and the troops of General Wilson would not be able to achieve decisive success during the winter.[51]

It was now clear to Stalin that the Red Army would arrive first. Churchill's trick hadn't worked.

9

During the last days of October, when the eventual landing on the Adriatic coast was still in dispute, the Mediterranean Command (or Churchill himself?) sent a special envoy to Moscow to check the up-to-date status of the Soviet (and Yugoslav) military plans. Shtemenko recalls the visit:

> Very shortly thereafter our allies tested our intentions. In late October Lieutenant-General Hammel [sic], a representative of the Allied command in the Mediterranean theatre, paid a visit to the General Staff. He met with Antonov and asked him to tell him about our plans for future actions in the Balkans. At the same time he requested information on the AVNOJ[52] Army's plans as regards actions to the west of Belgrade, and about its forces.
>
> Antonov flatly refused to give Hammel any information on the Yugoslav forces. 'We do not intend to move any farther in Yugoslavia. The task of fighting the Germans west of Belgrade is being handled by Marshal Tito's army, so it would be better to get the information you want from him.'
>
> As for the Soviet plans, Antonov repeated what had been said during the talks with Churchill and Eden. 'Our chief task is to take Hungary out of the war as quickly as possible, and our main thrusts will therefore be in that direction.'[53]

3

THE RETURN OF THE BOOMERANG

1

The Arrow-Cross Party[1] began its ferocious time in power in the early hours of 16 October with a bloody pogrom, probably the first one that Budapest had ever witnessed. The members of the party's militia (*Fegyveres Pártszolgálat*) broke into the Jewish houses and killed nearly 300 Jews, mostly women and children. The German tanks also participated in the 'action' by shelling the buildings.[2] The 'reprisal' raid was justified as a countermeasure against the Jews, who had fired shots upon the militia. (Some Jewish labour servicemen in possession of arms had offered resistance at couple of places a few hours earlier.)[3] The outrage did not stop there. In retaliation for the armed resistance shown by the labour servicemen, the militia rounded up several thousand Jews in the centre of Pest and herded them into two nearby synagogues. The would-be victims were saved from being murdered by the representatives of neutral countries and some outraged Hungarians. After energetic protestations, the synagogues were vacated and the Jews returned home under the cover of the night.[4]

Of course, the atrocities were not limited to Budapest only. On the night of 15/16 October, for instance, the entire Jólsva labour company – some 160 Jewish servicemen, mostly physicians, engineers and other professionals – was slaughtered in Pusztavám, a small village northwest of Székesfehérvár.[5]

The reaction of the ordinary Hungarians to atrocities such as these was symptomatic of how the majority of them had accepted the German occupation and the change of the regime with indifference and apathy. There were no organised protests while the acts of armed resistance were scarce and carried out only by 'professionals'. A considerable number of Magyars, poisoned by decades of paranoia, mistrust and ignorance, lacked the moral grounding to prevent the genocide that followed. A Holocaust survivor describes how this latent anti-Semitism was further fuelled by well-crafted propaganda:

> And after Stalingrad the extreme right wing of the press had been busy spreading the word that if Germany were to lose the war, the Jews would exterminate the Christians. And this was swallowed by adults, by people with degrees; the so-called middle class passed this depraved nonsense from mouth to mouth. As my old friend said, it short-circuited their brains. They were able to believe that the Jews would exterminate their own clients. And whom would they cheat, whom would they leave off, after that? And how could they believe, the sons of this brave Hungarian nation, that a handful of Jews would exterminate ten million Gentiles?

Even counting the Jewish babies in arms, there were no more than 150,000 of us left; weak, unarmed Jews. Couldn't the Gentiles conceive of resisting such an onslaught? After all, they would not have to kneel down and offer their necks to be cut …

Oh, this was the greatest suffering, the one meted out on one's intelligence. To have to swallow this thick spate of idiocy, to breathe this filthy smog instead of clean air; all these lies, all these stupefying inanities. To look on helplessly at the mental degradation of this country blessed with such human resources and talent, to witness the atrophy of reason, spirit, humour. When would we ever recover from the damage done to the mind and soul of this nation? There was one explanation for otherwise intelligent people believing these wild inanities about the Jews. When you usurp another people's jobs, businesses and properties, it is easy to believe all the bad things about them, to justify the hatred, and lull the conscience.[6]

The Magyars were so overwhelmed by the pace of the events that hardly any of them realised that Szálasi's coup would effectively terminate the 1000-year-old kingdom of Szent István and would turn their world upside down. Pandora's box was open, all the evils of man escaped and there was no closing it.

2

In the autumn of 1944 the fascist Arrow-Cross party, which had been returned to life by Sztójay's government, was Hitler's last political reserve in the Danube Basin. As a political structure it comprised members of different classes of society, ranging from aristocrats to lumpen-proletariat, united by nationalism, anti-Bolshevism and violent anti-Semitism. In many respects it was a carbon copy of its 'bigger brother', the NSDAP – the arrow-cross insignia, the armbands worn by the militiamen, the uniforms (green shirts) –the master race concept, demands for an ethnically pure state and admiration for order imposed through power. The core of the Arrow-Cross ideology was so-called 'Hungarism': the primacy of Hungarian values. After the war Veesenmayer characterised the instalment of the Arrow-Cross government as 'an ill-fated move'.[7] But the new regime had not been installed for its respectability; even though the Germans never took the Arrow-Cross movement seriously, they gave their full support to it, simply because after the sacking of the Sztójay's government there was no other alternative.

Of course, such a movement could not exist without a public figure with whom to identify. In this case, the role of the 'Führer' belonged to the party leader and founder Ferenc Szálasi, a retired Major of the General Staff and a man 'of little ability and less tact'.[8] He is described as a 'deeply religious, honest, unpretentious, and cheerful man; knowledgeable on a wide range of subjects; and a compassionate friend of peasants, workers, and soldiers. Above all, he was a zealous defender of Hungarian traditions and values and an indefatigable designer of the Hungarist solution, which envisioned a prosperous and peaceful Greater Hungary.'[9]

The tyrant was persuaded of the ability of ordinary Magyars to embody the principles of his ideology; in the course of his trial he recalled that during his travels throughout Hungary in the summer of 1944 he 'became convinced that most of people viewed Hungarism with great faith, enthusiasm, and love'.[10] Szálasi craved Hitler's support, but was anxious that the Third Reich viewed the Hungarist Empire not as a satellite state but as an independent and equal partner in the struggle against Communism. His ally, in turn, viewed him as an 'irritating fantast' and a 'dreamer, not a politician, who was obsessed with his 'sacred' mission.'[11] Had Germany won the war, Hitler definitely would have had no use for Szálasi and his plans for Greater Hungary.[12]

To his followers, Szálasi was a Magyar patriot who embodied all of the human virtues. His writings and speeches were read by few and understood by fewer, that is why the driving force

Ferenc Szálasi, the leader of the Hungarian National Socialist Arrow Cross Party, stands near a ruined building in Budapest. (Dénes Bernád)

of his movement was neither political, nor ideological, but social: the habitual hatred of the bourgeoisie and the militant anti-Semitism of the lower strata of the Magyar population. The latter groups had almost always associated the Jews with social inequality and viewed them as a class who had profited at the expense others. As a whole, the leaders, members and sympathisers of the Arrow-Cross party detested the very character of the society of the Horthy era, with its elitism and privileges.

3

The government had to decide immediately whether to accept as a fact the relentless advance of the Red Army and act accordingly, or to view the resolute intention of the Germans to hold Budapest, whatever the cost, as paramount. Szálasi's faith in the final victory of Nazi Germany was unshakable; his belief in the ability of the German armament industry to produce war-winning weapons was strong. ('That is why I opposed so emphatically Horthy's attempted putsch to gain a cease-fire,' he declared during his trial.)[13] The contribution of Hungary to the war effort became a central theme of his policies. On the night of 16 October, in one its first public declarations, the new regime announced his resolve not to surrender the country to the Bolsheviks and to hold firm to the terms of the alliance with the Third Reich ('the common struggle would be strengthened').[14]

Transition from the Horthy era to Arrow-Cross rule was swift and unchallenged. A flood of urgent orders and proclamations followed: the Jews were directed to resume wearing the

Yellow Star of David, a ban was placed on the assembly of more than three persons on the street, except at a tram stop. The civil servants and workers were ordered to return to their jobs and shops to reopen.[15] Shortly afterwards, Emil Kovarcz, a minister without portfolio in charge of national mobilisation and preparation for war, was given an instruction by Szálasi to mobilise all citizens of both sexes between the ages of 12 and 70 for either labour or military service. It was expected that more than a million Hungarians would be detailed.[16]

The *nyilas éra* (the Arrow-Cross era) officially began on 17 October, when Szálasi formed a fifteen-member 'government of national solidarity' and a three-member regency council and thus combined the positions of Regent and Prime Minister.[17] In addition to these, he created himself a new title: 'Leader of the Nation' (*Nemzetvezetö*). The latter position was legalised on 3 November, when both Houses of Parliament (only 104 deputies out of 370 turned up in the Lower House on that day) 'unanimously' adopted the new arrangement.[18]

An ambitious 'Plan of National Reconstruction' was prepared and approved by the Parliament on 2 November, which called for a complete transformation of Horthy's aristocratic Hungary into a 'Hungarist corporative' state by 1 March 1945, but nothing was actually done to this end; most of the ministers were either busy coping with everyday problems or were simply paralysed by the overall situation.[19] Though the transfer of power in all areas of the state apparatus was surprisingly rapid and sweeping. Every possible higher administrative position was filled with Arrow-Cross men, mostly from the lower and middle classes, aided by experienced officials who had served in Sztójay's government. Even though the 'Hungarist Empire' (*Hungarista Birodalom*) consisted only of several counties still nominally controlled by Szálasi's government, members of the Arrow-Cross party were appointed for all official posts in the Soviet-controlled East Hungary, Vojvodina, Transylvania and Ruthenia.[20] On the whole, the administrative infrastructure was inadequate, the majority of the Arrow-Cross officials lacked the necessary experience and the *nyilas* state barely functioned.

Szálasi was confident that the legitimacy of his Hungarist state would be sanctioned by international recognition. His government was seeking to establish normal ties with other countries and the 34-year-old Foreign Minister Baron Dr Gabor Kemény became the most tenacious promoter of the international probity of the Arrow-Cross government. In fact Hungary suffered near-total international isolation. Not only was the country already at war with the world's most powerful states, but after the news of the Arrow-Cross coup reached them, the Hungarian ambassadors in Ankara, Berne, Lisbon, Madrid and Stockholm refused to recognise Szálasi's government. Moreover, they did not resign but rather reaffirmed their loyalty to the Regent Horthy *en bloc* and retained possession of the embassies. The governments of the neutral countries either refused to recognise the Arrow-Cross government or adopted a noncommittal stance.[21]

The new regime quickly installed a reign of terror. Though this terror was nominally directed against the political opponents of the Arrow-Cross government and the Jews, it deeply affected all levels of society. In the few months they were able to hold onto power, Szálasi and his supporters liquidated tens of thousands of intellectuals, civil servants, clergymen and workers.[22] The terror was not only physical, it was mental as well; in November the officer corps and civil servants were ordered to take an oath of loyalty and obedience to Szálasi, Hungary and the principles of Hungarism. There were very few recusants.[23] Lieutenant György Hahn from an unknown artillery battalion recalled how he took the oath in a farmyard: '[the officers] stood in a circle as the Colonel mounted a heap of refuse to obtain a better view of his men. It was a symbolic moment. A fellow officer whispered, "Now look what we are taking an oath on: a dung heap!"'[24]

4

By the beginning of July all the Jews in the provinces had already been transferred to the death camps, but the planned deportation of the Budapest Jews (approximately 220,000), which was to take place on 25 August, had been prevented by order of the Regent.[25] Horthy did not stop the deportations on his own initiative, he was subjected to pressure by the Pope, the King of Sweden, President Roosevelt, other world leaders and the international press. Eichmann himself had left Hungary by the end of July and eventually on 28 September his *Sondereinsatzkommando* was disbanded,[26] but one of its leading members, the 'Advisor on Jewish Affairs' *SS-Hauptsturmbannführer* Dieter Wisliceny, remained behind 'just in case'.[27] However, the Nazis and their Magyar 'colleagues' had not abandoned their hopes of 'solving the Jewish problem' in Budapest and simply waited for a favourable opportunity. It came soon enough, although the Nazis were disappointed that valuable time had been lost. On 24 October Veesenmayer sent a memorandum to Ribbentrop, expressing his frustration: 'Fresh negotiations concerning the final solution of the Jewish problem in Hungary were started, with the partici-pation of German officials as advisers, only after 16 October this year.'[28]

By 15 October Auschwitz was already in its liquidation phase, but now the SS-empire was building underground factories for aircraft and V-2 missiles. The new construction projects needed labourers by the hundreds of thousands and as the Germans had complete control over Hungary, the underground tunnels were ready to accommodate the Jews of Budapest. On 18 October Vessenmayer and Gábor Vajna, the new Hungarian Minister of the Interior, agreed that 50,000 Jews, men and women, would be transferred to the Reich. All other able-bodied Jews were to be relocated to four labour camps and the remainder concentrated in a ghetto located on the outskirts of the Hungarian capital. In his message to Berlin, Vessenmayer added that Eichmann intended to demand another 50,000 Jews later.[29] Ribbentrop understandably did not object and insisted that the Hungarians should 'proceed with utmost severity against the Jews'.[30] And they did.

In the early hours of 20 October the Magyar police, accompanied by Arrow-Cross elements, raided the yellow-star-marked houses and seized all the men between the ages of 16 and 60. By the end of the day approximately 22,000 had been rounded up. The Jews were driven either to the racetracks at Kerepesi Street or to the KISOK sport ground:

We marched on in a somewhat resigned mood, the only sour note being the periodic shouts of our military escort on the left or right, reminding us to straighten out and step lively. It was a warm day. Some gentlemen were wiping their foreheads, many had taken off their hats. We marched on the side of the road. Occasionally we had to crowd over, when large trucks or armoured vehicles rumbled by. The drivers, Hungarian or German soldiers, looked down on us with indifference. Those passing us on carts or on foot gave us the once-over; occasionally a child or an old woman lugging a sack or a basket stopped to stare better. We did not hear any comments. Only two young housewives giggled on seeing us. I couldn't say that their laugh-ter was prompted by scorn or hatred; it was merely childish and unthinking. They laughed because we were being driven like helpless cattle.

We marched for an hour, two hours. We lost track of the time. The streets had been left behind us long ago. We had been so exhausted when we set out, but amazingly we still kept marching. We got the hang of it. But various minor problems began to arise. The man on my right kept saying he was dying for a drink of water. This gentleman used to be a wholesaler. (By now I had had a chance to exchange a word or two with my neighbours.) The one the left had a nail bothering his foot; it was beginning to be torture. The man ahead of me kept reaching back under his weighty knapsack: the straps were cutting into his shoulder. He wore a thin overcoat. Left and right we passed scattered small railway shacks, humble and homely villas, half-built houses that would not be completed for some time. Some of the buildings had suffered bomb damage. On fences and walls we saw swastikas daubed in green paint, and Szálasi's name in capital letters. On wooden fences we saw more SZÁLASI scrawls in chalk, some with *S* inverted. Other graffiti were faded by the years. I felt the onset of recurring nicotine cravings; of course smoking was out of the question.[31]

Not all of the 'labourers' reached their final destinations; some were shot en route. Others were attacked and robbed by the prostitutes from the nearby red-light district.[32]

As the lines of Jews were driven in the drizzling rain through the streets of the capital toward the racetracks amid the abuse of their fellow citizens, a little girl of four whose parents had been previously shot strayed away from the column. An Arrow Cross man grabbed the little thing and threw her back into the line with such vigour that she landed with her face on the muddy pavement, lacerating her skin. The onlooking crowd greeted this feat with laughter, roaring its approval.[33]

In the following days the 'mobilisation' was extended to women (between 16 and 40) and by 26 October the reserve labour force numbered around 25,000 men and 10,000 women.[34] The men were gathered into labour companies and sent to dig trenches around Budapest while the Jewesses were set to washing and mending soldier's clothes.

The transfer of the Jews meant for slave labour in the Reich began on 8 November.[35] However, there was one obstacle: as a result of the Allied bombing the railway transportation system had broken down, the trains to the west no longer could be dispatched and the Budapest Jews had to be marched out on foot. They were sent off in groups of 2000–4000 people and it took them 7–8 days to get to Hegyeshalom, a town on the German-Hungarian border. [36] By 13 November some 27,000 Jews of both sexes had been marched off.[37] Without food and water, the hapless victims were forced to walk in long columns over 200km through mud, rain and snow to the Reich's border. The attitude of their guards – soldiers and militiamen – was ruthless and monstrous, and the local peasantry was often hostile and abusive. Only some merciful locals, the Red Cross and the diplomats of neutral countries occasionally came to their aid. Along the route many Jews, already starved in the ghettos, died of exhaustion. The treks are remembered as the 'death marches to Hegyeshalom'.

The rest of the Jews, around 120,000 by the beginning of November, remained in Budapest. Some of them were rescued by merciful Christian Hungarians – neighbours, friends, relatives – while others found refuge in the so-called 'protected houses' set up in the Jewish upper-middle class area of Pest by a number of courageous men. They include the Swedes Raoul Wallenberg (emissary of the American War Refugee Board) and Per Anger (a secretary at the Swedish legation in Budapest), the Swiss Carl Lutz (the Consul of Switzerland), Friedrich Born (a representative of the International Red Cross), the Italians Angelo Rotta (Papal Nuncio) and Giorgio Perlasca (an acting Spanish Consul). These brave men and true heroes of the Hungarian bloodbath used their connections with the high-ranking Arrow Cross functionaries to grant recognition of the protective passes issued by their Missions and thus saved the lives of many thousands of Jews. Within a few weeks the number of Jews carrying such papers and living in the 'protected houses' rose from 15,000 to 33,000.[38]

As a result of the pressure from the representatives of the neutral states and the Vatican, on 12 November the Arrow-Cross government ordered all Jews holding foreign protective passes to be relocated to the 'protected buildings'.[39] Thus in District VI in Pest the so-called 'International Ghetto' came into existence. On 18 November the government informed the Jewish Council of Budapest about its decision to set up a ghetto for the remaining ('non-protected') Jews as well.[40] It was situated in the nearby District VII and would be known as the 'ordinary' ghetto.

Of course, the rescuers would have been powerless to save so many lives without the cooperation, full or grudging, of leading officials of Szálasi's regime. In particular, Wallenberg's circle of contacts included Kovarcz, Kemény, Dr Jószef Gera (the director of the Office of Party Development) and Ferenc Fiala (Szálasi's press chief and the editor of *Összetartás*, the Arrow-Cross main publication).[41]

Szálasi's state apparatus proved itself incapable of maintaining any semblance of discipline. Many of the district commanders often ignored the orders of their superiors and unprovoked attacks and random atrocities were daily occurrences. Sometimes it was difficult to determine whether the attackers were organised Arrow-Cross militiamen or opportunistic fanatics without party affiliation, who had been given weapons during Kovarcz's 'total mobilisation'. These young men brought shame on the Hungarist system they represented more than any other section of the state apparatus. Szálasi promised investigations and his ministers vowed to maintain law and order, but nothing changed.

5

For the ordinary Hungarians, those who were numbed with the sheer horror and preoccupied with the uncertainties of the future, the Arrow-Cross reign was some kind of bad dream, from which they could not awake:

> This sad and shameful period of our history was characterised by German terrorism, the total continuation of the war, the complete ruination of the country and the uncontrolled and frantic prosecution of the Jews. The irresponsible leaders who had gained power tried to justify their activities by posing as the heroic saviours of the homeland and branding the members of the former Horthy regime as traitors. These notions were proclaimed ceaselessly over the radio and through the press, along with the hero worship of the Germans. In summary, our *'foreign policy'* amounted to nothing more than slavery under Nazi Germany and the continuation of the hopeless war. The so-called *'domestic policy'* had but one point in its program: the unbridled persecution of the Jews, accompanied by terror.[42]

Before long an anti-German and anti-Arrow-Cross mood began to swell in the population. An onlooker, who lived in Buda at that time, recalls:

> After the Germans removed the Regent, the nation as whole turned against the Germans and the Arrow Cross. Even those who had supported Germany now felt revulsion at the activities of Szálasi's gang.[43]

The leading Magyar literary novelist of the 1930s, Sándor Márai, made the following entry in his diary:

> The Germans really are magicians. They have contrived the miracle that all decent people look forward with genuine fervour to seeing the Russians, the Bolsheviks, who will be arriving as true liberators. I too look forward to seeing the Russians. We have all come a long way since two days ago... two days, seven months, twenty-five years.[44]

In contrast, the majority of the ethnic Germans living in Hungary (the so-called *Volksdeutsche*) – who were locally known as 'Swabs'[45] – felt greater loyalty towards the Third Reich than to

Hungary.[46] 'The ethnic Germans of Hungary, who had had unlimited privileges and unlimited possibilities for development, changed almost overnight into an egocentric, grasping and demanding force in the country,' wrote a former member of the Hungarian parliament after the war.[47] Most of them gladly accepted service in the Waffen-SS and three of the SS-Divisions (18, 22 and 31) engaged in the defence of the Hungarian Plain were almost exclusively composed of *Volksdeutsche* volunteers and conscripts. The *Volksbund*[48] established a special police force, *Heimat-Schutz*, for the maintenance of public order, which was supplied with weapons and quickly turned into a paramilitary branch of the SS. After 15 October the *Volksbund* press became very powerful. The weekly *Deutscher Volksbote* (sub-title *N.S.-Kampfblatt*) used its columns to incite street fights and called for the massacre of 'traitors'. The papers kept repeating the the Nazi propaganda slogan, 'Hold out! The wonder weapon is on its way!'[49]

A wedge was driven between the *Volksdeutsche* and the Hungarians. Alaine Polcz, then a 22-year-old refugee from Transylvania, recalls his arrival in a village situated just west of Budapest:

> We went to a Swabian village, Ilonka's mother told her happily that her husband would be home Saturday on a two-day leave. 'He should not go back to the army,' I said. 'Dress him in civilian clothes and have him wait, hidden somewhere, for the Russians.' They looked at me very strangely. They belonged to the *Volksbund* … (They could easily have broken my neck.)[50]

Divisions existed not only between the Magyars and the ethnic Germans but throughout Hungarian society.

> What was odd about this friendly company was that a continual political tension existed between us. They believed in a German victory and waited every minute for the front to reverse. We waited every minute for it to come to an end; after all, our very lives depended on it. Only one solution presented itself: no one ever talked politics, we never argued about anything. We talked about literature, philosophy, people, the past. We told stories, we played games. The endless winter nights passed … Marci and his wife were anti-Semitic, I believe. They were not pleased in principle by our harbouring Jews, but they accepted it in practice.[51]

After the war Szálasi's regime was blamed for everything and became a useful alibi for some nationalists and revisionists. The Horthy rule, in turn, has often been described as a marvellous time. But it was Horthy who in late 1919 staged the counter-revolutionary 'White Terror', with up to 5000 victims, and who usurped the throne in 1920 and appointed himself Regent for life. It was Horthy's government that during the inter-war years imposed a series of anti-Jewish laws, advocated anti-Semitism and territorial revisionism, avoided fundamental social reforms and brought Hungary into the orbit of Nazi Germany. Finally, it was Horthy and his clique that declared war on the Soviet Union and joined Hitler's *Drang nach Osten*. An entire army was sent to certain death in the Don steppes. The *Honvédség* did not find glory in a faraway land. Moreover, many of its troops pillaged, plundered, raped and committed terrible crimes against the local population and POWs. In the end they were quickly defeated and their remnants followed the direction of the general retreat of the *Ostheer*. Now, two years later, the boomerang of hatred was returning.

4

THE COMPLEXITY OF THE SOVIET MILITARY PLANS

1

Even though the earliest Soviet plans for invasion of the Magyar lands dated back to 1940,[1] the General Staff of Red Army began to map out a detailed strategy for seizing the Pannonian Plain only at the end of August 1944, when Romania capitulated and the 2nd Ukrainian Front reached the southern borders of Hungary. But the remnants of the defeated Army Group South Ukraine, mixed with several newly raised Magyar divisions, offered fierce resistance along the Carpathian chain and it took Malinovsky a whole month to break into Transylvania. From the very beginning the conquest of the Hungarian Kingdom promised to be bloody and difficult.

In the meantime, several major political events occurred in the region that further shaped Soviet military strategy. Stalin, of course, did everything possible to use these events for his own geopolitical aims.

First, on 26 August the Bulgarian government announced that the country was breaking the alliance with Germany and a fortnight later declared war on its former ally. By that time the troops of Marshal Tolbukhin's 3rd Ukrainian Front had poured into the country. Before long Tolbukhin managed to concentrate the 57th Army in northwestern Bulgaria without any interference, and moved on Belgrade. For Stalin, however, the Yugoslavian capital was not much more than a way station on the way to Budapest.

On 29 August a national uprising erupted in Slovakia. The next day, when the news about the revolt reached Moscow, Stalin ordered the 4th Ukrainian Front and the 38th Army of the 1st Ukrainian Front to cross the Carpathians and link up with the Slovakian insurgents.[2] In doing so, he hoped to establish a solid base for a subsequent drive into the Hungarian Plain and to link up with the spearheads of the 2nd Ukrainian Front in the area of Csap and Nyíregyháza. The offensive that began on 8 September, however, ran into severe difficulties due to the mountainous terrain and determined enemy resistance. By the end of the month the vital Carpathian passes were still in German hands.

The consolidation of forces intended to advance on Budapest began on 15 September, when Malinovsky received instructions to bring the 46th Army and the Pliev Cavalry-Mechanised Group to Timişoara over the period 3–7 October. From there that grouping was to advance either along the eastern bank of the Tisza or along the eastern bank of the Danube, on Budapest.[3]

Stavka realised that a direct advance on Budapest from the south/southeast would be too risky since there were still strong enemy groupings on both flanks, in Yugoslavia and in the Carpathians. The situation required these forces to be destroyed (or engaged) first and only then could the offensive in the centre be unleashed. Having successfully conquered Eastern Hungary, the Soviet troops would move on Budapest simultaneously from several different directions.[4]

Following this basic plan, on 28 September the 3rd Ukrainian Front mounted the Belgrade operation. On the same day the 38th Army and the 4th Ukrainian Front resumed their offensive to seize the Dukla pass and Ungvár (Užhorod). Finally, on 6 October, Stalin's main force, the 2nd Ukrainian Front, struck in the centre, aiming to capture Debrecen with the 6th Guards Tank Army and Pliev's group.

2

From the very beginning the Soviet grand offensive in Southeast Europe did not go as planned. While Tolbukhin's troops and Tito's partisans steadily advanced on Belgrade, putting the capital within their grasp, the attempt of the 4th Ukrainian Front and the 38th Army to break into Hungary through the Carpathians was a total failure. The attack of Malinovsky's armoured formations on Debrecen from the south ran into severe enemy resistance too.

Despite the obvious military difficulties, shortly after the beginning of the Debrecen Operation Stalin began to gather forces for the subsequent drive on Budapest. With the peace negotiations with Horthy's emissaries in full swing, the Hungarian turnabout now seemed just days away and a powerful force was to be assembled to drive to the capital as quickly as possible. That is why on 8 October Stavka ordered the 2nd Ukrainian Front to pull out the 7th Guards Army from the Târgu Mureş (Marosvásárhely) area in Central Romania and by 20 October to deploy it south of Oradea (Nagyvárad).[5] On the same day the fresh 23rd Rifle Corps (three divisions strong) was directed to transfer from Galicia (Western Ukraine) to Timişoara.[6] Three days later, the full-strength 2nd Guards Mechanised Corps, originally intended for the 3rd Ukrainian Front, received orders to assemble in the vicinity of Arad, not far from Szeged.[7] Thus a powerful grouping, comprising some 20 divisions and an armoured corps, was to be assembled near Szeged by the end of October and, the Soviet planners believed, shortly afterwards it would enter the capital of their newest ally in triumph.

Straddling the Tisza, Szeged was viewed by the Soviet High Command as the most suitable springboard for a rapid advance on Budapest. It offered not only the shortest route to the capital, but also an opportunity for troops and supplies to be brought quickly across the military and logistical obstacle of the Tisza. Therefore on 8 October Malinovsky ordered the 46th Army to capture Szeged by 10 October and switch onto the defensive along the banks of the Tisza and Danube.[8] The following actions of the front were enmeshed with the progress of the peace talks with the Magyars.

As we already know, at midday on 13 October Malinovsky submitted to Stavka his plans for the next stage of the Debrecen Operation (up to 20 October). He proposed to using the Pliev Group to attack towards Nyíregyháza and Csap with the objective of speeding up the drive of the 4th Ukrainian Front into the Hungarian Plain, at the same time using the Gorshkov Cavalry-Mechanised Group to strike at the Satu Mare (Szatmárnémeti)–Carei (Nagykároly) area and thus to entrap the Axis forces retreating from Transylvania. At a later stage the 6th Guards Tank Army was to be used either to reinforce the cavalry-mechanised groups or to launch an attack of its own from Debrecen to Miskolc. As previously mentioned, for the time being Malinovsky intended to hold the 46th and 53rd Army in their defensive positions along the Tisza and when a favourable situation arose to regroup them to reinforce the Szolnok axis.[9]

Once the information about the Arrow Cross coup d'état reached Moscow, Stalin decided at first to gamble. Following the instructions of Stavka, on 16 October Malinovsky ordered the 46th Army within the next 24 hours to form a shock group of no less than six divisions in the Szeged area and on the morning of 18 October to attack towards Budapest.[10] This offensive, however, was never put into effect, most probably because Stalin realised that the moment for such a daring raid had passed. It was clear that the Hungarian deadlock could be broken by force of arms only. The time for diplomacy had gone.

Meanwhile on the morning of 17 October the corps of the left flank (31st Guards) of the 46th Army was directed to move westwards and by the end of 20 October to reach the Danube and secure the Baja–Zombor line.[11] This was intended to prevent the German troops retreating from Belgrade to counter-attack the army from the rear. During the next three days the corps advanced some 75km without facing much opposition and secured the objective.

The failed Magyar volte-face forced Stalin to act promptly. In the early hours of 18 October he signed two directives that clearly showed his determination to solve the 'Hungarian problem' once and for all. With the first one (signed at 02:00 MT) he directed the central grouping of the 2nd Ukrainian Front (6th Guards Tank Army, Pliev's and Gorshkov's cavalry-mechanised groups) to capture Debrecen and to destroy the enemy forces defending the vicinity of the town. The 46th Army was ordered to reach the Danube at Zombor and to form there a powerful grouping for a subsequent advance on Budapest.[12] The other directive, issued seven hours later, ordered the 3rd Ukrainian Front to start deploying in the Hungarian Plain.[13]

3

The entry of Tolbukhin's troops into the battle for Hungary was determined by both political and military factors. Amongst the political ones were the coup in Budapest and the Moscow conference, but the strategic plans and the preliminary agreements between Stalin and Tito were the most decisive. Therefore, it is no wonder that on 15 October Stalin ordered the 3rd Ukrainian Front not to advance beyond Belgrade.[14]

The strictly military factors were the situation in Hungary and the successful withdrawal of German troops from the Balkans. Soviet intelligence had noted construction of defensive lines on the Drava, Sava and Drina rivers that were intended to cover the retreat of the enemy. Very well fortified positions were also being prepared along the Bratislava–Maribor–Trieste line, which would allow the Germans to form a stable front from Hungary to Italy. Taking this into account, the General Staff perceived that if the Germans succeeded in withdrawing their forces to the Trieste–Bratislava line they would receive effective help from the Hungarian and Italian troops and would have more favourable flank position than the 2nd Ukrainian Front, the troops of which had advanced far to the north. There was a gap between the forces of Malinovsky and Tolbukhin, which was only weakly protected by the Red Army in the Zombor–Novi Sad area. Shtemenko recalls the decision-making process:

> To prevent German troop concentrations, as yet separated, from coming together in a solid front, the Third Ukrainian Front would have to launch active operations before the autumn and winter rains made the roads difficult. The main axis of advance could follow the valleys of the Drava and Mur rivers, through which forces of all types could pass freely; there we would have the best chance to form the wedge that the enemy so feared. This is why, when the 57th Army's corps was sent into the area of Sombor, the Army commander was told that an offensive to the west might be ahead.[15]

Following these considerations, on 18 October Stavka issued directive # 220244 ordering Tolbukhin by 25–27 October to position one rifle corps along the Danube bank at Zombor in order to protect Malinovsky's left flank. It was be reinforced with the recently reconstituted 4th Guards Army (eight divisions strong), which was to transfer from Galicia to Timişoara.[16]

4

Following the instructions in the Stavka directive of 18 October, from 19 to 21 October Malinovsky issued a series of orders aiming to regroup his troops for the forthcoming actions and to improve their jump-off positions.[17] The 46th Army, in particular, was tasked to reach the Baja–Kiskunfélegyháza line by 21 October and to hold firm.[18] The arriving 2nd Guards Mechanised Corps was directed to assemble in the vicinity of Szeged by 27 October.[19] It would not be alone; another armoured formation, the 4th Guards Mechanised Corps, was coming that way too. On 21 October the corps, which had just taken part in the liberation of Belgrade, was subordinated to the 2nd Ukrainian Front and ordered to regroup in the Vršac area.[20] Wasting no time, Malinovsky issued orders directing the corps to transfer to Szentes and thus to assemble in the immediate rear of the 46th Army. The move had to be completed by 25 October.[21]

In the meantime the fighting at the front continued unabated. On 19 October the German LVII Panzer Corps delivered a sudden blow to the Romanian positions at Szolnok. The critical situation there forced Malinovsky to commit the 7th Guards and 6th Guards Tank Armies. Further to the northeast, the Soviet forces finally succeeded in breaking through the Axis defence in the Debrecen area. The town itself fell into their hands on 20 October. Then Pliev's group advanced straight to the north, to Nyíregyháza, in an attempt to cut off the rear communications of the 8th German and 1st Hungarian Armies and to entrap them in the area west of Užhorod (Ungvár). The Germans, however, took full advantage of the narrow width of the Soviet penetration corridor and the vulnerable flanks of the Pliev group. On 22 October their armoured formations, supported by other German and Hungarian units, counter-attacked the Soviets near Nyíregyháza and managed to surround the spearhead of the cavalry-mechanised group. The latter suffered serious losses[22] and thus the Soviets once again failed to encircle the Axis troops.

The fact that the Axis efforts were diverted to the Nyíregyháza area allowed the 46th Army to advance to the west virtually unopposed. On 21 October the troops of its 31st Guards Rifle Corps seized Zombor and Baja and in so doing reached the Danube on a broad front. On the army's right flank, however, the situation did not develop as expected. Right from the outset it became clear that the northward drive of the 37th Rifle Corps would not be easy. The corps captured Kiskunfélegyháza during the evening of 23 October, after three days of heavy fighting. All its attempts to advance farther to the north and even to take Kecskemét were warded off by the Hungarian troops. The latter launched a series of fierce counterattacks and by the end of 26 October the corps switched over to the defensive.[23] Despite this minor setback, Malinovsky's order was accomplished and by 26 October the 46th Army secured the line that would become its springboard for the march on Budapest.

5

At the beginning of October the Soviet offensive along the Vistula and Narew rivers finally lost its momentum. Once again Stavka carefully evaluated different sectors of the front to determine the next objectives. It was clear that Poland, along the direct route to Berlin, offered the most attractive avenues of advance. On the other hand, the Germans were still keeping a considerable number of their panzer formations there. A successful attack would require a diversion of the German armoured reserves from the Berlin axis, so it was decided to shift the emphasis to the flanks. In the autumn of 1944 the flanks of the Soviet-German front ran through the East Prussia and Courland peninsula (in the north) and Hungary and the Balkans (in the south).

While in the north a heavy blow against the German army groups defending the Baltic corner was delivered almost immediately, in the south the failure of the Hungarian attempt to quit the Nazi camp called for a major reshape of Soviet military plans. So in the last days of October the General Staff produced a new plan, which differed from the previous ones because the goals set were to be achieved by military means only. The main forces of the 3rd Ukrainian Front were to be concentrated between the Danube and Tisza rivers in the area south of Kecskemét. From there Tolbukhin should attack to the north and northwestwards and thus assist the offensive of the 2nd Ukrainian Front.

Stavka hoped that the troops would advance at high speed and reach the Banská Bystrica–Komárom–Nagykanizsa line by 30 November and the city of Vienna by 30 December. It was expected that by New Year's Eve the southern wing of the Red Army would stand at the Vienna–Jihlava line, some 250–350km from its positions of late October. The achievement of these objectives would allow the Soviets to establish a firm base for a subsequent drive into Czechoslovakia and Central Germany from the south. Such a powerful onslaught, the Soviet General Staff officers believed, would divert Hitler's attention from the main (central) axis and would force him to move his main armoured reserves to Hungary. In turn, this would allow the Red Army to advance to Berlin from the east without much opposition. This would become the broad brush guideline for the conduct of the Soviet war effort in Central Europe.[24]

Special importance was attached to the capture of Budapest. It was estimated that the fall of the Hungarian capital would have a great effect on the political situation in the country and would undermine the morale of the Axis. The earlier plans for taking the city with the forces of the 2nd and 4th Ukrainian Fronts only were now revised and the 3rd Ukrainian was also brought in. 'It might seem that we had more than enough forces,' Shtemenko wrote after the war.[25] Budapest was not only a significant military and political objective; it was an important economic centre as well. There were 900 factories and plants situated in and around the city producing goods for Hungary and the Third Reich. In addition, Budapest was an important junction: at least seven major highways and eleven railways were running through it. Without the capture of the capital any further advance on Vienna would be out of the question; it would turn into a logistical nightmare.

The Soviet General Staff was well aware that the Hungarian capital was prepared for a long siege. In the region of Budapest the German command had created strong defensive lines, which, in the form of arcs, covered the city from the south and east (the so-called 'Attila line'). The enemy had significant stocks of arms, ammunition, foodstuffs, medical supplies and other resources. Everything possible was done to halt the advance of the Red Army at the gates of the Magyar capital. That was why for the Red Army it was very important to avoid being dragged into a costly frontal attack:

> At the General Staff we made an in-depth study of the impending actions by Soviet forces in the Budapest operation: their nature and the methods to be employed. The gist of our thinking as regards manoeuvres was that we should move around the city in the north and the south, using minimal forces in frontal attacks … Meantime the enemy was striving in every way to block our manoeuvres and our forward movement. It was important to him to compel us to make a frontal attack, the least promising for us, and fraught with heavy losses, and to provoke us to attack on the run without the requisite preparation. Such is the logic of war, when two forces with diametrically opposed aims come into conflict.[26]

5

'TAKE BUDAPEST AS QUICKLY AS POSSIBLE!'

1

Stalin ordered the attack on Budapest shortly before midnight on 28 October 1944. At 22:00 MT the headquarters of the 2nd Ukrainian Front received the following important directive from Moscow:

> Stavka of the Supreme Main Command orders [the 2nd Ukrainian Front] to go over to the offensive on 29 October between the river Tisza and the river Danube with the forces of 46th Army and the 2nd Guards Mechanised Corps with the objective of rolling back the defence of the enemy on the western bank of the river Tisza and taking the 7th Guards Army beyond the river Tisza. Subsequently, with the approach of the 4th Guards Mechanised Corps, a determined attack is to be made against the enemy's grouping, which is defending Budapest.[1]

Two popular theories circulate about the reasons why Stalin ordered Marshal Rodion Malinovsky, the commander of the 2nd Ukrainian Front, to unleash a powerful offensive on the Hungarian capital right after the bloody battle of Debrecen. According to the first, the Kremlin dictator wanted the city captured by 7 November, the anniversary of the October Revolution. This version, spread after the war by some former German generals, has no factual basis.[2]

The second theory came from Malinovsky himself. In 1965, in a book entitled *Budapesht–Vena–Praga*, the Marshal blamed Stalin for the failure of the Red Army to capture Budapest in the autumn of 1944. According to Malinovsky, on the evening of that fateful 28 October, the Supreme Commander had called him up at the headquarters of the 46th Army and ordered him in a resolute tone to seize Budapest as soon as possible:

> STALIN: It is absolutely essential that in the shortest possible time, in days even, you capture the capital of Hungary – Budapest. This has to be done no matter what it costs you. Can you do this?

> MALINOVSKY: This assignment could be carried out within five days, once 4th Guards Mechanised Corps moves up to 46th Army. This movement is expected to be complete by 1 November. Then 46th Army, reinforced by two Guards mechanised corps – 2nd and 4th – would be able to mount a powerful attack, which would come as a complete surprise to the enemy and in two to three days take Budapest.

STALIN: The Stavka cannot give you five days. You understand that it is because of political considerations that we have got to take Budapest as quickly as possible.

MALINOVSKY: I very definitely understand that we have to take Budapest in view of these political considerations. However we should wait for the arrival of 4th Guards Mechanised Corps. Only under these conditions will it be possible to count on success.

STALIN: We cannot consider postponing the offensive for five days. It is necessary to go over to the offensive for Budapest at once.

MALINOVSKY: If you give me, as of now, five days as an absolute maximum, Budapest will be taken. If we go over to the offensive without delay, then 46th Army, for sheer lack of forces, will not be able to develop its blow quickly, it will be inevitably get bogged down in heavy fighting at the very approaches to the Hungarian capital. Putting it briefly, it cannot sieze Budapest off the march.

STALIN: You are arguing all to no purpose. You don't understand the political necessity of mounting an immediate attack on Budapest.

MALINOVSKY: I understand all the political importance of taking Budapest and for that very reason I am asking five days ...

STALIN: I categorically order you to go over to the offensive for Budapest tomorrow.[3]

The transcript ends here, but it is accompanied by the following comment:

Stalin then hung up, which meant that the conversation was over. A few minutes later the telephone rang again. Army-General A.I. Antonov, the Deputy Chief of the General Staff, asked the precise time when the 46th Army would attack, in order to report it to Stalin.

Malinovsky spoke to Stalin and Antonov directly from the HQ of the 46th Army. And right then and there, he ordered the army's commander to attack on the morning of 29 October. Naturally, the attack developed slowly, and the German-Fascist command had time to transfer enough forces and materiel to organise a stiff resistance. That was the only reason why protracted battles were fought for Budapest. They were an eloquent testimony to misplaced haste or rather to error in deciding such an important strategical mission as the capture of the Hungarian capital. One could not help but remember the military leader's motto: 'I don't hurry, because I intend to act quickly.' We might point out that afterwards, Stalin avoided the subject of Budapest in his phone conversations with Malinovsky for quite a while.[4]

Malinovsky's disclosure quickly gained popularity in the West, but his claim that his armies were not prepared to launch an immediate offensive on the Magyar capital should be taken with a pinch of salt.

During the Soviet era the story about this phone conversation appeared in three other books: in 1970 it was entirely reproduced in the Marshal Matvei Zakharov's *Osvobozhdenie Yugo-Vostochnoi i Tsentralnoi Evropy* (*Liberation of Southeastern and Central Europe*); in 1971 it appeared again in another work of Zakharov, an article dedicated to Malinovsky, which was included in the first volume of *Polkovodtsy i voenachal'niki Velikoi Otechestvenoi* (*Commanders and Military Leaders of the Great Patriotic [War]*); and in 1972 it was briefly mentioned in the first biography of Malinovsky, a booklet titled *Soldat. Polkovodets* (*Soldier. Commander*), written by M. Gorbunov. Malinovsky's statement found a supporter in the person of Shtemenko, who in his memoir pretended to be revealing more facts on the circumstances surrounding this complicated decision:

One factor which to some extent figured in our hurrying up the attack on Budapest was the jingoistic optimism of the reports that L.Z. Mekhlis sent in on the breakdown and demoralisation of the Hungarian forces. He did a particularly good job of throwing the fat on the fire with his telegram of October[5] addressed to Stalin personally:
'The units of the Hungarian 1st Army opposing our front are in process of a breakdown and of demoralisation. Every day our troops take from 1000 to 1500, 2000 or more prisoners. On 25 October 1944, the 18th Army took 2500 prisoners, with whole units surrendering at a time… Owing to the turning movements of our front's forces, many Hungarian units are quite simply scattered; and individual groups of soldiers wander through the woods, some with arms and some without, while some have put on civilian clothes…'
With his reports, Mekhlis managed to stimulate Stalin's imagination, and the latter asked the General staff how we might best attack Budapest so as to take it as quickly as possible. Suspecting nothing, we replied that the best way would be to utilise the extensive bridgehead that had been seized by the left flank of the 2nd Ukrainian Front in the area between the two rivers: the Tisza and the Danube. Here it would not be necessary to force a river, and the enemy had fewer forces in this area than on the other sectors. Also, the 46th Army, which had advanced to that point, was relatively fresh. After breaking through, it could roll back the enemy's defences beyond the Tisza on the north, and thus facilitate a direct thrust toward Budapest by Shumilov's 7th Guards Army and the Romanian 1st Army coming from the east.
Having thought over the General Staff's idea, Stalin called Malinovsky and ordered that the 2nd Ukrainian Front should immediately capture Budapest. Even Antonov, who gave the Supreme Commander an unvarnished report on the situation, could not prove to him that the reports from Mekhlis did not correspond to the facts, especially in the area of Budapest.
I mention this episode because in the technical literature there have been frequent mentions of the fact that on October 29, 1944, the 2nd Ukrainian Front launched an offensive toward Budapest without adequate preparation or troop build-up. The first to write about this was Malinovsky, who had personally received from Stalin the order to take the Hungarian capital in the shortest possible time, 'literally in a matter of days'. Malinovsky asked for five days in which to set about accomplishing the mission, but the order he got was: 'Mount the offensive toward Budapest tomorrow.'
We confirmed this verbal order from the supreme commander by a Stavka directive dated October 28 at 2200 hours.[6]

The western historians that were then researching the battles on the Eastern Front took (and still take) Malinovsky's 'disclosure' and the subsequent Shtemenko 'revelations' at face value. For them the explanations of these two key Soviet officers were just another example of the sheer stupidity and brutality of Stalin. Ever since then, virtually all of the books issued in the West about the Soviet-German conflict have repeated uncritically the story about the 'unprepared' attack the 2nd Ukrainian Front had launched on Budapest. None of them has paid attention to the fact that the Shtemenko's and Malinovsky's version of the events was not supported by other, far more serious Soviet studies on the subject. How correct is their story? Did their description of events echo the actual military situation in Central Hungary in the last week of October 1944? What was the purpose of Malinovsky's visit to Shlemin's HQ on that day? What exactly had forced Stalin to order the attack?
Let us begin with the Shtemenko's claim that with his reports Mekhlis had managed to stimulate 'Stalin's imagination' by reporting that *Honvédség* was disintegrating. Even though

in terms of the losses sustained by the 1 Army (Hung) those reports proved to be correct,[7] Stalin was already well aware that the Magyar troops would not leave the Axis camp. A proof of that is the already-quoted Stavka directive that was sent on the evening of 24 October to Marshal Timoshenko, the 2nd and the 4th Ukrainian Fronts, regarding the treatment of those Hungarian forces that continued to fight against the Red Army.[8]

The number of prisoners taken by the 2nd Ukrainian Front after the arrival of the directive does not show any signs of disintegration either; from 25 to 28 October fewer than 4400 enemy troops had been captured and some of them were of course Germans.[9] Some more of Shtemenko's claims don't hold water either.

In April 1965, barely a month before *Budapesht–Vena–Praga* became available to the public, the *Voenno-Istoricheskii Zhurnal* (Military History Magazine) published an article by Shtemenko, entitled *'Kak planirovalas posledniaia kampania po razgromu Gitlerovskoi Germanii'* ('How the last campaign for the destruction of Hitler's Germany was planned').[10] In contrast to his later memoir, the article is quite frank and detailed. Regarding the planning of the Budapest offensive, Shtemenko wrote the following:

> In the zones of the 4th, 2nd and 3rd Ukrainian Fronts, on the other hand, the General Staff hoped for considerable success, essentially on the basis of political considerations. There were prospects for a headlong drive to the Moravska Ostrava–Brno line and to the approaches of Vienna, for the capture of Budapest, and for crossing the Danube. A considerable part of the enemy infantry in this area was made up of Hungarian divisions whose stability, in our estimation, might well be fundamentally undermined by the growing anti-war feeling and the atrocities committed by the fascists in their efforts to keep Hungary on the side of Hitler's Third Reich. The fall of the Szálasi regime would have taken the country out of the war and placed the German troops in a difficult situation. Unfortunately, these calculations proved to be wrong … In the course of this creative search, an overall major idea was born and developed, an idea which concerned the pre-requisites for the success of our operations in the main sector. The idea was to draw the enemy forces away from the central sector by means of active operations on the flanks of his strategic front. It was proposed to achieve this not only in Hungary and Austria, which were farther away from the main direction of our future offensive, but in East Prussia as well. This called for an energetic development of the offensive in the Budapest area and the carrying out of offensive operations in the Königsberg area.[11]

This statement, directly contradicts what he would write later in his memoirs:[12]

> The operation demanded long and careful preparation; all the more so since the autumnal season of bad roads had set in, and the rain was heavy. There was virtually no air action, and the artillery often had to be dragged along by hand. Any kind of transport would bog down in the washed-out roads. Under these conditions it was very hard to supply the front with all it needed, and even harder to effect regrouping and turning movements … Our hopes that we would have time to make thorough preparations for the operation were not fulfilled.[13]

What made him change his standpoint so radically? It is difficult to say, but one of the possible reasons was the fact that Malinovsky had brought his military career back to life. Shtemenko ended the war as a Deputy Chief of the General Staff and one of Stalin's favourites. Soon thereafter he was promoted to the rank of Army-General, Chief of the General Staff and Deputy Minister of Defence. After Stalin's death he was reduced in rank, overthrown and virtually disappeared from public life; but in 1956 Zhukov, then a Minister of Defence, lent a helping hand and appointed him chief of Soviet military intelligence. This did not last long and when

Above: Colonel Zhukov, commander of the 36th Guards Tank Brigade.

Left: Colonel-General Matvei Zakharov, the chief of staff of the 2nd Ukrainian Front.

in October 1957 Zhukov was relieved, Shtemenko's career nosedived again. In 1962 Zhukov's successor – Malinovsky – for some reason decided to restore his trust in Shtemenko and made him Chief of the Main Staff of the Soviet Ground Forces. In 1965, the mastermind of Stalin's conquest of Eastern Europe was already a Deputy Chief of the General Staff. The second blossoming of his career did not end here and continued even after Malinovsky's death in 1967. In 1968 Shtemenko was on top again and as Chief of Staff of the Warsaw Pact Forces plotted the invasion of Czechoslovakia. So in the late 1960s one of Stalin's favourites might have had a very good reason to be grateful to his new mentor.

The authors of the other two books mentioned above might have had their own good reasons to support the story about the 'hasty' attack on Budapest too. Matvei Zakharov was Malinovsky's Chief of Staff from May 1944 until the routing of the Kwantung Army in August 1945 and a co-editor of *Budapesht–Vena–Praga,* while Gorbunov was one of the ghostwriters who did the actual writing. As with Shtemenko's writings, there is a contradiction in Zakharov's works as well. In 1965, in an article published in a book of essays dedicated to the liberation of Hungary, Zakharov recalls that the Front Command had decided to launch an attack on Budapest from the south right after the fall of Debrecen, when the battle at Nyíregyháza was still raging.[14] If he is to be believed, on 2 November 1944, when the Soviet spearheads were at Budapest's doorstep, he and Malinovsky concluded that their decision to attack the Magyar capital without operational pause 'was the right one'.[15]

Unlike in the West, the official Soviet historiography never took seriously the Malinovsky-Shtemenko version, and with justification. In 1958 the then classified study *'Operatsii Sovetskih vooruzehennyh sil'* ('Operations of the Soviet Armed Forces'), prepared by the History Department of the General Staff, emphasised that the grounds for the Stavka decision were:

- the weak enemy defence of the eastern approaches to Budapest (the 350km long front-line between the Dukla Pass and Polgár was defended by 31 divisions and 3 brigades with an average frontage of 11km per division while the 250km line from Polgár to Baja was defended by only 11 divisions with an average frontage of 23km per division)
- own offensive was already in preparation: in October, sizable reinforcements were moved to the left flank of the 2nd Ukrainian , the 7th Guards Army, followed later by the 6th Guards Tank Army and 18th Tank Corps (we also saw that the 23rd Rifle, 2nd and 4th Guards Mechanised Corps were moved there too); furthermore, the 57th Army of the 3rd Ukrainian Front began to regroup into the area between Tisza and Danube immediately after the completion of the Belgrade Operation with the aim to attack Budapest from the south
- the apprehension that after the success at Nyíregyháza the German Command would regroup their forces (and the armoured formations in particular) to strengthen the eastern and southeastern approaches to the Hungarian capital (fully justified, as we shall see later).[16]

The fourth volume of the official *Soviet History of the Great Patriotic War* (published in 1963) makes it clear on what grounds the decision for attack had been reached:

> Having estimated the developed conditions, in particular the shaky political position of the ruling clique of Hungary and the weakness of the defence of the enemy facing the left wing of the 2nd Ukrainian Front, on 28 October Stavka of the Supreme Command sent a directive to the commander of the 2nd Ukrainian Front … to go over to the offensive.[17]

In his book of 1965, *Osvobozhdenie Vengrii i Vostochnoi Avstrii* ('The Liberation of Hungary and Eastern Austria'), Colonel Malakhov gives exactly the same reasons for the Stavka order as above.[18] Moreover, two years later, in his classic study *Osvobozhdenie narodov Yougovostochnoi Evropy* ('The Liberation of the Peoples of Southeast Europe'), Minasyan dared to contest Malinovsky's version.[19] Golubovich, who wrote the second biography of Malinovsky (published in 1983), threw more light on the political aspect of the decision, indicating that Stalin was motivated to forestall the Western Allies in Central Europe and the Balkans.[20]

Malinovsky's claims did not find supporters even amongst those who could benefit most from them: his former subordinates. Even in the dusk of their lives, these men were still officers who held their heads up high and kept their dignity. Despite the communist censorship and the nepotistic atmosphere of the Brezhnev era, the former army commanders did not use their publications for self-serving purposes. In an article published in December 1964 Shlemin described the events that preceded the attack on Budapest.[21] Being aware of the 'phone call story', in 1969 Shumilov nevertheless wrote that Stalin's principal motivation was desire to exploit the 'military–political situation' in Hungary.[22] In the 1980s Pliev wrote in his memoirs:

> Taking into account the strained and unstable political situation in Hungary and the importance of taking the country out of the war, already during the Debrecen Operation the leadership of the 2nd Ukrainian Front was preparing a decisive strike on Budapest. For that purpose, by the end of October considerable forces were massed on the Front's left flank.[23]

The wartime records of the 2nd Ukrainian Front do not give a definitive answer as to how surprising the Stavka directive was for Malinovsky and his staff. However, it is clear that by 28 October some preparations for attack in the sector of the 46th Army had already been carried out. Thus, for instance, on the evening of 25 October the 2nd Guards Mechanised Corps received orders to redeploy to Kiskundorozsma by 27 October, just to the northwest

Colonel-General Mikhail Shumilov, commander of the 7th Guards Army.

of Szeged. There it was to camouflage carefully all its tanks and trucks.[24] But that was not all: in the afternoon of 27 October the corps units began to study the routes by which they would move once the big offensive would be unleashed. The corps commander himself was told that the attack would take place in the sector of the 10th Rifle Corps, in the direction of Kiskunhalas.[25]

The other major formations intended to reinforce the effort of the 46th Army had gathered themselves together as well. Thus by the end of 28 October the entire 23rd Rifle Corps had assembled northeast of Makó.[26] And we already know that the 4th Guards Mechanised Corps, the slow regrouping of which was Malinovsky's main argument for postponement of the offensive, had been scheduled to complete its assembly on 25 October. On the night before the attack the bulk of its troops were in Szeged.

This is not all: there are some wartime documents that directly contradict Malinovsky's claim from 1965. For instance, the records of the 37th Rifle Corps, the force that was intended to deliver the initial blow and open the road to Budapest, clearly describe the offensive of 29 October as nothing but a continuation of the one that was halted on 26 October just north of Kiskunfélegyháza by the determined Magyar resistance: 'At 14:00 MT on 29.10.1944 the troops of the 37th Rifle Corps, after a brief artillery barrage, resumed the offensive and, having crushed the enemy resistance, developed their success to Kecskemét.'[27]

When in May 1965 Marshal Malinovsky revealed the 'truth' behind his failure to take Budapest quickly, Fyodor Kolchuck, the former commander of the 37th Rifle Corps and a retired general, was probably more than a little surprised.

2

The reasons that compelled Stalin to pick up the phone and order an immediate attack on Budapest were definitely complex; they were a mixed set of military – forestalling the regrouping of the German armour, the weak enemy defence in the zone of the 46th Army, the build up for offensive on the left flank of the 2nd Ukrainian Front that was in progress since mid-October – and political – the low morale of the *Honvédség*, the shaky political situation in Hungary, forestalling the Western Allies in Central Europe. One could add here the reports of Soviet intelligence; at the end of October it informed the Stavka that the powerful fortifications around the Hungarian capital were still unmanned.[28] From today's point of view the decision was warrantable.

Probably Malinovsky did indeed believe that Budapest would have fallen quickly had he been given five extra days. The condition of his forces after their advance across Eastern

Hungary was not good, the troops of the left flank had just crossed the Tisza and needed time for consolidation. After the debacle at Nyíregyháza most of the Front's armoured formations were in tatters. He knew in general terms that the Germans were beginning to shift their armoured forces from the northeast to the area southeast of Budapest and he was afraid that without proper preparation the enemy armour, in combination with the bad weather and the difficult terrain, would bring his forces to a halt short of the main objective. 'Making a decision, Rodion Yakovlevich was convinced that it was the right one, and consequently was always ready to defend it,' Zakharov wrote on the occasion of 'that' conversation with Stalin. 'Quite often, as is apparent from the cited example, it demanded some courage: the anger of the Supreme Commander did not promise anything pleasant.'[29] Nevertheless, Stalin's decision to ignore Malinovsky's request to increase the strength of the 46th Army by postponing its advance was perhaps the right one; had it started on 2/3 November, the attack would have faced a fairly impenetrable continuous defence line south of the Hungarian capital backed by six newly arrived German mobile divisions.

6

'WET, COLD AND TOTALLY DEPRESSING'

1

Had Malinovsky been given enough forces, he would have become the Brusilov of the Pannonian Basin (he had quite enough qualities for that) and the first Soviet Commander to enter deep into the Third Reich. But in the autumn of 1944 full priority was given to the Berlin axis and the flow of strategic reserves, replacements, new tanks and aircraft went there. In order to achieve his main military and political goal – crushing Nazi Germany and capturing Berlin before the Allies get there – Stalin took away two of Malinovsky's tank armies during the early summer of 1944 and two all-arms armies (after only nine days of fighting!) immediately after the conclusion of the Jassy-Kishinev operation in late August. With his last remaining tank army, which was a weak version of the 800+ tank-strong tank armies stationed in Poland, the 2nd Ukrainian Front looked like a one-armed boxer: ferocious, but predictable. The southern flank was not the top priority for the Soviet High Command, so it is no wonder that throughout the whole campaign in Hungary the overall numerical superiority of the Red Army never exceeded 2 to 1.

Malinovsky's main problems were the exhaustion of the troops and decline of manpower as a result of the bloody losses sustained during the October battles. Success in the Debrecen operation was bought with 19,713 killed or missing and 64,297 wounded.[1] No substantial replacements were provided to make up these losses.

Another major worry for Malinovsky and his staff was the severe tank shortage that occurred at the end of October. The Marshal had foreseen this problem and already had warned Stavka about it. On 20 October he reported to Moscow that in the recent engagements the Front had lost no fewer than 1229 tanks and SP guns[2] and requested an urgent delivery of 1347 armoured machines, instead of only 300 that were already underway.[3] The Front was now left with only two armoured formations fit for immediate frontline employment: the newly arrived 2nd and 4th Guards Mechanised Corps. Thus in late October Malinovsky found himself forced to conduct operations with relatively light mobile forces. This, in turn, deprived the planners of the 2nd Ukrainian Front of alternatives and made their moves easy to predict.

The remainder of the mobile troops were temporarily non-functional and were licking their wounds in the rear areas. The Pliev Cavalry-Mechanised Group (4th, 5th and 6th Guards Cavalry Corps; 7th Mechanised Corps and 23rd Tank Corps) would be ready for combat by 10 November while the 6th Guards Tank Army (5th Guards Tank and 9th Guards Mechanised Corps) and 18th Tank Corps would be committed again only in December. On the eve of the first assault on Budapest no less than 57–58 per cent of the Front's tank inventory was allocated in the 2nd and 4th Guards Mechanised Corps.[4]

2

The generally unsatisfactory combat performance of the Romanian armies was another headache for the leadership of the 2nd Ukrainian Front. The quality of the troops of this new Soviet ally varied from outstanding to poor. Even though some formations received high praise from the army commanders under whom they served,[5] many others were described as 'not suitable for employment in the main sectors of the front', undermanned, underarmed and hopelessly weak.[6] The overall impression was that the Romanians were using obsolete tactics. A Soviet liaison officer with the headquarters of the 4th Army reported, for instance, that the interaction between infantry and artillery was almost non-existent.[7] The author of this report paid special attention to the lack of efficient leadership in the Romanian infantry divisions: the senior officers were not leading from the front; the junior officers, on the contrary, were leading from the front, but at the same time, the casualty rate among them was very high; the replacements of the fallen junior officers were usually sergeants and privates with very limited man-management skills.[8]

The condition of the Romanian troops left much to be desired. Armed predominantly with a limited range of German-made weapons and machinery, they were very short of motor transport and engineering equipment and were in constant need of spare parts. Because of this the official establishments of the corps and divisions were seriously reduced. The infantry divisions were mostly composed of semi-literate peasants and the firepower of their horse-drawn artillery regiments was quite inadequate; their 100mm howitzers and 75mm field guns were considerably inferior to their German and Soviet equivalents. The same applied to the divisional anti-tank artillery: it was to consist of a single battery of six 75mm guns. The defencelessness of the Romanian infantrymen against the panzers became especially evident during the sharp German counter-attack at Szolnok (19–22 October) when in a mere 48 hours a whole division (4th Infantry) was taken prisoner and erased from the order of battle of the 1st Army.

The fact that the Romanian troops had proved themselves incapable of withstanding strong armoured attacks was becoming a serious problem and Malinovsky tried to cope with it by introducing two very different measures. He reinforced the VII Army Corps (Rom) with a towed anti-tank artillery regiment and he ordered Soviet barrier detachments to be placed behind the Romanians to prevent panic or unauthorised retreat.[9]

The ordinary Soviet combatants usually shared the low opinion of the Romanian troops that their Front commander had. Alexander Rogachev, a commander of the anti-tank battery in 1st Battalion, 18th Guards Mechanised Brigade of 9th Guards Mechanised Corps, found the Romanian infantry prone to panic and far inferior in combat to the German and Magyar infantrymen.[10] Another soldier – Tarassuk from the 53rd Rifle Division – heard good things of the ill-equipped new artillery allies:

> Amazingly, the Romanian artillery, which looked to me not to be specialists, had guns which were very much outdated in terms of construction and support equipment. I saw them moving on the roads quite often and they looked like they were from World War I. Yet, I heard our officers praise the action of Romanian artillery, unlike other units like the cavalry.[11]

On the whole, the morale of the Romanian troops was not very high. They were fighting in a hostile environment (the Romanians and the Magyars had been arch-enemies for centuries), their country was war weary, the Soviet occupation of the homeland did not raise the spirits and the defeat of the 4th Infantry Division was still fresh in the memory. Furthermore, during the previous battles the Romanian units had sustained considerable losses; between 21 September and 25 October the 1st Army alone had lost 8720 men (out of a strength of 67,347).[12] And last but not least, there was a considerable decline in motivation once Northern Transylvania was 'liberated' and the war was brought to the Hungarian Plain.

The low morale and hostile surroundings led to numerous incidents of indiscipline by the Romanian troops. Looting, rapes and other acts against the Magyar population became so widespread that on 14 October Malinovsky found himself forced to issue the following order:

> The Military Council of the Front has been made aware of a number of occasions when Romanian units break into, ransack and plunder private properties of the people of Transylvania and Hungary, pick out the last remaining household goods, rape women and children and abuse the locals in various ways. Those facts bring about negative moods among the local population.
>
> Romanian units should fight, not engage in banditry; their unacceptable behaviour in the territories of Transylvania and Hungary evokes feelings and moods against the Red Army that are not politically advantageous.
>
> In order to eradicate the habit of looting from the Romanian troops, the Military Council orders the Army Military Councils to immediately take the respective measures and issue a special order to the commanders of the Romanian divisions, requiring that they, in turn, should take all the necessary measures to immediately stop the cases of banditry and make sure that all such cases are investigated locally and those found guilty tried and punished severely … [13]

3

The 2nd Ukrainian Front was forced to begin the Budapest operation under less favourable conditions than it had had on the previous offensive. Of course, on paper it was still almost 580,000 strong, but, as we have already noted, the armoured formations had fewer tanks, the infantry and the cavalry had lost a lot of men. The most important disadvantage, however, was that now the frontline was half as long, which meant that the Germans would be able to regroup their armoured reserves much quicker and the concentration of the enemy troops would increase greatly.

The supply situation was difficult. By the beginning of November the rear services of the 2nd Ukrainian Front could provide the frontline troops with 1.5-2 ammunition sets, 2.9 'fills' of gasoline and 5.9 of diesel fuel. The 5th Air Army was provided with 5.9 fills of B-70 aviation gasoline, but the high-octane B-78, as usual, was in short supply: only 2.5 fills.[14] These quantities were inadequate to meet the demands of a large-scale action like the assault on Budapest.[15]

The logistic troubles of the 2nd Ukrainian Front were caused primarily by the narrow gauge of the Romanian railway network. But this problem was not something new to Malinovsky and his staff; already in September the railway stations near the Soviet-Romanian border were jammed with military goods urgently needed at the battlefield. The unpleasant situation forced the leadership of the Front to switch transportation from the railways to the highways. Thousands of vehicles were employed for the purpose. Day and night they were driving through the Carpathian passes, carrying munitions, fuel and provisions for the armies fighting in the *Puszta*.[16]

This was not the end of the supply nightmare for the 2nd Ukrainian Front. As the autumn went on, the rains turned the non-asphalt roads into quagmires impassable for most of the motor vehicles. Once again Malinovsky's logistic headquarters was forced to seek alternative methods for transporting the military goods. The Front was allowed temporarily to create 11 horse-drawn transport companies.[17]

The supply channel was not only slow, it was unsafe. From the beginning of September enemy diversion groups repeatedly attacked Soviet railway trains in Romania, setting fire to many wagons with munitions. Because of theses attacks, the command of the Front created nine security battalions to protect the rear area.[18]

The supply problems meant that the 2nd Ukrainian Front would begin a second major offensive in a row without adequate munitions stocks.[19] Malinovsky was well aware of this and on 19 October had begged Moscow to speed up the delivery of 900 tons of ammunition stuck in the Ukrainian town of Beltsy.[20] The ammunition was low not only because of the transportation difficulties; the non-stop combat led to a very high rate of munitions expenditure.[21]

The Front's medical services were also far from prepared for the offensive. Since the Budapest operation was about to begin without pause, there was no time left to drive the wounded to the rear. By 20:00 on 28 October the field hospitals of the 46th and 7th Guards Armies were filled beyond their theoretical capacity. The situation with the ambulance trains was even more critical; some of them were carrying three times the numbers they should. Moreover, because of the rapid advance of the mobile troops during the Debrecen Operation, some medical units were still many kilometres behind the ever advancing battle line. Despite these difficulties, the situation was quickly improved after the senior medical commanders managed to bring forward some hospital bases and even to create local reserves. When the first assault on Budapest began, each of the armies of the front's left wing (46th, 7th Guards and 53rd) had at its disposal from 5 to 9 field hospitals with 1500–2100 free beds.[22]

The other problems facing the command of the Front were the bad weather, the terrain and, of course, the enemy. By the end of October the Germans had not only managed to establish a continuous frontline from the Carpathians to the Balkans, but it was half as long as it was a month before. The canals that crisscrossed the Hungarian Plain were advantageous for defensive operations. Because of the poor weather and the autumn rains any kind of transport was bogging down in the washed-out roads. These terrain difficulties made the Soviet commanders very anxious:

> The generals and other commanding officers had frayed nerves. Even the imperturbable Malinovsky sometimes lost his equanimity. On one occasion Gen. I.V. Managarov, likewise a very even-tempered individual, asked Malinovsky to assign him additional traction equipment because of the bad weather. The front commander replied curtly and nastily. 'Get your traction equipment from the enemy!'[23]

The ordinary combatants were not in the best spirits either. The armistice that did not take place had a terrible effect on the mood of the exhausted Soviet troops and definitely contributed to the barbarity of the battle for Hungary. Furthermore, it was widely used by the Soviet frontline political agitators to enrage the soldiers. Gabriel Temkin, a Polish Jew who served as an infantryman in the 78th Rifle Division, recalls:

> Amongst us … there was great disappointment and anger when we realised that the Hungarians decided – that is how Red Army soldiers saw it – to stick with their German allies. *Voron voronu glaz nye vykluet* (crow will not pick out crow's eyes). Since it became clear that Hungary would not sign an armistice agreement, let alone change sides like Romania, hasty preparations for the forthcoming offensive began on our side, including political indoctrination on a scale and of a kind I had never witnessed before. The *Frontovaya Gazeta* (front newspaper) and *politruks*,[24] some dispatched from our corps or the army's HQ, were coming

one after the other to lecture about Hungary, Hitler's last satellite in Europe, and the most stubborn of all. The Hungarian troops, we were reminded, had together with their Nazi allies behaved abominably at Voronezh, on the Don, at Chernigov, and at Kiev. 'We are entering the enemy's den, we will avenge!'[25]

Even though at some places the Soviet soldiers were met with 'bread and salt',[26] establishment of good relations with the Hungarian populace was almost impossible. The Magyars had been frightened by the official Nazi propaganda, which was spreading myths about the Red Army[27] but many of them had heard about (and some even experienced themselves) the rape and looting by the advancing Soviet troops.[28] Grigory Chukhrai, a future film director and Palme d'Or winner at Cannes, who in the autumn of 1944 served as an officer in one of the divisions of the 7th Guards Army, recalled one comic incident:

> Later, in some small town, the inhabitants, led by the priest, locked themselves in from the Soviets in a church and decided to die all together. After great efforts, it was possible to convince them that nothing threatened them. On the church there was an inscription, with large letters in Hungarian and Russian, saying that the cathedral and the priests were under the protection of the Soviet Army. The priest thanked us, and the commander of the division, in an impulse of friendly feelings, made the priest dead-drunk, and the latter, not having reached his house, fell asleep on the asphalt. The commander of the division was censured for this.[29]

In an attempt to improve the situation, on 27 October the National Defence Committee passed a special resolution on the behaviour of the Soviet forces in Hungary and their relations with local civil authorities.[30] It instructed the Military Council of the 2nd Ukrainian Front to publish and distribute an appeal from the High Command of the Red Army to the population of the Soviet-controlled part of the country explaining the nature of the Soviet 'mission of liberation' and the goals of the military operations on Magyar soil. The text of the appeal was immediately drawn up by General Susaikov, the member of the Military Council of the Front, and printed in leaflet form for mass distribution:

> In pursuit of the enemy, detachments of the Red Army have set foot on Hungarian soil.
> As the Red Army sets foot on Hungarian territory, it is not led by the aim to occupy any part of it or to change Hungary's present social order.
> The entry of the Soviet detachments into the territory of Hungary has been made inevitable solely by military necessity, because German detachments and the armed forces of Hungary allied to Germany continue to resist…
> [The Red Army] has no other aim than to smash the enemy German army, and to wipe out the rule of Hitler's Germany in the countries subjugated by her.
> The Soviet military authorities do not intend to change Hungary's present social order and to introduce their own regime in the territories occupied by them.
> The private property of citizens shall remain untouched, and comes under the protection of the Soviet military authorities.
> The local authorities and all organs of local self-government, which were operating before the entry of the Red Army, should remain in place.[31]

The resolution was nothing more than a piece of political demagogy designed to smooth the way for the expansion of Stalin's empire. Whilst the Soviet leadership was demanding that the troops behave appropriately, it was violating its own professed principles of conservation of the 'existing social order'. On the same day the resolution was signed, Stalin ordered the military council of the 2nd Ukrainian Front to organise confiscation of all 'valuable' Hungarian industrial equipment, machinery and goods that were not directly related to the war effort and to transport them to the Soviet Union.[32] In many of the recently 'liberated' regions, under the pretext of mobilisation for 'three-day repair works', arrest of able-bodied males from 15 to 55 years and deportation to the USSR for forced labour began. Approximately 40–60,000 men were rounded up, put in camps and sent by boxcars to different parts of the USSR. Many of them never came back.[33]

The resolution of 27 October was followed by a propaganda avalanche, where every mass media instrument – newspapers, posters, leaflets, radio broadcasts and meetings – was put to use. The Soviet propaganda was at least partially successful and this was recognised even by the German command. On 15 November Colonel-General Johannes Friessner, the commander-in-chief of Army Group South, reported to Hitler:

> The very skilful propaganda of the Soviets and the propagandistic subversive activities of the deserted Hungarian generals makes an impression on large sections of the populace, as if after the Russian occupation of the country 'everything remains as it was' and only the fight against the German fascists counts. On the other hand, only little credence is given to the after-the-fact reports on Russian atrocities widespread by German propaganda.[34]

As a result of the prolongation of the struggle for the Hungarian Plain and the hostile atmosphere that surrounded the Red Army, lawless behaviour spread amongst the Soviet soldiers and the number of criminal acts committed against the local population grew with every passing day. There was a considerable decline in discipline. The senior commanders were appalled and at the end of October a series of strict orders prohibiting the mistreatment of the local population were issued.[35] All was in vain. Tarassuk, then a 19-year-old sub-machine-gunner from the 53rd Rifle Division, recalls:

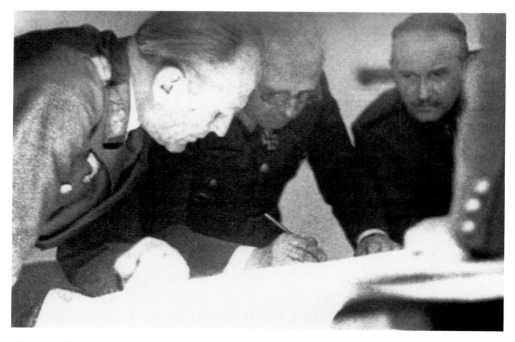

Kirchner, Friessner and Heszlényi discuss the military situation, autumn 1944. (Bundesarchiv)

Friessner (left) and Fretter-Pico (right). (Bundesarchiv)

We were given very frequent, I would say weekly, instructions on behaviour. We moved so much we crossed borders very often, especially between Hungary and Czechoslovakia; and so when crossing we were given a sermon on how to behave because one country was still an enemy – that was Hungary – and another was liberated, while a third was allied (that was Romania). My God, it was quite a mess. Of all the instructions, I remember well one sermon we received soon after crossing the Romanian border, when we were told, 'These people are allies, so behave nicely,' and so on. At this time there was no commissar, so it was the deputy battalion or regimental commander for political affairs (a major) who gave us the sermon.

Well, you know our regiment was not in charge of order in the town; but it was the commandant's squad from some other unit. In the evening the same man who gave us such a nice sermon was caught with two sergeants stripping a bag and watches from a woman.[36]

4

It did not take long for the command of Army Group South to recognise Soviet intentions to attack Budapest from the south. At 20:05 BT on 24 October the Chief of Staff of Hungarian 3 Army phoned Major-General Heinz von Gyldenfeldt, his colleague at the HQ of the Commander-in-Chief 'Southeast' (Army Group F) and asked him for cooperation in tracking enemy troop movements in the area between the Tisza and Danube. The Hungarian officer was afraid that the Soviets would begin to shift their forces from Belgrade to the north and the 4th Guards Mechanised Corps might move unnoticed.[37] Before long von Gyldenfeldt brought alarming news. At 18:50 BT the next day he called back and said that the 4th Guards Mechanised Corps had probably changed its course and now was heading north.[38]

The intelligence of the army group kept monitoring the redeployment of the enemy forces over the following days. At 10:45 BT on 26 October 1944 Major-General Hans Gaedcke, the

Chief of Staff of the 6.Army, informed Lieutenant-General Helmuth von Grolman, his counterpart in Army GrouP's HQ, that the Soviets had built a bridge over Tisza at Tiszabo (northeast
of Szolnok) and a large assembly of troops had been spotted at Vezseny.[39] Fifteen minutes later
Lieutenant-Colonel Marcks, the First General Staff Officer (Ia) of 6 Army, reported that the
two corps of the 6th Guards Tank Army were stationed south of Szolnok, but thanks to the
interception of the Soviet radio traffic it was already clear that they would not attack the
town.[40] This led Friessner to believe that Malinovsky was preparing an offensive in the sector
of Hungarian 3 Army and all the signs showed that it would begin within two days.[41] He knew
that he could repel the Soviet attack only if he managed to regroup his forces in time.

The regrouping was carried out quickly. Already on 25 October Friessner decided to keep
24 Panzer-Division in the area of Kecskemét as a reserve for 3 Army (Hung).[42] On the next day
the staff of the Hungarian 2 Army was ordered to move to Transdanubia and assume responsibility for the western bank of the Danube.[43] Thus the dangerous gap that had emerged in the
Zombor–Baja sector was filled and the border with Army Group F was sealed.

By 27 October the leadership of Army Group South still believed that the 2nd Ukrainian
Front would attack Budapest from two directions: from the south (with Shlemin's and
Shumilov's armies) and from the east (with 6th Guards Tank and 53rd Armies). So on that
day it was decided that 1 and 23 Panzer-Divisions would be deployed in the Hajdúdorog–
Hajdúnánás area (northwest of Debrecen), where they, together with Panzer-Grenadier Division
'Feldherrnhalle', were to be employed against an eventual attack of the 6th Guards Tank Army.[44]
One day later, however, it turned out that the tank army in question had only 36 tanks left and
therefore would be of little use in the forthcoming offensive.[45] Now it was clear that Malynovsky
would concentrate his main efforts in the Szeged–Szolnok–Kecskemét area only and Friessner
commanded all of his armoured forces to deploy behind the lines of Fretter-Pico's 6 Army.
Four of them ('Feldherrnhalle', 1, 13 and 23 Panzer-Divisions), which were still mopping up
the last few pockets of enemy resistance scattered around Nyíregyháza, were ordered to turn
over their positions to the infantry and move quickly to the southwest. As a result of this, the
German armoured forces were redeployed and brought much closer to the Hungarian capital,
which proved to be one of the most deceive decisions taken by the Axis camp during the battle
of Budapest. Following that order 1 and 24 Panzer-Divisions were attached to LVII Panzer
Corps, 'Feldherrnhalle' and 13 Panzer-Division to III Panzer Corps, while 4 SS-Police-Panzer-
Grenadier and 23 Panzer-Divisions were attached to the recently activated IV Panzer Corps.[46]
In order to consolidate the front along the Tisza and provide the panzer reserves attached to 3
Army (Hung) with better leadership and to increase the chances of repelling the impending
Soviet offensive on Budapest from the south, 3 Army (Hung) was subordinated to 6 Army. Thus
Armeegruppe Fretter-Pico was created (effective 29 October, 18:00).[47]

5

Friessner had enough reasons to worry about the integrity of his southern flank: the troops
of his army group were running out of strength, the Luftwaffe was short of fuel and the
Hungarians long ago had been adjudged unreliable military partners. Still worse, after the catastrophe in Romania in late August, where 16 experienced German infantry divisions had been
lost for good, Army Group South was permanently starved of infantry. From that moment on
it was able to form a continuous defensive line only with great difficulties and the battles were
fought predominantly with mobile formations. Friessner had no other choice but constantly to
shift his armoured forces from one sector to another. This imbalance between the panzer and
infantry divisions was one of the weakest characteristics of Army Group South and after the
war Gaedcke cited it as a key factor for the German defeat in Hungary:

I have written that our shortage of infantry in Hungary led to our defeat in the Puszta region. On the battlefield itself we won repeatedly, if I may exaggerate slightly, but we lost the campaign.

Let me explain. Let's say we were holding a series of strong points, as always, with weak forces. Say the Russians attacked on the left flank and our position was only under light attack and holding firm. What was the thing to do then? At night, we would quickly shift the mobile forces across from the right flank position to the left flank, leaving behind two or three armoured cars. In the morning we would suddenly drive back the enemy on the left flank with the forces that we had shifted earlier in the night. So in this sector, once again we were the victor.

But in the meantime, the Russians with their much larger forces would recognise the opportunity on the right flank. Consequently we would have to pull back our weak right flank position and then rescue the situation by rapidly returning the mobile forces back to the right flank. So it went: step by step backwards out of the Hungarian lowlands until we had withdrawn all the way to the Tokay [Tokaj] region.

This is a typical case of what happens when you lack infantry to hold positions grabbed by mobile forces.[48]

Such an order of battle was so unusual; by 29 October the ratio between the Axis mobile and infantry divisions defending the Tisza front was nearly 1:1. With such an OOB, how could one slow down the enemy infiltrating through the gaps? How do you increase the mobility of the troops or shield them from Soviet air attacks? For this, we must once again turn to the recollections of Gaedcke:

Normally they [the infantry divisions] were on foot. Of course, they would have been quickly lost if they had remained on foot. But they were numerically so weak that, with trucks they scratched up out of the supply trains and rear areas, etc., they were able to drive off. Of course, they also 'organised' any usable civilian trucks they found. So these divisions were, in actuality, partially motorised. Otherwise they would have never been able to keep pace with the armoured divisions.

I remember countless conversations with our subordinate corps commanders that went something like this: orders would be given, based on their own recommendations, to throw parts of a panzer division (after all these were far from full panzer divisions) over to the right flank. Then would come the question, 'What are we leaving on the left flank?' The answer was usually 'Why don't you leave a couple of tanks there to overlook the terrain – I don't have anything.' 'Sorry, we don't either.' So the position would be left empty and, at the latest by 9:00 or 10:00 in the morning, the enemy held the heights we had abandoned during the night. That's how you lose territory step by step.'[49]

The condition of the Axis troops in the eve of the first Soviet offensive on Budapest are well documented by surviving reports submitted by Friessner himself and his subordinates. In addition, the Commander-in-Chief of Army Group South held a number of phone conversations with Guderian, in which he described the terrible situation at the front. All of his pleadings were in vain as time and again the Chief of the German General Staff refused to send substantial reinforcements to the *Puszta*. On the evening of 27 October, when Friessner complained that his armoured formations were short of tanks and asked for urgent delivery of new machines, Guderian replied that 'for the time being this could not be done' and advised him to use the available maintenance facilities more effectively.[50] The losses sustained by Friessner's 11 German divisions (6 infantry and 5 panzer) during September and October exceeded 19,000 and they had received only 8500 replacements. Now their combined military value was no more than 21,000 combat personnel. The equipment shortfalls in the panzer divisions (from their authorised strength) amounted to 69 Panthers, 100 Pz IV and 29 heavy anti-tank guns.[51]

The leadership of Army Group South hoped to compensate for the lack of infantry with concentrated firepower, but the assets to achieve this – the GHQ artillery units – were available in very low numbers. The artillery situation was not good at all: by the end of October there were 10 GHQ artillery battalions with only 79 guns between them, as well as 4 assault gun brigades. Still worse, because the divisions that had been reconstituted recently were still short of organic artillery, six of the GHQ artillery battalions were attached to them on a permanent basis.[52] Thus the army group was left with only four GHQ artillery battalions that could be deployed at the focal point (*Schwerpunkt*) of the Soviet attack. In attempt to solve this problem, on 1 November Lieutenant-General von Grolman, Friessner's chief of staff, requested from OKH an urgent delivery of three artillery battalions and one rocket-launcher brigade.[53] 'This is of crucial importance for the outcome of the ongoing defensive battle,' von Grolman emphasised, but again Guderian turned a deaf ear to the plea.

Even where there was enough artillery, it was virtually immobile since there was a serious shortage of machinery to tow it. 'In a critical situation this could lead to a loss of valuable heavy weapons,' Fretter-Pico outlined in his monthly condition report.[54] The limited mobility of the Axis troops was not restricted to the artillery; owing to the overall lack of supply vehicles, the available truck carrying capacity was pushed beyond its limits and was wearing out quickly. The repair of the damaged vehicles was considerably hampered by the short supply of tires and spare parts. The panzer units were largely affected by this problem too; their constant use in difficult terrain led to a number of mechanical breakdowns among the tracked vehicles.[55] Some of the repair units were constantly short of spare parts.[56]

The war of attrition had affected not only machines, but men as well. The number of experienced combatants was constantly declining and the infantry replacements that had been sent to fill the gaps were inadequately trained. This problem was especially critical in the Waffen-SS formations. 'The cores of the battle-tested divisions are steadily melting away,' noted the commander of German 6 Army.[57] Based on the above considerations, in his monthly condition report Fretter-Pico assessed his infantry divisions as 'capable of limited defensive actions only'. On the other hand, he proudly claimed that 'the mobile formations, despite their declining combat value, are still a match for the numerically superior enemy.'[58]

For Friessner, however, the chief worry was the miserable condition of the Magyar troops. He made the point to Guderian on 27 October:

> My biggest concern is the state and the combat morale of all Hungarian formations, with very few exceptions. Now this concern grows more and more as it becomes clear that the enemy will attack during the next days at the Tisza with tanks that are now on the march. Already now it is possible to predict that the Hungarians will not hold on.
>
> 24 Panzer-Division and 4 SS-Police-Division, which are intended for support, are insufficient to prevent the collapse of the Hungarian battlefront. If I get no additional German formations to be placed at the disposal of the 3rd Hungarian Army as its backbone, it must be expected that the enemy will overrun the Hungarians and seize Budapest very soon.
>
> The Hungarian forces intended for the defence of Budapest and employment in the bridgehead are not even approximately sufficient to repulse a strong enemy attack, to say nothing about their morale.[59]

Other reports from the period in question express similar thoughts. 'The Hungarian artillery simply can't function properly due to the lack of signals equipment,' General Fretter-Pico complained to Friessner while the latter was at his headquarters in Kompolt on 27 October. A

A 75mm Pak 40 anti-tank gun, manned by a Hungarian crew, in action, autumn 1944. These low-silhouette guns were among the deadliest enemies of the Red armoured formations and accounted for a considerable amount of the Soviet tank and self-propelled guns destroyed on the Eastern Front. Unfortunately for *Honvédség*, the Hungarians received very few of them. (Mirko Bayerl)

comment from DVSt 3, the German liaison staff attached to the HQ of 3 Army (Hung), was even more forthright:

> The efforts of the staffs to strengthen the morale of the reserve and replacement divisions have produced only limited results. The will to fight, especially among the troops of 8 and 23 Reserve Divisions, is very weak. The infantry runs away when hit hard by artillery fire or when the enemy closes in. … The morale of 20 Infantry Division is weak too.[60]

The low combat efficiency of the *Honvédség* was determined by several factors, including inadequate training, shortage of motor vehicles, out-dated armament and, above all, low morale, a widespread defeatism born of the negative course of the war in general. In fact, by the end of October only the Air Force was still showing itself capable of fighting the Soviets on equal terms; the fighters claiming a good number of victories and the German commanders repeatedly praising the valiant performance of the parachute battalion. In such a situation the German leadership found itself with no other choice but to tighten control over the Magyar troops and deny them any freedom of action.

As a matter of fact, some form of control existed long before Szálasi's takeover. It had been imposed by the German liaison staffs that were permanently attached to every allied formation at divisional level and above. These staffs were used to advise the allies regarding the tactics and operations, as well as to spy on them.[61] But now the situation called for extreme measures, so on 28 October von Grolman ordered all Hungarian troops to be integrated into German formations, 'to improve the staying power of the Hungarian units'. The chief of staff of Army Group South was clear about how the newly reorganised alliance ought to fight:

> The Hungarian commanders-in-chief and commanders must understand that this measure follows from the current situation on the battlefield and that the Hungarian combatants will perform better under the immediate command of the better-armed and more experienced German forces.[62]

Within the rank and file of the *Honvédség*, this order produced deep anger and a sense of national humiliation. One of the training units quartered in Upper Hungary listened to the Arrow Cross minister of propaganda announcing their incorporation into the German army:

> For a time the recruits listened to the great man, then someone began singing 'Szózat', a patriotic Hungarian anthem with the opening lines 'To your country you must be steadily faithful, O Hungarian,/It's your crib and later your grave site that cares for you and covers you.' Others chimed in, and soon the minister's speech was submerged by a rolling anthem powered by hundreds of throats. Officers ran about, threatening punishment, but the anthem continued until the minister departed in a huff. The entire camp was then restricted to barracks for two weeks.[63]

This desperate attempt to restore some of the combat value of the *Honvédség* was not an overnight decision. It was actually preceded by two other, no less draconian moves. The first one was the decision to establish the so-called 'barrier lines' in the rear areas of the German 6 and 8 Armies, the sole purpose of which was to collect stragglers and 'fight the panic and desertions'.[64] The 'collected' Honveds, escorted by gendarmes, were to be sent to special camps, where they had to undergo hard training for 1–2 days, aimed at strengthening morale and restoring discipline.[65]

The second harsh measure was Friessner's order giving the commanding officers of the German troops a free hand 'to sack immediately all commanders of Hungarian Units and Formations who have proved themselves incapable in handling the tasks assigned to them and to replace them with energetic, suitable persons, regardless of their rank'.[66]

Of course, none of these measures ever produced the desired results and on 1 December 1944 Friessner went even further. He signed an order calling on his troops to machine-gun the surrendering allies: 'Who is too cowardly to die in honour, must die in disgrace!'[67] The *Honvédség* kept melting away nevertheless, the front around the Hungarian capital collapsed and 22 days later Friessner's military carreer was over.

Freissner never forgave the Hungarians. In the early 1950s he penned a memoir entitled *'Verratene Schlachten'* ('Betrayed Battles'). In it he blamed his former brothers-in-arms, the Romanians and the Hungarians, for the collapse of the entire southern flank of the German East Front in the summer and autumn of 1944. Even though it was more or less factually correct, the book in question immediately provoked a full range of angry responses from Magyar ex-officers in exile.

Their main point was the arrogant attitude of the Germans, especially in the closing months of the war. Many Magyar officers and soldiers felt humiliated by the complete subordination of the *Honvédség* to the German army and the elimination of the Hungarian Command. The Germans never recognised this as a failure because their army had few traditions in coalition warfare and none of the Nazi warlords had much experience of having to deal with allies. The superiority expressed in the memoirs of Friessner, Balck and Guderian is a clear proof of that.

6

Frissner's nemesis, arguably, was neither the Red Army, nor the unwilling Magyars, but the Nazi leadership: the deluded Hitler and the over-ambitious Guderian. On 27 October, when it was already evident that the Axis troops defending the Eastern Carpathians would avoid anni-hilation and the Pliev Group would be defeated at Nyíregyháza, Hitler issued an order about the future conduct of operations in the Hungarian Plain. Its content can be summarised:

- Army Group South must hold the Tisza defensive line;
- Enemy troops on the western bank of the Tisza river should be destroyed by the IV Panzer-Corps;
- The enemy in the front of the Armeegruppe 'Wöhler' (the German 8 Army and Hungarian 1 Army) should be defeated by a concentric panzer attack and the link with Army Group A restored;
- After the accomplishment of the above tasks, all armoured forces should be concentrated in the area between the Tisza and Danube for launching an attack to the south with the objec-tive of recapturing Szeged and establishing a steady connection with Army Group F.[68]

A couple of years back such limited objectives would have been achieved without much effort; but in the autumn of 1944 the Wehrmacht possessed neither the zeal, nor the means, for the successful fulfilment of these offensives.[69] Being aware of this, Friessner tried to protest ('The Russians will attack within the next two days … We must beat off the assault on Budapest first')[70] but in vain. The army group was left with no other choice but to obey and on the next day passed the relevant orders to the troops.[71] The ridiculous idea was not put into action only because the Red Army reached the outskirts of Budapest too soon. This would not be the last

A retreating German column in the Eastern Carpathians, autumn 1944. Up front is a captured Russian automobile, followed by a captured British truck and a SdKfz 251 medium armoured halftrack. (Charles Klement)

time Guderian bombarded Friessner's headquarters with sweeping plans that were meant to lead to the destruction of Stalin's southern wing once and for all.

The efficient conduct of operations in the *Puszta* was undermined not only by the unsatisfactory condition of the Axis troops and the unrealistic orders from above, but by the fact that Friessner himself was forced to deal with several different authorities. Unlike the Red Army, where all branches operating within a given area, including the air force and the troops of new allies, were placed under a single authority (Front) and directed by a single command (Stavka), Friessner's group could be characterised as an alliance of vassals, rather than a task force.

Hungary was where the boundary between two 'military worlds', the OKH and OKW, ran. Army Group South itself was under OKH, the General Staff of the Army, while its southern neighbour – Army Group F – was directed by OKW, the Armed Forces Command Staff. The rivalry between these two structures, which *de facto* operated as two parallel headquarters, existed at both an institutional and personal level and this was jeopardising the entire southern wing of the German front. Guderian is right when he states in his memoirs that the different branches demonstrated a 'firmly un-cooperative attitude' and their commanders-in-chief 'behaved like true republicans'.[72] This friction had a very negative impact on the overall situation in the south:

> In the area controlled by the Commander-in-Chief Southeast, Field-Marshal Freiherr von Weichs, Belgrade was lost during the same month. This area was still an OKW theatre of operations and was not controlled by the OKH, even though the Balkan Front was now certainly part of the Eastern Front. The boundary between the areas controlled by the OKW and the OKH ran through a village on the Danube near the mouths of the Drava and the Baja. This was utterly senseless. The Russians crossed the Danube at a point immediately south of this boundary between the two Supreme Command staff's areas, and therefore in the territory controlled by the Commander-in-Chief Southeast, who was concentrating his attention on his scattered fronts many miles away to the south.[73]

This was not all. During late summer Hitler chose Transdanubia as a place where to rebuild some of the divisions designated for the counteroffensive in the Ardennes. By late October the Hungarian Plain was no longer a quiet area, but those divisions remained under the control of OKW and were unavailable either to Guderian or Friessner. At the same moment when the army group was starved of infantry, six divisions were completing their training just northwest of Budapest. To make things more absurd, some of the divisions were Waffen-SS and even OKW could not move them without Himmler's permission. Still worse, the Arrow Cross leadership was constantly voicing its own opinions and the Luftwaffe air and ground units deployed in the area only 'cooperated' with Army Group South, but were not subordinated to it. When Friessner had to make a decision he had to consider the possible reactions of OKH, OKW, SS, the Hungarians, as well as the Führer. This meant repeated delays in the decision-making and nerve-wracking complications when urgency was required.

Meanwhile, the troops in the field, who had no clue about the grandiose scenarios, were too busy trying to survive than to think about strategy. 'The condition of the German troops is good, they could be used in full swing,' was Friessner's judgment on their physical shape, but the same could not be said about their minds. Even though the war was still not technically lost, it had become a lost cause long ago. In the previous two years the Wehrmacht had suffered defeat after defeat and every military catastrophe had caused a serious breakdown in morale and discipline. The lawless nature of the war in the East had corrupted the souls of many and it is no wonder that when the German forces fell back onto allied Hungarian soil they sometimes misbehaved to the point of criminality. Since the war no longer could be measured in victorious campaigns, the combatants in field grey began to measure it in short-term gains from looting. 'Whatever house you enter, you'll be told that something has been stolen,' the residents of Makó complained to General Zakharov. 'They even took away the furniture.'[74] The German leadership tried to prevent such robbery and on 3 October 1944 Friessner issued a special order on the subject that was announced through widely distributed leaflets:

> Lootings are rising to a threatening degree. Stealing of small animals, furniture, especially behind the frontlines, conducted under the excuse of saving these things, shows that troops, in which such incidents occur have bad morale and suffer from the absence of good leadership.
>
> I emphasise:
>
> Whoever is found guilty of looting – looting is an appropriation of another's property, including the abandoned houses, without a relevant requisition order – will be court-martialled immediately.
>
> From now on I will call to account the commanders of the guilty ones, if it can be proven that they have tolerated these actions.
>
> Instructions have to be conveyed immediately and in the clearest form. These have to be repeated at fixed dates four times a week. Every officer should ensure that every soldier is aware that stealing, looting, is against the honour of the German soldier.
>
> Gross violations are punishable by summary execution.
>
> The longer the war lasts, the more important is the strict discipline of the troops.
>
> I rely on a considerable number of my decent soldiers …[75]

A similar order was declared by Fretter-Pico on 17 October,[76] but nothing changed – plundering had long since ceased to be viewed as a crime by the Landsers of the Eastern Front.

The ordinary combatants needed no more indications to know that the Soviet attack was imminent and that it would be huge. Another bloody battle was ahead, just like every day, but by now even the recently arrived units were already war-weary and discouraged. 'The operations on the Thieß [Tisza] offered little satisfaction since there was hardly any visible success and yet one had to remain ready for action and prepared for an enemy attack,' wrote a member of Heavy Panzer-Battalion 503. The grey autumn sky, the dull days and the sticky mud did not raise anyone's spirits either. 'It was wet, cold and totally depressing.'[77]

7

MIND GAMES

1

Malinovsky did not want to carry out the dictator's order to attack Budapest immediately, but he was well aware that obeying orders was part of his duties as an officer. 'Rodion Yakovlevich put all his energy and skill into the assigned task,' recalls General Zakharov, his Chief of Staff.[1] The HQ of the Front immediately began planning the forthcoming offensive and in less than two hours the official plan was prepared:

1   The 46th Army with the attached 2nd Guards Mechanised Corps was to attack at 14:00 on 29 October in the general direction of Kecskemét and Budapest.
2   The main strike was to be delivered by the army's right flank (10th Guards Rifle, 37th Rifle and the 2nd Guards Mechanised Corps) while the left flank (31st Guards Rifle Corps) was to advance along the Danube bank.
3   The Solt–Lajosmizse–Nagykőrös line was to be secured by the end of 30 October.
4   By the end of 30 October the 2nd Guards Mechanised Corps was to reach the Alberti–Örkény line.
5   On the morning of 30 October the 7th Guards Army (with four rifle divisions) and 'the Romanian army' (three divisions) was to launch an offensive with its left flank in the general direction of Budapest. By the end of the same day the Nagykőrös–Tószeg line was to be secured.
6   During the first day of the offensive the 5th Air Army was to concentrate its efforts on the support of Shlemin's army, while from 30 October some of its air units were to be directed towards rendering assistance to the attack of 7th Guards Army.[2]

Once the order went down to the armies and corps, the first reaction was shock followed by a deep sense of anxiety. Stepan Grechko, then chief of the operations department of the 5th Air Army's staff:

On that same day General Goryunov, not having fully recovered, returned from the hospital. Having learned from Seleznev's report about the task assigned to the army, he at once rushed off to the Front's HQ to beg them for a couple of days for the adjustment of interaction with the all-arms armies. The visit was ineffectual. The redirection of the air force should be completed by the dawn of 29 October – such was the requirement of the Stavka.[3]

The planning of the offensive was carried out in a great hurry and the staffs of the Front, 46th, 7th Guards and 5th Air Armies, as well their subordinated units, worked furiously. A sleepless night was guaranteed for everybody. Preparation for this new mission, which would go down in history as Operation *Budapest*, was carried out 'simultaneously on all aspects, conducted continuously, without a minute of rest during the remainder of the night'.[4] Many senior commanders made on-site visits to the troops in the field to check their combat readiness. Despite the great hurry, by the dawn report after report saying 'everything is ready for the fighting' began to arrive in the HQ of the 2nd Ukrainian Front from the subordinate formations.

2

This plan deserves consideration from a modern perspective. One of its most obvious features is the fact that the 2nd Guards Mechanised Corps was to be committed once the way through was cleared by the infantry. Afterwards the corps was to advance to the Magyar capital at full speed and by the dusk of 30 October it was to reach the Alberti–Örkény line, some 20km ahead of Shlemin's rifle divisions. But this corps was not Shlemin's sole force; if we assume that it was the second echelon of the 46th Army, then the arriving 4th Guards Mechanised Corps and 23rd Rifle Corps were the third one.[5] Their commitment would not only surprise the Axis defenders, but would back up the efforts of 2nd Guards Mechanised Corps to take Budapest from the march.

Speaking of Budapest, we come to the next feature of Malinovsky's plan, namely that no long-range objective was assigned to the attacking armies, nor a deadline, such as when to capture the Magyar capital. This was typical of the Soviet way of planning: the objectives of the next stage of the operation are only set when the forces have met the objectives of the previous one.

The timing was quite unrealistic. The distance between Kiskunfélegyháza (the springboard of the new offensive) and the Alberti–Örkény line was nearly 80km and it had to be covered in less than 36 hours. This would have been a tall order for a large mechanised formation even under peacetime conditions. The road network on the Hungarian Plain was not extensive and at that time of the year most of the roads had become virtually impassable owing to mud. It was not difficult to figure out that the Axis troops facing the 2nd Guards Mechanised Corps would try to block the major crossroads and at the same time to attack its vulnerable supply lines.

The initial objective assigned to Shlemin's infantry was also overambitious. For instance, during the first day of the operation the right-flanking divisions were to occupy three big towns at once: Kecskemét, Lajosmizse and Nagykőrös. Even though initially they would face only Hungarian troops, this hardly seemed realistic, especially given the most recent experience of the 37th Rifle Corps with the Magyars at Kiskunfélegyháza. Moreover, on 28 October the corps' intelligence reported that 'through reconnaissance and observations it was determined that in the Kiskunfélegyháza area the enemy is assembling up to 100 tanks, as well as is bringing in new forces.'[6] Although this report had overestimated the strength of the arriving Axis reinforcements, it was nevertheless a clear warning of the troubles to come.

One could easily accuse Stalin and the Stavka of demanding unrealistic results as a matter of course. But this, apparently, was not the case: in 1942 the new Soviet infantry field manual established guidelines for the planning of offensive operations and stressed the assignment of realistic missions and timetables to the attacking troops.[7] The next version of the manual (issued in 1943) kept following that line of thinking. Moreover, stemming from the combat experience gained during the previous three years and the recent changes in the German tactics, in May 1944 the Soviet High Command issued strict instructions to the Fronts with regard to the planning of offensive actions. According to them, the primary objective of a rifle corps during the first day of the attack was the breaching of the main enemy line of defence. The daily missions of the divisions and regiments were to remain unchanged.[8] The breaking of the enemy's

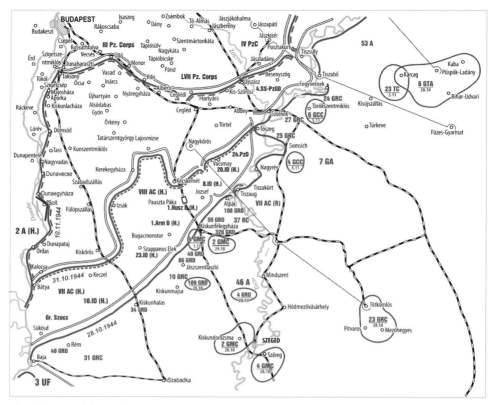

The offensive of the 46th Army and 7th Guards Army (29 October – 6 November 1944).

forward defences was to be followed by a second phase, during which fresh mobile reserves were committed to exploit the success of the infantry and thrust in depth.

A close analysis of some of the battle plans developed by Malinovsky's Operations Department reveals that they suffer from one and the same defect: they were always very ambitious and the initial objectives assigned to the exploitation forces were way too distant.[9] So the blame for the unrealistic schedule should go to Malinovsky and his staff planners. (No case is known where a Soviet formation achieved a penetration of nearly 80km during the first day of an offensive and the 2nd Guards Mechanised Corps would be no exception.)

Returning to the battle plan developed on 28 October; the role of Shumilov's 7th Guards Army was to screen the right flank of Shlemin's army and tie down part of enemy reserves. The 46th Army was to be the sword, which was to pierce the Axis defence, while the 7th Guards Army was to be the shield.

Perhaps the most characteristic feature of Malinovsky's plan was that no specific objectives were given to the armies of the Front's right flank (53rd, 27th, 40th, 4th Romanian and Pliev's group) and they were to continue their drive to the west. Nevertheless, this grouping played an important role in the plans of Stavka for a quick capture of Budapest; its advance towards Nyíregyháza and Miskolc was to pin down the German armour, thereby preventing its redeployment to defend the capital.[10] By 28 October, this force, which was holding a front of 200km between Vitka and Tiszab , consisted of 22 rifle and 3 cavalry divisions, 2 fortified regions, 1 tank and 1 mechanised corps plus 10 Romanian divisions.[11] The 4th Ukrainian Front, which had just taken Ungvár (Uzhgorod) and Csap, would support these operations by attacking to the west and crossing the Ondava River, further tying down Axis divisions.[12]

3

Whether because Malinovsky was present in the HQ of the 46th Army or because the situation gave them no other choice, the battle plan developed by Shelmin's staff was nothing but an expanded version of the directive received from the 2nd Ukrainian Front. Around midnight of 28/29 October the following orders were sent to the troops:

- The 37th Rifle Corps, with 7th Artillery Division (less the 11th Light Artillery Brigade), 48th Guards Mortar Regiment, 991st and 1505th Self-Propelled Artillery Regiments, and one engineer-sapper battalion, was to penetrate the enemy defence between Alpár and Kiskunfélegyháza and by the end of 30 October to secure the Nagykőrös–Lajosmizse line.[13]
- The 10th Guards Rifle Corps, with 45th Cannon Artillery Brigade, 462nd Mortar Regiment, 437th Anti-Tank Artillery Regiment and 1897th Self-Propelled Artillery Regiment, was to penetrate the enemy defence southwest of Kiskunfélegyháza and by the end of 30 October to secure the Lajosmizse–Szabadszállás line.
- The 31st Guards Rifle Corps, with one engineer-sapper battalion, was to penetrate the enemy defence northeast of Baja and by the end of 30 October to secure the Szabadszállás–Solt line.
- The 109th Guards Rifle Division was to assemble in the vicinity of Kiskunmajsa not later than 20:00 on 29 October; then it was to be subordinated to the 10th Guards Rifle Corps.
- The 4th Guards Rifle Division was to be kept in reserve, in readiness to develop the success of the 2nd Guards Mechanised Corps.

By the morning of 29 October the tank units of the 2nd Guards Mechanised Corps were to assemble south of Kiskunfélegyháza in readiness to advance along one of the two axes Kiskunfélegyháza–Kecskemét or Kiskunmajsa–Kecskemét.

By the end of 30 October the corps was to secure the Alberti–Örkény line. Upon the accomplishment of this objective, its forward detachments were to advance towards Pilis and Gyón, capture both settlements and hold them until the arrival of the main forces. The corps was to be unleashed once the infantry secured the Jozsef–Puszta Páka–Bugacmonostor–Szappanos Elek line. From that moment on the following artillery units were to be subordinated to the corps: the 11th Light Artillery Brigade (of 7th Artillery Division), two battalions of the 48th Guards Mortar Regiment, two battalions of the 45th Cannon Artillery Brigade, and two regiments of the 9th Anti-Aircraft Artillery Division.[14]

4

Like their colleagues in the other ground and air formations, the staff of the 2nd Guards Mechanised Corps spent the night of 28/29 October planning the entry of the powerful armoured formation into the battle of Budapest. At around 22:00 on 28 October General Sviridov was called to the HQ of the 46th Army where he was informed that his corps had been placed under Shlemin and that it would go into battle on the very next day. Depending on the situation, the corps would be unleashed either in the sector of the 10th Guards Rifle Corps (at Kiskunmajsa), or at the boundary of the 10th Guards Rifle Corps and 37th Rifle Corps (at Kiskunfélegyháza). Whatever the point of entry, the objective of the corps was the same: to capture Kecskemét, secure the Alberti–Örkény line and from there to advance on Budapest.

Following these verbal instructions, Sviridov and his officers developed a plan, which included the following points:

- The corps would relocate to a new area (to the west of Kistelek), which was situated much closer to the front.
- The corps would attack in two-echelon formation; the first echelon was to consist of the 4th and 6th Guards Mechanised Brigades reinforced with the 1509th and 251st Self-Propelled Artillery Regiments respectively, the second one was to comprise the 5th Guards Mechanised Brigade and 37th Guards Tank Brigade (reinforced with the 30th Guards Heavy Tank Regiment).
- The troops would receive two coded orders: 'Volga' 3333 ('Get ready to go!') and 'Eagle' 5555 ('Launch the attack!').
- The scout parties and the forward detachments of the first echelon brigades were to be placed within the battle line of the rifle divisions; once the enemy defence was breached, the scouts and forward detachments would follow the infantry closely to the József ranch–Puszta-Páka–Szappanyos line (halfway between Kiskunfélegyháza and Kecskemét) and from there they were to surge forward as a spearhead of the offensive.
- The enemy strongholds encountered in the path of the brigades were to be eliminated by enveloping attacks.
- Owing to the importance of speed, the biggest strongholds encountered were to be bypassed and left to the rifle divisions for mopping up.[15]

The Soviet manuals and military academies recommended the deployment of troops in echelon in an offensive and it proved beneficial in many large battles. The other basic principles of the Soviet art of war were the concentration of force, all-arms offensives and the establishment of 'long-range' mobile groups. The latter were formed around tank armies, combined cavalry-tank groups or single armoured corps. Their task was to exploit into open country in the enemy rear; they were to fragment the Axis forces rather than encircle them, thrust the deep rear and leave the business of mopping up the isolated pockets to the follow-up echelon (the infantry). In order to provide the long-range groups with more 'tools', they were usually reinforced with additional artillery (see below) and maintained close liaison with the air force.

The momentum of the Soviet offensive operations was set by a system of forward detachments. These small but powerful fighting advance guards were the spearheads of the mobile groups. Their tasks were to defeat the German armoured reserves in 'meeting engagements', brush aside the enemy defensive positions erected in the path of the mobile group, seize key road junctions, river crossings and the like, and hold them until the parent formation arrived.

The 2nd Guards Mechanised Corps was no exception and each of its brigades formed forward detachments of their own. Thus the 4th Guards Mechanised Brigade created a forward

Lieutenant-General Karp Sviridov, commander of the 2nd Guards Mechanised Corps.

detachment consisting of a reconnaissance company, the 23rd Guards Tank Regiment, 2nd Motorised Rifle Battalion, 1509th Self-Propelled Artillery Regiment and an artillery battalion of 76mm towed guns.[16] The detachment of the 6th Guards Mechanised Brigade had a similar composition, while that of the 37th Guards Tank Brigade would comprise the 2nd Tank Battalion and two companies of the 30th Guards Heavy Tank Regiment.[17] As we will see later, it was much the same story with the arriving 4th Guards Mechanised Corps.

5

Operation *Budapest* bore many similarities with another hastily prepared lightning offensive that had ended just a month before: Operation *Market Garden*, Montgomery's disaster. They were born out of ambition to hasten the end of the war by exploiting certain apparently weak spots of the German front. They were ultimately pursuing a political goal – to seize as much territory as possible before the arrival of other allied armies. Both plans were a gamble and the masterminds behind them naively believed that once a hole in the frontline was torn open, hundreds of tanks would pour through it and soon would reach Berlin and Munich, respectively. Powerful armoured formations were to be involved in both, but they would be denied any opportunity for manoeuvre, since they would be forced to advance along a single road. The main objectives were several key bridges over big rivers. *Market Garden* had ended in defeat. The similarities did not strike Stalin.

6

46th Army was a relatively fresh formation. Throughout October it did not see much intensive combat and during the second half of the month some of its rifle divisions were replenished.[18] The 31st Guards Rifle Corps had been just relieved from its previous engagement at Zombor by the troops of the 75th Rifle Corps of the 3rd Ukrainian Front and by 28 October the army was holding a 120km front from Alpár to Baja.

Like most of the Soviet late-war all-arms formations, the 46th was somewhat short of infantry, but strong in artillery. By 29 October it managed to achieve an average gun density of 14.1 tubes per kilometre along a 120km front, which gives a rough estimate of nearly 1700 guns and heavy mortars available.[19] Taking into account that the weight of the attack would fall on his right flank, Shlemin considerably reinforced the 10th Guards Rifle and 37th Rifle Corps with artillery from the army's pool:

- The 10th Guards Rifle Corps received the 45th Cannon Artillery Brigade, 462nd Mortar Regiment, 437th Anti-Tank Artillery Regiment and 1409th Anti-Aircraft Artillery Regiment (of 38th Anti-Aircraft-Artillery Division).
- The 37th Rifle Corps received the 7th Artillery Division (less 11th Light Artillery and 105th Super-Heavy-Howitzer Artillery Brigades), 48th Guards Mortar Regiment and 1405th Anti-Aircraft Artillery Regiment (of 38th Anti-Aircraft-Artillery Division).

The sector of the 31st Guards was considered of secondary importance and that corps received no artillery reinforcements. The 2nd Guards Mechanised Corps was given the 11th Light Artillery Brigade (which was to be employed mainly in an anti-tank role), the bulk of the 48th Guards Mortar Regiment, 981st and 993rd Anti-Aircraft Artillery Regiments (of 9th Anti-Aircraft-Artillery Division). The 46th Army itself formed a 'long-range artillery group' (9th Guards, 17th and 45th Cannon Artillery Brigades), which was further divided into two groups attached to the 10th Guards and 37th Rifle Corps respectively. The 24th Anti-Tank Artillery

Brigade formed the Army's anti-tank artillery reserve.[20] The breakthrough of the infantry was to be supported by three SU-76-equipped self-propelled artillery regiments (991st, 1505th and 1897th) with a total of 53 self-propelled guns between them.[21]

The forces intended for the exploitation of the initial success were to be deployed in the area south of Szentes. By the end of 28 October the full-strength 2nd Guards Mechanised Corps, Shlemin's main strike force, was assembled northwest of Szeged. The 4th Guards Mechanised Corps was to deploy east of the town too, but it was delayed by the limited capacity of the Danube crossings and the bad weather, the heavy rains had turned the roads into quagmires. By 28 October the corps's personnel with the artillery and the wheeled transport managed to assemble at Szeged, but the tanks detrained there only on the next day, when the attack was already underway.[22] The situation with the 23rd Rifle Corps (68th Guards, 99th and 316th Rifle Divisions), which was to assemble in the vicinity of Pitvaros, was similar. Although the corps command arrived on 28 October, some of its troops were still underway.

On the eve of the offensive the two mechanised corps had the following strength:

- 2nd Guards Mechanised Corps: 16,045 men, 248 tanks and self-propelled guns, 79 guns of all calibres, 154 mortars, 8 'Katyusha' rocket launchers, 98 armoured cars and personnel carriers.[23]

- 4th Guards Mechanised Corps: 13,403 men, 124 tanks and self-propelled guns, 74 guns of all calibres, 137 mortars, 7 'Katyusha' rocket launchers, 45 armoured cars and personnel carriers.[24]

By 29 October the 7th Guards Army and the Romanian 1st Army of General Macici (operationally subordinate to the 7th Guards Army) – a total of 8 Soviet and 3 Romanian divisions – were deployed along a 55km front at the Tisza between Tiszabő and Alpár. The 24th Guards Rifle Corps with its 81st Guards Rifle Division was holding a bridgehead on the western bank of Tisza at Nagykörü (west of Fegyvernek) while the 25th Guards Rifle Corps held another one at Tószeg. Between 25 and 29 October more than 12,000 men, approximately 700 guns and mortars and over 1000 trucks and tractors were moved to the bridgeheads.[25] The Romanians had troops on the western bank of the Tisza as well: the 19th Infantry and 9th Cavalry Divisions. By 29 October they were busy improving the footholds at Alpár and Tiszaug respectively. Perhaps the biggest lack in this numerically impressive allied force was the absence of close-support tanks or self-propelled guns; neither Shumilov nor Macici had a single armoured vehicle under his command.

Malinovsky planned to employ Colonel-General Kravchenko's 6th Guards Tank Army at a later stage of the operation along the Budapest axis. For that purpose on 26 October it was pulled out of the front and stationed in the vicinity of Kaba and Karczag for refitting. The army had

Colonel-General Sergei Goryunov, commander of the 5th Air Army.

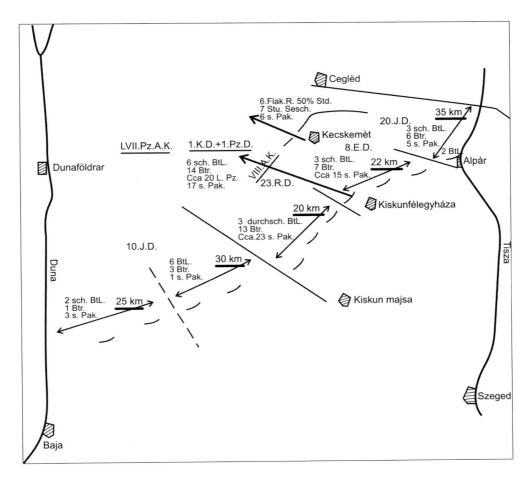

The disposition of the 3rd Hungarian Army on the eve of the Soviet offensive, and the German assessment of the probable route of the Soviet advance, 24 October 1944.

suffered very heavy losses during the previous two months (especially in tanks) and it was not until the beginning of December that it was made operational again.

The 5th Air Army under Colonel-General Goryunov was in charge of close air support. Two of its corps were deployed at the airfields of Pitvaros and Szarvas, while the third was in the vicinity of Turda. Of all of the formations of the Army, only the pilots of 6th Guards Air Fighter Division, which had been responsible for the air cover of the 46th Army, were familiar with the terrain. On 1 November the Army's inventory numbered 925 serviceable aircraft: 450 fighters, 295 ground-attack planes, 145 bombers, 22 reconnaissance and 13 artillery-spotter/fire-correction aircraft.[26] In addition, I Romanian Air Corps with about 100 combat aircraft was subordinated to Goryunov's army, thus granting the Soviets a comfortable supremacy in the air.

7

Friessner's plan to beat the Soviet attack was simple. As his army group had a reasonable number of armoured formations but not enough infantry, he intended to employ once again his favourite 'hit-and-run' tactics, the purpose of which was not to keep control of territory, but to inflict damage on the advancing enemy and immediately regroup to another area to slow down the Soviet advance. This tactic further benefited the Axis troops because the Red armour could not operate off the main roads during that time of the year. Every settlement between the Tisza and the capital was to be turned into a strongpoint, from where the German panzers would be able to strike the exposed Soviet flanks. This way of fighting worked perfectly for the army group during the battle of Debrecen and now Friessner hoped that he would be able to trick Malinovsky once again.[27] (The best counter to such flexible defence was the two-pronged armoured attack, each wedge guarding only its outer flank, while the enemy strongpoints caught in between the wedges were annihilated. This perhaps explains in more detail why Malinovsky was not keen to begin the offensive without the 4th Guards Mechanised Corps.)

'Hit and run' tactics required one condition to be met – the presence of mobile troops on the battlefield – but by the beginning of the Soviet onslaught there were none between Kecskemét and Budapest. Actually, there were only weak Magyar forces in the zone of Shlemin's attack. By 24 October they were deployed as follows (in order from southwest to northeast):

- The Sükösd sector (25km long): part of 10.Infantry Division[28] with 2 weak battalions,[29] 1 artillery battery and 3 heavy anti-tank guns.
- Kiskunhalas sector (30km long): the bulk of 10.Infantry Division[30] with 6 battalions, 3 artillery batteries and 1 heavy anti-tank gun.
- Kiskunmajsa–Kiskunfélegyháza sector (20km long): 23.Infantry Division[31] with 3 average battalions, 13 artillery batteries and 23 heavy anti-tank guns.
- Kecskemét sector (22km long): 8.Reserve Division with 3 average battalions, 7 artillery batteries and 15 heavy anti-tank guns.
- Alpár–Tószeg sector (35km long): 20.Infantry Division with 3 weak battalions, 6 artillery batteries and 5 heavy anti-tank guns.
- Reserve of LVII Panzer Corps (in the rear of 10.Infantry Division): 1.Huszar-Division and 1.Armoured-Division with 6 weak battalions, 14 artillery batteries, 20 light tanks and 17 heavy anti-tank guns between them.
- Reserve of VIII Army Corps (northwest of Kecskemét): Flak-Regiment 133 (Luftwaffe), 7 assault guns[32] and 6 heavy anti-tank guns.

Thus on the eve of the offensive the entire front of Colonel-General Heszlényi's 3rd Hungarian Army (some 135km in length) was defended by only 17 infantry battalions (11 of which were very weak), 7 Huszar battalions, 44 batteries, 20 tanks, 7 assault guns and 70 heavy anti-tank guns.[33] The sole German unit available to Heszlényi was the Flak-Regiment 133. There were still no operational reserves in the army's rear. Malinovsky could have found no better moment to open his attack in full force!

Knowing that the Soviet mobile troops could move only on good roads, Heszlényi had deployed most of his forces in the Kecskemét area to bar the Kiskunfélegyháza–Budapest road, the only asphalt motorway leading into the capital from the southeast. In that sector the Magyar engineers had put a good deal of effort into trying to hamper the attackers. Barbed wire and minefields protected the approaches to the trenches and the main roads were also mined.[34] At the army's right flank, however, there were no fortifications at all. The artillery situation was equally dismal; the guns were not only low in number but they also stood in open emplacements, easy targets for the Soviet pilots and artillerymen. Apparently, the main defensive line of the 3rd Hungarian Army could hardly be described as a serious obstacle.

Being aware of the weakness of the Hungarian front, in the days preceding the Soviet onslaught Friessner tried his best to reinforce his ally. As previously mentioned, on 25 October the army group directed 24 Panzer-Division to deploy in the vicinity of Kecskemét. On the next day the Magyar 5 Reserve Division was also placed under Heszlényi.[35] Neither of these formations, however, was fully deployed in the endangered area when Shlemin's onslaught began.

Already on 25 October the 24th Panzer was thrown against the Soviet and Romanian bridgeheads at Tószeg and Nagyrév respectively. (The Romanian one was wiped out; the Soviet one shrank, but survived.)[36] Despite the requests of Friessner and the insistence of OKH that the division must be urgently pulled out of combat and assembled at Kecskemét to parry the impending Soviet offensive, Heszlényi did not oblige immediately.[37] It was only on 28 October that the panzer-division was withdrawn and deployed east of Kecskemét. Even then its infantry element (Panzer-Grenadier Regiment 21) was left in the area south of Tószeg to strengthen the weak Magyar 20 Infantry Division.[38]

Lieutenant-General József Heszlényi, commander of the 3rd Hungarian Army.

Was Heszlényi's decision to employ on 25 October the 24 Panzer-Division in the area south of Szolnok, instead of placing it immediately in reserve very close to Kecskemét, the correct one? It is difficult to say. To keep a whole panzer division in the rear when the bridgeheads of the 7th Guards Army on the Tisza's western bank were dangerously mushrooming was a luxury that he really could not afford. Its resolute counter-attacks effectively reduced the size of the Soviet footholds and prevented Shumilov from bringing across enough forces. The result was that when on 30 October the 7th Guards Army joined the battle for Budapest, it was not able to deliver the desired all-out assault because of the limited size of the available jump-off points.

The assembly area chosen for 24 Panzer-Division after it was released from combat on 28 October deserves comment. This former East Prussian cavalry division[39] was stationed south of Nagykőrös, which allowed it immediately to intervene in case of an enemy attack from the east (that is, by the 7th Guards Army). But it was deployed at the far side of Kecskemét (when viewed from the south) and therefore it could not be employed immediately in the case of a Soviet head-on assault on the town. There is no doubt that the 24th Panzer would have effectively barred the southern approaches to Kecskemét in the afternoon of 29 October. But it was not there and Sviridov's tanks moved up the road to Budapest virtually unopposed.

It is interesting to know that 24 Panzer-Division was deployed at Nagykőrös on purpose. The commander of Hungarian 3 Army believed that the Soviets would not attack Kecskemét from the south, but along the Alpár–Kiskunfélegyháza line, with the focal point at Alpár. Keen to forestall the supposed enemy offensive, on 30 October he ordered the LVII Panzer Corps (the 24 Panzer-Division and the left-flank troops of the Magyar VIII Army Corps) to launch an attack of its own and recapture Alpár and Tiszaujfalu.[40] Heszlényi also awaited an attack from the Kiskunmajsa–Kiskunhalas area towards Soltvadkert and Kiskőrös, i.e. to the northwest.[41] Perhaps in an attempt to deal with this threat, on 28 October he pulled Hungarian 1 Armoured Division (less one battalion) out of the front and placed it as his reserve at Jakabszállás (southwest of Kecskemét).[42] In so doing, on the eve of the Soviet offensive he had tactical armoured reserves on both sides of Kecskemét. One of them (the Hungarian division), however, was pretty weak, whereas the other (the 24th Panzer) was deployed too far in the rear. And neither of them was standing in the path of the Red armoured avalanche.

The Soviet *maskirovka* (deception) was very successful in this instance. It concealed the actual direction and strength of Shlemin's attack and tricked Heszlényi into misplacing his tiny armoured reserves. It is very difficult to say what would have happened had the 24 Panzer-Division barred the southern approaches to Kecskemét in the afternoon of 29 October. It didn't and the Soviet tanks rolled northwards virtually unopposed.

8

Being well aware that the troops available to Heszlényi would be nowhere near enough to halt the forthcoming powerful Soviet offensive, Friessner began to transfer additional reserves to 3 Army (Hung) immediately after the victorious conclusion of the battle for Nyíregyháza. The first formation that received orders to move to the southwest was 1 Panzer-Division. On 27 October it was instructed to hand over its sector to 4 Mountain Division and move to Kecskemét, where it was to be assigned to LVII Panzer Corps.[43]

Friessner, was not sure about the long-term intentions of the Soviet Command and that is why he decided not to rush the rest of his armoured formations into battle too soon, but to keep them in reserve and wait. Thus on 28 October when it became apparent that an attack of the Soviet 6th Guards Tank Army in the Nyíregyháza–Debrecen sector was very unlikely, the 23 Panzer-Division was ordered to deploy in the Jászberény–Jászapáti area as Fretter-Pico's reserve.[44] On the same day two more divisions became reserves: the Panzer-Grenadier

A Flakpanzer IV *Wirbelwind* of Heavy-Panzer-Battalion 503 in Budapest on the day after the Arrow Cross putsch. The rapid fire from the four 20mm barrels of these self-propelled anti-aircraft also made them very effective against ground targets. (Dénes Bernád)

Division 'Feldherrnhalle' was directed to assemble north of Mezőkövesd, while the Hungarian 2 Armoured Division went to the vicinity of Gyöngyös.[45]

More reserves were freed on 29 October. Then the 13 Panzer-Division was taken from 8 Army and given instructions to transfer to Cegléd. The Assault Gun Brigade 228 was also pulled out of 8 Army's front and subordinated to 6 Army's IV Panzer Corps.[46] Upon its arrival it was to replace the Heavy Panzer-Battalion 503. The latter, in turn, was to be withdrawn to the rear and assembled in the vicinity of Abony as IV Panzer Corps' tactical reserve.[47]

Friessner's decision to take all his armoured formations off the frontline and deploy them in the rear was reasonable. First, these divisions were worn down by the intense combat that they had been involved in throughout October. They needed some time to replenish and recuperate. Second, the leadership of Army Group South was still not sure whether the enemy would attack in the Kecskemét area only, or thrust to Budapest from the southeast and east as well. That is why Friessner placed his main operational reserves in areas that were equidistant from all potential threats. On the other hand, this meant that in the case of a Soviet breakthrough at Kecskemét, he would not be able to employ them en masse, but piecemeal, in the order of their arrival at the battlefield. This is exactly what happened.

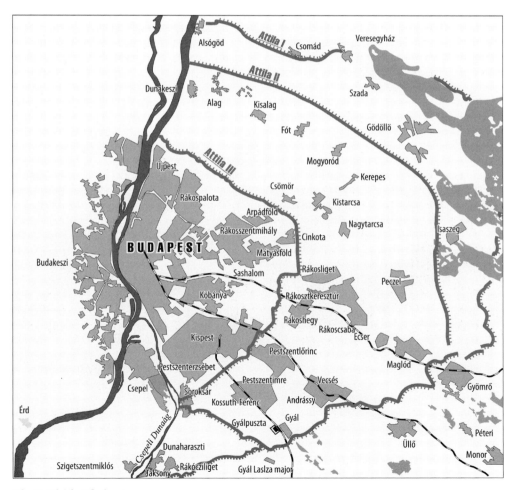

The 'Attila' fortified system.

9

The fact that by the beginning of the Soviet offensive there were no operational reserves in the rear of the 3rd Hungarian Army does not mean that Budapest was left defenceless. Actually, a considerable force guarded the Hungarian capital, but it could not be used to strengthen the southern front without Hitler's permission since it was under the direct command of Keitel's OKW. On 25 October Hans von Greiffenberg, Wehrmacht Plenipotentiary General in Hungary, told Lieutenant-Colonel Schäfer, the first Operations Officer of Army Group South, that the following troops were available for the defence of the Magyar capital:

- VI Army Corps (Hung) with one division[48] and six independent battalions.
- 22.SS-Cavalry-Division with 12,918 men and 1993 Hiwi,[49] 24 heavy anti-tank guns and 57 other artillery pieces.
- Battle Commandant 'Budapest' with 1950 men.
- 146 Flak guns in Budapest and 20 Flak combat groups on the eastern side of the Danube.

The combat value of these troops, officially known as 'The Budapest Group', however, was far from high. The 22nd SS, entrusted with the defence of the western bank of the river in the segment south of the capital, was still undergoing training, to be completed by 1 December. Owing to the lack of motor vehicles it was virtually immobile. The Flak artillery of Budapest suffered from the same problem; most of these 146 guns were in fixed positions.[50]

The troops intended to defend Transdanubia (the region lying west of the Danube) were in even worse condition. According to von Greiffenberg's report, they consisted of 31 SS-Grenadier Division (still forming, with only 1370 men issued with rifles), three police regiments (approxi-

Hungarian paratroopers march down a Budapest street in their way to the front, 30 October 1944. Shortly afterwards they would man their positions in the 'Attila I' line. (Author's Collection)

mately 3000 men, with mortars being their only heavy weapons), SS Tartar Brigade (800-strong, but very unreliable), Grenadier Reserve Regiment 44 and three Flak detachments.[51] These units could hardly protect Transdanubia in case of a Soviet attack across the river.

10

In Hungary, as elsewhere in Europe, the Nazi leadership had placed high hopes on a series of military fortifications to halt the drive of the Red Army towards the heart of the Reich. In the *Puszta* there were three such barriers erected in the path of the Malinovsky's and Tolbukhin's soldiers: 'Margit' (*'Margarethen'*), 'Karola' and 'Attila'. The 'Margit' Line ran from the river Drava in the south past the lakes Balaton and Velence to the Mátra mountains in the north. Its purpose was to contain the advance of the Soviet troops to the west and northwest, to prevent the fall of Vienna and the loss of the precious Nagykanizsa oilfield. In the north the 'Margit' Line linked with the 'Karola' Line, which was meant to protect Upper Hungary. This was not all; behind 'Margit' and 'Karola' there were several more subsidiary lines with tender names ('Susanne', 'Sabine', 'Senta', 'Selma', 'Klara'), still in the process of construction.

Budapest itself was shielded from the east by three semicircular defensive belts called the 'Attila' lines, after the famous Hun ruler. Their form was like a horseshoe and their main assets were the anti-tank ditches. The ditches were some 5–6m wide and up to 10m deep.[52] Since they were too wide and too deep to be crossed by a tank without help from the engineers, the tank might become an easy target for the anti-tank guns. In order to prevent the enemy engineers and infantrymen from assisting the armour, additional fortified pionts – machine gun

Hungarian Minister of Defence Beregfy in the trenches of 'Attila I' line, in the section held by 22 SS-Cavalry Division, November 1944, in the suburbs of Pest. On Beregfy's right stands SS-Sturmbannführer Karl-Heinz Keitel, the eldest son of Field-Marshal Keitel. During the initial stages of the battle of Budapest Keitel was in charge of SS-Cavalry Regiment 17 of that division. On 12 December he was wounded in action and later was evacuated from the city. (Mirko Bayerl)

pits, battery emplacements, trenches and bunkers – were integrated into the defence system.

The wings of each belt ended at the Danube. The outermost one, the 'Attila I' Line, was quite far from the city, running through the villages of Dunaharaszti, Vecsés, Gödöllő and Alsógöd. 'Attila II' was only partly constructed. (For instance, it had no anti-tank ditch.) It was situated along the Soroksár–Pécel–Kerepes–Mogyoród–Fót–Dunakeszi line and it joined 'Attila I' near the village of Maglód. 'Attila III' was situated near the border of Pest and ran through several of its suburbs, including Csepel, Pestszenterzsébet, Rákoskeresztúr, Rákospalota and Újpest.[53]

The anti-tank ditches of the 'Attila' Lines were dug by hand. Such a serious construction project required the employment of considerable numbers and the Hungarian High Command mobilised a lot of units. Amongst them were the Slovakian Technical Division, forced labour troops of the Jewish population of Budapest and civilians recruited in the area. Construction continued on the earthworks even after the Soviet attack had begun; on 1 November the army group reported that there were some 28,000 men engaged in construction activities in and around the Magyar capital.[54] The effort was fully justified: Malinovsky's spearheads were effectively stopped at the first 'Attila' Line and it was not until New Year's Day that the 2nd Ukrainian Front breached the third belt of the defensive system.

11

In the previous chapter we already saw how Guderian, despite Friessner's objections, imposed his decision for a powerful armoured attack from Kecskemét to the south and demanded the annihilation of the enemy deployed between the Danube and Tisza rivers. Being a true soldier, the commander-in-chief of the army group had no other choice but to obey. On 28 October he issued an order about the future conduct of the operations of the armies of the right flank:

- Effective 29 October, 18:00, the Hungarian 3 Army and the German 6 Army would be consolidated under a single command, Armeegruppe Fretter-Pico.
- For the time being the 3 Army (Hung) was to concentrate its efforts on the repelling of the upcoming enemy offensive, especially along the Budapest highway. At a later stage, after the arrival of strong panzer formations, the army was to launch an attack with the objective of destroying the enemy armoured corps between the Danube and Tisza and establishing a close connection with the neighbouring Army Group F. 'Thus the entire area between the two rivers will fall in German hands,' says the document about the final objective of the Heszlényi's army.
- 6 Army, in conjunction with the 3 Army (Hung), was to defend Tisza and concentrate its efforts on repulsing an eventual enemy attack upon Budapest (from the east). One armoured battle group under IV Panzer Corps was to be held in reserve near Jászberény. It could be used on the southern flank of the Armeegruppe 'Wöhler'[55] as well.
- The armies were to focus on building of the 'Karola I' Line; the Budapest bridgehead (that is, the 'Attila' positions) and 'Karola II' Line were to remain the responsibility of the Hungarian General Staff, while the army group itself was to take care of the construction of the 'Margit' Line.[56]

12

Having paid a visit to the Fretter-Pico headquarters on 27 October, the next day Friessner went to Budapest 'to discuss with the new Hungarian leadership various questions concerning the army group'.[57] Much to his surprise, at the gates of the Royal Palace he was met by a ceremonial guard battalion dressed in full parade uniform. 'Needless to say, I wasn't flattered

Szálasi's government; seated, left to right: Lajos Reményi-Schneller (Minister of Finance); Gábor Kemény (Minister of Foreign Affairs); Ferenc Szálasi (Prime Minister); Károly Beregfy (Minister of the Defense); Lajos Szász (Minister of Economy and Communication). Standing, left to right: Ferenc Rajniss (Minister of Religion and Education); Count Fidél Pálffy (Minister of Agriculture); Gábor Vajna (Minister of Internal affairs); Béla Jurcsek (Minister of Public service); Emil Kovarcz (Minister of Country Mobilization and Military Equipment); Ferenc Kassai (Minister of Propaganda and National Defense); Emil Szakvári (Minister of Industry); Emil Szöllősi (Deputy Prime Minister). (Author's Collection)

by this unnecessary peacetime performance,' Friessner recalls. 'It reminded me of the last act of *Götterdämmerung*.' Meanwhile the army group commander was approached by the Szálasi's wing-aide-de-camp, who informed him that these honours were intended for him as 'a token of gratitude of the Hungarian government and the Hungarian nation' for the successful conclusion of the battles at Debrecen and Nyíregyháza. Szálasi himself and his whole Arrow-Cross government awaited him upstairs, in the audience hall:

> After having expressed my thanks, I was asked to report to the gathered members of the government on the situation. I took this opportunity to emphasise the gravity of the situation and to leave no one in any doubt that the country was threatened by a catastrophe, which could be avoided only if Hungary, as well as Germany, mobilised all the available forces, without exception, to rebuff the common enemy, as well as the Hungarian troops putting up heavy resistance to the Russians.[58]

Being a career officer, Minister Beregfy did not believe in miracles. In the follow-up discussion, he preferred shorter, simpler alternatives to Friessner's bombast:

> Holding the Tisza line will avoid the downfall of Hungary and safeguard important regions and industries (like Miskolc, for example). In the case that the Tisza line cannot be held, then the Danube line attains primary importance. This will allow the extraction of vital raw materials in the Balaton area to continue undisturbed. The Hungarist reign will continue to be a fundamental factor too, as long as that line is secure. The third option is the most pessimistic – [the country will be abandoned and] all national human resources capable of mobilisation will be deployed east of the Prague–Salzburg line, where they will wait for a counter-offensive to take place.[59]

Beregfy also proposed, based on a lack of weapons, that the number of the Magyar divisions be reduced from 24 to 14 by December and the freed manpower be used as a labour force by German industry.[60]

The proposals of the Hungarian defence minister were fully supported by Szálasi and probably by the other members of the government. The Arrow-Cross leader asked first whether the Tisza line could be held and when he was told that this could not be done ('there are

General Károly Beregfy, Szálasi's Minister of Defence in the Castle Hill district in Buda on the day after the Arrow Cross putsch. The armbands indicated adherence to the Arrow Cross movement, which supported Hitler in the continuing the struggle against the Soviet Union. (Dénes Bernád)

strict orders from the Führer forbidding any withdrawal, but it is defended only by weak Hungarian troops', Friessner replied) he declared that the entire *Honvédség* should be disbanded and replaced by a completely new army. 'If I had enough weapons I would immediately put 500,000 men under arms. But since there aren't any, the Hungarian armies will be reduced to four divisions each,' Szálasi continued. 'Then we will concentrate our effort in industrial support by delivering a large enough workforce for the Third Reich's economy'.[61] Apparently, for this self-professed defender of Magyardom the turning of his countrymen into slaves of another regime was in tune with Hungarist values.

The Prussian-trained mind of the commander of Army Group South refused to accept the arguments of his allies. In the 1950s he even accused them of being paralysed by defeatism ('they intended to do nothing'). None of the members of the Arrow-Cross cabinet was alive by then to defend himself. Finally, the conference was declared over and Friessner headed back to his field headquarters. He left the capital with a heavy heart:

> While in Budapest, I realised that the population had no clue about how serious the situation at the front was. Everywhere I was still seeing scenes of the deepest peace and, unfortunately, this poured some bitter drops into the festive cup for the victories at Debrecen and Nyiregyhaza.[62]

8

THE RACE

1

On the morning of 29 October the commander of 23rd Rifle Corps, Major-General Grigorovich, together with his chief of staff, Colonel Andryushchenko and his chief political officer, Colonel Orlov, set out in two jeeps for Arad to introduce themselves to their new CiC, Marshal Malinovsky. The Sunday morning trip to the HQ of the 2nd Ukrainian Front was slow. The traffic in the opposite direction was heavy: it was rush hour for the supply trains of the frontline troops of 46th Army and trucks and carts loaded with fuel, ammunition and other goods surged northwards. Nevertheless, Andryushchenko remembered the drive as a carefree and almost enjoyable experience:

> It was a clear autumn day. Embraced by the first frosts, yellow leaves were falling softly from the trees. On either side of the road every now and then we could see unharvested cornfields and vineyards. On the crater-pitted ground there were blackened skeletons of broken guns and burned-out tanks with swastikas. Everything pointed to the fact that there was war here recently, which had left behind it ruin and desolation.[1]

Because of the upcoming meeting, both Grigorovich and Andryushchenko were nervous when at midday the jeeps finally arrived in the forest east of Arad, where the Front's HQ was located. The Marshal's quarters had been set up in a mansion. Once the officers were let in, Malinovsky greeted them warmly and shook their hands. Andryushchenko's first impression of the Marshal was that he was 'tall and broad-shouldered. His eyes stared intently and were very friendly… On his round face every now and then appeared a warm smile. We could see that he was in a good mood.'[2]

Malinovsky listened carefully to Grigorovich's report without interrupting him. After that he asked the General a couple of questions about the numerical strength of the corps' troops and their morale. With the short meeting concluded, the Marshal was in a hurry to fly to Shlemin's field HQ and witness the beginning of Operation *Budapest*. His farewell words were prophetic: 'The fighting is expected to be hard. The Nazis know that they are doomed and they will fight like condemned men.'[3]

Major-General Mikhail Grigorovich, commander of the 23rd Rifle Corps.

Marshal Rodion Malinovsky, commander of the 2nd Ukrainian Front.

2

While Grigorovich and Andryushchenko were still en route for Arad, the giant Soviet war machine slowly began to roar into life. Most of the units were preparing for the battle to come, others were already fighting. Those were, as usual, the close support air units, the IL-2-equpped Shturmovik regiments of the 3rd Guards Assault Air Corps. Since early in the morning, they had been attacking previously selected targets: strongholds and communications.[4] A total of 116 sorties were flown[5] until in the afternoon the weather deteriorated. The Hungarians fought back as best as they could and 1 Armoured Division claimed to have shot down two Shturmoviks,[6] but, on the whole, their anti-aircraft defence was too weak to trouble the aerial terror hurled against them.

3

The Soviet assault on Budapest began at 14:30 MT on 29 October, when 46th Army opened its attack on a 95km front stretching from Rém to Alpár. In the sector of the 37th Rifle Corps (32km) it was preceded by a 30-minute intensive artillery bombardment delivered by 1120 guns, howitzers and heavy mortars. (In the zone chosen for the attack of the 10th Guards Rifle Corps that preparation lasted only 5 minutes instead of the originally planned 30, since it appeared that there were no significant enemy fortifications.)[7]

Watching from his forward command post, Shlemin could see the devastating effect the artillery preparation was having on the enemy defence. The bombardment was still in progress when the commander of 46th Army, who was in a hurry to meet the assigned objectives, asked Malinovsky to release his main force, the 2nd Guards Mechanised Corps. The coming darkness, which would not allow the corps to form its battle line, was a far bigger concern

KEY

Symbols:

Motorized Staff Company/ Battery

Panzer-Grenadier Company (armored)

Field Gendarmerie Platoon

Panzer Staff Company (Pz V)

Panzer Staff Company/ Battery (Pz IV)

Panzer Company (Pz IV)

Panzer Company (Pz V)

Supply Company

Panzer Maintenance Company

Staff Company (armored)

Anti-Tank Company (Nashorn)

Panzer- or Anti-Tank Company (StuG)

Anti-Tank Company (Marder)

Panzer Staff Company, regimental (Pz V)

Panzer Staff Company (King Tiger)

Anti-Tank Staff Company (Hetzer)

Heavy Panzer-Grenadier Company (armored)

15-cm Howitzer Battery (towed)

10.5-cm Howitzer Battery (towed)

10.5-cm Howitzer Battery (towed, horse-drawn)

Panzer-Grenadier Company (motorized)

15-cm Heavy Infantry Gun Company (SP)

Reconnaissance Company (armored)

Anti-Tank Staff Company

Anti-Tank Company (towed)

Anti-Tank Company (PzJg IV)

Staff Reconnaissance Company (armored)

Light Reconnaissance Company (armored)

Anti-Tank Company (Hetzer)

Panzer Company (King Tiger)

Panzer Flak Platoon (Moebelwagen, 3.7-cm)

Panzer Flak Platoon (Wirbelwind, 4x2-cm)

Panzer Company (Pz IV/70 A)

10.5-cm Howitzer Battery (SP, StuH 42)

Heavy Cavalry Squadron

Cavalry Squadron

Heavy Panzer-Grenadier Company (motorized)

Light Flak Battery (2-cm, towed)

15-cm Howitzer Battery (SP)

10.5-cm Howitzer Battery (SP)

15-cm Heavy Infantry Gun Company (towed)

Radio Company (armored)

Engineer Company (armored)

Engineer Company (motorized)

Telephone Company (armored)

Telephone Company (motorized)

Anti-Aircraft Company/ Platoon/ (2-cm, SP)

Panzer-Grenadier Anti-Aircraft Company (armored)

Flak Platoon (4x2-cm, SP)

Maintenance Company (non-armored)

Reconnaissance Company (VW Scwimmwagen)

Radio Company (motorized)

Panzer Company (Pz IV/70 V)

Panzer Staff Company/ Battery (Pz III)

8.8-cm Flak Battery (towed)

Medium Flak Battery (3.7-cm, towed)

for Shlemin than the still unbroken Magyar resistance.[8]

The Marshal, who was located with Shlemin and Sviridov at the HQ of 46th Army, immediately sanctioned the request. At 14:20 MT the codeword 'Volga, 3333' was transmitted to the 2nd Guards Mechanised Corps, followed two minutes later by another one: 'Eagle, 5555'. Ten minutes later the armoured beast rumbled forward.[9]

The first echelon – the 4th and 6th Guards Mechanised Brigades – left its parking positions and moved up the road. The reconnaissance companies scouted ahead of the main force. Their armoured cars (Soviet-made BA-64s and open-topped American M3 scout cars) and half-tracks (lend lease M3s) drove forward at full speed. Behind them hundreds of vehicles – T-34s, Joseph Stalins, self-propelled guns and Studebakers – slowly crept northwards.

By 17:30 MT the long grey columns had outpaced the infantry of the 10th Guards and 37th Rifle Corps and came in contact with the enemy at several points northwest of Kiskunfélegyháza. Alexander Kanevsky, a platoon commander in the reconnaissance company of the 6th Guards Mechanised Brigade, recalls the encounter vividly:

> Overtaking each other, the tanks rushed forward and dissolved into the inky darkness. The signalmen feverishly worked. The air above our heads shivered and vibrated. With a rustle, as if scratching the illuminated sky, shells flew, anti-tank rounds whistled, splinters squealed. The *Katyushas* started to 'talk', uncovering their fiery stings. This whole orchestra was playing a deadly rhapsody to the enemy.[10]

Meanwhile, everywhere the attack was going as anticipated. After about two hours, aerial reconnaissance reported 'the enemy is in retreat.'[11] Malinovsky's biggest fear – that the Axis troops might halt the drive of his Front during the initial phase of the operation – had nott materialised so far. In the course of the afternoon Shlemin's infantry advanced between 8 and 15km.[12]

On the left flank the offensive of the 31st Guards Rifle Corps was gaining momentum. The gamble to launch an attack there without any artillery preparation paid off, since only a sporadic enemy resistance was encountered in the sector. The successful advance of General Bobruk's troops threatened the Magyar regimental group 'Szücs'[13] with encirclement and forced the latter to withdraw to the north. In the centre the 10th Guards Rifle Corps was also progressing well. The 86th Guards Rifle Division began to envelop the Hungarian 23 Reserve-Division, while the 49th Guards Rifle Division reached the southeastern limits of Bugacmonostor by nightfall.[14]

Major-General Sergei Bobruk, commander of the 31st Guards Rifle Corps.

Major-General Fyodor Kolchuk, commander of the 37th Rifle Corps.

The most dynamic events, however, took place in the zone of the main attack. Since most of the resources of 46th Army (approximately 40 per cent of the entire order of battle) had already been gathered to the immediate rear of 37th Rifle Corps, the Hungarian positions facing the army's right flank were overrun with ease. The forces of General Kolchuk approached Kecskemét from two directions. The enemy losses were mounting; the forward two regiments of the 108th Guards Rifle Division alone took about 150 prisoners of the disintegrating 8 Reserve Division.[15] Kolchuk's other two divisions also got their share of POWs: the 59th Guards captured more than 150, while the 320th captured approximately 50.[16] Apparently, the Hungarian front would not hold out long against the growing Red onslaught.

At several places, however, the Magyar troops offered stiff resistance. The Infantry Regiment 24 (8 Reserve Division) reported destroying 2 Katyusha rocket launchers and 7 T-34 tanks. 1 Armoured Division claimed 2 armoured cars, while 1 Huszar-Division claimed 1 tank.[17] Some Magyar warriors chose to fight to the death rather than let themselves be captured. Amongst them, for instance, was the entire 1/15 Artillery Battery, which was destroyed in a bitter hand-to-hand fight.[18] But all those acts of bravery and self-sacrifice were not enough to turn the tables. The Soviets kept gaining momentum throughout the afternoon and the evening.

In a situation of increasing danger, when the Soviets were about to break through the main defence, the only way to avoid a total collapse of the Magyar VIII Army Corps was to pull back several kilometres to the north and try to form a new line just south of Kecskemét. To accomplish the withdrawal in an as orderly a fashion as possible, it was essential the Soviet spearheads be slowed down by counter-attacks. They were delivered predominantly by 1 Huszar Division, which had a very good reputation amongst the German commanders, and by three battalions of 1 Armoured Division.

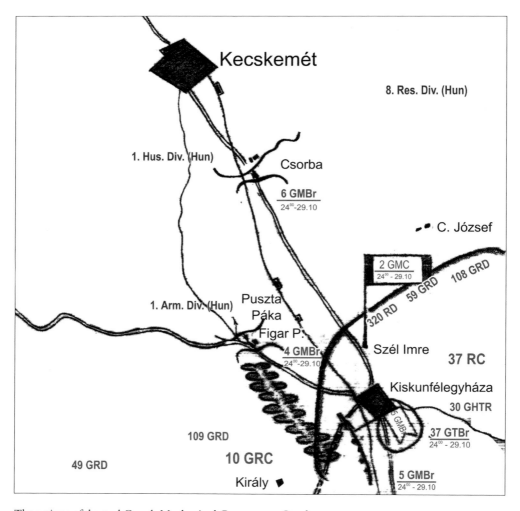

The actions of the 2nd Guards Mechanised Corps on 29 October 1944.

The first significant counter-attack was launched at around 19:00 MT when 6 tanks accompanied by a company of infantry (about 100 men) hit the 320th Rifle Division south of Kecskemét. One hour later up to 160 Hungarian troops supported by two tanks counter-attacked the 179th Guards Rifle Regiment (of 59 Guards Rifle Division).[19] Both counter-attacks, however, were far too weak to pose a threat to the Soviet divisions and were beaten back with ease.

The Hungarians, now mostly scattered remnants, still tried to offer resistance. They not only repeatedly counter-attacked, but also frequently opened fire from ambush positions. These tactics benefited from the terrain: low hills covered by wind-blown sand, many farmsteads, grassland farms and isolated courtyards. 'The enemy tried to convert every settlement or farmstead into a strongpoint,' Shlemin recalls.[20] But 46th Army quickly found a remedy: each regiment formed an assault detachment comprised of a rifle battalion supported by tanks and artillery. The heavy guns engaged the targets with direct fire. Under their cover the infantry and the armour approached the buildings and then stormed them. Often part of the detachment (a company or platoon) bypassed the makeshift bunker and simultaneously attacked it from the flanks and the rear. Thus the strongholds were eliminated one after another and before long the last pockets of resistance were silenced. Shlemin's troops were now free to continue their drive to the north.

The 2nd Guards Mechanised Corps was still the spearhead. By midnight 6th Guards Mechanised Brigade reached the vicinity of Csorba, just to the south of Kecskemét. At the same time its left-flank neighbour, 4th Guards Mechanised Brigade, approached Szél Imre, where it was counter-attacked by Magyar 1 Armoured Division. The resistance of the Hungarians was sporadic at best. Even though tanks and assault guns often supported their counter-attacks, their efforts were too weak to stop Sviridov's armoured avalanche. The brigades surged on through the night and when dawn broke 30 October, the faint shapes of Kecskemét appeared in the mist ahead of the Soviet scouts.

4

What was the reaction of the German command to Shlemin's onslaught? Did they insist the panzer divisions redeploy faster to the battle zone? Did they call the Luftwaffe to strike the enemy armoured columns? Did they order the rear area commanders to employ all troops at their disposal to block the roads? No, they did not. There was no reaction at all. Messages coming from the Hungarian staffs were simply not taken seriously and no one in Friessner's headquarters believed that the Soviet attack on Budapest had begun.

It is not known how many times Magyar officers or German liaison officers warned their superiors about the mounting danger, since the war diary of Army Group South does not record any such warning. What is sure is that warnings had been submitted and one of them, signed by Heszlényi at 21:40 BT, survived the war:

> The Russian grand offensive began with artillery bombardment. Tanks and assault guns broke through between Zsank [sic] and Alpár. The main thrust fell on 1 Huszar-Division, whose positions were attacked at 12:30 BT by 5 infantry divisions and 1 independent mortar brigade. At 14:00 BT another 1.5–2 divisions attacked between Baja and Kiskunmajsa. After these attacks, our troops were forced to withdraw after heavy fighting …[21]

Every officer in the chain of the command, and every field commander in every army, would have paid attention to a message like that; but not in Friessner's army group. The deep mistrust of the abilities of the Hungarians to fight, let alone to give trustworthy intelligence information, had made the Germans judge the situation according to their own prejudices. The effects of such neglect could be seen even at divisional level. The recollection of Major Rudolf von Knebel-Doeberitz, then First General Staff Officer of 24 Panzer-Division, of the situation around Kecskemét during the last two days of October is exemplary:

> Well, from the top we received very little [intelligence]; and our own reconnaissance battalion the previous night[22] reported it had heard loud tank noise; but, since we were in the approach phase, it did us little good. That was the only intelligence we had. Please, remember that at that time, we were under 3rd Hungarian Army, and their reconnaissance effort was weak … the Hungarians had almost nothing in that respect and there was no real interaction. So I used to send an armoured reconnaissance patrol to the Hungarian army headquarters or corps headquarters, usually led by an old experienced staff-sergeant or sergeant-major; and what the Hungarians did was, as soon as they arrived, they included them in their war council and asked them questions about the situation and how the troops were deployed. This way I was able to get some information of the deployment and the commitment of the Hungarian troops and their intentions. This was the only way I could get it.[23]

In a situation like this, it is not surprising that the views of the German leadership prevailed. At 17:50 BT Lieutenant-Colonel von dem Planitz, the chief of staff of LVII Panzer Corps, informed Army Group South that 'in the afternoon the Russians have gone over to the offensive on a broad front between the Danube and Tisza, in the sector between Rém and Kiskunfélegyháza, launching a number of attacks in battalion strength.' He added 'this is not the anticipated big offensive.'[24] At 20:00 BT Gaedcke further backed this verdict: 'these are only reconnaissance attacks that precede the main offensive. No tanks have been seen yet.'[25] Perhaps most of the German staff officers went to bed that night convinced that the southern front was still firm and the main battle was yet to come.

In the meantime 24 Panzer-Division, which had been placed under LVII Panzer Corps with the task of assembling east of Kecskemét for an attack southwards, was dashing through the darkness. The columns were stretched over many kilometres. While the spearhead, Panzer-Reconnaissance Squadron 24, was about to run right into the enemy's midst, the main battle force, Panzer-Grenadier Regiment 21, was still far behind; it only disengaged from its previous operational area east of Jászkarajenő at 22:30 BT.[26] The regiment could not arrive before midday on 30 October, but the start of the attack by the divisional armoured group was scheduled for early in the morning.[27]

As they drew near to Kecskemét shortly after midnight, the scouts of the reconnaissance squadron heard the rumbling noise of approaching tanks. A strong Russian armoured formation was coming its way! The staff of the division was warned about this by radio, but since precise information was lacking they could only guess the size of the force. 'We were under the impression that the Russian tank units that bypassed us had between 400 and 500 tanks,' von Knebel-Doeberitz recalls.[28] Before long the armoured cars of Panzer-Reconnaissance Squadron 24 clashed with forward detachments of 2nd Guards Mechanised Corps and a firefight broke out in the *Puszta*. The brief night battle, however, did no harm to Sviridov's spearheads and they kept advancing northwards. Now all hopes of holding Kecskemét were pinned on Lieutenant-Colonel Kurt Hortian and the gunners of his Flak-Regiment 133.

5

With its nearly 64,000 inhabitants, before the war Kecskemét had been one of the biggest settlements in the Hungarian Plain. Now only about 7000 were still in the town, the rest had fled before the Red Army.[29] This ghost town was still the natural gateway to Budapest since the only asphalted road to the capital from the southeast ran through it. Being aware of this, the Magyars fortified the premises and turned the town into a fortress. General Sviridov apparently had no clue about this, so he decided to take Kecskemét with a coup de main.

The attack began at dawn. The 4th and 6th Guards Mechanised Brigades, which during the night had drawn near the place, regrouped and marched on Kecskemét at full speed. The frontline of the 1 Huszar-Division was penetrated quickly and the latter retreated to the northwest. At around 07:00 MT the forward detachment of the 6th Guards Mechanised Brigade reached the southern suburbs of the town. There it was met by intense artillery and machine-gun fire. A member of the 6th Brigade recalls the assault clearly:

Our brigade was moving directly on Kecskemét. Ahead of us were the 'thirty fours' of Major Kataev's 25th Regiment with submachine gunners riding on them. Having formed a line of battle, the tanks advanced to the buildings. Ahead of them the black tops of the shell bursts were growing constantly. The enemy, goodness knows where from, struck with armour-piercing shells. Suddenly, a soft yellow flame crept out from under the stern of one of the tanks and captured at once its body. Dense smoke tumbled down from the viewing hatches. But the other 'thirty fours', manoeuvring, breaking the battle order of the defenders, continued to move towards the outskirts of the town.[30]

The forward detachment of the 4th Guards Mechanised Brigade, which at 07:00 MT reached the southwestern edge of Kecskemét, ran into similarly bitter resistance. The enemy troops (identified as Infantry Regiment 24 and Huszar-Regiment 2), who had positioned themselves in bunkers and houses, met the attackers with accurate artillery and machine-gun fire and stalled them.

By 09:00 MT it was already clear that both brigades would not be able to take the town by a swift charge. The daring assault had brought unexpected losses. The 4th Guards Mechanised Brigade had lost 4 tanks, 2 trucks and 1 BA-64 armoured car.[31] The 6th Guards Mechanised Brigade fared no better: 4 tanks had burned out, another 2 had been knocked out, 1 armoured halftrack and 1 BA-64 armoured car were charred wrecks; 10 men had been killed, 17 others wounded.[32] The initial plan hadn't worked out.

The unpleasant situation forced Sviridov to rethink his tactics. He summoned his deputies to develop a new plan. As usual, the decision-making process was aided by intelligence. Newly obtained information from corps intelligence and the scout patrols of the 6th Guards Mechanised Brigade revealed that Kecskemét was a real fortress surrounded with trenches and with heavy weapons in place. It was believed that the defence was manned by troops that had fallen back from the broken front as well as by the newly arrived units of the 1 Huszar-Division.[33]

After hearing the reports, Sviridov decided this time to combine frontal assault with close envelopment. The objective now was to bypass and isolate Kecskemét, cut the avenue of retreat for the garrison, take the town by storm and continue the drive to Budapest. He decided to keep attacking Kecskemét frontally with the 6th Guards Mechanised Brigade and the main body of the 37th Guards Tank Brigade, and at the same time to outflank it to the east with the forward detachment of the 37th Guards Tank Brigade, and to the west with the 4th Guards Mechanised Brigade. The 5th Guards Mechanised Brigade would follow in the wake of the latter.[34]

The defence of Kecskemét was not as strong as it seemed to the staff of the 2nd Guards Mechanised Corps. Contrary to the intelligence assessments, the main body of 1 Huszar-Division was deployed farther to the west. Moreover, the Soviets could not know that Colonel Orbay, acting commander of the 8 Reserve Division, had refused to send his troops into the town, despite orders to do so. To Orbay, the whole idea was 'simply absurd'.[35] He had no intention of letting his troops be trapped and cut off. But he did nothing to prevent their desertion from the battlefield, either: at the end of the day Fretter-Pico's staff reported:

> As a result of a strong enemy attack, the Hungarian 8 Infantry-Division was scattered and now is being assembled northwest of Kecskemét. The runaway units of the division were rounded up by our Flak battle group in the vicinity of Kecskemét.[36]

So, in the morning of 30 October only the Luftwaffe Flak-Regiment 133 protected Kecskemét and there was very little infantry around.[37] To make things worse, panic broke out amongst the remaining population of the town and there were some 300 POWs to be deslt with by the garrison. Nevertheless, the courageous 41-year-old Hortian decided to take the fight to the enemy and his gunners met them with a hail of shells and bullets. The terrain provided an excellent field of fire and the deadly 'eighty-eights' poured round after round into the advancing tanks. The Soviet attack had stalled; but for how long?

6

It was not until the morning of 30 October that Friessner's staff realised the full magnitude of Shlemin's attack. At 07:45 BT Lieutenant-Colonel Marcks, 1st General Staff Officer of Armeegruppe Fretter-Pico, phoned the headquarters of Army Group South in Mátraháza to say that the Russian grand offensive had already begun.[38] An emergency conference was called immediately. No details had reached them yet, but it was already clear that the *Schwerpunkt* was the Kecskemét sector, so the leadership of the army group decided to counter-attack the Russian wedge with 24 Panzer-Division (from the east) and the Magyar 1 Armoured-Division (from the area southwest of Kecskemét).[39]

During the next few hours the individual pieces of the puzzle gradually came together. Alarming news kept coming from the front: 'The Russian armour has penetrated into the southern outskirts of Kecskemét, infantry follows behind'; 'at least 15 Russian tanks have been spotted at Jakabszállás'; 'Hungarian 8 Reserve Division is retreating down the road to Budapest'; '23 Reserve Division is falling back in disarray.' Before noon a POW interrogation shed more light on Soviet intentions. The information elicited was that 2nd Guards Mechanised Corps had 105 operational tanks and its troops had been ordered 'to have reached Budapest by the evening'.[40] Now there was no doubt: a great danger was mounting in the south.

Friessner and his officers undertook a series of countermeasures. Since no other branch could react faster than the air force, at 09:35 BT Lieutenant-Colonel Schäfer, 1st General Staff Officer of Army Group South, called his counterpart in Air Fleet 4 and asked for the immediate intervention of the Luftwaffe.[41] Before long, General Deichmann directed a considerable part of his I Air Corps to the endangered zone. The Axis close support aircraft hit the advancing Soviets hard. At the end of the day, the Air Fleet 4 claimed to have destroyed 5 tanks, 1 armoured car, 60 trucks and 20 horse-drawn wagons, all of them in the area of Kecskemét.[42]

The Luftwaffe alone could not halt Malinovsky's march on Budapest, strong ground troops were necessary, especially armour. So throughout the whole day the officers of the operations section of the army group monitored the status of the troops regrouping from the northeast.

A building in Mátraháza, in which the headquarters of the Army Group South was situated during the first battle of Budapest. (Bundesarchiv)

1 and 23 Panzer-Divisions were due to arrive first; the former was assembling north of the Cegléd–Örkény line, the latter was moving down from Jászberény to Cegléd. Both divisions could be thrown into combat the following morning. The other divisions meant for Fretter-Pico, however, were still far away; 'Feldherrnhalle' desperately needed a short break, while the 13th Panzer had not yet been released from Armeegruppe 'Wöhler'.[43]

The next logical step for Friessner was the reorganisation of the newly constituted Armeegruppe Fretter-Pico. With the forces available or still in transit, the army group commander intended to form two powerful shock formations comprising no less than five armoured divisions, with which to strike back. In doing so, he subordinated 1 Armoured Division (Hung), 1, 23, and 24 Panzer-Divisions and the Heavy Panzer Battalion 503 to the staff of LVII Panzer Corps, which was to lead the first group.[44] The creation of the second one (III Panzer Corps with 'Feldherrnhalle' and 13 Panzer-Division) was discussed with OKH.[45]

The Magyar troops were also reorganised. The left flank forces (Group 'Szücs', 10 Infantry Division and 23 Reserve Division) of 3 Army were placed under the staff of the newly arrived VII Army Corps (Hung), while those fighting on both sides of Kecskemét – 1 Huszar-Division, 8 Reserve Division and 20 Infantry Division – remained under VIII Army Corps. The latter was additionally reinforced with the inexperienced 5 Reserve Division, which had just arrived from the rear.[46]

Friessner also requested the General Staff to release some of its reserves, namely the 277 Volksgrenadier-Division that was rebuilding in the Komárom region.[47] Hitler had other ideas; he wanted that division to be kept for the forthcoming operation in the Ardennes. So OKH gave up the inexperienced 22 SS-Cavalry-Division and the worthless 153 Field-Training-Division, which were immediately placed under Fretter-Pico.[48] By subordinating the 'Budapest Group' (22 SS-Cavalry-Division and the staff of the Hungarian VI Army Corps) to Fretter-Pico, Friessner had extended the Armeegruppe area of responsibilities to include the Magyar capital.[49]

Attempts to consolidate the crumbling front included some desperate measures, directed mainly against the Hungarian allies. For instance, von Grolman requested that the Hungarian authorities block the roads leading southeast of Budapest with strong gendarme checkpoints to collect stragglers, deserters and retreating units. The security of the so-called 'Pest bridgehead' was to also be strengthened.[50]

7

The planned double attack against the flanks of 2nd Guards Mechanised Corps had little prospect of success; the troops involved were simply too few in numbers to cause any serious harm to Malinovsky's main armoured formation. For instance, the Magyar 1 Armoured Division had only a handful of obsolete Hungarian-made Turan and Nimrod tanks and two batteries of the attached Assault Gun Battalion 7, which were equipped with StuG IIIs.[51] The situation with the East Prussian 24 Panzer-Division was no different; the former cavalrymen could field approximately 20 operational panzers, some of them being Pz IV/70 (A) tank destroyers.

The Hungarian armoured division attacked with up to 30 armoured vehicles accompanied by infantry. It struck the right flank of the 109th Guards Rifle Division southwest of Kecskemét and thus seriously threatened the boundary between 10th Guards Rifle Corps and 37th Rifle Corps.[52] The large-calibre guns of the 7th Artillery Division saved the situation. The hero of the day was Sergeant Arkady Kukin from the 877th Regiment of the 25th Howitzer Artillery Brigade. The 30-year-old former gold digger from Kazakhstan moved his 122mm howitzer forward and aimed it through the sight. Three tanks were knocked out. Before long his crew was killed and Kukin himself was wounded in both legs. Nevertheless, he continued the fight and despite the pain managed to set fire to an assault gun. Then a direct hit destroyed the

A battery of Soviet divisional 122mm M-30 howitzers in action in the Budapest area, November 1944. (The Photo Archive of the Ministry of Defence of Bulgaria)

howitzer and silenced it for good. When the enemy infantry surrounded the position, Kukin fired back with his pistol, leaving the last bullet for himself. On 24 March 1945 he was posthumously made a Hero of the Soviet Union.[53]

After the failure of the counter-attack, 1 Armoured Division occupied a defensive perimeter some 2km southeast of the Helvetia railway station (8km southwest of Kecskemét). It managed to contain the enemy pressure for a while, but mostly because the Soviet thrusts in this sector were still fairly weak.[54] The division, however, was no longer capable of undertaking offensive actions. For Heszlényi that setback was hardly a surprise; he had bet his stakes on the 24th Panzer, anyway. Earlier in the morning he had informed Fretter-Pico that his 'insignificant forces will be able to hold the front only if the attack of 24 Panzer-Division proves to be a success'.[55] It was all or nothing.

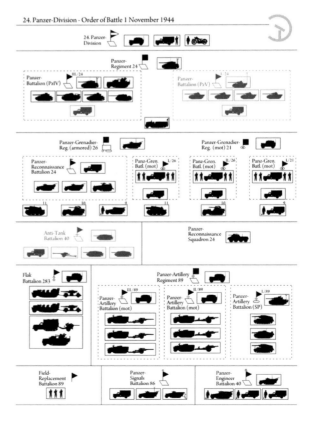

8

In the meantime 24 Panzer-Division managed to create a mini-crisis on the other flank of the Soviet wedge. The former cavalry division was not only understrength, but also part of it was still en route to the battlefield. What was available, however, was thrown into combat in full accord with tactical regulations, which strongly advocated the employment of *Kampfgruppen* (battle groups). Usually, the panzer-divisions formed two battle groups: one that comprised mostly motorised elements (truck-borne infantry and towed artillery), and another consisting of the available armour. Since the main component needed to build the 'motorised' battle group, the Panzer-Grenadier Regiment 21, was still lagging behind, initially only the armoured battle group was thrown into combat.[56]

In the morning the armoured battle group struck Shlemin's right-flank divisions, the 59th and 108th Guards, southeast of Kecskemét. The first attack was against the 59th Guards. At 09:30 MT a battalion of infantry supported by 9 tanks and some armoured halftracks hit the 183rd Guards Rifle Regiment.[57] It was repulsed at the cost of one panzer and one half-track.[58] Over the next couple of hours the Soviet regiment managed to advance farther to the north and approached the Kecskemét–Szolnok railway.

At 10:00 MT another counter-attack followed, this time farther to the northeast. At Kisfái (a small settlement and railway station situated to the southeast of Kecskemét) 17 panzers and infantry of battalion strength attacked the 305th Guards Rifle Regiment of the 108th Guards Rifle Division.[59] This one was also beaten back.

Even though the initial German pressure was contained, General Kolchuk, commander of 37th Rifle Corps, was well aware that his rifle troops were too weak to fight the panzers alone. At around 11:00 MT he sent a personal plea to Sviridov, literally begging him for 'assistance in repulsing the enemy tank group to the north'.[60] Sviridov, however, could not answer Kolchuk's cry for help because all his brigades were already engaged.

The East Prussians did not give up and kept attacking with their usual determination. There was no continuous frontline in the *Puszta* and the German armour wandered back and forth searching for weak points in the Soviet battle order. Thus at 11:30 up to 15 tanks came out of the forest north Koháry Szent Lőrinc[61] and attacked the boundary of the 305th and 308th Guards Rifle Regiments. The guardsmen turned them back. The failure forced the armoured group once again to shift its focal point, now to the northwest. At 12:00 MT it struck the 183rd Guards Rifle Regiment at Kisfái with 10 tanks and an infantry battalion.[62]

The lack of success forced the command of 24th Panzer to rethink tactics. Apparently, the series of small-scale probing attacks did not work against the mobile enemy defence. They

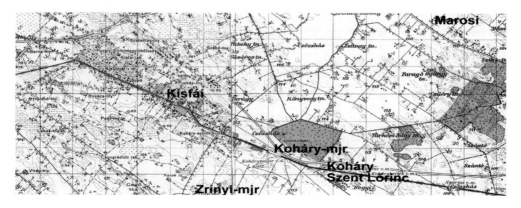

The area where the 24 Panzer-Division launched its counterattacks on 30 October 1944.

decided to assemble the entire strength of the armoured group into a powerful 'fist' and smash the Soviet flank with a single, bold stroke. Up to 30 tanks were assembled for that purpose in the forest east of Koháry-major.[63] After a brief pause to regroup and replenish, the Germans tried their luck again.

The blow fell on the 308th Guards Rifle Regiment's 3rd Battalion that had just taken Koháry Szent Lőrinc after house-to-house fighting. At 14:00 MT 18 panzers moved in on the positions of Lieutenant Lazarev's platoon (13 men and an anti-tank rifle) at the railway embankment. 12 more advanced against his left-hand neighbour, 305th Guards Rifle Regiment. The artillery soon engaged them. Of those 18 machines 3 were quickly knocked out by the 76mm guns of 245th Artillery Regiment, but the rest kept moving forward. As the panzers came closer and closer, another one was stopped when it took an anti-tank rifle shot. But almost immediately an explosion eliminated the anti-tank rifle team and Lazarev himself took the place of his fallen men. With six rounds he immobilised two more tanks, but this was not enough to stop the rest. After a burst wounded him and damaged the rifle, Lazarev, determined not to allow the enemy to break through, threw himself under the leading tank with grenades. The tank blew up. Inspired by the self-sacrifice of their commander, the rest of the platoon counter-attacked and pinned down the accompanying panzer-grenadiers with automatic fire and hand grenades. Then the anti-tank artillery arrived on the scene, making any further advance of the panzers impossible.[64] For his courage and sacrifice, Georgy Lazarev was posthumously made a Hero of the Soviet Union.[65]

It seemed that even the most determined resistance would not be able to contain the zeal of the East Prussians that afternoon. They attacked again at 15:30 MT when 31 tanks, in a two-echelon formation, rolled out of the forest west of the Koháry Szent Lőrinc railway station and smashed the left flank of the 305th Guards Rifle Regiment. The panzers and the panzer-grenadiers advanced straight to the south, but soon enough they were intercepted by the Soviet artillery and turned back.[66]

The ever-increasing German counterblows now threatened the rear communications not only of the 37th Rifle Corps, but also those of the 2nd Guards Mechanised Corps. This time Sviridov reacted immediately to the menace. He ordered the commander of 37th Guards Tank Brigade to divert one battalion to the southeast and halt the enemy counter-attack.[67] At least one tank company of the 1st Battalion was placed in ambush west of Zrínyi-major. With their guns facing to the northeast, the crews waited patiently for the Germans to appear.

The Soviet tank men did not have to wait long. At around 16:30 MT 28 panzers set out from the vicinity of Kisfái. They bypassed the positions of the 183rd Guards Rifle Regiment (of 59th Guards Rifle Division) and surged to the southwest, aiming to cut off the Kecskemét–Kiskunfélegyháza motorway, the main Soviet supply line.[68] Before long they ran straight into the guns of the T-34/85s. Around ten German machines were knocked out in quick succession and the East Prussians were beaten back again.

Having finally dealt with the vigorous enemy counter-attacks – eight had been repulsed since the morning! – at 17:00 MT the 108th Guards Rifle Division went over to the offensive again. The 308th Guards Rifle Regiment succeeded at last in securing the entire area around Koháry–Szent–Lőrinc, while on its right the 311th Guards Rifle Regiment made a deep penetration to the north. The latter captured the small village of Marosi, the Szt. Király forest (just to the west of Marosi) and cut off the main road between Kecskemét and Szolnok.[69]

A reconnaissance group led by Lieutenant I. Zakharchenko distinguished itself during the battles in the vicinity of the Szt. Király forest. First it attacked the firing position of a Hungarian artillery battery and captured it together with its guns. The Kecskemét–Szolnok motorway was not far from there and Zakharchenko decided to set up an ambush hoping someone would come along. Some half an hour later two German staff cars were captured. Their passengers,

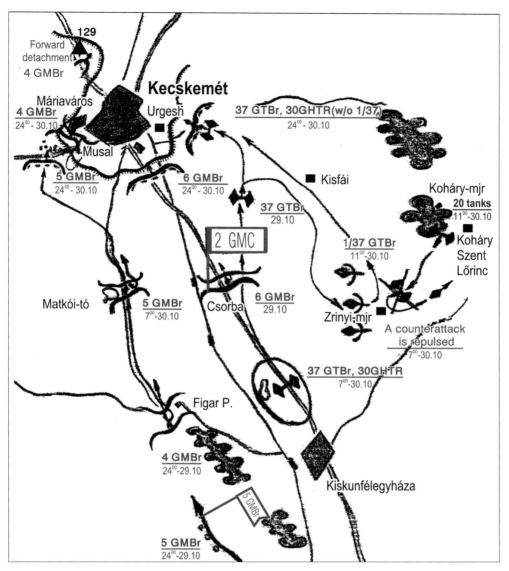

The actions of the 2nd Guards Mechanised Corps on 30 October 1944.

several officers of 24 Panzer-Division, were shocked that the Russians had advanced so deep – and that their military service to the Reich had ended in such a way. They were hurriedly led into Soviet captivity.[70]

By nightfall the 108th Guards were occupying very favourable jump-off positions for the next phase of the offensive and the fighting gradually calmed down. It was the time to make up the profit and loss acount. The division claimed the following losses amongst the enemy: 380 officers and men, 11 artillery guns, 3 mortars and 9 machine guns destroyed; 15 tanks knocked-out and 499 Axis troops taken prisoner. The 108th, in turn, had lost 32 killed and 110 wounded, as well as 2 76mm guns, 2 45mm anti-tank guns, 3 120mm mortars, 8 heavy machine guns, 11 light machine guns and 1 truck.[71]

9

While the right-flank elements of Sviridov's and Kolchuk's corps were desperately trying to seal off the enemy penetrations east and southeast of Kecskemét, the main body of the 2nd Guards Mechanised Corps continued slowly, but steadily, to encircle the town.

Until the evening Sviridov's left pincer (4th Guards Mechanised Brigade and 1509th Self-Propelled Artillery Regiment) remained pinned down west and southwest of Kecskemét. It simply was not able to overcome the Magyar defence established there by elements of the Reserve Regiment 24 (of 8 Reserve-Division) and Huszar-Regiment 2.[72] The stalemate was broken after 19:00 MT when a breakthrough was finally achieved. Heaving encountered very little opposition (the small Hungarian rearguards standing in the way were simply brushed aside), by midnight the forward detachment of 4th Guards Mechanised Brigade reached Hill 129, thus cutting off the main road to Budapest.[73] On the other side of the town, however, where 37th Guards Tank Brigade was fighting, events took a far more dramatic turn.

Initially, everything went well for 37th Guards Tank Brigade. In the early afternoon the forward detachment (the 2nd Battalion, two companies of the 30th Guards Heavy Tank Regiment, infantry riding on tanks) severed the railway and main road northwards, destroying the forward command post of 24 Panzer-Division in the process. One high-ranking officer was killed and the Axis units deployed in the area sustained heavy losses.[74]

The account of Major von Knebel-Doeberitz helps us get a sense of the chaos that reigned in this part of the *Puszta* during the afternoon of 30 October 1944:

> There were no boundaries because everything was a great mix up of different units. Russian and German all mixed up in great confusion. The Russians, who were on our right flank, had their vehicles mixed up with our vehicles and no one really knew what was happening. The 21st [Panzer-Grenadier] Regiment, came from the north to our sector – at that time our division CP [Command Post] had been overrun by the Russians – though we were all still alive. What I did when the regiment approached, I got into my vehicle and went up to them and personally led the regiment into the combat area where they were to be committed.[75]

The Germans had been caught off guard by the daring Soviet tank raid, but early in the afternoon, the 'northern' battle group of 24 Panzer-Division (the reinforced Panzer-Grenadier Regiment 21) arrived and changed the balance on the battlefield. At around 15:00 MT it launched a violent counter-attack from the northeast. Lieutenant-Colonel Korotkov, brigade commander, was now in a very difficult situation: he had to deal simultaneously with two threats.

The first one was in the north. Since the infantry unit deployed nearby (179th Guards Rifle Regiment of the 59th Guards Rifle Division) had inadequate numbers of troops on hand and would not be able to withstand the German onslaught, Korotkov decided to meet the latter with the bulk of his own brigade. The second threat was deep in the south, between Kisfái and Koháry Szent Lőrinc, where, as we already know, the armoured battle group of 24 Panzer-Division had just launched a powerful attack, trying to drive a wedge between the 59th and 108th Guards Rifle Divisions. In order to deal with this new threat, Korotkov shifted his 1st Tank Battalion to the southeast, as mentioned.[76]

Korotkov's guardsmen tried to resist the counter-attack of Panzer-Grenadier Regiment 21 as best as they could. The fierce fighting raged throughout the afternoon and the evening. This is confirmed by the German records. At 18:40 BT the 1st General Staff Officer of Armeegruppe Fretter-Pico reported that the northern battle group of e 24 Panzer-Division had reached a point 3km east of Kecskemét, while the southern one had crossed the Kecskemét–Kiskunfélegyháza road.[77] Nevertheless, no contact with the garrison had been established as yet.

By the evening the 37th Guards Tank Brigade was no longer able to withstand the enemy pressure and the Germans had fragmented it into three groups. The forward detachment (the reinforced 2nd Tank Battalion) found itself surrounded by enemy infantry 1km northeast of Ürges (a southeastern suburb of Kecskemét). Its situation was worsening because shortly before midnight the Axis artillery joined the battle and began to shell the trapped battalion. The exact location and condition of the 3rd Tank Battalion was unknown to Korotkov, since radio communication was lost. The only thing that he knew (from the last report before the communication breakdown) was that the battalion was busy repulsing attacks by enemy armour and panzer-grenadiers somewhere southeast/east of Kecskemét. The situation of the brigade's motorised rifle battalion was not very clear either, since it had been split into groups and assigned piecemeal to the tank battalions.[78] The worst was yet to come: around midnight 24 Panzer-Division finally succeeded in opening a corridor to Kecskemét and now both Soviet tank battalions were isolated.

10

In the meantime, a battle of equal ferocity was raging at Kecskemét. The garrison was under pressure from three sides, but was holding out. At Máriaváros, a southwestern suburb of Kecskemét, the 4th Guards Mechanised Brigade was desperately trying to break in. At Musal (a southern suburb) and Ürges the entire 6th Guards Mechanised Brigade, part of the 37th Guards Tank Bridge, and half of the 'Joseph Stalins' of the 30th Guards Heavy Tank Regiment, were pinned down. The Axis machine gun-, mortar and artillery fire was murderous, and the repeated attacks of the Luftwaffe were paralysing.

Attempting to break the deadlock, Shlemin ordered the 320th and 59th Guards Rifle Divisions to enter the battle for the town. The former arrived from the southwest, the latter – with two regiments – from the southeast, leaving the 183rd Regiment to guard the deep eastern flank. (As we already know, in the afternoon it would be nearly routed by 24 Panzer-Division.) Both divisions mounted a resolute attack on the southern perimeter of Kecskemét, but achieved very little success. The 59th Guards, for instance, captured the power plant and part of the town's factory, but was not able to advance farther.[79]

In the meantime Sviridov reinforced his left flank with the 5th Guards Mechanised Brigade, but even this did not change things; the gunners of Hortian's Flak-Regiment were fighting like lions. Some leftovers of 8 Reserve Division supported them: III Battalion/Reserve Regiment 24 and one engineer company, as well as 3 Battery/Assault Gun Battalion 7. The joint effort produced a wall of fire and the Soviet casualties mounted. The number of Soviet tanks reported as knocked-out by the Flak regiment increased from 5 in the morning to 20 by the end of the day.[80] One more was claimed by a Hungarian assault gun, while another was captured intact.[81] A further 7 tank kills were credited to the Third Reich's most decorated pilot, Hans-Ulrich Rudel.[82]

The fierce resistance encountered by the Soviets at the gates of Kecskemét did not break their will. On the contrary, they began to fight more resolutely, even to the point of self-sacrifice. Today it is hard to imagine how ferocious those battles really were and what exactly had motivated Captain V. Dolya from the 23rd Guards Tank Regiment to keep fighting in his burning tank to the very end. But he and his three crewmates did it. Having received several direct hits, Dolya's blazing T-34 kept rolling forward, crushing enemy anti-tank guns and machine guns under its tracks. The tank even managed to break into the town, where soon thereafter, it detonated. [83] The death of the heroes was in vain; no one followed them in and 'fortress' Kecskemét remained in Axis hands.

The defenders of Kecskemét, the three battalions of the Flak Regiment 133 (I/25, I/28 and 147), possessed considerable firepower: approximately 36 heavy 88mm and 120 light 20mm anti-aircraft guns.[84] It served them well during the day, but with the approach of the night the lack of infantry protection raised serious worries at German headquarters. It was feared that the Russians might infiltrate the Axis positions under cover of darkness and eliminate the guns.[85] All attempts to find additional troops failed; the divisions that could provide them were either engaged in combat or were still underway. In order to save the Flak regiment from annihilation, Fretter-Pico proposed that Kecskemét be abandoned and a new front be created north of the town employing Hortian's guns and 24 Panzer-Division. The staff of the army group immediately rejected this plan and von Grolman reminded Gaedcke about the order from OKH to destroy all enemy troops to the north of Szeged.[86] Finally, at around 02:00 BT, 24 Panzer-Division established contact with Flak Regiment 133. Good news, at last!

11

In terms of casualties inflicted, 30 October was a successful day for 46th Army. Its units reported 25 tanks and self-propelled guns knocked out, 8 aircraft shot down, 27 guns captured and more than 1300 enemy troops taken prisoner.[87] But the principal objective of the day, the Alberti–Örkény line, was not met. The main reasons for this failure were identified later on:

> … unimaginative frontal attacks against a fortified place [Kecskemét] that led to unnecessary losses; slowness, indecision and lack of manoeuvrability of the units of the [2nd Guards Mechanised] Corps; lack of interaction between the different arms branches; the dispersal of the armoured forces and their employment in the mopping up of small enemy pockets of resistance.[88]

Understandably, Shlemin was furious. At the end of the day he dictated the following order, addressed to all corps commanders:

> None of the four corps (2nd Guards Mechanised; 10th Guards, 31st Guards and 37th Rifle Corps) has accomplished the mission for 30 October. The main reasons that have kept them from meeting the mission objectives are poor cooperation between the infantry with artillery and tanks, and inadequate manoeuvre of the tanks and artillery on the battlefield.
>
> 1   The assigned mission must be accomplished on 31.10.1944.
> 2   The commander of 2nd Guards Mechanised Corps must show greater resolve in accomplishing his mission. The anti-aircraft artillery must accompany the brigades, the troops must avoid battles for enemy strongholds, and bypass them instead and manoeuvre on the battlefield. The attached field artillery must accompany the brigades.
> 3   In order to combat the enemy tanks more effectively, the corps commanders must place the artillery within the infantry formations and carry out careful reconnaissance to detect the enemy tanks in time. The appearance of enemy tanks must not stop the advance of the infantry, which has to be protected by the artillery.
> 4   The army offensive must be resumed during the night of 30/31 October, not later than 03:00 MT. By that time the forward repositioning of the artillery must be completed.[89]

The advance was running behind schedule and the offensive was losing momentum. The pressure was on. It was clear to everybody in the HQ of the 2nd Ukrainian Front that the current situation was entirely favourable to the enemy; it was winning the Germans time to redeploy their armoured formations to the endangered zone.[90] Malinovsky was breathing down Shlemin's neck; if 46th Army were to have any hope of getting to Budapest before the arrival

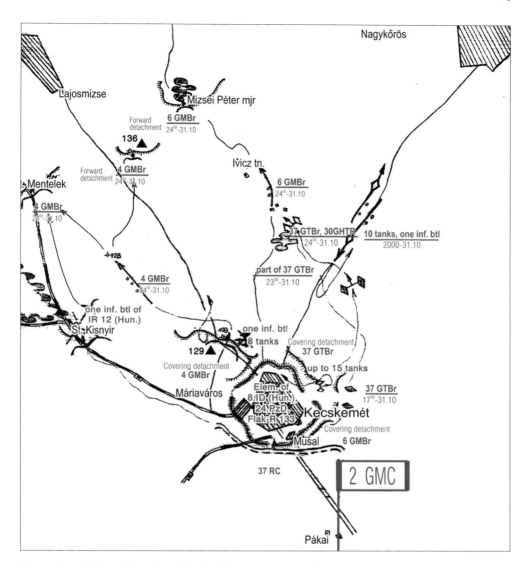

The actions of the 2nd Guards Mechanised Corps on 31 October 1944.

of the bulk of the German reserves, it had to break the deadlock at Kecskemét as soon as possible. The situation demanded decisive action and the only one who could deliver it was the 48-year-old Lieutenant-General Karp Sviridov, commander of 2nd Guards Mechanised Corps.

12

The pressure from above left Sviridov no choice but to urge more resolute action from the leading brigades. He also finally abandoned the idea of capturing Kecskemét by a direct assault and began to regroup his forces for a pincer attack. Thus the 6th Guards Mechanised Brigade, which had spent the day in fruitless attacks against the southeastern perimeter of the town, was relieved during the night by the infantry of 37th Rifle Corps.[91] The brigade was assembled in the field and at first light resumed its drive to the north.

The attack in the morning of 31 October was a complete success, but it was no joyride. The right pincer (6th Guards Mechanised Brigade, 37th Guards Tank Brigade and 30th Guards Heavy Tank Regiment) had to fight its way through determined resistance. Small groups of enemy tanks and assault guns, backed by infantry, repeatedly counter-attacked the vulnerable flanks of the task force. Time and again, the Axis close support aircraft dived on the Soviet armour, which was advancing in a single column because the ground on either side of the road was too soft. It finally broke into open country and Kecskemét was completely encircled. 24 Panzer-Division was split into two groups. The staff of Panzer-Artillery Regiment 89 and some of its artillery units, parts of I Battalion/Panzer-Grenadier Regiment 26 and Panzer-

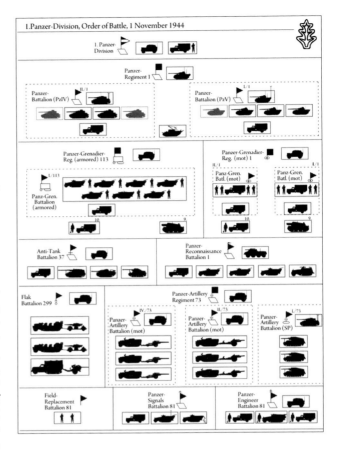

Engineer Battalion 40 were trapped in Kecskemét, where, together with Flak Regiment 133, they formed a battle group under Colonel von Uslar-Gleichen. The rest of the division was engaged in combat north and northeast of the town.[92]

Shortly afterwards, however, the East Prussians counter-attacked from the north. They not only destroyed two Soviet tanks, but most importantly, succeeded in re-establishing contact with the surrounded garrison.[93] Thus they managed to secure an avenue of retreat for Uslar-Gleichen's group (the Kecskemét–Budapest road), which they kept open until the end of the day.

The left pincer of the corps (4th and 5th Guards Mechanised Brigades) initially encountered very little opposition. The 5th Guards, who had now taken the lead, even managed to surround one battalion of the Infantry Regiment 12 (Hung) in the vicinity of the Kisnyir railway station. The Battalion's situation was hopeless and in the course of the day it was wiped out.[94] The advance of Sviridov's western task force along the Budapest–Kecskemét motorway, however, would get tougher: pretty soon both brigades would run into a much stronger opponent, 1 Panzer-Division.

13

1 Panzer-Division (also known as 'the oak leaf division' after its insignia) began to assemble in the vicinity of Lajosmizse in the morning of 31 October. Since the German panzer divisions comprised many types of vehicles, while redeploying to another area they were not only divided into units, but often were broken into subgroups based on the equipment they used.

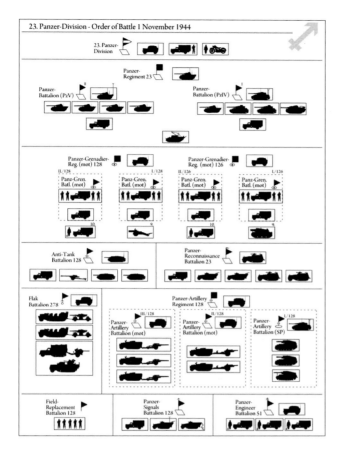

23. Panzer-Division - Order of Battle 1 November 1944

Thus the wheeled elements moved on the roads in columns, while the tracked elements, notorious for high mechanical attrition rates, were transported by rail. The transfer of a panzer-division from one point to another was a sophisticated and time-consuming logistical operation. The relocation of the 'oak leaf division' was no exception.

Panzer-Engineer Battalion 37 was the first of its units that appeared on the battlefield. On 30 October it had been subordinated to Hungarian 1 Armoured Division,[95] probably with the mission of supporting its offensive actions. The Hungarians, however, had been in constant retreat ever since, so the only thing that the German combat engineers could do was to build roadblocks. The sound of the approaching battle and the not-so-distant roar of Sviridov's tanks had probably scared many of them, since the battalion lacked any heavy weapons with which to confront the Soviet armour.[96] The makeshift road obstacles offered only an illusory hope. Needless to say, the arrival of the one of the forward units of their parent division was a real relief to the troubled combat engineers. This was Panzer-Grenadier Regiment 1, which in the morning occupied the perimeter around Lajosmizse and in so doing barred the southern route to the town.[97]

As usual, the division was spearheaded by its reconnaissance element, Panzer-Reconnaissance Battalion 1, whose armoured cars and halftracks immediately began to scout the area south/southeast of Gyón. Before long enough intelligence was collected and Captain Dr Koehler, the battalion commander, forwarded it to the divisional HQ. This allowed Major-General Thunert and his staff by midday to build a complete picture of the enemy.[98] Most of the division – the tanks, the rest of the panzer-grenadiers and the artillery – was yet to appear. They would arrive piecemeal in the course of the next couple of days.

Despite the absence of the armoured core, 'the oak leaf division' was already part of Friessner's plans for halting the advance of the 2nd Guards Mechanised Corps towards Budapest: it was to hold fast the area of Lajosmizse and thus prevent the Soviets from rushing to the northwest.

In these plans the two major roles would be taken by 1 Armoured-Division (Hung) and 23 Panzer-Division. The Hungarians, as on the day before, were to attack Kecskemét from the west and thus to strike Sviridov's apparently exposed left flank. 23 Panzer-Division, which, like 1st Panzer had just begun to arrive, was to deliver a powerful blow from the area of Nagykőrös to the south and link up with the surrounded defenders of Kecskemét. The attack of 23rd Panzer was scheduled for 10:30 BT.[99]

As one might expect, the offensive of the Magyar armoured division failed to materialise. The fast-moving Soviet spearheads simply forestalled it; the Hungarians were attacked 'by a superior enemy force' even before they managed to occupy the designated jump-off area. It was only by 17:00 BT that they managed to repel the Soviet attacks and stabilise the front.[100] After that the division abandoned the Kerekegyháza area, withdrew to the northwest and by the end of the day assembled its exhausted battalions 4–5km southwest of Lajosmizse. Its new mission was to protect the road to Tatárszentgyörgy.[101] Given its condition, 1 Armoured Division was incapable of anything more than that. In contrast, the forward elements of 23 Panzer-Division, which was considered one of the best in the Wehrmacht, managed to cause a lot of headaches to the Soviets.

The counter-attack of 23rd Panzer from Nagykőrös to the southwest, which was scheduled for the morning, was considerably delayed because of an unanticipated problem: the retreating Hungarian troops had blown up a bridge too prematurely.[102] So the division went into combat only at midday. Its units were committed to battle in order of their arrival.

Naturally, the first that headed into the unknown were the patrols of Panzer-Reconnaissance Battalion 23. After a short while, they radioed that they had seen strong enemy columns moving from Kecskemét to the northwest towards Lajosmizse. (These were, of course, some elements of the 2nd Guards Mechanised Corps.) The northern Russian flank looked temptingly vulnerable and one battle group (Panzer-Grenadier Regiment 128 reinforced with two battalions of Panzer-Artillery Regiment 128) attacked it vigorously. Later on, the battle group disengaged and moved closer to Kecskemét. III Battalion/Panzer-Artillery Regiment 128, which followed closely behind, managed to set up positions just 6km northwest of the town. From there its heavy 15cm howitzers delivered a hail of fire on the Soviet infantry concentrations and armoured columns.[103]

In the afternoon the engagement evolved into fierce tank versus tank duels. A tank battle took place northwest of Kecskemét, near the road to Budapest, where a battle group of the 23 Panzer-Division was engaged. Another battle group of the same division was involved in heavy fighting in the area between Nagykőrös and Kecskemét.[104]

Farther to the west, at Lajosmizse, Panzer-Grenadier Regiment 1 (reinforced with one artillery battalion) was finally committed to action. During their first contact with the enemy, the panzer-grenadiers of the 'oak leaf division' managed to knock out two Soviet tanks.[105] By the end of the day they had repulsed yet another attack (presumably by the 4th Guards Mechanised Brigade), claiming five more tanks.[106]

When dusk fell, it was clear to both sides that the German counter-attack had shot its bolt. By 18:30 MT both newly arrived panzer-divisions began a fighting withdrawal to the northwest and northeast respectively. The brigades of the 2nd Guards Mechanised Corps, in turn, quickly formed reinforced forward detachments and resumed their offensive. Shortly afterwards they cut the Kecskemét–Nagykőrös and Kecskemét–Budapest motorways and advanced to the north and northwest.[107] Even so, that day the situation was very dynamic and the German commanders had not yet given up hope of regaining the initiative in the *Puszta*.

The desperate attempts of 23 Panzer-Division to link up with the defenders of Kecskemét continued well into the evening. It was pitch dark when the Germans struck again. At 20:00 up to 10 tanks and a battalion of infantry[108] launched an attack along the Nagykőrös–Kecskemét road and surprised the covering detachment of the 6th Guards Mechanised Brigade from the rear. They had been left by Sviridov to block the escape of the defenders of Kecskemét. The attack cut off the supply route of the 6th and 37th Brigades. Sviridov kept his head and decided not to break off his own attack, but to push back the Germans with the forces already in place and at the same time to continue the drive to the northwest with the main body of the corps. So he ordered the covering detachment to pin down the attackers and radioed 37th Guards Tank Brigade to turn back some of its tanks and riding infantry and open up the supply route

An armoured halftrack of 23 Panzer-Division rolls by the remnants of a destroyed Soviet supply column somewhere between Kecskemét and Budapest, late October/early November 1944. (Mirko Bayerl)

King Tigers of Heavy-Panzer-Battalion 503 somewhere between Kecskemét and Budapest, late October/ early November 1944. (Mirko Bayerl)

again. The order was carried out immediately and by 23:00 MT the situation in the corps' rear was restored. Having found itself counter-attacked from different directions, the German battle group fell back to the northeast.[109] The 6th Guards Mechanised Brigade quickly exploited the gap that now opened in the Axis line and by midnight its forward detachment reached the Mizsei Péter major (cattle farm).[110]

The brigades of Sviridov's left pincer (the 4th and 5th) did not gain much ground either. The fact that such a formidable obstacle as Kecskemét was behind them did not put a spring in their step. Pretty soon they came under attack from two different directions. We have already seen how 1 Panzer-Division managed to halt their advance on Lajosmizse. 23 Panzer-Division also caused them problems with its sudden raids against their open northern flank. Thus (presumably in the evening) the forward detachment of 4th Guards Mechanised Brigade was counter-attacked near Hill 129 by an infantry battalion supported by 8 tanks. The assault was beaten back with heavy losses to the Germans and the detachment resumed its advance along the road to Lajosmizse. By midnight both brigades were at the gates of the town: the forward detachment of the 4th had reached Hill 136, while the spearhead of the 5th was in the vicinity of Méntelek railway station.[111]

Meanwhile, 37th Rifle Corps stormed the southern perimeter of Kecskemét, where heavy fighting erupted. Two Soviet divisions (59th Guards and 320th) put pressure on the von Uslar-Gleichen battle group, raising worries in the headquarters of Army Group South that the defenders would not hold out for long. The surrounded troops were running low of ammunition and fuel. The fall of the 'fortress' seemed imminent.

14

There was no fixed frontline in the area of Kecskemét and the battle deteriorated into a chaotic mess. Brigadier-General Bela Temesy, commander of 8 Reserve-Division, recalls a bizarre incident that occurred during the retreat of his formation after the breakthrough of the Soviet armour:

> All of a sudden two tanks overtook me from the left. They went ahead at high speed. They even collided lightly with some Hungarian tanks. All of us believed that these were German tanks. There were some angry Hungarians who threatened the tanks with hand-grenades for their impertinence. On one occasion, when the road looked very narrow for the tank, one of its crewmen poked his head out of the hatch and called out to the column 'to the right' – in Hungarian, and waved his hand. When the tanks reached the head of the column, one man again poked his head out of one of them and fired into the first tank with a submachine gun. Then the Hungarian soldier there angrily decided to fire a *Faustpatrone,* even it was a German tank. The tank burst into flames at once. In reply, the other tank fired with his main gun at the column, but did not hit anybody, fortunately. Then another Hungarian soldier released a *Faustpatrone* at that tank. It also burst into flames. It turned out that these were actually two Soviet T-34s, which wanted to get to the head of the column to knock out one or two tanks there, and in so doing to block up and capture the whole column.[112]

The Soviet armoured columns advancing northwards were vulnerable to aerial attack. Despite the extensive anti-aircraft fire and fighter protection, the German and Hungarian pilots of the Air Fleet 4 had yet another successful day: they claimed the destruction of 10 tanks, 50 trucks, 20 horse-drawn wagons and a considerable number of anti-aircraft guns.[113] Six of the tank kills were credited to Rudel. The famous 'tank buster' vividly recounts one of those successful missions:

Colonel Hans-Ulrich Rudel (middle), the famous German tank killing ace, examines damage to a Soviet T-34-85 tank in the company of some Hungarian officers and German pilots, Hungary, November 1944. The Luftwaffe in Hungary included several units specialising in anti-tank combat but their effectiveness against the Soviet armour was grossly inflated: according to the after-action report of the commander of the armoured and mechanised troops of the 2nd Ukrainian Front , during the Budapest Operation (29.10.1944–13.02.1945) only ten tanks were lost as total write-offs due to aerial attacks. (Dénes Bernád)

With the few aircraft left to my wing, including the anti-tank flight, I often take off on a sortie in the area S.E. of Kecskemet. Our aircraft strength ... has been so greatly reduced that one day I go out alone, escorted by four FW 190s, to attack the enemy's armour in this area. As I approach my objective I can hardly believe my eyes; a long distance north of Kecskemet tanks are moving along the road; they are Russians. Above them, like a bunch of grapes, hangs a dense umbrella of Soviet fighters protecting the spearhead ...

I come down and make an attack. One tank is on fire. Two FW 190s are weaving about me trying to draw off a few Lag 5s. The two others stick to me, manoeuvring as I do; they have no intention of leaving me alone, which is bound to happen if they engage in aerial combat with any of the Ivans. Twenty or thirty Lag 5s and Yak 9s now turn their attention to us ...

Meanwhile I attack another tank. So far they have not run for cover, doubtless believing that they are sufficiently protected by their fighters. Again one bursts into flame. The Red Falcons are circling overhead and making the craziest hullabaloo; they all want to give advice on the best way to shoot down my Ju. 87. ... Now they come back again, from different angles in fact, and I'm glad that my fifth tank has used up my last round of ammunition, for if we keep up this game much longer we cannot count on a happy ending. The sweat has been pouring off me all the time, though it is very cold outside; excitement is more warming than any fur jacket. The same is true for my escort.[114]

15

The vigorous resistance did not prevent 46th Army from advancing. In the HQ of Army Group South the staff officers followed with heavy hearts the progress of Shlemin's offensive. The exact location of the spearheads of 2nd Guards Mechanised Corps were not known and Fretter-Pico's chief of staff, General Gaedcke, was afraid 'that the Russians may already have captured Lajosmizse'.[115] But even after hearing the latest reports, the leadership of Army Group South believed that they could still turn the tide. They felt that a decisive counterblow could be launched once they had gathered their armoured reserves. So Fretter-Pico received instructions to hold his present positions and wait for reinforcements. After their arrival he was to form two shock groups under Breith (III Panzer Corps) and Kirchner (LVII Panzer Corps) to destroy the enemy troops and recapture Szeged.[116] In an attempt to galvanise the command of Armeegruppe Fretter-Pico into prompt action, in the evening von Grolman informed them that they would be reinforced with three SS-divisions (8, 18 and 22) that should be used en masse in the area between the Danube and Tisza.[117]

16

In the afternoon of 31 October the 59th Guards Rifle Division finally succeeded in crushing the determined enemy resistance and by 17:00 MT had penetrated into the eastern and southern parts of Kecskemét. At the same time, the 320th Rifle Division entered the southwestern perimeter.[118] By dusk both divisions reached the town centre. The garrison of the 'fortress' was now completely abandoned to its fate. Perhaps it had no radio contact with the HQ at all, otherwise in the evening Gaedcke would not have said to von Grolman that he seriously doubted 'whether 24 Panzer-Division and Flak-Regiment 133 [were] still in the town'.[119] The battle group had not left Kecskemét yet, but they were preparing a breakout; von Uslar-Gleichen was well aware that lack of fuel and ammunition meant the end of it and made the decision on his own initiative to break through to the north during the night.[120] The Soviets suspected this as well; throughout the day many soldiers of 59th Guards Rifle Division heard detonations in the city, a sure sign that the surrounded enemy troops were destroying valuable objects and may attempt an escape soon.[121] The swift action of the trapped opponent nevertheless caught them completely off guard. 'Thanks to the careful preparation and the strict ban on firing,' says the combat history of 24 Panzer-Division, 'the battle group managed to break out under cover of darkness without appreciable losses of men, vehicles or equipment.'[122]

The history of the 24th Panzer has been slightly economical with the truth here; according to a report of 46th Army of 1 November, the Soviet troops were still mopping up the last pockets of resistance in the town.[123] This means that either von Uslar-Gleichen had left some troops behind as rearguards, or that the Germans, as in the Don steppe or the Libyan desert, had fled and left their junior allies to their fate. Whatever the truth, on the first day of November the battle for Kecskemét was over. Shlemin reported an impressive victory: up to 2000 enemy troops killed; 38 tanks and self-propelled guns, 4 armoured halftracks, 40 motor vehicles, 240 horse-drawn carts, 23 guns, 22 mortars, 40 machine guns destroyed; 724 soldiers and officers, 24 guns, 19 machine guns, 350 rifles and 11 vehicles captured.[124] At the same time he lost the race for Budapest there and then; the resolute defence of Kecskemét won Friessner time to regroup his reserves and erect an impregnable barrier between the Soviets and the Hungarian capital.

17

While 37th Rifle Corps and Sviridov's tanks were fighting a battle of life and death in the vicinity of Kecskemét, the other two corps of 46th Army were moving northwards virtually unopposed. On the far left flank, on 30 October the 40th Guards Rifle Division captured the beautiful winemaking villages of Dusnok, Miske and Hajós. Farther to the east 34th Guards Rifle Division advanced along the Kiskunhalas–Kiskőrös road and approached Keczel.

In the meantime a disaster was looming for the Magyar 23 Reserve-Division. In the morning of 30 October 10th Guards Rifle Corps penetrated its defensive line and pushed its left flank some 4–5km to the northwest, as far as Bugacmonostor.[125] Before long the division was scattered and it was only in the afternoon that order was restored and its regiments began to assemble in the area southeast of Izsák.[126] They attempted to establish a semblance of defence in that area, but at 16:00 BT the Soviets attacked once more, the unfortunate Hungarian formation was caught off guard and scattered again.[127]

The lack of organised resistance allowed 10th Guards Rifle Corps to encircle a considerable part of the Magyar division. One or two regiments were caught in the trap and by the end of the day were annihilated in the vicinity of the Szabó hamlet (some 20km to the southwest of Kecskemét). The catastrophe was total: the command post of the division was overrun; the divisional commander was killed; his deputy, alongside with several other staff officers and approximately 500 troops, were taken prisoner.[128] At the nearby airfield of Izsák 49th Guards Rifle Division captured 48 aircraft, mostly unserviceable.[129] Izsák itself fell into the hands of the Soviets at around 02:00 MT. On the morning of 31 October the attackers decided to take a break and stopped their advance 4km north of the town.[130] By that time, there was no enemy in front of them.

The Red onslaught was proving far too powerful for the Hungarian defence; Heszlényi's army was falling apart under the pressure of the Soviet rifle divisions. On the extreme western flank Group 'Szücs' retreated as far as Kalocsa and before long was trapped there. 10 Infantry Division stopped at Soltvadkert (northeast of Kiskőrös). The remnants of the 23 Reserve-Division were fleeing in panic and only the elite 1 Huszar-Division was trying to offer an organised resistance. Lieutenant-Colonel Emil Tomka, the commander of 2/I Hussar Battalion, recalls 30 October as a confusing day, during which his unit was forced to relocate several times:

On 30 October, while crossing the highway from Kecskemét to Jakabszállás, I drew back from the new dangerous outflanking move to the coverer of the countryside there, and succeeded in establishing communication with the regiment's headquarters, as well as with units of the reserve regiment. Because the Russians on my left continued their advance to the west, by the orders of the regiment and the headquarters of the reserve regiment, we withdrew 8km behind the Kecskemét–Izsák railway line, where it was possible to take up a supportable defensive position in the open country amongst the farms. To the west of me the Schmerzing detachment from the reserve hussar regiment (under the command of Lieutenant-Colonel Egon Schmerzing) took up its defensive position. The battlefield position of both regimental headquarters was northwest of me, in a farm at nearly one-kilometre distance.

The regiment got together in Kerekegyháza, as far as the available force could be called a regiment. I had some 300 people altogether, but more than 25 per cent of them had to be left with the horses and the supply point. The situation of II Battalion was still worse. For the time being Captain György Szunyogh stood in for Major Dienes-Oehm, who had perished as a hero.

The regiment took a defensive position northwest of Kerekegyháza … From the other units of the division – 1st Hungarian Hussar Division – I had the following information: the division headquarters was in Tatárszentgyörgy, and the reserve hussar regiment was in retreat on the way to Tatárszentgyörgy. The 3rd Hussar Regiment had retreated to Kunszentmiklós, and to the west of it, the 4th Hussar Regiment was also in retreat.[131]

The German command tried desperately to set up a new defensive line between Kiskörös and Kecskemét using the still intact 1 Huszar-Division and stragglers of 23 Reserve-Division collected by officers and the field gendarmerie. It was an impossible task:

> The Hungarian troops are in full retreat, despite the fact that the enemy pressure is weak. The lack of German infantry is felt in that area, which is covered mostly with bushes, and therefore could not be defended by tanks alone. That's why the ground couldn't be held.[132]

During the night of 30/31 October the Soviet forward detachments succeeded in pushing the rearguards of 10 Infantry Division farther to the north and in the morning that division found its left wing pushed up to the Soltvadkert–Kaskantyú line (just to the east of Kiskörös). In the middle the situation was no better: the garrison of Keczel, numbering some 300 troops, was surrounded and wiped out. The survivors – approximately 100 men – surrendered to the Soviet 34th Guards Rifle Division.[133] The Axis command had no other choice left than to order 10 Infantry Division to establish a new defence running from Dunapataj (on the Danube) to the village of Akasztó (northwest of Kiskörös).

In the meantime, to its left 23 Reserve-Division had been scattered to the four winds and now a gap emerged in the very centre of the Magyar 3 Army's front. In attempt to close that gap, 1 Huszar-Division was directed to form a defensive position at Könscög (a railway station southwest of Kecskemét) and extend its left flank to cover the breach.[134] But that could not be done. During the morning of 31 October Fretter-Pico's headquarters reported that '23 Infantry Division doesn't exist anymore and 10 Infantry Division won't be able to hold out for long.'[135] Another crisis was mounting and it would not take the Russians long to exploit it; shortly before noon Gaedcke phoned Friessner's staff and reported that 'strong enemy columns are moving up the Kiskunhalas–Soltvadkert–Kiskörös road.'[136] These were 4th Guards Mechanised Corps and 23rd Rifle Corps. Malinovsky had just played his last two trump cards.

18

When the men of Lieutenant-General Vladimir Zhdanov's 4th Guards Mechanised Corps arrived in Hungary, they were quite shocked by the cold reception they received from the local populace. Having just left Yugoslavia, where crowds of friendly people were giving them 'bottles of fresh wine, bouquets of late autumn flowers and baskets full of fruits', the liberators of Belgrade found that the Magyars 'were frightened and demoralised', says the official history of the corps.[137]

Zhdanov, however, had other troubles to worry about than the absence of cheering crowds. His arrival into the headquarters of the 2nd Ukrainian Front was frosty as Malinovsky was angry at the slow deployment of the corps' troops. The Marshal was in a hurry to throw the armoured formation into the battle of Budapest as soon as possible and was unmoved by all the protestations of the corps commander that the retreating enemy had demolished the bridges and the rains had softened the roads.

Despite being involved in heavy battles during its route to Belgrade, the 4th Guards Mechanised Corps was still in relatively good condition. The troops, however, needed five or six days to rest and repair the equipment.[138] Malinovsky, however, wanted the armour now and immediately after their arrival in Szeged on 29 October they went to the battlefield. Long columns of tanks, trucks and armoured cars moved up the road to Kiskunfélegyháza. An onlooker would have noticed the animal insignia on the vehicles: bears, lions, elephants and other wild species.[139] Those were the symbols of Zhdanov's corps since the Jassy-Kishinev operation and perhaps many of its members truly believed that they made them invincible in battle.

Lieutenant-General Vladimir Zhdanov, commander of the 4th Guards Mechanised Corps.

Colonel Nikitin, commander of the 14th Guards Mechanised Brigade.

The 'wild' corps was to enter into action together with the 23rd Rifle Corps of Major-General Mikhail Grigorovich. The commanders met on 30 October in Shlemin's headquarters to work out a detailed plan for a joint offensive. It took them three hours to reach a conclusion. In order to provide the tanks with extra infantry support, one of the divisions (68th Guards) was subordinated to Zhdanov. The other two (99th and 316th) were to carry out a forced march of 80km overnight and by 10:00 MT on 2 November to assemble in the vicinity of Solt –Szabadszállás. From there they were to attack along the Danube to Budapest.[140]

In order to catch up with the tanks, the 68th Guards Rifle Division was to be made fully mobile.[141] The trucks were to be provided by the 4th Guards Mechanised Corps.[142] Zhdanov, however, did not have enough of them. So the riflemen were mounted on a variety of vehicles: captured trucks, horse-drawn carts taken from the supply units or requisitioned from the local population. The gathering of the transport was undoubtedly a time-consuming business and soon it would become obvious that the 68th Guards would not be able to meet the timetable.

Zhdanov intended to merge the 68th Guards with his own troops and thus to create large combat teams drawn in two-echelon formation. Two of his mechanised brigades (14th and 15th) would form the first echelon, while the third one and the tank brigade would follow behind. The combat teams of both echelons were to advance to the north in two parallel wedges, with the main forces being concentrated in the right-hand one. The mission of the left wedge was to shield the corps' left flank against eventual enemy attacks from the western bank of the Danube.[143]

The spearhead of the right wedge – Colonel Nikitin's 14th Guards Mechanised Brigade, reinforced with the 200th Guards Rifle Regiment of 68th Guards Rifle Division, 1512th Anti-Tank Artillery Regiment and 129th Guards Mortar Battalion (M-13 *Katyusha* rocket

launchers) – was directed to assemble south of
Szabadszállás, attack towards Kunszentmiklós and
by 11:00 MT on 2 November to capture Ócsa, one
of the villages outside Budapest.

The first echelon of the left wedge was to consist
of 15th Guards Mechanised Brigade (Colonel
Andrianov), reinforced with the 202nd Guards
Rifle Regiment (of 68th Guards Rifle Division)
and one battalion of the 527th Mortar Regiment.
It was tasked to move past Fülöpszállás and Solt,
then advance along the riverbank and not later
than 11:00 on 2 November to take three small
settlements on the Danube: Taksony, Rákócziliget
and Szigetszentmiklós.[144]

The second echelon was to be composed of
Colonel Goryachev's 13th Guards Mechanised
Brigade (with 198th Guards Rifle Regiment of
68th Guards Rifle Division and the remainder of
e 527th Mortar Regiment) and Colonel Zhukov's
36th Guards Tank Brigade (plus 352nd Guards

Colonel Andrianov, commander of the 15th
Guards Mechanised Brigade.

Heavy Self-Propelled Regiment and a howitzer battery of 68th Guards Rifle Division).
Zhukov's brigade was to follow the tracks of the 15th Guards and by 11:00 MT on 2 November
was to take Dunavarsány (a village located just south of Taksony), while Goryachev's group was
ordered to capture Alsónémedi, situated just northwest of Ócsa.[145]

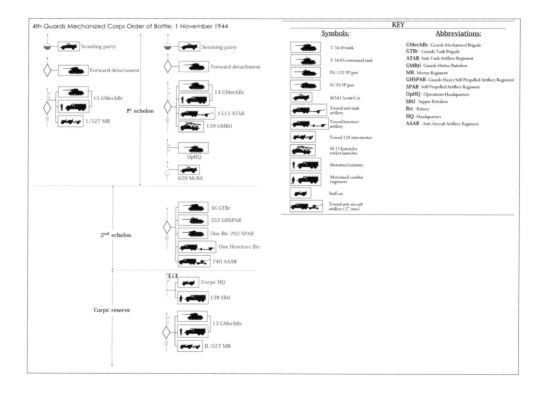

On the whole, this was a very good plan, but it never worked out the way it was supposed to. The 68th Guards Rifle Division failed to catch up with Zhdanov's tanks, probably because of the lack of transport at the outset. The forward elements of 68th Guards left their deployment areas at Csongrád (east of Kiskunfélegyháza) at 18:00 MT on 1 November, at the very moment when the leading brigades of Zhdanov's corps entered the battle for Budapest. Thus when General Grigorovich's three rifle divisions began their journey to the front there was a 70km gap between them and the 4th Guards Mechanised Corps.

Zhdanov's and Grigorovich's troops experienced serious difficulties during their advance to the north. The road network in that part of the *Puszta* was less dense, there was no asphalt, and because of the bad weather the terrain was boggy and 'it was impossible to pass through the surrounding fields.'[145] Nevertheless, the drive of both corps to the growing gap in the Magyar defence continued. Their appearance on the battlefield would be a complete surprise to Fretter-Pico and his staff; the Axis intelligence believed that both formations were still in the vicinity of Szeged.[146] Fortunately for Fretter-Pico, however, the scale of the redeployment undertaken by Friessner would be sufficient to deal even with this as yet unknown threat.

19

The overall success of 46th Army during the battles on the last day of October – and in particular the excellent performance of 2nd Guards Mechanised Corps – allowed Malinovsky to begin detailed planning of the next stage of the offensive. The new phase was to lead to the swift capture of beautiful Budapest, the main prize in this murderous competition between the forces of Stalin and Hitler.

Shortly before midnight of 31 October Malinovsky submitted personally to Stalin his ideas about the quick conquest of central Hungary and the seizure of the capital. In summary:

- On the right flank of the Front the 40th Army and the Romanian 4th Army (five Soviet and seven Romanian divisions), in close cooperation with the southern flank of the 4th Ukrainian Front, would launch an attack in the general direction of Miskolc.
- The 53rd Army (seven Soviet rifle and two Romanian mountain divisions) would force the Tisza river and advance towards Füzesabony (southwest of Miskolc). The offensive would commence on 10 November.
- The 27th Army (ten divisions) would regroup to the southwest, to Szolnok, and on 10 November would mount a powerful attack with eight of its divisions in the direction of Jászárokszállás (north of Jászberény).
- The 7th Guards Army (eight Soviet and three Romanian divisions) would continue its attack and with ten of its divisions would advance in the general direction of Tura (north of Zsámbok).
- The 46th Army (nine divisions and the 2nd Guards Mechanised Corps) would keep advancing on Budapest from the south and southeast. It would be reinforced with the 4th Guards Mechanised Corps and the 23rd Rifle Corps.
- The 6th Guards Tank Army (the 5th Guards Tank Corps and 9th Guards Mechanised Corps) would be assembled behind the 7th Guards Army and used to exploit the success in that sector.
- The Pliev Cavalry-Mechanised Group (the 4th and 6th Guards Cavalry Corps; 23rd Tank Corps) would be assembled behind the 27th Army and thrown into combat there.
- The Gorshkov Cavalry-Mechanised Group (the 5th Guards Cavalry Corps and 7th Mechanised Corps) would be assembled behind the 53rd Army and employed in that sector.

In brief, by 10 November Malinovsky intended to attack the Axis forces defending the area between the Danube and Tisza simultaneously from several different directions with a powerful force consisting of 36 rifle divisions, three cavalry corps, four mechanised corps and two tank corps.[147]

Stalin approved Malinovsky's plan but also made same changes. (The 6th Guards Tank Army, for instance, would not be committed to combat in November, most probably because it was still too short of tanks.) Following the corrections made by Stavka, in the afternoon of 1 November the Command of the 2nd Ukrainian Front issued detailed orders to the 40th, 7th Guards and 46th Armies about the continuation of the offensive.[148] Shlemin's army, in particular, was directed thus:

- By the end of 3 November to seize Budapest and secure the Pánd–Isaszeg–Újpest–Budakeszi–Érd line.
- Its 4th Guards Mechanised Corps, reinforced with one truck-borne division of the 23rd Rifle Corps, was to attack in the direction of Solt–Dömsöd–Budapest and by the morning of 2 November to reach the Ócsa–Dunaharaszti–Szigetcsép line. The other two divisions of the 23rd Rifle Corps were to follow behind.
- By the morning of 2 November the right flank of the army was to secure the Cegléd–Örkény–Kunszentmiklós line.
- In the meantime the 2nd Guards Mechanised Corps was to reach the Monor–Üllő–Inárcs line.
- One rifle corps was to protect the army's left flank along the Danube bank.

Today it is difficult to say to what extent Shlenmin shared Malinovsky's views on the situation, and in particular, the optimistic assessment of the Front commander that Budapest would be taken within the next 48 hours. What we know for sure is that Shlemin and his operations department fine-tuned Malinovsky's plan and distributed the tasks among the subordinate formations:

- The 37th Rifle Corps, with all available forces, by the morning of 2 November was to secure the Cegléd–Muzsik[149] line.
- The 10th Guards Rifle Corps, with all available forces, by the morning of 2 November was to secure the Muzsik–Örkény–Kunszentmiklós line. Upon the arrival of the 23rd Rifle Corps it was to hand over the Kunszentmiklós sector to the latter.
- The 31st Guards Rifle Corps, was to secure the Kunszentmiklós–Tass line. Upon the accomplishment of this mission, it was to turn the front of the 34th Guards Rifle Division to the west and task it with the protection of the entire Danube bank from Tass down to the boundary with the 3rd Ukrainian Front.
- The 2nd Guards Mechanised Corps: by the morning of 2 November it was to secure the Üllő–Inárcs line. Subsequently, it was to advance (northwards) with the mission <u>by the end of 3 November to capture Budapest</u> and reach the Kerepes–Isaszeg line.
- The 4th Guards Mechanised Corps, coupled with one truck-borne division of the 23rd Rifle Corps, by the morning of 2 November was to secure the Alsónémedi–Rákócziliget–Szigetszentmiklós–Tököl line. Subsequently, it was to advance with the mission <u>by the end of 3 November to capture Budapest</u> and reach its northern limits along the Újpest and Rákospalota line; at the same time, using specially detached advance teams, it was to secure the main city's bridges over the Danube.
- The 23rd Rifle Corps: to subordinate one rifle division (the 68th Guards) to the commander of the 4th Guards Mechanised Corps with the mission to accompany the armoured elements of the latter; the division in question was to be made truck-borne by

the use of the motor vehicles of the corps. With the rest of its forces, by the morning of 2 November the corps was to reach the Szabadszállás–Solt line and after that to advance in the wake of the 4th Guards Mechanised Corps. The corps' staff was <u>to take all measures to increase the mobility of the units and to prevent lagging behind the 4th Guards Mechanised Corps</u>[150]

It is obvious now that Malinovsky's plan of capturing Budapest was unrealistic. It seems that he and his staff officers were unaware that Friessner's reserves were arriving,[151] nor did they have the slightest idea how formidable the 'Attila' line was. Otherwise it is difficult to explain on what grounds they believed that such a big city, situated on both banks of a large river, could be occupied in a single day. It is possible that they believed the enemy was actually retreating and abandoning the area. This is (indirectly) confirmed by an entry in the war diary of the Front: 'Aerial reconnaissance reported a long column of trucks and horse-drawn carts heading northwards to Cegléd; in the area of Budapest there are seven intact bridges over the Danube.'[152] Soon Shlemin's troops would pay dearly for this incorrect assessment, if that is what it was.

20

Friessner spent 1 November in attempts to consolidate his reserves to the south and southeast of the Hungarian capital and thus to erect a firewall in the path of the Soviets. In doing so he had to overcome many difficulties, which strangely had nothing to do with enemy actions. In the morning it became clear that 'Feldherrnhalle', 13 Panzer-Division and 8 SS-Cavalry-Division were still en route and could be used only on the following day.[153] Moreover, 22 SS-Cavalry-Division and 18 SS-Panzer-Grenadier Division, though nominally under Army Group since the previous day, had not yet departed because they still had not received permission from Himmler. Friessner went mad: the latest intelligence indicated that the entire 6th Guards Tank Army was moving to Szolnok[154] and he wanted to block that route with the 18th SS. Von Grolman called OKH and OKW several times throughout the day, but the reply was always the same: 'Reichsführer SS cannot be reached now and without his approval Fegelein[155] cannot sanction the transfers.'[156] With every call Friessner's chief of staff was getting more and more nervous. The rather large straw that broke the camel's back was when he learned from the German Plenipotentiary General in Slovakia that the 18th SS had no military value whatsoever. Von Grolman phoned the OKW headquarters and started yelling at poor von Buttlar-Brandenfels, the chief of the Operations Section in OKW. Finally, approval was given in the late afternoon and both inexperienced SS divisions went to the front.[157]

On the battlefield the situation remained unchanged: the Soviets attacked vigorously while the Germans and Magyars desperately tried to halt them. Chaos reigned and the Command of Army Group South was still one step behind events. During the night Friessner had ordered the LVII Panzer Corps to destroy the enemy spearhead that had sneaked north of Kecskemét, but in the morning he found out that Hungarian 1 Armoured Division was 'smashed the other night at Kerekegyháza'.[158] That was not all: no one knew for sure where 1 Huszar-Division was positioned.[159] Now it was crystal clear that Kirchner would not be able to carry out Friessner's order. The forces of Kirchner's corps were no longer capable of maintaining any semblance of interaction and every one of them was fighting a battle of its own.

After the breakout from Kecskemét, Flak-Regiment 133 and Uslar-Gleichen's battle group parted. Lieutenant-Colonel Hortian, the hero of the battle for Kecskemét (in November he would be awarded a Knight's Cross for his bravery there), led his men to the northwest. They reached the vicinity of Lajosmizse and wasting no time began to establish a blocking line there. This proved to be a welcome feature to the thinly held positions of 1 Panzer-Division. The

An assault group of 37th Rifle Corps attacks down a street in Kecskemét during the fierce fighting for the town in late October/early November 1944. (The Photo Archive of the Ministry of Defence of Bulgaria)

blocking line was tested almost immediately: at around 23:00 BT on 31 October the Flak-gunners repulsed the attack of a Soviet rifle battalion supported by 10 tanks.[160]

Uslar-Gleichen's battle group joined hands with its parent formation and during the course of the night of 31 October/1 November they formed a 'hedgehog' position some 6km north of Kecskemét. During the same night they repelled a Soviet attack of battalion strength.[161] This was just a prelude to the main enemy onslaught. At 05:00 MT on 1 November the 37th Rifle Corps simultaneously attacked in two directions: the 59th Guards Rifle Division (reinforced with 476th Rifle Regiment of the 320th Rifle Division) launched an offensive northwestward, along the Kecskemét–Lajosmizse motorway, while the 108th Guards Rifle Division approached Nagykőrös from the south.[162] Thus the 24th Panzer was caught between a rock and a hard place.

The 24th found themselves pressed from all sides and throughout the day repelled one attack after another. There were no prepared positions in that area, so they used the full potential of their artillery and mortars to repel the Soviet attacks.[163] Finally, the division fighting under the insignia of the leaping horseman managed to escape the trap and took up positions east of the Kecskemét–Nagykőrös road. There at around 22:00 BT on 1 November a contact with the scouting patrols of 23 Panzer-Division was established.[164]

For 23 Panzer-Division, 1 November was yet another day of crises. First, at 8:00 Romanian troops penetrated into the southeastern districts of Nagykőrös. They were driven back by a swift counter-attack launched by Panzer-Reconnaissance Battalion 23 supported by 5 tanks.[165]

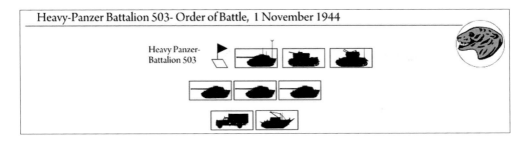

Heavy-Panzer Battalion 503- Order of Battle, 1 November 1944

Heavy Panzer-Battalion 503

But the main task of the day remained the reestablishing of ground communications with the trapped 24 Panzer-Division. In doing so, at 13:30 BT the armoured battle group of 23 Panzer-Division attacked to the south in the direction of Kecskemét.[166] Here, for the first time since the beginning of the Soviet offensive, the Heavy Panzer Battalion 503 was brought into play. Even the presence of the monstrous King Tigers did not break the Soviet defence. Freiherr von Rosen, a member of the Tiger battalion, recalls the ferocity of that engagement:

> Our attack proceeded further along the road to Kecskemet. All of a sudden, the 2./schwere Panzer-Abteilung 503 encountered strong anti-tank guns. From my position, I was unable to participate. The lead vehicle, commanded by Leutnant Brodhagen, went up in flames. The terrain on both sides of the road offered limited observation, consisting of vineyards and gardens with bits of meadow and fields in between. In the meantime, dusk was falling and the visibility got worse and worse. One could only pick out the enemy positions by the muzzle flashes of the guns as they fired. Those were the only aiming points available for fighting the enemy in the twilight. There was no way frontally to attack the Russians in this instance.[167]

Perhaps this attack did not bother Shlemin that much; in his evening report he evaluated the strength of the attackers as not very significant ('two infantry battalions supported by 10 tanks and 10 assault guns').[168] The Soviet troops not only repulsed it, but also advanced farther to the north and by the end of the day the 108th Guards Rifle Division reached the southern outskirts of Nagykőrös.[169] To cover Shlemin's main breakthrough force, a considerable part of the 5th Air Army had already been directed to the Nagykőrös–Lajosmizse area. Shturmoviks and Bostons time and again pounded the Axis columns and assembly areas, thus softening up the enemy's tougher units.

21

From the moment when Kecskemét became the focal point of the struggle for Hungary, both Malinovsky and Friessner rushed the bulk of their air forces to that area. The Fw-190s fighter-bombers, the tank-busting Ju-87 Gs and Hs-129Bs repeatedly attacked Sviridov's tanks and Kolchuk's infantry, inflicting serious damage. At the same time, the Hungarian and German Messerschmitt Bf 109 pilots, amongst whom there were many famous aces, like Hartmann, Bakhorn and Lipfert, did their best to control the autumn sky. This resulted in a whole series of aerial dogfights.

The role of the Axis pilots was not limited to the slowing down of the Soviet advance. Just like in the Blitzkrieg days of old, the actions of the panzers in the *Puszta* were coordinated with I Air Corps and received maximum close air support. Thus the attacks of 24 Panzer-Division on 30 October east of Kecskemét were significantly assisted by General Deichmann's pilots.[170] The same applied to the counter-attack mounted by 23 Panzer-Division in the afternoon of 1 November south of Nagykőrös.[171]

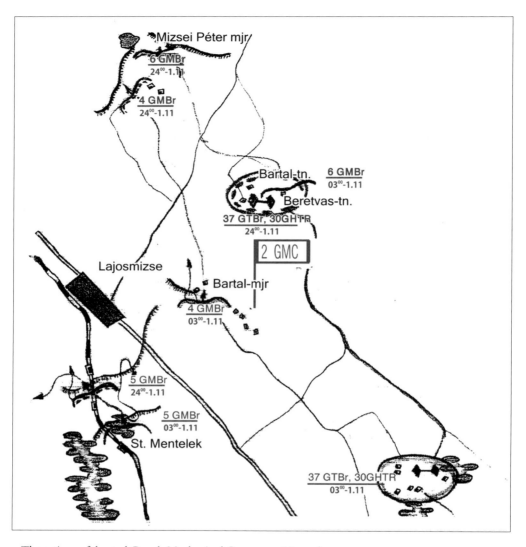

The actions of the 2nd Guards Mechanised Corps on 1 November 1944.

The neutralisation of the Luftwaffe required total commitment from General Goryunov's men, who were also tasked with clearing the way for the ground troops. Right from the beginning of Operation *Budapest* they flew hundreds of sorties a day, weather permitting. One of those days when the pilots of 5th Air Army gave no respite to the Axis divisions was 1 November.

That afternoon, when 23 Panzer-Division began vigorously to counter-attack the right flank of 37th Rifle Corps south of Nagykőrös, the Shturmoviks of the 131st Guards Assault Air Regiment were called for help. Fifteen trucks and about two battalions of infantry were spotted in the vicinity of the town and seven Il-2s immediately attacked them with bombs and cannon fire. The pilots employed their favourite tactics – the 'Circle of Death' – in which the Shturmoviks flanked the enemy, successively dived to make individual attack runs, climbed out to rejoin the formation and dived again. According to the report of the group commander, the attack destroyed six trucks and more than 150 troops were killed or scattered. The Germans were forced to cease the counter-attack and fell back to the north.[172]

On the same day two groups of bombers (nine Bostons in each) led by the commander of the 48th Bomber Air Regiment, Major V.P. Koly, successfully attacked Axis troop concentrations in the vicinity of Cegléd. Shortly afterwards the same targets were bombed by two more groups of the same strength, this time led by the commander of the 452nd Bomber Air Regiment Major A.A. Panichkin. This attack was a success, too. The Bostons of the 48th and 453rd Bomber Air Regiments also attacked enemy strongholds at Abony and Cegléd, which were bombed with good effect from a medium height.[173]

The Soviet fighter pilots were as busy. For instance, the chief mission of the 85th Guards Fighter Air Regiment on that day was to protect the ground troops against Axis aerial attacks. A group of six La-5s of 85th Guards Fighter Air Regiment under Captain M.S. Mazan especially distinguished itself. In the area between Lajosmizse and Kecskemét they intercepted a large group of Axis Fw-190 fighter-bombers escorted by Bf 109 fighters. In the dogfight that followed Mazan's group reportedly shot down four enemy aircraft. Not far from there another group of six La-5s led by Captain N.S. Artamonov (177th Guards Fighter Air Regiment), claimed two Axis fighters.[174]

In the most critical moments of the air battle on 1 November, the 'regular' Soviet fighter groups were supported by the so-called 'Group Sword', who flew Yaks.[175] The group in question had been established in the 151st Guards Fighter Air Regiment (13th Guards Fighter Air Division) from very experienced pilots with the purpose of conducting 'free hunt' missions.[176]

22

Having seen how fruitless the efforts of the armoured groups were, in the afternoon of 1 November Fretter-Pico decided to cancel the attack, pull out 23 and 24 Panzer-Divisions and assemble them farther to the north. Friessner approved that decision ('it is a correct one'). But the Soviets detected the withdrawal of the German divisions almost immediately and wasting no time, deployed part of the 2nd Guards Mechanised Corps in the wood northwest of Nagykőrös.[177] Yet another gap in the Axis defensive line was in the making: that between 1 and 23 Panzer-Divisions.

Shlemin, was actually far more concerned about the Lajosmizse sector than about the situation at Nagykőrös. His first attempt to capture that important road junction on the way to Budapest failed. Using the momentum generated after the capture of Kecskemét, he directed the 2nd Guards Mechanised Corps to the northwest to seize Lajosmizse from the march. His hopes rested on the assumption that the enemy defence was still very disorganised, and that the night would conceal the approach of the Soviet mechanised groups.

Exploiting the wide gaps in the Axis defence, in the early hours of 1 November Sviridov's forward detachments got nearer to the town. At around 03:00 MT the 6th Guards Mechanised Brigade captured Beretvas-tanya (a hamlet). At same time 4th Guards Mechanised Brigade began a battle for Bartal-major (a cattle farm). Its mission turned out to be very difficult, because the brigade's troops received heavy flanking fire from Lajosmizse. The third element of Sviridov's first echelon, the 5th Guards Mechanised Brigade, seized Mentelek railway station, but was not able to go on.[178]

In attempt to reinforce the thrust of 2nd Guards Mechanised Corps and take Lajosmizse as quickly as possible, after 05:00 MT two Soviet rifle divisions joined the battle. The 59th Guards Rifle Division advanced from the southwest, along the Kecskemét–Budapest highway (mentioned above), while the 49th Guards Rifle Division attacked straight from the south. Right from the start, however, the Soviet 'shock group' ran into very determined resistance and throughout the day was not able to capture the town.

Being well aware that the Soviets would concentrate all their efforts on capturing Lajosmizse and thereby freeing the highway to Budapest for their mechanised formations, Kirchner began to gather all available forces in the vicinity of the town in the morning. In addition to the reinforced Panzer-Grenadier Regiment 1, which had been deployed there since the previous morning, now the Panzer-Grenadier Regiment 113 (reinforced with II and III Battalions/ Panzer-Artillery Regiment 73) was brought urgently from the southwest (Szabadszállás area) and positioned to the left of the former. The badly battered Hungarian 1 Armoured Division, which was now under 1 Panzer-Division, was ordered to occupy the perimeter around Ladánybene (6km southeast of Tatárszentgyörgy and 4km west of Lajosmizse) and thus to protect the right flank of 1st Panzer.[179] In so doing Kirchner succeeded in building a thin, but nevertheless continuous semicircular defensive line that effectively prevented the enemy from taking or outflanking Lajosmizse.

The Axis troops put up a desperate fight. Their main problem was that, despite the reinforcements, there were still gaps in their defensive line. The Soviets, of course, infiltrated at several places and even the positions of Panzer-Artillery Regiment 73 were attacked. During these clashes the artillerymen sustained losses, which included two very experienced battery commanders – Captain Müller and Captain Wojak – who were both killed in action.[180] The German artillery battalions were widely dispersed and therefore were not able to hit the attackers with massed artillery fire.

The Germans repeatedly counter-attacked themselves. At midday about 25 tanks accompanied by infantry struck the 49th Guards Rifle Division west of Lajosmizse. The Soviet artillery, however, reacted very quickly to the threat and knocked out seven tanks.[181] The rest turned back. A little while later a battalion of infantry and six tanks attacked the left flank of 59th Guards Rifle Division near the town and attempted to push it to the southeast. The most powerful counter-attack of the 'oak leaf division' was yet to come. In the evening Shlemin informed Malinovsky that 'an enemy infantry regiment supported by 45 tanks is repeatedly counter-attacking 49th Guards Rifle Division in the direction of Hill 132.'[182] The Axis battle group 'advanced very little' and sustained serious losses ('10 enemy tanks have been set on fire', says the evening report of 46th Army).[183]

The vigorous German resistance did not prevent the Soviets from advancing and by the end of the day 476th Rifle Regiment (the one that was borrowed from the 320th Rifle Division) finally penetrated into the southeastern perimeter of Lajosmizse.[184] Farther to the northeast, the 4th and 6th Guards Mechanised Brigades also made some headway. Their first attempt to break into open country northwest of the Bartal-tanya–Bartal-major line was beaten back by 1st Panzer with the crucial help of the Luftwaffe ground attack aircraft. (The latter claimed to have destroyed 11 Soviet tanks some 8km northeast of Lajosmizse.)[185] In the evening both brigades still reached Mizsei Péter[186] and this forced the Command of the panzer-division to stretch its thinly manned defensive line farther to the northeast and deploy the Panzer-Engineer Battalion 37 and Panzer-Reconnaissance Battalion 1 north of the settlement in an attempt to contain the Russian advance along the Kecskemét–Budapest motorway.[187] This movement was to no avail because the withdrawal of 23 Panzer-Davision to the northeast of Nagykőrös had already torn open a gap in the Axis front and now the left flank of the 1st Panzer was hanging in the air. The 'oak leaf division' was forced to retreat north.

The successful Soviet advance on that day forced Friessner to reorganise his southern wing once again. In order to strengthen the defensive line and tighten the control over the Hungarians, he placed the Magyar VII and VIII Army Corps under the III and LVII Panzer Corps respectively. Thus two strong task forces were established under Fretter-Pico: Panzer Groups 'Breith' and 'Kirchner'. Fretter-Pico himself received instructions to stop the enemy at the Kunszentmiklós–Kecskemét–Szolnok line.[188] General Breith, whose staff had just arrived from the Nyíregyháza area, was entrusted with the responsibility of defending Budapest from the south. For that purpose he was given the four divisions still in transit (8 and 22 SS,

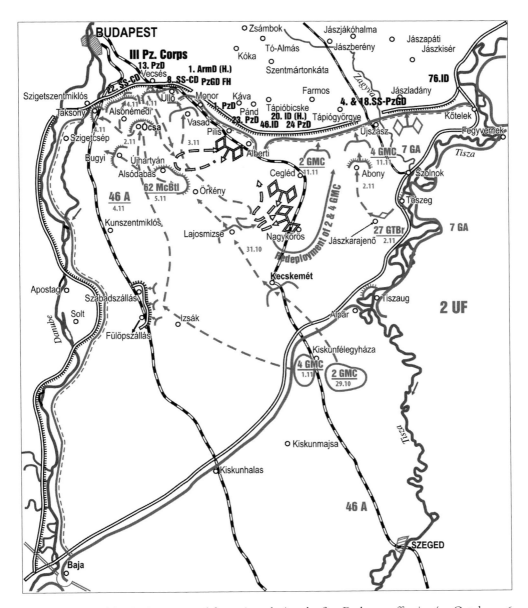

The operations of the Soviet armoured formations during the first Budapest offensive (29 October – 6 November 1944), events described in Chapters 8, 9 and 10.

'Feldherrnhalle' and 13 Panzer). Friessner was sure that with these divisions he would be able to plug the gap between the two Hungarian corps and finally defeat Shlemin at Kecskemét. While giving these orders he could not take into account the fact that barely an hour before the 4th Guards Mechanised Corps had begun to sneak through that gap. Malinovsky and Shlemin had outplayed him: throughout the day they used Sviridov's and Kolchuk's corps as a shield to absorb the full weight of the German counter-attacks and thus screened the route of advance of Zhdanov's and Grigorovich's troops. These were intended to be the sword that was to deliver the coup de main against Budapest.

23

As mentioned, the sudden appearance of 4th Guards Mechanised Corps on the battlefield north of Kiskőrös in the afternoon of 1 November was a complete surprise for Fretter-Pico. He actually believed that Malinovsky was trying to create one more wedge that would strike from the vicinity of Szolnok straight to the north. In so doing, the intelligence department of Armeegruppe Fretter-Pico assessed that the Soviets would screen the eastern flank of 46th Army and at the same would strike deep into the rear of the German 8 Army.[189] The Germans could not have been more wrong.

The leading brigade of the 4th Guards Mechanised Corps, Colonel Nikitin's 14th Guards, went into the battle at around 18:00 MT on 1 November. Between Fülöpszállás and Szabadszállás it encountered a strong line of defence facing east that was manned by elements of the Hungarian 23 Reserve and 1 Huszar-Divisions. Once the Soviets came into view, the Magyars, who had a considerable number of artillery pieces, opened fire and forced them to turn back. Then the Soviets decided to bypass Fülöpszállás, but the engineer reconnaissance detachments that had been sent forward reported that the approaches to the village were heavily mined and there was no way round. Access to the motorway along the Danube's bank was now blocked and the 15th Guards Mechanised Brigade, which had to advance separately along the river, had to seek another route.

The situation required a substantial change of the original plan. Wasting no time, Zhdanov decided to merge both wedges into one and place 15th Guards Mechanised Brigade immediately behind the 14th Guards. In order to not lose momentum, the enemy stronghold at Szabadszállás was to be bypassed as quickly as possible.

Partially hidden in the evening darkness, the tanks and trucks moved through the soft fields. Moving over the muddy ground was a nightmare and often the stuck vehicles had to be manhandled. Zhdanov himself was in the midst of the first echelon to supervise and control the decisive outflanking manoeuvre. It was completed in less than two hours and at 20:00 the 14th Guards struck again. Some 10km northwest of Izsák the hastily organised enemy defence was broken down with ease.[190] Before long General Zhdanov could hear in the headset the first reports from Nikitin: 'The Hungarians are running away … The Hungarians are coming forward to surrender with hands raised.'[191] The road to Budapest was finally open.

9

STALIN AD PORTAS!

1

The eyes of the world were now focussed on Budapest. The news about the Soviet victory at Kecskemét and the rapid drive of the Red Army towards the Hungarian capital hit the front pages of newspapers worldwide. The headlines of the articles in *The Times* in London read like a countdown: 'Drive Towards Budapest' (31 October); 'Progress In Hungary' (1 November); '35 Miles From Budapest' (2 November); 'Growing Threat To Budapest' (3 November); '9 Miles From Budapest' (4 November); 'Closing In On Budapest' (6 November). On the other side of the Atlantic, the headlines of the *Washington Post* were similar: 'Russians Drive To 43 Miles Of Budapest' (31 October); 'Last Budapest Key Captured by Reds' (2 November); 'Soviet Tanks Hammer Gates To Budapest' (5 November); 'Soviet Tanks Smash Into Budapest' (6 November). The *New York Times* joined the chorus on 1 November on its front page:

RED ARMY SMASHES TOWARD BUDAPEST
New Drive Is 44 Miles from Hungarian Capital

Russian troops, smashing toward Budapest in a renewed offensive in which more than 200 Hungarian towns and villages were seized, yesterday drove to within 44 miles southeast of the Hungarian capital and broke into the streets of Kecskemet, Hungary's fourth city.

It continued inside:

Since Admiral Horthy begged for an armistice, only to be choked off the air by his Nazi betrayers, we have had no real news from Hungary. Now Berlin, evidently in some alarm, tells us that Russian armies have driven to the very center of the country and that the roar of Russian guns can be heard in Budapest.

On the next day the battle of Budapest was again on the front page:

RUSSIANS 32 MILES SOUTH OF BUDAPEST
Sweep through Kecskemet on road to capital in drive to knock out Hungary

Hungarian infantry with a Schwarzlose heavy machine gun during a battle on the Tisza river in November 1944. (Dénes Bernád)

LONDON, Thursday, Nov. 2 – The Red Army thrust within thirty-two miles of Budapest yesterday in a great drive rolling rapidly northwestward across the Hungarian plains between the Danube and Tisza Rivers.

The world was holding its breath: The Russians are coming! Some were excited, many others were terrified: never before had the Red Army had been so close to the heart of Europe. Now not only Budapest was falling, but also Vienna, Prague and even Milan and Munich were within the grasp of Stalin's spearheads.

Marshal Malinovsky, however, had no clue as to what the world's newspapers were saying about the actions of his troops. He was preparing to visit the war-torn Kecskemét to meet a very interesting man and was very impatient to hear what that man had to say. It was 2 November, Thursday, the most decisive day of the first battle of Budapest.

2

While most of the POWs that surrendered in Kecskemét were other ranks, the Soviets also hooked one really big military fish: Colonel-General János Vörös, the last Chief of the Hungarian General Staff of Horthy's era. Right after Szálasi's takeover Vörös had escaped with his wife from Budapest and hid disguised as a monk in Kecskemét until the front passed through. He reported to the Red Army once the town was cleared and Malinovsky immediately was informed about it. This time 'the catch' was so extraordinary that the Front commander decided to attend the interrogation in person. So, on 2 November, he, his chief of staff, General Zakharov, and the head of the Front's intelligence department, General Povetkin, went to Kecskemét to chat with Vörös.

Vörös was open and talkative, but it is difficult to say whether the leadership of the 2nd Ukrainian Front learned something really important during the interrogation. After all, Vörös had been 'out of office' since mid-October and therefore not in touch with the latest events. On the other hand, he was still a professional officer and therefore well aware of the military realities in

Hungary. He warned that the Germans were viewing the Pest area as a large bridgehead capable of 'accommodating' seven full-strength divisions. Vörös even gave his interrogators the numbers of two divisions that could be used for the defence of the bridgehead: 22 SS (in Budapest) and 18 SS (at Komárom and Győr). He also tried to temper the enthusiasm of the Soviets by claiming, officer to officer, that the seizure of the capital would be by no means an easy task:

> Part of the city is situated on the eastern bank of the Danube, on a flat terrain, and is less suitable for defence. That part of the city situated on the western bank of the Danube is built on high ground that commands not only the eastern part, but the whole area of the bridgehead. This part of the city could be seized only by pincer attack from the northwest and west.[1]

The interrogation of the former Chief of the Magyar General Staff hardly changed Malinovsky's perspective on the situation. On the previous day he had received eight situation reports from 46th Army and all of them ended on a positive note: 'The offensive is going according to plan.'[2] The messages that arrived from Shlemin's HQ until mid-day of 2 November had the same optimistic spirit. The last one even declared that 'the armoured vanguard of the army has reached the approaches of Budapest.'[3] Zakharov was in good spirits too: 'The conversation with Vörös confirmed the correctness of our decisions.'[4] It seemed that nothing could prevent the Red Army from entering the Hungarian capital in triumph within the next 24 hours.

3

The rapid advance of the Soviet mechanised forces towards Budapest and the disintegration of the Hungarian 3 Army forced Friessner once again to take urgent measures to consolidate the crumbling front. In the late evening of 1 November he ordered Fretter-Pico to build a new front running from the Danube bank to Örkény with the available units of the arriving 13 Panzer and 'Feldherrnhalle' Divisions and thus to block the path of Soviet troops approaching from Kunszentmiklós. (These were Zhdanov's corps and Grigorovich's truck-borne riflemen.) The other two formations still in transit – the 8 SS and 22 SS-Cavalry-Divisions – were to be used to halt the enemy forces advancing to the east of Kunszentmiklós (Sviridov's corps and the right wing of 46th Army) and later on, in cooperation with the other armoured formations already fighting there (1, 2. and 24 Panzer-Divisions), they were to launch 'an offensive

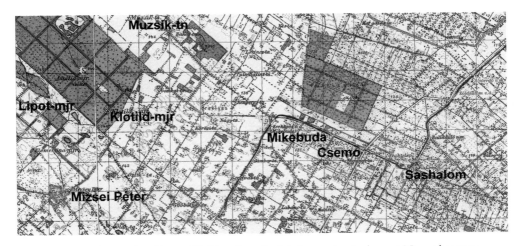

The area where the 1 and 23 Panzer-Divisions launched their counterattacks on 2 November 1944.

action' in the Kecskemét–Szolnok area. The plan also contained one very unrealistic detail: 'a German battle group' was to be transferred to a small bridgehead held by the Hungarians at Dunaföldvár[5] and from there it was to strike the Soviets deep in the rear.[6]

Once he received the order, Fretter-Pico immediately gave detailed instructions to the forces in the field. The Hungarian 10 Infantry-Division was directed to build a new line between Solt and Szabadszállás (in fact it was already overrun by Zhdanov's tanks, but obviously the communication between the Hungarian and the German staffs continued to be very poor) and regroup part of its troops at Kunszentmiklós. The spearhead of Sviridov's corps was to be encircled and destroyed in the vicinity of the Kelemenke settlement by concentric counterattacks from the area of Lajosmizse to the east (1 Panzer-Division) and from the vicinity of Cegléd to the southwest (23 Panzer-Division).[7]

4

Whilst in the HQ of 6 Army Fretter-Pico's operations officers were preparing for the counter-attack, the battle in the *Puszta* continued unabated. Even during the night there was no rest for the retreating Axis troops. Shlemin's men were putting heavy pressure on them: 86th Guards Rifle Division (in cooperation with 14th Guards Mechanised Brigade) captured Kunszentmiklós, the 49th Guards Rifle Division took Tatárszentgyörgy, at 05:00 MT on 2 November the 108th Guards Rifle Division began the attack of Nagykőrös, while at around the same time the 476th Rifle Regiment of 320th Rifle Division entered the northeastern perimeter of Lajosmizse.[8] Thus all of the major strongholds that Friessner was counting on to contain the Soviet onslaught were about to be lost.

In the meantime, Friessner's main concern, 2nd Guards Mechanised Corps, had advanced even farther. Just before midnight Malinovsky's order was transmitted down to Sviridov and the corps was assigned a new objective: by the morning of 2 November to secure the Monor–Üllő–Inárcs line and later to seize the southeastern edge of Budapest.[9] The night offered protection and the powerful armoured formation, spearheaded by the reconnaissance parties, used this advantage to rush forward virtually unopposed. As a result of this impetuous advance, not only did the Soviet 4th and 6th Guards Mechanised Brigades get far closer to the capital, but also LVII Panzer Corps was forced to change the starting point of the attack of 1 Panzer-Division, since during the night the latter had withdrawn from Lajosmizse to the area east of Örkény.[10]

As scheduled, the German counter-attack against the right wing of 46th Army commenced in the morning of 2 November. A battle group of 1 Panzer-Division comprising a tank company (seven Panthers under Lieutenant Hutter) and a reinforced battalion (II/Panzer-Grenadier Regiment 1 of Captain Becker, strengthened with anti-tank-, anti-aircraft and heavy infantry guns) struck the left flank of 2nd Guards Mechanised Corps (presumably the 4th Guards Mechanised Brigade) at Lipot-major (a farmstead just to the east of Örkény). The Germans succeeded in capturing the farmstead, which was their immediate objective, and thus temporarily blocked the Soviet supply traffic. Several kilometres of ground had been won, but any further advance proved impossible due to the fierce Soviet resistance. Hutter's panzers formed a semi-circular defence and repulsed a couple of enemy tank-supported counter-attacks, knocking out some T-34s in the process. In the meantime, the semi-automatic light Flak guns of Becker's battalion set fire to several Soviet trucks. And that was it. In the afternoon the action was called off and the battle group was radioed to disengage and withdraw to the west.[11]

On the opposite flank of the Soviet penetration the 23 Panzer-Division achieved even less. At first its main body was deployed south of Nagykőrös, where early in the morning it covered the retreat of the 24 Panzer-Division to the north. Then it retreated northwards as well and assembled near the village of Sashalom, some 8km southwest of Cegléd.[12] In that area, chosen as a springboard for the upcoming attack, a strong armoured group was built. The group, led by Lieutenant-Colonel Prinz zu Waldeck und Pyrmont, the commander of Panzer-Regiment 23, consisted of Panzer-Regiment 23 (Pz IVs, Panthers and assault guns), Heavy-Panzer Battalion 503 (18 operational King Tigers), an armoured battle group of 24 Panzer-Division (5 Pz IVs and several armoured halftracks), Panzer-Grenadier Regiment 126 (which accompanied the panzers on foot) and the howitzers of II/Panzer-Artillery-Regiment 128.[13]

At 09:40 BT the armoured group attacked from the area between Sashalom and the Kistelek ranch and advanced westwards along the local railway line, in the direction of Becker's men. Shortly after the start it ran into a tough opponent: the 6th Guards Mechanised Brigade. A fierce firefight erupted between the German spearhead and the Soviet tanks that were supported by motorised infantry. Two of these tanks were reportedly knocked out, but the 23rd Panzer also sustained losses: three of its assault guns were put out of action. The Germans managed to smash through that defence and rolled forward, knocking out several more enemy tanks.[14] Approximately 1km northwest of the Mikebuda railway station, however, they encountered fierce enemy resistance once again.[15] The Soviet anti-tank guns, skilfully positioned 'on the edge of marshy terrain amongst long-lying vegetation', immediately engaged the Panthers and before long the offensive came to a halt. The situation required the urgent employment of the heaviest tanks and the cry rang out: 'Tigers to the front!' What happened next was described by one of the members of the heavy panzer battalion, Freiherr von Rosen:

The situation initially looked very sticky, but after a short time we had knocked out ten anti-tank guns. Several anti-aircraft guns, trucks and other equipment were abandoned; the Russians had quickly pulled out under pressure from the Tigers. After that line of resistance had been broken, we then advanced as a spearhead even deeper behind the Russian lines. Our mission was to reach a designated point about 25km away and link up with 1 Panzer-Division, which was advancing to meet us from Örkeny. That would cut the Russians advancing towards Budapest off from their supplies. However, that was not what happened. After we had advanced another three kilometres, the company encountered enemy tanks in difficult, uphill terrain. The enemy armour was well concealed on the edge of the woods and was not spotted until after it had opened fire.

After the first of the Russian tanks had been set on fire, the others took off into the countryside. Our attack continued. In order to advance more rapidly, the riflemen rode on our tanks. Only the two lead tanks of the company moved without infantry mounted on them. We put kilometre after kilometre behind us in that manner. The Russians could emerge from behind the corner of every patch of woods and, after a while, we encountered enemy tanks again. We spotted enemy tanks in an isolated farmstead at 1500m and immediately opened a firefight. We noticed a particularly brilliant firefight from several of the Russian tanks. That was our first encounter with the Stalin tanks with a 12.2cm gun and very heavy armour. What would be the outcome of that engagement? Then the first Stalin tank was in flames! Onward! The attack sector became increasingly marshy in places.

Feldwebel Seidel and his Tiger 313 hit a soft spot; it was immediately buried to the track guards.

We couldn't stop then; we had to go on. It was already getting noticeably dark, and we had several more kilometres ahead of us. So I left Feldwebel Weigel and his tank to protect Tiger 313. However, it was easy to see that the terrain was too unfavourable. There was no firm ground for the recovery tanks to negotiate.

We made it to the objective of our attack by dark, a road intersection in the midst of the woods. Security was established in all directions. We established radio contact with 1 Panzer-

Division, but they were still far away. A link-up with 1 Panzer-Division in the foreseeable feature seemed to be ruled out. Once again we were in the midst of the Russians and deep behind their lines. We had used up half of our fuel. From near and far we could hear the characteristic sound of Russian tanks.[16]

The German attack was finally stopped dead 1km south of Klotild-major, less than 5km from Lipot-major where Captain Becker's troops were still holding their perimeter.[17] In a desperate attempt to dislodge the enemy, the panzer-grenadiers dismounted and attacked on foot, but again without success. Soon the armoured battle group had to deal with yet another threat: the 59th Guards Rifle Division, which was steadily approaching from the south. In order to protect his open left flank, Prinz zu Waldeck und Pyrmont decided immediately to turn part of his forces to the southeast and counter-attack the advancing Soviets in the open field south of the railway. At 18:00 MT infantry of battalion strength accompanied by nine armoured vehicles attacked southward from the vicinity of the Csemo railway station. The 179th Guards Rifle Regiment, however, managed to repel the thrust and after its end reported knocking out three assault guns.[18]

The struggle lasted several hours. The armoured battle group claimed to have knocked out 7 tanks, 13 anti-tank guns, 18 trucks and 1 light anti-aircraft gun.[19] It, in turn, lost four assault guns as total write-offs and the Tiger tank of Lieutenant Rambow, which had been set on fire by a Soviet anti-tank gun.[20] Since all attempts to break through had failed, at around 20:00 an order came from LVII Panzer Corps to break off the attack and return to Sashalom.[21] The return was hard, across the swampy terrain. Thirteen King Tigers and several other panzers were recovered, but one Panther and at least one King Tiger had to be blown up.[22]

Friessner decided to cancel the counter-attack in the afternoon. It was not an easy decision for him; the latest information was that both battle groups were steadily advancing towards each other (whether this was correct is moot). It was obvious that the rapid drive of 4th Guards Mechanised Corps along the Danube and the progress of 2nd Guards Mechanised Corps were threatening 1 Panzer-Division and the newly arrived battle group of 'Feldherrnhalle' with encirclement. Still worse, as Gaedcke reported, 3 Army (Hung) was 'non-existent' and it was urgently necessary to build a new continuous front just to the south of the 'Attila' line using the available German forces. In a situation like this, when there was a huge gap in the middle and the flanks of Breith's and Kirchner's divisions were hanging in the air, this was the only decision that Friessner could have made. And at 16:00 BT he ordered the cancellation of the counter-attack.[23]

In his postwar memoir Friessner explained its failure by the fact that the Soviets had employed new tactics:

> They had learned from the battles for Debrecen and Nyíregyháza. The two cauldrons[24] forced them to be more cautious now. Their motorised formations moved on the roads not in large columns, but in echeloned armoured groups of 20 to 30 tanks, closely followed by the infantry with the assigned artillery.[25]

Friessner is totally wrong here; Malinovsky and Shlemin did not use any new tactics during the opening stage of the battle for Budapest. The Soviet corps commanders simply followed the principles outlined in the later Red Army field regulations, which strongly advocated the employment of well coordinated all-arms groupings. Unlike Pliev, Sviridov and Kolchuk (commander of the 37th Rifle Corps) had paid attention to the security of their vulnerable flanks and never allowed the enemy to catch them off-guard. The excellent tactical skills demonstrated by both generals during the counter-attack of LVII Panzer Corps found recognition

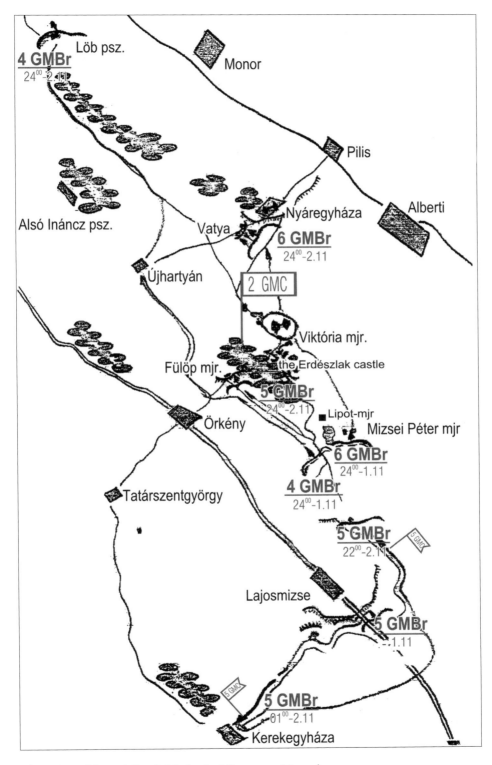

The actions of the 2nd Guards Mechanised Corps on 2 November 1944.

even in the war diary of Army Group South: in the afternoon of 2 November it recorded the complaint of Fretter-Pico that 'I and 23 Panzer-Divisions are not able to advance farther because the 2nd and 4th Guards Mechanised Corps have erected strong anti-tank gun barriers at their flanks.'[26]

5

Even though Fretter-Pico's counter-attack did not achieve its main objective, it nevertheless managed to contain the Soviet thrust for a significant length of time. Both German battle groups were standing in the path of Shlemin's main forces. These two 'hedgehogs' were about to form one spiky ball. There was no way to smash them and the only way to deal with them was to bypass them.

We have already noted how bloody and desperate was the struggle of the eastern 'hedgehog', 23 Panzer-Division, through the day. The actions in which the western 'hedgehog' – I Panzer-Division – was involved were no less fierce. They broke out in the early hours of 2 November, shortly after the division abandoned Lajosmizse, and occupied the perimeter around Örkény. There it was joined by a battle group of the 'Feldherrnhalle' Division,[27] which had just arrived from the north. Thus reinforced, I Panzer put up a maniacal defence, stalling the Soviet armour and infantry all day.

The Russians tried to break the defenders by simultaneously attacking them from the southwest (with the 86th Guards Rifle Division), from the south (with the 49th Guards Rifle Division), from the southeast (with the 109th Guards Rifle Division) and from the east and northeast (with the 2nd Guards Mechanised Corps). The taking of Örkény was of primary importance to them, because the Kecskemét–Budapest motorway ran through it. As long as it was in German hands it would be like a huge roadblock and no Soviet supply truck would ever move up that road. The Germans reportedly inflicted 'heavy losses' on the attackers.[28] In the afternoon the 49th Guards Rifle Division finally reached the southern outskirts, but by late evening it still had not broken in.[29]

The Soviet pressure from the east was especially strong. Initially, everything went well for Sviridov's troops. At 01:00 MT on 2 November the General ordered 5th Guards Mechanised Brigade to regroup from Kerekegyháza to Mizsei Petér-major and thus to position itself behind the 4th and 6th Guards Mechanised Brigades. Subsequently it was to advance along the right side of the Kecskemét–Budapest motorway.[30]

In the morning the leading two brigades (4th and 6th) made a deep penetration along both sides of the motorway. By midday their forward detachments reached Újhartyán, while the main body of the corps moved to Viktória-major.[31] At that time, as we already know, the flanks of both brigades came under attack from the west and east respectively. This forced Sviridov to pay more attention to his flanks and for several hours the advance stalled. Moreover, because of the actions of Becker's battle group, which had occupied the forested area between Lipot-major and Erdészlak castle, Sviridov was not able to commit his reserve (37th Guards Tank Brigade and 30th Guards Heavy Tank Regiment) to reinforce the thrust of the 4th and 6th Guards to Budapest. Instead of sending them northwards, the General ordered the tank brigade and the heavy tank regiment to turn to the west and smash the dogged resistance of Becker's battle group.[32] In the late afternoon two regiments of 109th Guards Rifle Division came to the aid of the tank units, but even this powerful force was not able crush the defence of I Panzer-Division at Erdészlak castle. When darkness fell, Becker's men were still holding their perimeter.

The efforts of 2nd Guards Mechanised Corps finally produced results in the late evening. Heaving repulsed two small-scale counter-attacks, by midnight 6th Guards Mechanised Brigade reached the southern approaches of Nyáregyháza, where it was stopped by a strong enemy rearguard consisting of up to 20 tanks and 5 or 6 self-propelled guns. The 5th Guards Mechanised Brigade, which in the meantime had been committed to action, at 22:00 MT encountered stiff resistance southeast of Örkény. This forced the riflemen to dismount from the tanks and approach the German position on foot. By midnight the brigade had reached Fülöp-major. This actually decided the battle; at once the German defence began to collapse. The 'Feldherrnhalle' group found itself isolated at Örkény and was forced to conduct a fighting withdrawal to Újhartyán, while the main body of 1 Panzer-Division was pushed to Ágaston-major (just southwest of Erdészlak castle). Now there was a corridor between them, which the 4th Guards Mechanised Brigade immediately exploited and advanced as

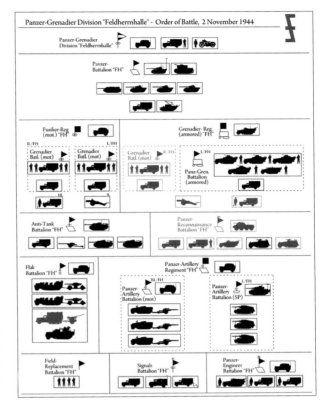

far as Löb-puszta.[33] It was midnight of 2/3 November. Monor, Üllő, Vecsés and the other villages close to Budapest were now within reach of Sviridov's spearheads.

For Shlemin, the German double counter-attack was not a serious threat: the situation reports submitted by his staff throughout the day do not even mention it. The final daily report sent to Malinovsky did not ring any alarm bells either: 'The 2nd GMC is being attacked by 1 Panz.Div. and 8 Inf.Div.'[34] What these documents do not say, however, is that Kirchner's counteractions, though unsuccessful, had seriously reduced the Soviet chances of capturing Budapest from the march. As at Kecskemét, Sviridov failed to secure the immediate objective assigned to him (the Monor–Üllő–Inárcs line) and thus allowed the enemy to deploy his reserves along the 'Attila I' line. The 48 hours lost at Kecskemét and the 24 hours lost on 2 November had profound consequences for the Soviet offensive in Hungary: what had been planned as a bold stroke to knock Hungary out of the war quickly, became a stalemate, and the campaign would continue until the spring of 1945.

6

The Axis troops began to man the formidable 'Attila' line and its approaches almost immediately after the start of Shlemin's onslaught. Not only were a considerable number of powerful Flak guns brought from the capital, but all combat-worthy elements deployed in the Budapest area were ordered to the front. When the first of Zhdanov's tanks arrived at the gates of the Magyar capital on midday of 2 November, they faced an enemy that was ready and waiting.

In the days that preceded the assault, troops of relatively good quality were placed in position. The inexperienced 22 SS-Cavalry-Division was deployed in the westernmost segment of the 'Attila I' line – Sector A. It would face its baptism of fire at Taksony, Dunaharaszti and Alsónémedi. There it was to be supported by the elite Hungarian I/1 Parachute Battalion. The assault artillery group of Major-General Billnitzer (up to five Hungarian assault gun battalions), which was equipped with both German and Hungarian-made machines, was placed in Sector B. Since there was never enough infantry in the *Puszta*, three German police battalions were sent to Sector A and one to Sector B.[35]

Meanwhile, a number of other units had been mustered between the Tisza and the Danube for the defence of the capital and were moving at full speed to the front. The first ones to arrive were Panzer-Grenadier-Division 'Feldherrnhalle' and 13 Panzer-Division, forward parties of which appeared on the battlefield in the morning of 2 November; 8 SS-Cavalry-Division would arrive the next day. The hastily reconstituted 12 Reserve Division (actually, the merged remnants of the Hungarian 4 and 12 Reserve Divisions) would follow shortly afterwards. A lot of artillery units were underway, too. Finally, on 2 November, 18 SS-Panzer-Grenadier-Division began to entrain for the Budapest area. Thus in the first days of November Army Group South succeeded in assembling a powerful force numbering more than 100,000 men in the vicinity of Budapest.[36] The quick capture of the Magyar capital was no longer possible. The Soviets did not know that yet.

REDEPLOYMENT OF GERMAN RESERVES TO BUDAPEST

	Panzer-Grenadier Division 'Feldherrnhalle'	8.SS-Cavalry-Division 'Florian Geyer'
Arrived by 3 November 1944	Division Staff Fusilier Regiment 'FH' Anti-Tank Battalion 'FH' (less the assault guns) Artillery-Regiment-Staff 511	SS-Reconnaissance Battalion 8 SS-Flak Battalion 8 (5 x 8.8cm, 6 x 3.7cm and 10 x 2cm guns) SS-Cavalry Regiment 15 (4 Squadrons)
En route to the front	Panzer-Engineer Battalion 'FH' Signals-Battalion 'FH' Artillery Battalion I./77	SS-Flak Battalion 8 (the rest) SS-Anti-Tank Battalion 8 SS-Engineer Battalion 8 SS-Cavalry Regiment 16 SS-Cavalry Regiment 18
Departed on 3 November 1944	Panzer-Battalion 'FH' Anti-Tank Battalion 'FH' (the assault guns) I.Battalion/Panzer-Artillery Regiment 'FH' (self-propelled)	
Scheduled to depart in the morning of 4 November 1944	I.Battalion/Grenadier Regiment 'FH' (armoured halftracks) Staff/Grenadier Regiment 'FH'	

7

In the previous chapter we saw how the 4th Guards Mechanised Corps succeeded in finding a gap in the Axis defence at Szabadszállás and subsequently broke out into open country. Spearheaded by a strong task force, the 14th Guards Mechanised Brigade, the corps dashed through the cold autumn night towards the first objective, Kunszentmiklós.

The town of Kunszentmiklós played an important role in the Axis plans for the stabilisation of the crumbling front. In the evening of 1 November Fretter-Pico, for instance, informed Army Group South HQ that he intended to establish a blocking line between Solt and Szabadszállás with 10 Infantry-Division (Hung) to stop the Soviet thrust from the south and thus to gain time for the scattered remnants of various Hungarian units to regroup in the vicinity of Kunszentmiklós.[37] But these plans were not to be realised: the Soviet tanks moved far too fast!

The defence of Kunszentmiklós was entrusted to 1 Huszar-Division, which during the previous four days had been badly mauled and the morale of its men was sinking. ('The combat worth of this division has declined considerably,' General Kirchner observed in his evening report, and pointed out that it was retreating in the face of 'insignificant enemy forces.')[38] It is no wonder then that when in the early hours of 2 November the 14th Guards Mechanised Brigade, in cooperation with the 86th Guards Rifle Division, attacked Kunszentmiklós from the south and east, the Hungarians quickly abandoned the town and fell back to the north.

The terrain north of Kunszentmiklós was boggy, the only road was just 4m wide and ran through marshes. Some tanks got stuck and had to be towed out. Near Kis-major (a farmstead), some 10km north of the town, the Hungarians had set up a blocking position manned by two infantry companies supported by two mortar batteries, two artillery batteries and 4 self-propelled guns.

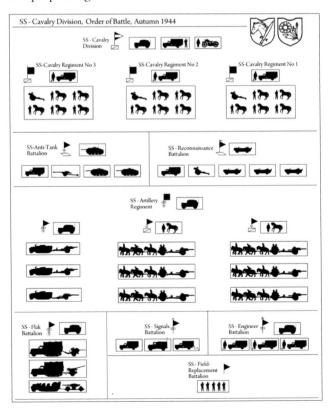

The forward detachment of the 14th Guards gave the defenders no chance. It attacked the position at full speed, crushed it and forced the Hungarians to flee. Herding before them the panicked remnants of the once proud Magyar hussar division, on the morning of 2 November the Soviet tanks reached F. Ürb - puszta (just south of Bugyi) and entered that 'manor' literally 'on the shoulders of the retreating enemy'. The blocking position encountered there was also crushed immediately and the survivors, 'tossing away their weapons', fled.[39]

At around 10:00 MT on 2 November, 14th Guards Mechanised Brigade entered Bugyi and captured it after a brief action. A scouting party of 13 Panzer-Division, which had been sent there by the

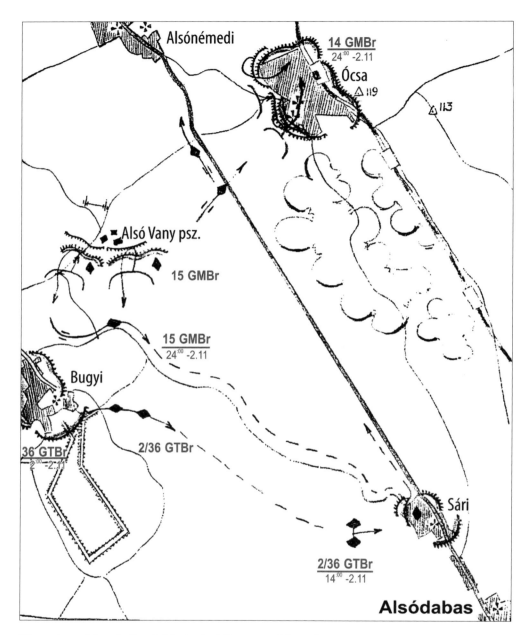

The actions of the 4th Guards Mechanised Corps on 2 November 1944.

divisional commander, General Schmidhuber, was caught by surprise and fled in panic. One motorcycle messenger, however, was not able to escape and was taken prisoner. It turned out that he was a very important catch, because he was carrying with him staff maps and documents.[40]

The fall of Bugyi, which stood so close to Budapest, was troubling news for the Axis command. At the moment the news hit them, elements of 13 Panzer-Division began to arrive in the area. Armoured Reconnaissance Battalion 13, the eyes and ears of the division, was the first unit that appeared on the battlefield. It was followed by Panzer-Grenadier Regiment 66, which in the morning had received orders from Schmidhuber to set up positions south of Ócsa. Very soon, however, the scouts reported that the Russian tanks had already overrun the areas earmarked for the organisation of defence. Still worse, it turned out that the Magyar troops that had been garrisoned there had simply disappeared.[41] Once again, no luck for the unfortunate '13th'! Destroyed in Bessarabia during the summer and repeatedly employed as a 'fire brigade' throughout the battle for Debrecen, it was now caught in the eye of the Soviet storm. Once again the tankers and the panzer-grenadiers were to be pushed into action before anyone had time even to draw breath. Their old enemy, 4th Guards Mechanised Corps was coming their way.[42]

It was time for action and Schmidhuber decided to retake Bugyi immediately. One of his battalions attacked from the northeast. Overcoming the resistance of the Soviet tanks, the panzer-grenadiers reached the northern perimeter of the village, but were not able to advance any farther and shortly afterwards were driven back. Together with the other newly arrived elements of 13th Panzer, they formed a thin defensive line between the villages of Alsónémedi and Ócsa.[43]

In the meantime, 14th Guards Mechanised Brigade continued its march northeast. Moving off road and overcoming marshy terrain, at 13:30 MT Nikitin's men seized Ócsa. While approaching the village they destroyed a Hungarian baggage train and captured an airfield with 10 aircraft. At the railway station of Ócsa they captured several trains, including one ambulance train.[44]

With the capture of Bugyi and Ócsa the main forces of Zhdanov's corps, which until then were moving in the wake of Nikitin's brigade without seeing any combat, were finally able to form a battle line and approach the objectives assigned to them. At that time, however, it turned out that both flanks of the corps were not screened, so General Zhdanov found himself forced to use part of his troops for their protection. The 14th Guards Mechanised Brigade formed a hedgehog defence in Ócsa and thus secured the right flank, whilst 36th Guards Tank Brigade did the same in Bugyi, protecting the left one.[45] The village of Sári,[46] which was now situated deep in the rear of the corps, was still in enemy hands and thus barred the main supply route, the Kecskemét–Budapest motorway. Understandably, free passage on that road was essential for the rest of the offensive, so Sári was to be taken immediately.

The mission was assigned to the 2nd Battalion of the 36th Guards Tank Brigade. Sári was swiftly attacked from the west and by 14:00 MT the village was completely cleared. The Soviet assault was so surprising that when the first tanks appeared on the streets most of the garrison was resting in the houses. A panic broke out, the confusion was total and the defenders offered very little resistance. (The Soviets lost 1 tank, 1 killed and 2 wounded.). Up to 40 German officers and men had lost their lives, another 11 had been taken prisoner, 1 tank had been destroyed and 40 motor vehicles had been captured.[47] The Soviet corridor had been widened. Now came the moment for the second echelon (the 13th and 15th Guards Mechanised Brigades) to enter the scene.

Command of Army Group South had very few troops in that area (22 SS-Cavalry-Division had not yet arrived), so the only thing it could do was to track with a heavy heart the approach of the Soviet mechanised formations. Alarming messages were arriving at frequent intervals: 'The Russian tanks and infantry have captured Bugyi' (at 9:40 BT); 'the Russians are advancing from Bugyi to Alsónémedi' (11:40 BT); 'Russian tanks are standing before Alsónémedi, another group of tanks is trying to attack towards the Danube bank' (15:15 BT); 'the enemy has captured Ócsa and, according to aerial reconnaissance, has entered Alsónémedi as well' (16:15 BT).[48]

After the capture of Ócsa the 4th Guards Mechanised Corps kept moving to the northwest, but now there were clear signs that its advance was losing momentum owing to increasing opposition. During the evening 15th Guards Mechanised Brigade attempted to reach the Danube bank at Taksony, but was stopped at the Alsó Vany puszta (farmstead), where it encountered vigorous resistance.[49] The Magyar paratroopers, who had taken a stand at Alsó Vany, successfully withstood the attack of the 'Swallow Brigade'. They had four 75mm anti-tank guns, but it was another weapon from their arsenal that deserves our attention: here, perhaps for the first time, a powerful Hungarian-made rocket launcher, 44 MSZR, also known as *Szálasi röppentyű* (Szálasi's rocket) was used. An officer of the parachute battalion vividly recalls the first employment of the weapon:

> During those days tests took place of a new weapon made in Hungary – the Szálasi-rocket, right in the defensive zone of my troop. This rocket was a recoilless weapon, like the bazooka, which was launched by electric ignition from a wheel-stand. The head of the rocket was much bigger than that of the bazooka, and they used to say that it had a really great splinter effect. The trial launching was successful and the projectile resembling an enormous club set off in the direction of a farm that was 3km away, where Soviet tanks were supposed to assemble. The projectile flying through the air could be followed visually for a long time. It produced a strong booming sound in the air, then a flash of lightning could be seen from the direction of the farm and a sound like an artillery shell hit could be heard'.[50]

The actions of 13th Guards Mechanised Brigade were not successful either. Having captured Alsónémedi in the afternoon, in the evening the 'Deer' brigade was stopped in front of the anti-tank ditch situated 3km north of the village.[51] Second Lieutenant Géza Marosújvári of the Hungarian parachute battalion gives a vivid account of what happened there:

> The offensive … started in the afternoon. The 1/2nd Parachute Company went into defensive position south of Soroksár under the command of First Lieutenant Endre Juhász. The leading five T-34s shortly reached the anti-tank ditch (in front of the defensive position) …

I remember vividly that scene! There was a deadly silence, only the growling of the Soviet tanks and the scratch of their tracks could be heard. Night was falling swiftly, but we saw the Soviet infantry that followed the tanks crouching in the ditch beside the highway. Our orders were not to open fire on the infantry until the tanks had been knocked out. The tanks advanced with short stops, covering each other, but they stopped short before the bridge. At that moment the anti-aircraft guns hidden in the acacias along the road fired, the tank-killing groups deployed near the bridge also fired with their bazookas. There was heavy infantry fire in addition and the infantrymen following the tanks threw themselves down on the ground. As a result of the unexpected fire, all five tanks were hit and remained immov-

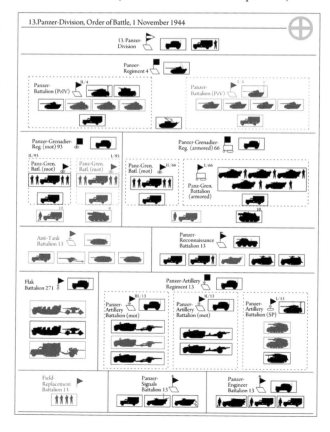

able. As far as I remember, one of the burning tanks tried to withdraw, but Sergeant János Tóth stopped it with a hand-grenade bundle; his face and arms were heavily burnt and wounded.

About 8 pm the Soviet offensive started again and with the throwing in of twenty tanks; the chaotic battle in the defensive position lasted all night. Many tanks were knocked out by teller mines and by armour-piercing shells, but the Soviet troops quickly towed away the knocked-out tanks to a safe place. A T-34 was hit on the highway, at about 200m behind the defensive position, and exploded ...[52]

This was the first clash of a Soviet unit with the 'Attila' line and it could safely be said that the fortification passed the test. Its presence allowed Fretter-Pico for the first time since the beginning of Shlemin's onslaught to establish a continuous frontline south of Budapest. It ran from Dunaharaszti to Üllő and was held by the newly arrived 13 Panzer-Division and 22 SS-Cavalry-Division. The former was probably represented by only two battalions that in the afternoon had been deployed north of Bugyi and Alsónémedi. Their intervention, however, was crucial in preventing the Soviets from breaching the 'Attila' line. The drive of 4th Guards Mechanised Corps, which had covered 110km in less than 24 hours, was finally checked.

Perhaps if Zhdanov had had enough infantry and heavy artillery at his disposal, his troops would have met the objectives assigned to them. But on that afternoon the entire 23rd Rifle Corps was still many kilometres behind and could not lend a helping hand. The insufficient road network and the soft terrain did not allow Grigorovich to commit his troops to battle quickly enough. (In particular, at 16:00 MT the temporarily motorised 68th Guards Rifle Division was still moving through Kunszentmiklós.)[53] Thus Zhdanov found himself forced to use two of his brigades for flank protection and was able to attack the 'Attila' line with only two brigades. Their strength was quite inadequate for knocking the Axis troops out of their positions.

8

Despite the fact that in many places the Soviet advance had been considerably slowed, in the afternoon of 2 November Friessner and Fretter-Pico were still struggling to consolidate the front. Especially critical was the situation in the centre, where the gap between Alberti and Abony was not yet closed and the German troops fighting there were *de facto* encircled. It was clear to the leadership of Army Group South that upon the arrival of the reserves still en route the hole would be plugged, but in the meantime the endangered forces must be saved. We already know that in the evening 23 Panzer-Division broke off its attack and withdrew to the northeast. Similar orders were issued to the other troops that were in danger of being cut off: a battle group of the 'Feldherrnhalle' Division (at Újhartyán), Becker's battle group (still engaged at the Lipot farmstead) and the main body of 1 Panzer-Division (at the Ágaston farmstead, northeast of Örkény).[54] The retreat of these forces was carried out after dark in most difficult conditions, through a terrain of forests and small lakes, with frequent clashes with the advancing enemy. It was not until the afternoon of the next day that the last of these wandering units reached the Axis frontline.

For Malinovsky and Shlemin, 2 November was a day of mixed fortunes, as the troops of 46th Army made significant territorial gains but failed to penetrate into Budapest. Sviridov's corps was slowed by the German counter-attack, Zhdanov's formation was contained in front of the 'Attila' line, while the three fresh divisions of Grigorovich's 23rd Rifle Corps were delayed by the terrain. Most of the other divisions saw heavy fighting.

Apart from the dogged resistance encountered by 4th Guards Mechanised Corps, at the western flank of Shlemin's army another problem began to emerge: the bridgehead of Solt. It was held by the troops of 10 Infantry-Division that had been pushed aside by Zhdanov's brigades the previous evening. Once bypassed, the Magyars did not lose their heads but quickly formed a defensive perimeter around Solt and, with their backs to the Danube, put up a stubborn opposition. For the next ten days the Solt bridgehead would be like a thorn in the flesh of the Soviets and would pin down the entire 34th Guards Rifle Division that otherwise would have been used for the capture of Budapest.

On the right flank of the 46th Army there was heavy fighting, too. By 11:00 MT the 476th Rifle Regiment of 320th Rifle Division captured Lajosmizse.[55] The nearby town of Nagykőrös, however, turned out to be a much harder nut to crack. Early in the morning of 2 November it was attacked by 108th Guards Rifle Division, which cooperated closely with the SU-76-equipped 1505th Self-Propelled Artillery Regiment. The Germans had no intention of holding the place and in order to facilitate the retreat of 24 Panzer-Division to the north, 23 Panzer-Division was ordered to halt the 108th Guards south of the town.[56]

Early in the morning 23rd Panzer, with 22 tanks accompanied by infantry, struck the 108th Guards from the direction of Nagykőrös. 'The counterattack was beaten back' says the morning report of 46th Army.[57] Then it was the turn of the Soviet guardsmen to attack and they employed the entire might of their division to accomplish the mission assigned to them. The town was stormed simultaneously from three sides. The 311th Guards Rifle Regiment advanced from the east, the 308th from the north, while the 305th quickly infiltrated the place and before long was engaged in combat for the railway station. A fierce street battle erupted everywhere, but the Soviets did not allow themselves to be pinned down. Their assault groups moved rapidly, bypassing the encountered pockets of resistance.[58] By midday the defenders (Panzer-Grenadier Regiment 128) abandoned the town and it finally fell into Soviet hands.[59] From that moment on the entire 37th Guards Rifle Corps began gradually to turn to the northeast. Its next objective was Cegléd.

9

The battle for air supremacy over the *Puszta* continued unabated. Now its focal point shifted to the area of Cegléd. The main mission assigned to the I Air Corps remained unchanged: 'With all possible means to destroy the enemy tanks and pound its motorised units.' The Luftwaffe air units were also ordered to support their allies' counter-attacks, a task that was considered of primary importance.[60]

The German airmen, as usual, were in the thick of the battle. Throughout the day the fighter-bombers repeatedly pounded Slemin's forward detachments and troop concentrations in the area east of Budapest.[61] But the Hungarian fighter pilots, to whom we paid little attention so far, were very active, too. They not only carried out several low-level attacks against the Soviet ground troops, but were also engaged in fierce aerial combat. On 2 November two pilots of the Magyar 102/4 FS fighter squadron southeast of Cegléd – 1st Lieutenant György Bánlaky and Sergeant Lajos Molnár – shot down an Il-2 and a La-5 respectively. The Hungarians lost Lieutenant László Frankó who went missing during that action.[62]

The commanders of the Soviet air and ground units were seriously concerned about the high level of activity of the Axis air forces. They did their best to shield the troops in the field with a considerable number of anti-aircraft guns and fighter cover, a fact that immediately found recognition in the German reports.[63]

In their efforts to stop the Luftwaffe, the Soviet commanders were helped by the ground troops and by the weather. For example, on 2 November the rapid advance of the Soviet tanks and infantry forced the II/JG 52 and 102 FS fighter groups to abandon the Ferihegy airfield (just north of Vecsés) and move to Budaörs, west of the Danube.[64] The next day the rain clouds grounded the entire Air Fleet 4. The 5th Air Army did not rely only on such secondary bonuses but attempted to cripple the Luftwaffe units itself. Events on 2 November can serve as an example.

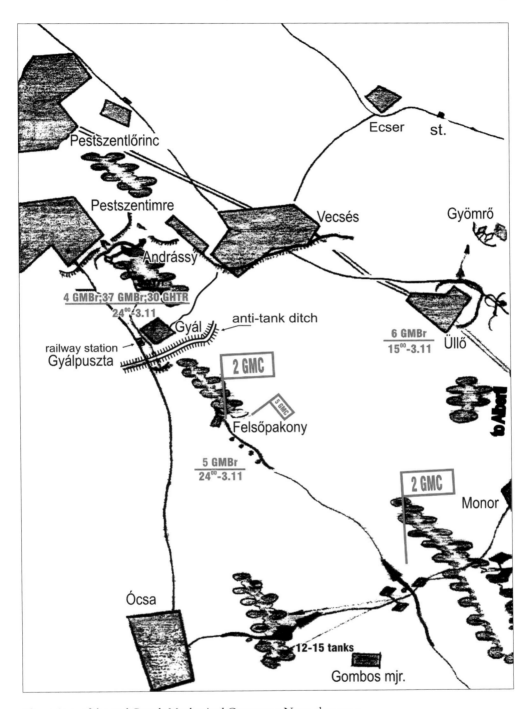

The actions of the 2nd Guards Mechanised Corps on 3 November 1944.

Soviet aerial reconnaissance reported that on the Tápiószentmárton airfield (where the German SG 2 and part of the SG 10 ground–attack groups were stationed) there were more than 50 enemy aircraft. Colonel Shuteev, commander of 7th Guards Assault Air Division, decided to launch a powerful attack on this tempting target. The Il-2s of the 130th Guards Assault Air Regiment took off and headed for the enemy air base. They were accompanied by the La-5s of 92nd and 486th Fighter Air Regiments. Just before the objective was reached, the group was met with intense anti-aircraft fire. Having foreseen this, Captain Prolygin, the group leader, ordered six specially chosen Shturmoviks, the crews of which had been briefed, to silence the Flak guns immediately. In the meantime, patrolling Axis fighters appeared, but they were engaged by the La-5s and effectively pushed aside. The main group of Il-2s was now able to deliver a scorching attack on the airfield, which it did from a height of less than 800m. Upon return to home base, Prolygin reported the destruction of 15 enemy planes and 3 Flak batteries.[65]

The actions of the Shturmoviks, of course, were not limited to the enemy airfields only. Their primary target continued to be the Axis ground troops. The latter felt horribly exposed when were attacked from the air. Major von Knebel-Doeberitz of 24 Panzer-Division vividly recalls that feeling:

> We, for the first time, encountered fighter-ground attack aircraft (we called them 'the butchers') that were able to fire rockets to their rear. This meant they used to overfly the German lines, and the rockets were fired to the rear to hit the deployed ground forces, and when we thought it was all over it really started. They flew very low. The only chance we had was with the 4-barrelled anti-aircraft guns – 20mms.[66]

10

On the night of 2/3 November, both Shlemin and Sviridov narrowly escaped death. In the early hours of 3 November a single Axis plane (identified as a Ju-88) dropped five high-explosive bombs that exploded very close to field HQ of 46th Army. Luckily for the Soviets, neither Shlemin, nor any of his closest entourage, was harmed.[67]

Sviridov's brush with death was different. Shortly after midnight the first echelon of the staff of 2nd Guards Mechanised Corps (its operations section), accompanied by some combat elements, set out from Luiza-major (just to the northwest of Viktória-major) and followed the tracks of the fast moving 4th Guards Mechanised Brigade. In the forest near Gombos-major they all of a sudden ran into an enemy column of truck-borne infantry of battalion strength accompanied by 12–15 tanks, which was retreating from the vicinity of Ócsa toward Monor. (It presumably belonged to 1 Panzer-Division.)

Soviet infantrymen armed with sub-machine guns mount T-34-85 tanks before they go into a battle in the vicinity of Budapest, late autumn 1944. (Author's Collection)

The forested terrain and the bad road prevented the Germans from quickly forming a battle line. The five tanks at the disposal of the corps' command and the platoon of submachine-gunners from 37th Guards Tank Brigade that accompanied them immediately opened intense fire. Whilst the shocked Germans were still trying to pull themselves together, the Soviets used the moment to occupy the nearby crossroads. The way forward for the Germans was now blocked and this allowed the corps' staff to be pulled out of the dangerous spot and to resume its drive to its final destination, Felsőpakony.

The German column, despite its numerical superiority, was forced to retreat. Having sustained some losses, it turned to the south, toward Inárcs, probably in search of an alternative escape route. There it once again clashed with some elements of the corps, this time the reserve of Sviridov's intelligence section. In order to help the latter, the General ordered a small battle group to be formed, consisting of five T-34 tanks of the 37th Guards Tank Brigade and 2 JS-2 tanks of the 30th Guards Heavy Tank Regiment. The hastily organised battle group managed to intercept the Germans and scattered their column. After that it continued to patrol along the corps' main supply route, thus providing security for the rear echelon elements arriving from the southeast.[68]

11

The actions of the forces deployed on the flanks of Shlemin's army allowed 2nd Guards Mechanised Corps to step up the pace of its own drive towards Budapest. The fierce counter-attacks of 1 and 23 Panzer-Divisions did little harm to Sviridov's brigades and they continued their advance to the northwest along the Cegléd–Budapest railway. It was so swift, that when on the night of 2/3 November the forward detachment of 6th Guards Mechanised Brigade entered the town of Üllő, all was peaceful. A member of the brigade recalls what happened next:

> As a result of the skilful manoeuvre undertaken by our brigade commander, we broke into Üllő. In the houses the lights were on; the Budapest power station was working, trains loaded with infantry and artillery were arriving at the train station. The appearance of scouts with armoured cars and tanks with Red Stars on the streets of the town proved to be a complete surprise for the local garrison. The Hitlerite officers, sleeping in their soft beds, were not allowed to dream their sweet dreams to the end. Half-dressed, they were running out into the streets, attempting to fire back. The more sensible of them raised their hands …
>
> Everything calmed down by the morning. The town was breathing out the heat and smoke of the earlier battle. The narrow streets were clogged with rammed armoured carriers, crushed guns, rumpled amphibians and passenger cars. And corpses …[69]

Approximately 200 Axis troops lost their lives in the battle. Another 100 ('from privates to colonels, Nyilasists with arrow-cross armbands on their sleeves, youths from the pro-Fascist militarised organisation *Levente*') were taken prisoner. At the railway station the company of Senior-Lieutenant Nikolai Evsyukov captured a train with two locomotives that was crammed with military goods and weapons.[70]

Despite the spectacular victory, Colonel Kanevsky – the brigade's commander – kept his emotions in check and did not press his units to continue their advance on Budapest immediately. In a situation like this, when the shining Magyar capital seemed to be within the reach of his men, he acted very professionally by stopping them and ordering scouts to reconnoitre the area and bring reliable information on what lay ahead. Before long that 'reliable information' was delivered in the persons of two captured high-ranking officers (a Hungarian and a German), who confirmed Kanevsky's misgivings: a strong German formation (the

'Feldherrnhalle' Division) was coming that way.[71] Wasting no time, the brigade occupied the northern, northwestern and western perimeters of Üllő and began preparing for the battle ahead. The infantrymen dug deep into the hard ground, tanks and anti-tank guns were placed in ambush positions over all likely routes.[72]

Kanevsky's other decision – to withdraw from Vecsés, which some units of his brigade had just captured – was reasonable and even brave. Vecsés was actually quite a large place, with a population amounting to about 15,000. Even though it was the last major settlement before the Magyar capital, Kanevsky was well aware that the troops under him were not strong enough to defend simultaneously both Üllő and Vecsés. He chose to gather all his forces around Üllő and defend that important jump-off point no matter what. So when that morning the advance parties of the 'Feldherrnhalle' Division reported to General Breith that they had captured Vecsés without a fight, the commander of the III Panzer Corps was very surprised.[73]

12

'This morning the Russian attack on Budapest reached its climax,' wrote von Grolman in the war diary of Army Group South on 3 November.[74] Indeed, it seemed like the Soviet tanks and riflemen were pouring from everywhere. The front was far from consolidated despite the fact that all available Axis forces were already engaged in the battle.

The Soviet penetrations in the area of Vecsés and Pestszentimre were especially troubling for the German command since the settlements were situated deep behind the 'Attila I' line. (Sviridov's corps had managed to penetrate 'Attila I' in the morning of 3 November probably because the fortifications in that sector had been left unmanned.) So for the troops assembling southeast of Budapest (Breith's III Panzer Corps) the restoration of the integrity of the 'Attila I' line became the main objective.

In a situation like this the only way to prevent a breakthrough is to give the enemy no rest: to counter-attack , to try to seize the initiative and remove the enemy's major jump-off points. This is how the troops under Fretter-Pico spent the day of 3 November: they counter-attacked the advancing Red Army time and again.

13

The town of Üllő was situated about 20km southeast of Budapest. When shortly after midnight of 2/3 November it fell into the hands of 6th Guards Mechanised Brigade, there were still no Axis troops in that sector available to seal of fthe Soviet penetration. Still worse for the Germans and the Hungarians, the fact that the town had been lost to the enemy was (probably) still unknown to the Axis command. Or at least it seemed so to Lieutenant Rambow from Heavy-Panzer Battalion 503, when his column of 12 damaged King Tigers (some of them in tow), which was slowly moving from Cegléd to Budapest, encountered outside Üllő 'a Russian anti-tank obstacle, totally by surprise'. For Rambow the situation was 'abominable': with all these disabled and immobile Tigers he could not defend himself. The Russians, of course, immediately open fire with their anti-tank guns and set fire to the leading tank, Tiger 300. The crew baled out, but the panzer was lost for good. Despite the intense enemy fire, Rambow and his men managed to cut the tow cable and disengage. The group moved back to Pilis and thus the remaining tanks were saved.[75]

Rambow's sudden encounter with the enemy tank killers was clear proof that the Soviets had taken Üllő. The town was a major road and railway junction. In the eyes of the German command, it was one of those dangerous jump-off points from which Shlemin would launch his final assault on the capital. As such, it was to be smashed without delay. The earlier, the

A knocked-out T-34-76 tank from the 6th Guards Mechanised Brigade of the 2nd Guards Mechanised Corps on the outskirts of Budapest, autumn 1944. (Dénes Bernád)

better. There was a serious problem, though: the force that was intended to launch the assault in question, 8 SS-Cavalry-Division, had still not reached its final assembly area (Vecsés) owing to fuel shortages and only SS-Reconnaissance Battalion 8 had arrived so far.[76]

The first German attack commenced in the early hours of 3 November. 6th Guards Mechanised Brigade was pressed from three sides: a battle group of the 'Feldherrnhalle' Division attacked from Vecsés to the southeast; elements of 8 SS-Cavalry-Division struck from the north, while another battle group of the same division struck from the northeast.[77] The main blow fell on the battalion of Major Babich, which was attacked on a narrow front by approximately 15 tanks and several infantry companies. The attackers were supported by a hail of artillery and mortar fire.

The defenders remained calm. Despite the murderous bombardment (the whistling mortar shells proved to be especially deadly), the riflemen, machine-gunners, the anti-tank rifle crews and the tank killers armed with anti-tank grenades and 'Molotov cocktails' waited patiently in their trenches and foxholes for the German tanks to approach. When the distance dropped down to 200m, Babich ordered his men to open fire. The machine guns, the anti-tank rifles and the 45mm and 57mm anti-tank guns fired at once from what amounted to point blank range. The leading German tank was hit, then another one was set ablaze, but the rest kept rolling forward. They were threatening to smash the positions of the company of Senior-Lieutenant Nikolai Evsyukov (the one that captured a train with two locomotives at the Üllő railway station a few hours earlier). Evsyukov took the situation in his stride and urged on his men. Having left his command post, in full view of the enemy, he used flares to direct the artillery fire. Babich in the meantime was helping him by ordering all companies to concentrate their fire on the enemy infantry and thereby to separate it from the tanks. Nevertheless, some of the panzers managed to reach the battalion's positions and began to crush the trenches and the emplacements, smashing several machine guns, anti-tank rifles and guns. It was only then that the German attack was finally checked.[78]

The first German attack was followed by another one at 15:30 BT, and then another. By late evening the attackers were halted for good by the determined resistance of 6th Guards Mechanised Brigade, the battle group of the 'Feldherrnhalle' Division northwest of the town and the two battle groups of 8 SS-Cavalary Division, 1km northwest and 1km north of the town respectively.[79] All these assaults were repelled thanks to the excellent leadership of Colonel Kanevsky, the brigade's commander, and the bravery of his men. Some of them died as heroes, including Evsyukov who posthumously became a Hero of the Soviet Union.[80] The setback did not discourage the Germans; they would now attempt to take Üllő during the night.[81]

14

While in the first hours of 3 November 6th Guards Mechanised Brigade was still clearing Üllő of the enemy, the 'shock group' of 2nd Guards Mechanised Corps (the 4th Guards Mechanised Brigade, 37th Guards Tank Brigade and 30th Guards Heavy Tank Regiment) was rolling to the northwest. This time it was spearheaded by a reconnaissance engineer platoon of the corps' 55th Guards Engineer Battalion, commanded by Senior-Lieutenant Voronov. Voronov had received his mission personally from Lieutenant-Colonel Miroshnichenko, corps' engineer commander: to check whether the bridge over the stream south of Inárcs was still standing, and if it was intact, to seize it and hold it until the arrival of 4th Guards Mechanised Brigade.

Voronov's men reached the objective early in the morning of 3 November. The bridge was intact, but was guarded by sentries. Voronov decided to attack the crossing simultaneously from two directions. The combat engineers struck with the first rays of dawn. Their attack was swift and sudden and the precious bridge was secured in no time. Ten Axis troops were killed in the firefight, two machine guns were captured, as well as 100 kg of explosives, which, no doubt would have been used for the demolition of the bridge. About 30 minutes after the last shots were fired, the forward units of 4th Guards Mechanised Brigade arrived from the south and began to cross.[82]

It was still the morning of 3 November when Sviridov's 'shock group' approached Gyál. In a swift action similar to that described above, the forward detachments of 4th Guards Mechanised Brigade and 37th Guards Tank Brigade managed to eliminate the enemy demolition teams, which had been tasked with destruction of the bridge spanning the anti-tank ditch that ran immediately to the south of the village. Wasting no time, both brigades moved their tanks and vehicles across the ditch and captured Gyál.[83] Then the task force advanced farther north and reached the eastern perimeter of Pestszentimre, which actually became the deepest point of Soviet penetration during Malinovsky's first offensive on Budapest.

'The situation at Budapest is getting worse,' Gaedcke complained to von Grolman.[84] One of the main reasons behind his complaint was the breakthrough of Sviridov's brigades in the area between Pestszentimre and Üllő. As result, the left flank of 22 SS-Cavalry-Division had been pushed aside, the 'Attila I' line had been penetrated and there were still literally no troops in the path of the Soviet tanks, with the exception of SS-Reconnaissance Battalion 8 deployed north of Vecsés. The word 'gap' was frequently used in the day's German documents when referring to the situation in that sector. The only way to close that gap was to smash the Soviet penetration corridor by attacking it with the newly arrived 13 Panzer-Division.

In the morning Schmidhuber received orders from Breith to attack from Pestszentimre to the southeast. By that time the bulk of his division was still assembling in the vicinity of the town.[85] (The rest of the division, save the non-operational tanks, arrived throughout the day.) As usual, before the attack it formed two battle groups: armoured and non-armoured. The armoured battle group was made up of Major Gehrig's II Battalion/Panzer-Regiment 4 (which was equipped mostly with Panthers) and I Battalion/Panzer-Grenadier Regiment 66

SdKfz 251/21 armoured half-tracks from I Battalion/Panzer-Grenadier Regiment 66 of 13 Panzer-Division, Hungary, autumn 1944. Originally designed for anti-aircraft defence, these halftracks were armed with triple-mount 15mm automatic cannon with a very high rate of fire. With this cannon the halftrack possessed a firepower that was enormous for a lightly armoured vehicle. It is no wonder that it was effective against ground targets also. Panzer-Grenadier Division 'Feldherrnhalle' was the only other German formation in Hungary that was lucky enough to have these vehicles in its order of battle. (Mirko Bayerl)

(equipped with armoured halftracks, including a considerable number of SdKfz 251/21 vehicles outfitted with triple-mount 1.5cm automatic cannons). The mission of Gehrig's group was to engage the Soviet armour and push it back.[86]

The other battle group consisted of Staff/Panzer-Grenadier Regiment 66 (Major Schöning), II Battalion/Panzer-Grenadier Regiment 66 (motorised infantry), to which one police battalion was subordinated together with a Hungarian tank company with 4 obsolete Škoda light tanks. The task of Schöning's group, which was to be supported by II Battalion/Panzer-Artillery Regiment 13, was to take Vecsés and from there to assist the counter-attack of Gehrig's armour.[87]

In the afternoon Sviridov's tank men and infantry managed to advance a little farther and by 16:00 BT reached the southern limits of Pestszentimre but were then stopped.[88] Soon enough they would find themselves caught in a very dangerous situation.

Pestszentimre was a typical suburb of Budapest. Populated mostly by factory workers, it consisted of one- or two- storey buildings, 'box-houses', small agricultural gardens, vineyards and a couple of estates. The narrow streets were perfect for ambushes and offered excellent hiding places for guns and armour. The Germans, of course, did not miss the chance to exploit these features and wasting no time unleashed hell on the Soviet spearheads.

The fierce counter-attack delivered by 13 Panzer-Division was initially successful and allowed it to advance some 3km to the southeast of Pestszentimre.[89] Up to 50 armoured vehicles struck 4th Guards Mechanised Brigade, the Axis artillery pounded its positions and the casualties began to mount. Amongst the badly wounded were the brigade's Chief-of-Staff, Lieutenant-Colonel V.N. Khokhlov, commanding officer of the 23rd Guards Tank Regiment, Major I.I. Chichev, and even the brigade's commander himself, Lieutenant-Colonel M.I. Lyaschenko. Anxiety and something approaching panic broke out in the ranks, most of whom were inexperienced recruits; communication with corps HQ was lost.

At this critical moment Major-General V.N. Baskakov (corps' deputy commander) and Colonel A.N. Samokhin, corps' artillery commander, arrived at the brigade's forward command post. General Baskakov quickly became acquainted with the situation and with the plan of action of the brigade's commander. After a brief exchange of opinions with the staff officers present, he ordered the corps artillery to bombard the area where the Germans were assembling for their next counter-attack. At the same time 37th Guards Tank Brigade, coupled with the 'Joseph Stalins' of the 30th Guards Heavy Tank Regiment, were directed to launch a counter-attack of their own.

The well-coordinated actions of all these units finally turned the tables and the Germans were defeated. In the battle, which lasted from 16:00 MT up until midnight, the troops under Baskakov claimed to have inflicted serious losses: 'almost 30' armoured vehicles were put out of action and 'a considerable number of enemy dead were left on the battlefield.'[90] 13 Panzer-Division was not able to gain any more ground and by the end of the day Breith reported that its advance had been stopped dead in its tracks in the area just north of Gyál owing to 'a strong anti-tank defence'.[91]

A Soviet JS-2 heavy tank of the 30th Guards Heavy Tank Regiment from the 2nd Guards Mechanised Corps close to Budapest, November 1944. (Author's Collection)

15

We already saw how in the evening of 2 November the 13th Guards Mechanised Brigade (the 'Deer Brigade') was stopped in front of the anti-tank ditch situated 3km north of Alsónémedi, while the 15th Guards Mechanised Brigade (the 'Swallow Brigade') was prevented from reaching the Danube bank at Taksony by the brave Hungarian paratroopers. But the battle did not die down at dusk.

Having received strict orders to enter Budapest the next day (3 November), 4th Guards Mechanised Corps resumed its attacks shortly after midnight. At 00:30 MT the combat engineers of 13th Guards Mechanised Brigade began to clear the mines protecting the anti-tank ditch south of the Gyál Laslza major. It was a near-suicidal mission since it was carried out under constant machine-gun and artillery fire. Nevertheless, it was a success and it allowed the brigade's 2nd Rifle Battalion to overcome the ditch and advance one step closer to the Magyar capital. Once the riflemen approached the farmstead, however, they were pinned down again by intense enemy machine-gun, mortar and artillery fire.[92]

The news that the Soviets were now across the anti-tank ditch disturbed SS-*Brigadenführer* August Zehender, commander of 22 SS-Cavalry-Division. German command counted very much on this obstacle and it was essential to restore the position immediately. Zehender ordered a counterstrike to be launched. Since the massed bombardment did not produce the

A German soldier inspects the turret of a knocked-out T-34-76 somewhere in the Budapest suburbs. Once again, the insignia (a deer) suggests that the tank had belonged to the 13th Guards Mechanised Brigade of the 4th Guards Mechanised Corps. (Mirko Bayerl)

desired results, his inexperienced troopers and policemen[93] were thrown into fierce counter-attacks that followed one after another:

- At 13:30 MT Axis infantry, 'more than a battalion strong', attacked the centre of the position of the brigade. At the same time a smaller group of infantry (presumably of company strength) struck the brigade's right flank, most probably in an attempt to outflank it. The battle lasted until 15:00 MT. At around 15:30 MT the attackers, having already sustained bloody losses, fell back to their original positions.

- At 16:00 MT the Germans, with about two companies of infantry, accompanied by a single assault gun and three armoured halftracks, tried their luck again. Supported by a hail of artillery fire, they desperately tried to push the 2nd Rifle Battalion back behind the ditch. Colonel Goryachev, the commander of the 'Deer Brigade', responded immediately to this new treat by sending three tanks north of ditch. With their help, the guardsmen stood their ground and the SS were repulsed again.

- At 18:30 MT about two battalions of Axis infantry, this time supported by tanks and assault guns, unleashed yet another violent storm on the Soviet foothold north of the ditch. The members of the 2nd Battalion once again fought like lions, but this time the enemy pressure was way too heavy and at around 20:00 MT they were pushed to the south and now were literally fighting with their backs to the ditch. But Zehender's men were already very exhausted, too, and at around 21:00 MT they ceased their assault.

- The Germans regrouped and at 22:30 MT made one final try to eliminate the 2nd Battalion, but again without success.[94]

The 15th Guards Mechanised Brigade also attempted to use the darkness to achieve its mission, which was to capture Dunaharaszti and Taksony and thus to clear the entire Danube bank, up to Budapest, of the enemy. When the order arrived, the brigade was engaged in battle at Alsó Vany. Still worse for Colonel Andrianov, the brigade's commander, the lack of good roads and the swampy terrain denied him use of all of his troops. He decided to leave a small rearguard (3rd Rifle Battalion, two tanks and two 76mm artillery batteries) northeast of Alsó Vany, their task to engage the attention of the enemy still occupying the farmstead, while the bulk of his forces moved to Alsónémedi to use the latter as a jump-off point for his attack. Having received General Zhdanov's permission, shortly before midnight the brigade pulled out of combat and set out for Alsónémedi. It marched through Bugyi, Sári and Alsónémedi and by 03:00 MT was on the northern outskirts of the latter.

When the 'Swallow Brigade' finally arrived at the jump-off point (some 2km northwest of Alsónémedi), it came under intense fire from Hills 112, 114 and 119. At 05:00 MT on 3 November its rifle battalions, supported by tanks, formed a battle line and advanced on Rákócziliget and Dunaharaszti. The Hungarian paratroopers were awake and waiting. They met the attackers with fierce artillery fire and succeeded in knocking out one tank and two armoured halftracks. The Soviet riflemen were pinned down and forced to take cover approximately 500m northwest of Hill 112.

The setback didn't discourage Andrianov. Determined to defeat the enemy as quickly as possible, he sent out scouting parties. The information brought by them, however, was not what he wanted to hear: there was an irrigation canal about 2m deep, filled with water, in front of the brigade. The bridge across it had been blown up; along both banks of the canal the Hungarians had dug trenches and now there were up to 12 machine guns in each of them. Still worse, there were three heavy self-propelled guns in waiting at the southeastern limits of Rákócziliget, while another six batteries supported the defenders of Dunaharaszti. All attempts by Andrianov's troops to gain ground were beaten back.

The defensive success apparently had encouraged the Magyar paratroopers and at around 22:00 MT they mounted a counter-attack supported by self-propelled guns. The confused battle in the dark lasted more than 90 minutes and in the end, the Soviets prevailed.[95] The paratroopers fell back.

Thus Zhdanov for a second day in a row failed to enter Budapest. The reason behind the lack of success was the same as on the day before: 4th Guards Mechanised Corps was fighting alone, with open flanks and without heavy artillery, infantry protection or close air-support. It was the open flanks that forced Zhdanov to leave 14th Guards Mechanised Brigade in Ócsa (where it was shelled all day long from the direction of Gyál) and 36th Guards Tank Brigade in Bugyi and Sári. The bad weather grounded the dreaded Shturmoviks and Bostons at their airfields for a vital 24 hours.

The force intended to help Zhdanov's men to push into Budapest, 23rd Rifle Corps, spent the day en route to its final assembly area. The corps saw its first battle on Hungarian soil at 04:00 MT on 3 November, when one regiment of 316th Rifle Division attacked from the march and captured Dunavecse, a small town right on the Danube's bank, about 100km south of the Magyar capital.[96] At midday the spearhead of the corps (68th Guards Rifle Division) reached Bugyi, but it was only in the late afternoon that it began joining the struggle of 4th Guards Mechanised Corps.[97]

16

On the opposite flank of Shlemin's army, 37th Rifle Corps was about to achieve its next spectacular victory: less than two days after the capture of Kecskemét, the troops under General Kolchuck were about to take Cegléd. Even though it was not as big as Kecskemét, Cegléd was an important component of the puzzle. Since time immemorial, the place had been a junction of many vital routes and a gateway to the Great Hungarian Plain from the west. It was a cornerstone of the Axis defence of Budapest.[98]

After a brief pause, 37th Rifle Corps resumed its drive towards Cegléd at 05:00 MT on 3 November.[99] The 59th and 108th Guards Rifle Divisions advanced along both sides of the Nagykőrös–Cegléd motorway, but right from the outset encountered fierce resistance from 24 Panzer-Division and the Hungarian 20 Infantry Division. As the Soviets approached the town, the Axis opposition grew. It did not take Kolchuck long to realise that a pincer movement was the best way to take the place, instead of frontal assault. He attempted to bypass it to the west. This manoeuvre was only partially successful. Although by nightfall Cegléd was still in German hands, both Soviet divisions were now much closer to their objective than they were in the morning and this created the preconditions for taking it by storm without delay. By midnight the outer pincer (the 59th Guards Rifle Division) was in position in the farmlands southwest of the town, while the regiments of the 108th Guards Rifle Division stood barely 1km south and southwest of Cegléd.[100] There was no doubt: Cegléd was falling. So, General Kolchuk decided that the offensive should not stop during the night.

It was the 108th Guards Rifle Division that took the brunt that day. Owing to the constant bombardment by the German long-range cannons and self-propelled howitzers positioned in the vicinity of Cegléd, 108th Guards advanced to the north and northwest very slowly, especially during the morning.[101] The Axis resistance further intensified in the afternoon. In particular, at around 16:30 MT the division repulsed a battalion-strong enemy counter-attack supported by 10 tanks against its left flank around Zöldhalom railway station (just southwest of Cegléd). The 108th Guards succeeded in inflicting a terrible defeat on the defenders: by the end of the day it claimed up to 300 Axis troops killed, with another 200 taken prisoner.[102]

17

As the day wore on General Kirchner gradually came to the realisation that Cegléd most probably would have to be abandoned. He ordered the artillery of 24 Panzer-Division (with the subordinate Heavy Artillery Battalion 844) to leave its positions at the northern outskirts of the town and deploy 4–5km farther to the north and northeast.[103] At the same time, he was still determined to hold the perimeter and this is something that he declared in his evening report to Fretter-Pico. He was also desperate to preserve his badly mauled panzer units as a reserve for powerful counter-attacks.[104]

The bulk of the forces of LVII Panzer Corps at that moment were panzer-divisions (1, 23 and 24) and they were doing the fighting. How did Kirchner intend to muster the bare minimum of infantry in the vicinity of Cegléd and how did his superiors intend to help him in this? Kirchner's plan was quite simple:

1. To stop the Russians at Cegléd with the fearless 24 Panzer-Dvision and thus to allow the retreating 1 and 23 Panzer-Divisions to conduct an orderly fighting withdrawal to the northeast and subsequently to establish a continuous frontline along the Monor–Alberti railway, thereby closing the gap between Üllő and Cegléd.

2. To use the infantry forces at his disposal (the Magyar 20 Infantry Division), as well as those promised him by Friessner (the German 46 Infantry Division) to strengthen the front at both sides of Cegléd and in so doing to relieve 24 Panzer-Dvision.[105]

3. To attack with 24 Panzer-Dvision from Cegléd to the east and thus to close the gap between his corps and IV Panzer Corps.[106]

The implementation of the first step of this plan worked fine, because, as usual, 24 Panzer-Division performed well. Its first mission was to cover the retreat of 23 Panzer-Division after the cancellation of the counter-attack by the latter in the area east of Lipot-major.[107] This mission was accomplished and by the morning of 3 November 23rd Panzer assembled at Alberti.[108] The stiff resistance allowed the sappers of Panzer-Engineer Battalion 40 to prepare the crossings over the Gerje árok stream (just southwest of Cegléd) for demolition.[109]

Then 24th Panzer formed a defensive perimeter around Cegléd. A semicircle, its western/northwestern shoulder was protected by 23 Panzer-Division. Its eastern/southeastern shoulder, however, was practically on its own. That sector was nominally defended by the Hungarians (20 Infantry Division), whose frontline extended to a point 3km east of Abony and thereby was intended to serve as a link between Kirchner's corps and IV Panzer Corps.[110] It was this sector that became a source of constant trouble for Kirchner: throughout the day it was permanently under pressure from the Soviet and Romanian troops of 7th Guards Army advancing from the south. German intelligence believed that on the next day (4 November), Shumilov's army would concentrate all its efforts against the thinly held Cegléd–Abony line in order to free the Szolnok–Budapest motorway and thus to screen the eastern flank of 46th Army.[111]

The relationship with the Hungarian troops was deteriotating. The Magyars fought half-heartedly at best, and many of them were far more concerned about their own lives than the missions assigned to them. In addition, the artillery of 20 Infantry Division was critically short of ammunition.[112] In a desperate attempt to force them back into battle, in the morning 24th Panzer began to collect the retreating units of the Hungarian division and to gather them in Cegléd. They were helped by VIII Army Corps (Hung), 'gendarmes' from which established a blocking line.[113] The assembled stragglers were finally put in position on both sides of the town.

Despite all these problems, the former East Prussian cavalry division fought with vigour and even though the defensive perimeter was constantly shrinking under the pressure of the Soviets, it was shrinking incrementally and slowly. The weather conditions were nightmarish: it rained heavily and there was mud everywhere, which made any withdrawal or regrouping almost impossible.[114] Nevertheless, the 24th Panzer succeeded in its main mission – to keep the Russians away from Cegléd – and when night fell, the frontline had stabilised not far from the southern limits of the town.

18

The main reason why Shlemin failed to take Budapest on 3 November was that the brigades of both 2nd and 4th Guards Mechanised Corps were forced to fight a lonely battle all day long. Their actions were not supported either by the air force (which was grounded by the bad weather), or by infantry, heavy artillery and assault engineers (all those were still dragging behind). As in many other instances, the infantry on foot failed to catch up with the tanks. This was, of course, by no means a problem confined to 46th Army: at that time the overwhelming majority of the Soviet rifle divisions were on foot with horse-drawn train support. The number of motor vehicles available per division (100–150), was barely adequate to cover the most urgent needs. This made those divisions slow to manoeuvre. When that day the Red mechanised spearheads pushed through the gaps in the Axis defence, no one followed closely behind them to fill and exploit those gaps. Perhaps the problem of slow infantry advance would have been partially solved if Malinovsky had employed some (or all) of his cavalry corps in the sector of Shlemin's army. Even though the cavalry formations did not possess heavy artillery either, their advance would not have been handicapped by blocked roads or bad terrain. At that moment, however, the three guards cavalry corps were still recuperating in the rear areas behind the Tisza.

The infantry also had to deal with small enemy pockets left behind. Zhdanov's and Svidov's highly mobile units bypassed them, but once the infantry attempted to follow in their wake, it encountered a strong and unexpected opposition. Thus the 34th Guards Rifle Division remained pinned down at Solt throughout the entire first half of the month, whilst in the morning of 3 November the 316th Rifle Division was forced to deal with the garrison of Dunavecse. The most critical delay, however, occurred in the sector of General Rubanyuk's 10th Guards Rifle Corps.

In the early hours of 3 November the 86th Guards Rifle Division took Gyón, 49th Guards Rifle Division completely secured Örkény, and 109th Guards Rifle Division was engaged northeast of it.[115] This was reported by Shlemin's HQ as a success, but at that moment the distance between Rubanyuk's rifle divisions and Sviridov's brigades was at least 50km, which would lead to problems. Shortly afterwards the 10th Guards Rifle Corps advanced a little farther and 'overcoming stiff enemy resistance' by 9:00 MT reached the Alsónémedi–Inárcs–Újhartyán–Muzsik line.[116] The Soviet mechanised and infantry formations were still separated by a wide gap.

The stiff resistance in question came from the three German battle groups defending the Gyón–Örkény–Újhartyán triangle: 'Wolff' (Fusilier Regiment 'Feldherrnhalle' reinforced with a company of towed anti-tank guns), 'Bradel' (Panzer-Grenadier Regiment 113 reinforced with elements of II/Panzer-Regiment 1 and Anti-Tank Battalion 37) and *'Huppert'* (Panzer-Grenadier Regiment 1 reinforced with self-propelled I/Panzer-Artillery Regiment 73 and part of I/Panzer-Regiment 1). German command was well aware that any further defence of that area would lead to certain destruction of the isolated battle groups and radioed them to pull back to the northeast and assemble in the vicinity of Pilis.[117]

Lieutenant-General Ivan Shlemin, commander of the 46th Army.

Lieutenant-General Ivan Rubanyuk, commander of the 10th Guards Rifle Corps.

The fighting withdrawal of 1 Panzer-Division from the Újhartyán area began at 02:00 BT on 3 November.[118] It was spearheaded by Panzer-Reconnaissance Battalion 1, Panzer-Engineer Battalion 37, as well as by some of the towed howitzer batteries of Panzer-Artillery Regiment 73. The retreat was carried out at night, in cold and wet weather, over bad roads, forested terrain and with minimal visibility. Nevertheless, by dawn the scouts, the combat engineers and the artillerymen succeeded in breaking through the Soviet columns with minimum casualties and securing the designated assembly area.[119] At first light Panzer-Reconnaissance Battalion 1 occupied the perimeter around Monor, Panzer-Engineer Battalion 37 was set to defend the area of Pilis, while the howitzers of Panzer-Artillery Regiment 73 (together with the Hungarian Rocket Launcher Battalion 151) were positioned to the northeast of that line.[120] The withdrawal of the main battle groups, however, proved to be much more difficult than the Germans hoped.

The first to bale out was the battle group of Colonel Bradel. The 35-year-old Knight's Cross holder Ernst-Joachim Bradel was not only a highly decorated officer, but also a very experienced combat leader. As an Eastern Front veteran, he was not new to dangerous situations and was well aware that his regiment must escape the trap as quickly as possible. Like the other battle groups, Bradel's began its withdrawal shortly after midnight of 2/3 November. Right from the outset, however, it found itself in the midst of Sviridov's mechanised columns advancing northwards. This forced the regiment to split into several smaller groups, which, in turn, led to repeated night clashes and skirmishes with the Soviets. (One such clash, which proved nearly fatal for Sviridov's staff, has already been described.) At one point Bradel's armoured halftrack almost collided with a T-34 and with the tank about to deliver a coup de grâce, one of the staff officers, Senior-Lieutenant Markl, knocked the steel monster out.[121]

The life of the commander was saved and the regiment continued its move to the northeast. It accomplished its move rather quickly and by 11:00 BT managed to occupy a defensive line between Monor and Pilis.[122]

The next mission of the reinforced Panzer-Grenadier Regiment 113 was to hold fast. One of the factors that helped the exhausted panzer-grenadiers to stand firm was the powerful support they received from the artillery. The latter was deployed in a way that allowed it to cover all possible routes of enemy approach: II Battalion/Panzer-Artillery Regiment 73 was placed at Monor, while III Battalion of the same regiment took up positions near Pilis.[123]

It was the 7th Battery of the latter battalion that distinguished itself most on 3 November. The battery, deployed to protect the gap in the frontline between Nyáregyháza and Alberti, placed its four 15cm heavy howitzers near a wooden mill southwest of Pilis. By midday the battery's artillery observers, who had set up their post in the mill, reported that a Soviet mechanised unit was approaching in the direction of Nyáregyháza and was about to take cover in a farm situated not far away from the mill. Immediately a powerful artillery barrage involving all neighbouring batteries was called for on the farm and the enemy unit was shattered. The Soviets reportedly lost three T-34 tanks, two armoured cars and two self-propelled guns, while another of their SPGs was damaged.[124]

The breakthrough of Wolff's regiment was much more time-consuming than Bradel's, since it was chosen to act as a rearguard and thus to cover the escape of the main body of 1st Panzer. This crack SA-unit[125] accomplished its mission brillinatly and succeeded in delaying the advance of a considerable part of the Soviet 49th and 109th Guards Rifle Divisions for several crucial hours. Though being slowly but steadily encircled, by 11:40 BT it was still holding the perimeter between Újhartyán and Máté-tanya (a small hamlet half-way between Vasad and Nyáregyháza).[126] In the afternoon the regiment managed to break through the enemy ring and reach the friendly lines at Monor.[127] Upon its arrival it immediately took over the positions of Bradel's men, because they were urgently needed to rescue the endangered Panzer-Grenadier Regiment 1 of Colonel Huppert.

The heaviest burden fell on the shoulders of Huppert's men that day. They failed to break out during the night and when the dawn broke were still in close contact with the enemy. Throughout the day the withdrawal of the 1st continued, but it was considerably hampered by the heavy autumn rain and the repeated Soviet attacks.[128] The battle group, which already had sustained considerable losses during the defence of Örkény,[129] continued to lose a lot of troops; in the evening 46th Army reported that more than 300 German and Hungarian officers and men of the 1 Panzer-Division, 8 and 10 Infantry Divisions (Hung) had been taken prisoner in the Inárcs–Újhartyán area.[130]

Army Group South HQ decided to launch an armoured attack and rescue Huppert's 'wandering pocket' out of this mess.[131] The attack in question commenced in the afternoon, when the Panzer-Grenadier Regiment 113, together with an assigned armoured battle group, struck from the vicinity of Pilis to the southwest. In the evening, the exhausted men of Huppert's group finally reached the lines.[132]

19

The descriptions of the battles on 3 November in the area between Monor and Cegléd would not be complete without mention of the actions of 23 Panzer-Division near Alberti. As we already know, in the morning of 3 November, thanks to the valiant rearguard actions of 24 Panzer-Division, the 23rd Panzer retreated undisturbed to Alberti and occupied a defensive perimeter there. Having achieved some stability in that sector, German command then decided to put the Soviets under pressure by posing a threat to the rear communications of the 109th

Guards Rifle Division that was approaching Nyáregyháza from the south. An order was issued to 23 Panzer-Division to cut the enemy supply route on both sides of Dánszentmiklós (halfway between Örkény and Alberti).[133] Immediately a small armoured battle group ('Fischer') was formed, which consisted of seven tanks and 4 Company/Panzer-Reconnaissance Battalion 23.[134] At 14:00 BT it attacked southwestwards and reached the crossroads near Antonia-major (just south of Dánszentmiklós).[135] The enemy resistance encountered was quite weak and Fischer's group succeeded in capturing the village of Dánszentmiklós, as well as two farmsteads: Antonia-major and Muzsik-tanya. During the same afternoon another attack was launched, this time by the left flank of 23rd Panzer, which struck from Alberti straight to the south. Some 4km south of the town, however, it ran into a strong Soviet infantry formation well-equipped with anti-tank guns and its advance stalled.[136]

Throughout the afternoon the pressure of the 109th Guards Rifle Division gradually increased. The forces responsible for the defence of 23rd Panzer's left flank (the Alberti–Ceglédbercel sector [137]) – the grenadiers of Panzer-Grenadier Regiment 128 and the artillerymen of III Battalion/Panzer-Artillery Regiment 128 – fought back hard. They withstood the intense fire and even claimed the destruction of one Soviet self-propelled gun.[138] The leadership of the division, however, became afraid that the Soviets might strike Group 'Fischer' in the flank and decided to pull it back. An order was issued calling on the units to withdraw to their original jump-off positions during the night.[139] In the evening a rearguard detachment consisting of elements of Panzer-Reconnaissance Battalion 23 and the Anti-Tank Battalion 128 relieved Fischer's group at Muzsik-tanya. The latter immediately moved to Alberti to prepare for another mission.[140]

20

By the end of 3 November the 10th Guards Rifle Corps finally managed to secure the gap between its rifle divisions and the 2nd Guards Mechanised Corps. The enemy forces that had confronted Rubanyuk's troops throughout the day, however, were not destroyed and succeeded in escaping to the northeast. This allowed Kirchner, for the first time since the beginning of the Soviet offensive, to establish a firm and continuous defensive line. It was running from Monor to Cegléd and was erected roughly along the railway connecting these two towns. Its presence now allowed Fretter-Pico to squeeze 46th Army into a much smaller space than Malinovsky and Shlemin had expected and thus to deny them room for manoeuvre. The shape of the front-line now allowed the Germans to consider a counter-attack in the flank of the Soviet wedge. But did Kirchner have enough forces for such a bold strike?

Apparently, Kirchner did not think that the troops under him were sufficient to deliver a decisive blow on the Soviet formation attacking Budapest. This is confirmed by the condition report he sent to Fretter-Pico in the evening. According to it, the Heavy-Panzer Battalion 503 was temporarily out of action due to 'heavy combat losses and maintenance difficulties'. The 1, 23 and 24 Panzer-Divisions could be used only for small-scale offensive operations, because the long battles had drained their strength in both men and material. The tank situation was nearly catastrophic: 1 Panzer-Division had three operational Pz IVs and two assault guns; 23 Panzer-Division was down to one Pz IV, three Panthers, four assault guns and sixteen Jgpz IV tank-destroyers; 24 Panzer-Division fared no better: three Pz IV/70 (A), five Pz IV and two assault guns. Kirchner also requested an urgent delivery of personnel and materiel replacements for the aforementioned divisions. The limited fuel stocks were barely enough for 'insignificant local actions'.[141]

21

There is no doubt that for Shlemin, 3 November was a day of great disappointment. None of his 'wedges' was able to breach the Axis defence and the enemy resistance was increasing with every passing hour. Nevertheless, he decided not to change the main battle plan, but to regroup part of his heavy artillery in the sector of the 10th Guards Rifle Corps and try to break into Pest in the morning. By the end of the day 46th Army's HQ issued the following orders to the troops:

- 37th Rifle Corps was to transfer part of the 7th Artillery Division to the neighbouring 10th Guards Rifle Corps, while with the bulk its forces was to secure Cegléd and the area west of it.
- 10th Guards Rifle Corps with the 7th Artillery Division, and in cooperation with 2nd Guards Mechanised Corps, was to secure Kerepes, Rákosszentmihály and Rákoscsaba; from there it was attack the northern part of Pest.
- 2nd Guards Mechanised Corps was to advance in the direction of Rákosztkerestur and Pest.
- The mission of the 4th Guards Mechanised Corps was the same as on the previous two days: to secure the Dunaharaszti area first and then to drive through Pest from the south as far as Újpest and Rákospalota; at the same time, with specially detached advance teams, to secure the city's main bridges over the Danube.
- With part of its forces the newly arrived 23rd Rifle Corps was to secure the crossings over the Csepeli Dunaág[142] at Ráckeve and Dunaharaszti, while the main body of the corps, in close cooperation with 4th Guards Mechanised Corps, in the morning of 4 November was to capture the southern part of Pest and the city's main bridges.
- 31st Guards Rifle Corps was to secure the entire Danube bank from Tass to the south.[143]

The above plan can be summarised as follows: the Hungarian capital would be taken by coup de main using two powerful combined groups of infantry and armour, with that in the centre (the 10th Guards Rifle Corps and 2nd Guards Mechanised Corps) being the strongest; another predominantly infantry force (37th Rifle Corps) would keep rolling back the Axis defences southeast of Budapest. It was by no means a bad plan, but had one very weak point: in the previous days the frontline had taken the shape of a bulge and now the army's right flank was overextended; the link between 10th Guards and 37th Rifle Corps was thin and was not too well sited for defence. As we shall see, the Germans would exploit this vulnerability to the full.

Troubles would hit 46th Army soon enough, but on the night of 3/4 November Shlemin was still full of optimism that his troops would succeed at last in breaking the Axis defence. What gave him a confidence boost was the arrival of the entire 23rd Rifle Corps, three divisions finally assembled in the sector of 4th Guards Mechanised Corps. Thus on 4 November 'Fortress Budapest' for the first time would be stormed in accordance with the principles of military all-arms doctrine – with infantry, tanks, heavy howitzers, combat engineers and close air support.

As an officer who had a solid practical and theoretical background in military leadership, Shelimin was well aware that in a situation where the enemy still has not exploited all his reserves, only constant aggressive actions are likely to lead to victory. In a fight where the two opponents are of roughly equal strength, it is necessary to make extra efforts not to lose momentum. That is why Shelimin ordered the attacks to continue ceaselessly during the night. There would be no respite for the defenders of Budapest!

22

The first formation that began to implement Shlemin's orders was 37th Rifle Corps, which under the cloak of night continued to envelop Cegléd. General Kolchuk's troops also succeeded in making the first breach in the Axis defensive perimeter: at around 21:00 BT on 3 November 24 Panzer-Division reported that two Soviet infantry companies had infiltrated into the southwestern part of the town, but were stopped by a fierce German counter-attack. The Soviet pressure, however, continued to grow and this forced the defenders to blow up the bridges over the Új árok canal and fall back to the town.[144]

In the early hours of 4 November 108th Guards Rifle Division, supported by 1505th Self-Propelled Artillery Regiment, entered the southern edge of the town where it immediately became engaged in heavy street fighting. They now learned that the Germans and the Hungarians had transformed Cegléd into a mini-fortress: the attackers encountered prepared obstacles, some of the key buildings had been converted into strongholds and there were wooden bunkers at the street crossings.[145] The defenders also had strong fire support.

The stiff resistance forced the Soviets to change their tactics and in the morning the division began to outflank the place. The 311th Guards Rifle Regiment bypassed Cegléd to the east; the 305th Guards Rifle Regiment captured the railway station and reached the western limits, while the 308th enveloped the town from the west, thereby protecting the left flank of the division. Before noon the 311th and 305th Regiments launched a simultaneous all-out assault on Cegléd, which proved to be a success: at 16:00 BT they captured the centre of the town and three hours later the settlement was completely cleared of its Axis defenders. Up to 400 of them were reportedly killed or wounded, while another 90 were taken prisoner.[146]

The unit that perhaps distinguished itself most in the bitter street fighting for Cegléd was the 1st Battalion of the 311th Guards Rifle Regiment. Advancing together with the open-topped SU-76s of the 1505th Regiment, the battalion captured one anti-aircraft and one mortar battery and then successfully repulsed a counter-attack of two enemy companies. The hero of the day was Junior-Sergeant K. Alexeev. When his platoon commander was wounded, Alexeev took up the command. At one of the intersections they collided with a group of Axis soldiers. Fire was exchanged and Alexeev's men were quicker and succeeded in killing several of the enemy troops from a close range, surrounded the rest and forced them to surrender. During that action Alexeev himself personally killed eight enemy troops and took three more prisoner.[147]

In a desperate attempt to restore the situation, General Kirchner brought in reinforcements: the Grenadier-Regiment 42 (of the German 46.Infantry Division) by midday was urgently trucked to the sector of 24 Panzer-Division. At around 16:00 MT the regiment mounted a fierce counter-attack ('a battalion of infantry supported by 10 tanks', according to the Soviet reports) from the direction of Varnyas (a small place just northeast of Cegléd) against the outer flank of 311th Guards Rifle Regiment. The guardsmen withstood the German pressure and repulsed it.[148] Their excellent performance was acknowledged even by Kirchner, who put the failure of the counter-attack down to 'tough enemy resistance'.[149]

One of the reasons cited by the staff of LVII Panzer Corps for the fall of Cegléd (as usual) was the low morale and defeatism of the Hungarian forces. As one of Kirchner's reports stated,

> … the just-arrived replacements for the 5th and 20th Hungarian Infantry Divisions are infected by communist ideology. The Hungarian officers, despite their willingness, are unable to prevent the flight of the troops and their desertion to the enemy.[150]

The commander of the Magyar 20 Infantry Division did not agree with such assessments and after the war gave his own view on the morale of the Axis troops defending Cegléd:

On the evening of 4 November, I visited General Nostitz,[151] who was in his headquarters north of Cegléd. That encounter with this neither friendly nor cold, neither polite nor rude German general is not one of the pleasantest memories of my life! When I entered his room, he greeted me with the question: 'Where are your troops from here to here,' and pointed to the area on the map west of Cegléd. After hearing this, I wanted to ask him the same question regarding Nagykőrös and Cegléd. Because when he mentioned that hundreds of healthy Hungarian soldiers were retreating without orders to Budapest, I also had seen German troops in retreat who, without engaging in combat operations, just fired one or two shots from time to time. But they were not walking, they were not ragged, unarmed and were not worn down as our Honveds, they were sitting in trucks, they had weapons in their hands and drove in convoys. That was the difference, but I couldn't tell Nostitz this, who told me not only with words, but also with a gesture, that 'all' were gone. I told him that the last combat-ready troops of the division, the battle group Bottond, were still holding the assigned defensive position. Although they consisted of only about two [infantry] battalions and three artillery battalions, I was sure they would not run away! On the other hand, I had to admit that I had no more soldiers west of Ceglèd and that I couldn't send more there. He shared my opinion that it didn't make sense to catch the men who run away from the troops at night and put them together again with the fighting troops on the next day at the front. They would desert again on the following night …[152]

There is further evidence of bad morale amongst the German troops beyond Tömöry's testimony; the widespread looting carried out by many of the retreating Landsers is a case in point. One of them, Adolf Shihel [sic] of Artillery Battalion 844, confessed during his interrogation that in Cegléd he had seen 'many German soldiers crushing the showcases and taking away the goods from the shops. All jewelry and watch stores were plundered.'[153]

23

The mission of the day for the 59th Guards Rifle Division was, in cooperation with 109th Guards Rifle Division (of the 10th Guards Rifle Corps) to capture Alberti. The jump-off point of the attack of the 59th Guards, which began at 06:00 MT, was the local railway line running west of Cegléd. The advance of the guardsmen through the cold semi-darkness of the morning of 4 November was initially successful and by 11:00 MT they were already fighting for Irsa, the southeastern suburb of Alberti.[154] But there their progress was halted by the mobile German defence.[155]

All attempts of the Soviet guardsmen to take the town by pincer attacks were beaten back by the fierce resistance of its defenders (23 Panzer-Division). When in the afternoon the 59th Guards Rifle Division finally managed to drive a wedge between Alberti and Ceglédbercel, 23rd Panzer began repeatedly to counter-attack with armour and infantry. At 16:30 MT about two infantry companies, accompanied by six tanks, advanced from the vicinity of Hill 147 (north of Alberti) to the southeast. Some fifteen minutes later another four tanks attempted to drive the Soviets to the south near Hill 193 (east of Alberti). Of course, all these Axis attacks were repulsed.[156]

At around 17:00 MT the Germans tried again, counter-attacking the positions of the 179th Guards Rifle Regiment east of Dánosi puszta (manor) just south of Alberti with two Pz IV tanks and seven armoured half-tracks.[157] The counter-attack was repelled and both tanks were reportedly knocked out. At the end of the day the 59th Guards claimed to have inflicted much greater losses on the enemy than it suffered itself,[158] but this did not help it win the struggle for Alberti. By nightfall this important junction on the way to the capital was still firmly in Axis hands.

24

In the centre of 46th Army's front, Shlemin's strongest 'shock group' (the 10th Guards Rifle Corps and 2nd Guards Mechanised Corps) experienced similar difficulties.

During the day 109th Guards Rifle Division advanced on a broad front between Monor and Alberti. By 11:00 MT one of its regiments reached Nyáregyháza, while another reached Dánosi puszta (just south of Alberti). Their forward detachments even succeeded in cutting the Cegléd–Budapest railway line some 3km west of Alberti.[159] Neither of the two regiments, however, was able to gain more ground during the rest of the day owing to the stiff enemy resistance and frequent counter-attacks of armour-supported infantry. In the meantime, the third regiment approached Monor and spent the rest of the day trying to capture it.

'Stiff enemy resistance' was not just an empty phrase. It was a realistic appraisal by the command of the 109th Guards. Since the morning that division had been embroiled in a titanic battle with elements of the two of the best German panzer divisions: the 1st and the 23rd. The latter repeatedly counter-attacked with small armoured battle groups, which, according to Kirchner, were very successful in inflicting heavy casualties on the Soviets.[160] At dawn on 4 November one such battle group of the 23 Panzer-Division attacked from the vicinity of Alberti to the west and struck the 109th Guards on its undefended eastern flank. The outcome was a painful defeat for the Soviet division and the Germans captured a fine amount of booty: three anti-tank guns, six heavy and seven light machine guns, 40 rifles and sub-machine guns and one German-built truck. Forty-nine dead bodies were counted on the battlefield and two Soviet soldiers were taken prisoner. As result, not only were the Russians temporarily pushed away from Alberti (to the west), but also the Germans managed to restore their defensive perimeter around Irsa.[161]

In the morning of the same day another small armoured battle group comprising six tanks, four armoured halftracks and a self-propelled artillery battalion (I /Panzer-Artillery Regiment 128) was tasked with freeing the road from Alberti to Pilis. The group was halted by an enemy anti-tank position 1km short of the town and one German assault gun went up in flames instantly. The Germans fired back and destroyed two Soviet anti-tank guns. Then the *Wespe* and *Hummel* self-propelled howitzers were brought into play and unleashed hell on the enemy troops that had assembled in the forest 1.5km northwest of Alberti. The latter reportedly sustained heavy losses and thus the Soviets were softened up. Now the German armour was able to resume its drive forward and the small Soviet pockets encountered in the process were quickly eliminated. Two more anti-tank guns were destroyed shortly after the attack was resumed and afterwards, near Pilis, another four were captured. At 10:00 BT the group finally reached Pilis where contact with 1 Panzer-Division was established. Thus the mission was accomplished and the precious armoured vehicles were free to be employed in another critical sector.[162]

1 Panzer-Division did not join the offensive actions immediately because in the morning of 4 November Huppert's Panzer-Grenadier Regiment 1, which, as we already know, reached Pilis only at the end of the previous day, was still taking over the positions of Panzer-Engineer Battalion 37 and Bradel's Panzer-Grenadier Regiment 113 in the vicinity of the town. Once Bradel's regiment was relieved, it was immediately used to form a 'shock group' comprising all of the operational armoured vehicles of the 'oak leaf division'.[163] Some relief! Thus a new Battle Group 'Bradel' came into existence that consisted of I Battalion/Panzer-Regiment 1, a company of armoured halftracks of Panzer-Grenadier Regiment 113, Panzer-Engineer Battalion 37 and most of I Battalion/Panzer-Artillery Regiment 73.[164] At around midday it launched a powerful counter-attack against a combat team of the 109th Guards Rifle Division that had infiltrated through the forest southeast of Pilis and eliminated it.[165]

In the afternoon the 109th Guards made a penetration east of Nyáregyháza and in the evening its left-flank regiment even infiltrated into the southern limits of Monor.[166] Thus by the end of 4 November the frontline of the division was running from Irsa to Monor, but the Germans were

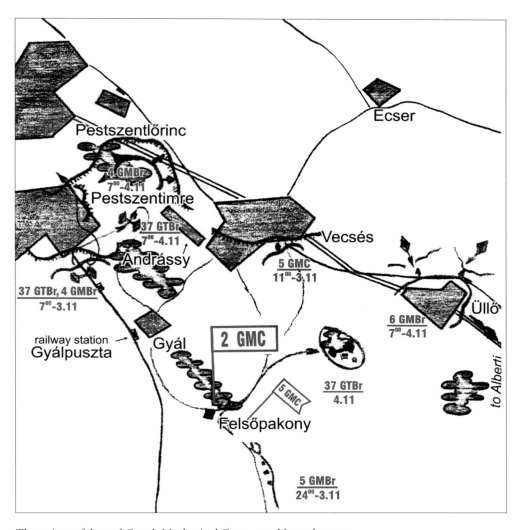

The actions of the 2nd Guards Mechanised Corps on 4 November 1944.

still in possession of all major strongholds in that segment of the Cegléd–Budapest railway line (Irsa, Alberti, Pilis and Monor). Throughout the day their repeated counter-attacks succeeded in wearing down the units of the division and now its front was not only overstretched, but also riddled with holes. Kirchner would not miss the chance to exploit them and the next day would launch a resolute counter-attack that would tear apart the 109th Guards' front, advance deep into Shlemin's rear and thereby put the final nail in the coffin of Malinovsky's Budapest offensive.

25

The town of Üllő, so desperately defended by 6th Guards Mechanised Brigade throughout 3 November, continued to exercise both Soviet and German commands the next day. Initially, it seemed that the Germans would prevail: at 03:00 BT on 4 November Panzer-Grenadier Division 'Feldherrnhalle' and a battle group of 8 SS-Cavalry-Division 'Florian Geyer' simultaneously attacked the place from the southeast and west.[167] The troops of the 6th Guards

An SS-trooper of 8 SS-Cavalry Division 'Florian Geyer' in the trenches of the 'Attila' line, autumn 1944. (Mirko Bayerl)

Mechanised Brigade fought intensely and managed to contain the fierce two-pronged assault. As later Breith reported, the German attack was called off because of the 'unexpectedly strong enemy resistance encountered at the edge of the town'.[168] The defeat did not discourage the SS-cavalrymen, the SA-troops and their commanders and they began to prepare for another try. They did not know that the 49th Guards Rifle Division was approaching from the south and its sudden appearance would turn the tables in favour of the Soviets.

Having set out from Vasad at around midnight, 49th Guards Rifle Division arrived in the vicinity of Üllő just in time to prevent it from falling back into German hands. Right from the early morning, the guardsmen found themselves involved in furious clashes with the Germans. perhaps the most fearsome one took place at around 08:20 MT. The right flank of the division came under a surprise attack of enemy infantry of regimental strength accompanied by 20 tanks, which advanced on Üllő from the east.[169] Sources from each side disagree on what happened next. According to a Soviet report, the attack was repulsed.[170] According to the German reports, one Soviet regiment was caught off guard while approaching Üllő from the south. It sustained heavy losses and one of its battalions was completely destroyed.[171] Whatever the truth, this attack was only a prelude to the hellish day that awaited the men of the 49th Guards.

Immediately after, the Soviet division turned to the west and entered Üllő . In the meantime Breith struck again: his 'Feldherrnhalle' and 'Florian Geyer' divisions launched their usual attack from two directions (western and southeastern).[172] This time they succeeded in recapturing a considerable part of the town and reached its centre.[173] The Soviet response was immediate and resolute. The guardsmen of the rifle division and the mechanised brigade formed assault groups and began to push the Germans back. Fighting street-to-street, house-to-house, by the next morning the assault groups succeeded in completely retaking the central and the northern parts of the town.[174]

Apart from the fierce Soviet resistance, it was the critical situation at the nearby town of Vecsés that forced Breith to call off the attack on Üllő again. During the struggle for Vecsés the elements of 'Feldherrnhalle' and 'Florian Geyer'[175] had already sustained heavy losses, and fearing that the bloodbath in Üllő would bleed these two crack divisions white, he ordered the attacking troops to pull back and establish a defensive perimeter along the northern limits of the town.[176] His anxiety was compounded by an intelligence report predicting that the Soviets were gathering together the 2nd and 4th Guards Mechanised Corps and on the following morning would use them to deliver a powerful pincer attack from the vicinity of Vecsés in a northerly direction, to enter Budapest from the east and northeast.[177] Fretter-Pico and Breith decided to pull the battle group of 'Florian Geyer' out of Üllő and assemble the entire SS-Cavalry-Division in the Pestszentimre–Vecsés sector to counter probable enemy assaults from Gyál to the north.[178] In turn, the Magyar 1 Armoured Division, which had enjoyed a short rehabilitation at Rákoscsaba, was ordered back to the front and tasked with the defence of the Vecsés–Üllő sector.[179]

Two officers of the 1509th Self-Propelled Artillery Regiment (2nd Guards Mechanised Corps) died heroic deaths during the gruesome battle for Üllő on 4 November: the regimental commander, the 35-year-old Lieutenant-Colonel Mikhail Laugutin, and the deputy political officer, the 35-year-old Major Semyon Sulin. On 24 March 1945 both officers were posthumously awarded the distinction of Hero of the Soviet Union.

Laugutin led his men very skilfully and contributed to the repulsing of three enemy counter-attacks. His SU-76 self-propelled gun was constantly in action and Laugutin and his crew were credited with seven tank kills.[180] Eventually their SPG took a direct hit and exploded killing all the men inside.

Sulin, like his commander, was constantly with the troops, encouraging them all the time to hold out and fight back. When during one of the attacks the Germans were about to encircle a Soviet unit, he jumped into a self-propelled gun and personally led a counter-attack. The SU-76s closed in on the enemy and opened up devastating fire from point blank range. Sulin's SPG reportedly destroyed two tanks and up to 50 enemy troops. Sulin himself was killed during the action.[181]

A knocked-out Soviet SU-76M self-propelled gun, Hungary, autumn 1944. (Dénes Bernád)

26

The key element of Shlemin's 'shock group', 2nd Guards Mechanised Corps, resumed its offensive in the early hours of 4 November. As on the previous day, a task force consisting of the 4th Guards Mechanised Brigade, 251st Self-Propelled Artillery Regiment, 37th Guards Tank Brigade and 30th Guards Heavy Tank Regiment was aimed at the heart of the capital.

Shortly after midnight the 4th Guards Mechanised Brigade, coupled with the 251st Self-Propelled Artillery Regiment, launched an attack on Gyál, but at around 05:00 MT 13 Panzer-Division counter-attacked and pushed the guardsmen out of the village.[182] In the morning, however, the Soviet task force struck again. Having left a small detachment at the southeastern limits of Pestszentimre to protect its extended left flank, at 07:00 MT the bulk of the task force launched an attack to the northwest towards Pestszentlőrinc.[183] The powerful thrust of about 30 Soviet tanks supported by infantry (presumably the 4th Guards Mechanised Brigade) ejected the German combat outpost from the northern part of Gyál and advanced. Further to the east, another Soviet combat team (presumably 37th Guards Tank Brigade) forced the Axis units protecting the southwestern approaches of Vecsés to fall back to the western and southwestern outskirts of the town. The desired breakthrough towards Budapest failed to materialise: shortly afterwards the Soviets were halted by stiff Axis resistance on both sides of Felsőhalom.[184] Soon enough they would realise that they had fallen into a trap.

Having halted Sviridov's armoured avalanche, the defenders (elements of the 13th Panzer and Hungarian assault guns and infantry of Billnitzer's group) counter-attacked and recaptured the tactically important Hill 129 (just to the northeast of Pestszentimre). Reportedly, during that battle 20 out of 35 Soviet tanks were destroyed and an infantry battalion accompanying them was completely decimated.[185]

The semi-forested area between Pestszentimre, Pestszentlőrinc, Vecsés and Andrássy[186] witnessed some very savage fighting throughout the rest of the day, but the Soviets gained no more ground. Just the contrary, they were forced to switch over to the defensive. Now came the moment for General Schmidhuber to undertake a powerful armoured thrust of his own. In the afternoon his 13 Panzer-Division attacked with tanks from Pestszentimre to the southeast with the objective of securing the northern bank of the Nagy Lecsapoló canal that flowed along the southern limits of Vecsés and Gyál. If the Germans had met their objective, they definitely would have succeeded in encircling Sviridov's task force; but they had not. Having advanced some 3km, the panzers were halted at Hill 120 (just east of Gyál) by determined Soviet resistance (presumably the 4th Guards Mechanised Brigade).[187]

By the afternoon it was clear to Sviridov that the main body of his corps was stuck in a bottleneck. His left flank (4th Guards Mechanised Brigade) was now under pressure, but still worse, the constant threat hanging over the corps' right flank (the repeated German attacks in the vicinity of

The disposition of the Axis and Soviet troops south of Pest by the end of 4 November 1944.

Vecsés and Üllő) forced Sviridov to pull 37th Guards Tank Brigade out of the battle and move it to Alsóhalom as his reserve.[188] The taking of Budapest was no longer an objective.

The relatively fresh 5th Guards Mechanised Brigade was just a little more successful that day. Having also started its attack at 07:00 MT, it quickly crossed the anti-tank ditch south of Vecsés and by 11:00 MT penetrated into the southern part of the town. There it was somehow halted by the troops of 8 SS-Cavalry-Division 'Florian Geyer'.[189] By that time the brigade was joined by the 260th Guards Rifle Regiment (of 86th Guards Rifle Division), which had just arrived from the south.[190] Meanwhile the Germans (the 'Florian Geyer' and 'Feldherrnhalle' divisions) brought in reinforcements, launched a resolute counter-attack and chased the Soviets out of the town.[191]

In the afternoon the Soviets (presumably 260th Guards Rifle Regiment) made another try. This time they attacked from the southeast, probably in an attempt to outflank the town from the east.

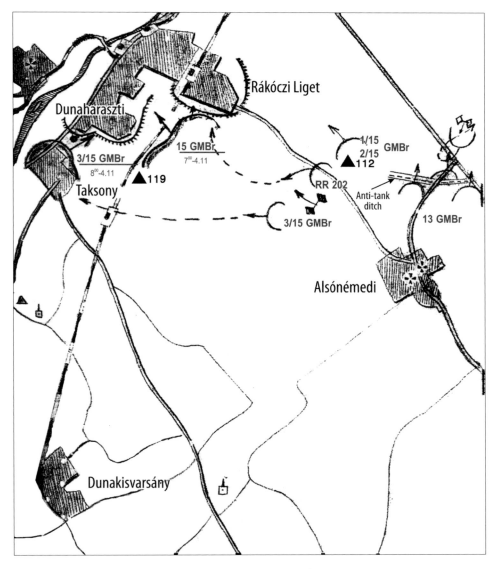

The actions of the 4th Guards Mechanised Corps on 4 November 1944.

But at around 16:00 near Hill 137 (3km northeast of Vecsés) the regiment was counter-attacked by German infantry and 30 tanks and was driven back to the southern edge of the town.[192]

There was no respite for the Axis defenders of Vecsés: at 17:00 MT the 5th Guards Mechanised Brigade attacked again with some of its units and succeeded in capturing the western edge of the town.[193] Thus the battle for Vecsés ended in stalemate: the Soviets were unable capture the place, the Germans could not secure it completely. The struggle for the town would resume on the following morning and would continue with growing ferocity for two more days.

The 86th Guards Rifle Division spent 4 November trying to survive in the narrow bottleneck between Gyál and Vecsés. The division left its last assembly area (just north of Alsónémedi) shortly after midnight and moved northeastwards with a forced march. It arrived in the sector of 2nd Guards Mechanised Corps on the morning of 4 November and immediately launched simultaneous attacks to the west/southwest (to recapture Gyál) and to the north (to take Vecsés). The coordinated actions with the units of Sviridov's corps produced very little results, however.

27

At Shlemin's left flank another 'shock group' (the 4th Guards Mechanised Corps and 23rd Rifle Corps) launched an all-out assault on the Axis positions in a final attempt to break into Pest.

The arrival of the long-awaited 23rd Rifle Corps allowed General Zhdanov to employ at last the full potential of his mechanised corps and send into battle all four brigades. The news that the rifle divisions had caught up with his tanks definitely lifted a heavy burden from the General's shoulders, since for a third day in a row his corps was trapped in that bottleneck (Bugyi–Dunaharaszti–Ócsa) that offered almost no room for manoeuvre. But by the end of 3 November the 68th Guards Rifle Division strengthened Zhdanov's spearhead, 316th Rifle Division (with two regiments) took over the duties of 36th Guards Tank Brigade of garrisoning Bugyi, while the 99th Rifle Division was deployed in Alsónémedi, thereby securing the rear of the first echelon.

The failure to secure the Dunaharaszti–Taksony area on the previous day taught Colonel Andrianov, commander of 15th Guards Mechanised Brigade, an important lesson: it is always preferable to outflank a stronghold rather than undertake a frontal assault. Now reinforced with the 202nd Guards Rifle Regiment (of the 68th Guards Rifle Division), he sent two battalions of the latter towards the southeastern edge of Dunaharaszti to envelop the enemy position to the south. At the same time, two of the brigade's rifle battalions (1st and 2nd) attacked along the road in the direction of the eastern and southeastern limits of Dunaharaszti. After some heavy fighting, by 11:00 MT the combined task force of the 'Swallow' Brigade's tanks and the riflemen of the 202nd Regiment reached the railway box that was 1.5km south of Dunaharaszti.

By that time the brigade's 1st and 2nd Battalions, which had advanced along the road to Dunaharaszti, reached Hill 114, where they were halted by the committed resistance of the Hungarian paratroopers. The hill itself was captured thanks to the courageous action of Major Lyakhovets, commander of the 37th Guards Tank Regiment, who, together with seven soldiers, stormed the Magyar positions and held them until the main force arrived.[194]

The fighting throughout the rest of the day continued to be very heavy and this is acknowledged by the Axis accounts. The Hungarian Parachute Captain Edömér Tassonyi gives us his recollection of the clash:

> The Russian attack at Dunaharaszti also collapsed, within assault distance, after a gun battle lasting many hours; there the front-line was firmly kept, many Russian tanks were knocked out. After midnight the Russians stopped the attack and withdrew their tanks … Our losses then, as well as later, were heavy, mainly because of the endless mortar fire.[195]

Even though the powerful Soviet attack on Rákócziliget and Dunaharaszti did not accomplish its objective, it nevertheless managed to conceal the pincer attack of Andrianov's 3rd Rifle Battalion, which early in the morning attacked Taksony. By 08:00 MT the battalion had completely secured the village.[196] The sudden appearance of the Soviets on their right flank was undoubtedly a nasty surprise for the exhausted Hungarian paratroopers and the troops of 22 SS-Cavalry-Division.

As on the previous day, 13th Guards Mechanised Brigade continued to hold the tip of the Soviet penetration and in particular the miniature bridgehead on the northern side of the anti-tank ditch south of Gyál Laslza major. Determined to eliminate that threat at any cost, the Germans (22 SS-Cavalry-Division) resumed their attacks against the bridgehead early in the morning of 4 November. At 08:15 MT a battalion-sized attack supported by eight tanks and self-propelled guns slammed the Soviet positions. After nearly two hours of fierce close-quarter fighting the German assault was repelled. Throughout the day men of the SS division made several more attempts to push the brigade as far as Alsónémedi, but they were beaten also back.[197]

The area in the vicinity of Gyál saw some heavy fighting as well. At around midnight on 3/4 November the 14th Guards Mechanised Brigade, now coupled with the 200th Guards Rifle Regiment (of 68th Guards Rifle Division), began to advance northwards along the Kecskemét–Budapest railway line. At 00:30 MT the spearhead of the 'Elephant Brigade' reached the southern limits of Gyál where it encountered heavy resistance. Throughout the rest of the night the guardsmen of both units slowly infiltrated into the village, but when the morning came it was still far from secured.

The 1st Rifle Battalion, operating on the brigade's left flank, reached the railway station of Gyál, but since it faced strong enemy resistance there, the battalion commander decided to bypass Gyálpuszta to the west and continue the advance in the direction of Hill 122. The manoeuvre proved to be successful and before midday the battalion was already on its way to Kossuth-Ferenc.[198]

In the meantime the 2nd Rifle Battalion stormed Gyál and by 04:30 MT had managed to capture two blocks. It immediately signalled that the tanks and self-propelled guns of 2nd Guards Mechanised Corps were standing on the far side of the irrigation canal running southeast of the village. Nevertheless, when at 05:00 MT the German garrison defending Gyál launched a counter-attack to restore the situation, Sviridov's tanks opened fire and most of the shells struck the positions of the battalion. The result of this friendly fire was five wounded Soviet soldiers. The bizarre occurrences involving Sviridov's troops did not end there.

After they finished with their 'blue on blue', the tanks and self-propelled guns of 2nd Guards Mechanised Corps crossed the canal and entered Gyál from the east. Shortly afterwards the Germans counter-attacked again and Sviridov's troops fled in panic, leaving behind two intact SU-85 tank destroyers, which apparently had been abandoned by their crews. Then the 2nd Rifle Battalion the 'Elephant Brigade' counter-attacked in turn and managed to recapture the two self-propelled guns. (One was fully operational, the other had a broken track.) Several skilled artillerymen of the battalion under Senior Sergeant Ponomarev immediately manned both guns and used them against the enemy until their ammunition was spent. After that sentries were put to guard the 'booty'.

Heaving repulsed the enemy attack, the brigade continued to clear the village, house-by-house. At 13:00 MT most of Gyál was already in the hands of the 'elephants'. By that time the spearheads had reached a point 400m south of Hill 122. But the brigade alone was too weak to continue its drive forward on to Budapest and this turned out to be the deepest point of Zhdanov's penetration.

In an attempt to reinforce the night offensive of 14th Brigade, at around midnight of 3/4 November General Zhdanov ordered 36th Guards Tank Brigade to join the 'elephants'. The

A unit of Soviet heavy artillery moves on Budapest, late autumn 1944. It is using fully-tracked Ya-12 tractors to tow 152mm ML-20 gun-howitzers. Note the considerable distance between the vehicles, which was mandatory, because of the frequent Axis aerial attacks on the Soviet columns in the immediate rear of the front. (Author's Collection)

tanks of the 36th Guards set out for Gyál at 02:40 MT on 4 November, but once they reached Ócsa they were halted (probably by a traffic jam). The brigade resumed its forward movement only at 11:00 MT, but it was hardly an orderly march. There were no good roads around, the terrain was marshy and softened by the rains and this forced the tanks to use the railway embankment to reach the battlefield. Tank by tank, battalion by battalion, they rolled slowly to the north until all of them assembled near a farm situated 1.5km south of Gyál. However, very few of the guardsmen saw action on that day; at 14:30 MT a tank company of the 1st Tank Battalion was ordered to enter the village and give full support to 14th Brigade. Shortly afterwards the company was engaged in combat approximately 1km southwest of the Gyálpuszta railway station.[199] But it was too little, too late; by then it was already evident that Zhdanov's corps would not be able to penetrate into the Hungarian capital.

28

Many soldiers of 14th Brigade distinguished themselves on that day during the battle for Gyál. Amongst them, for instance, was the crew of the T-34 tank commanded by Junior-Lieutenant Isakov, protecting the brigade's left flank. The brave crew not only beat off ten enemy counterattacks, but later, when an attack was ordered, their tank was the first to crush the enemy defensive position, destroying an assault gun, four machine gun nests, two field guns and killing ten soldiers in the process.

Private Kashen Bulatbekov, an infantryman of the 2nd Battalion, faced a counterattacking group of Germans and Hungarians during the street fighting in Gyál. He let them get nearer and then from close range, opened fire with his sub-machine gun, killing or wounding 18 of the attackers and taking two prisoners.

Another infantryman of the 2nd Battalion – Private A.D. Konovalov – performed a similar remarkable feat of bravery. Like Bulatbekov, he allowed the attackers to get close and then managed to put out of action six of them with hand grenades and shot down three others with his rifle.

Junior-Sergeant A.F. Maslov was forced to deal with a different kind of enemy. As a gunner in a M17 Lend-Lease halftrack, he was in charge of the anti-aircraft protection of the brigade. He did his job well and from 2 to 4 November succeeded with his quadruple .50 calibre machine gun in shooting down two Bf-109s.[200]

29

For the vast majority of the population of Budapest the news that the capital had become a frontline city came as a shock. There was no need of official announcements; from 2 November onwards they could hear the constant thunder of the artillery guns. The 'scenes of the deepest peace' seen by Friessner during his visit to Szálasi on 28 October were gone now. Anxiety and the beginnings of panic began to spread amongst the residents of the capital; some shops closed and the traffic began to disappear. The stream of refugees arriving from the south and southeast made the situation even more depressing. Questions without answers were bubbling in everyone's mind: How long it is going to last? Will we survive?

On 4 November an event took place that added extra stress to the already nerve-wracking situation: at midday three sections of the Margit Bridge, in the segment between Pest and the Margit Island, were blown up. During that part of the day the traffic was dense and the explosion claimed the lives of a 'considerable number of civilians'; two full streetcars fell into the river.[201] Erwin Leichter, a 21-year-old christened Jew from Budapest, was one of those who witnessed the accident:

> … I sat in the garden enjoying the picture-postcard view of Budapest and its well-known landmarks … I could see the widest bridge on the Danube, the multi-spanned Margaret Bridge … As I watched, something extraordinary seemed to happen. It seemed that two or three spans of the bridge began very slowly to sink downwards at the midspan. The streetcars stopped moving, and then, ever so slowly, began sliding on the downslopes towards the water. I could see buses, cars and people trying to scramble up the slopes; then suddenly everything cascaded into the river with the collapsing spans. Only then did the sound of the explosion and the pressure wave hit me … By accident, the Germans had blown up the bridge.[202]

With the approach of the 46th Army to Budapest, demolition plans were laid by the Germans, which included destruction of the Danube bridges. On 4 November 1944, with fierce battles going on in the suburbs, German combat engineers unintentionally set off the charges under the Margit Bridge. Several cars, trucks and even two full trams were on the bridge when the accident happened. (Dénes Bernád)

General von Greiffenberg, the Plenipotentiary General of Wehrmacht in Hungary, meets Friessner at the airport of Budapest, autumn 1944. (Bundesarchiv)

Amongst the casualties were about 40 German combat engineers.[203] An investigation revealed that the blast had occurred because something (or someone) had ignited by accident the fuse of the charges that the engineers had been installing under the bridge.

It seemed that the only person in Budapest who remained calm during those so dramatic first days of November 1944 was Szálasi. On 3 November he summoned the country's political elite to the Marble Hall of the Royal Palace in Buda to take an oath as 'a leader of the nation'. His post-acceptance speech was ridiculous as usual; most of it was dedicated to the relations between Hungary and Japan, then to other things, and despite the fact that the thunder of the guns could already be heard in the Castle District area, he made no comment on the military situation. He did that later, with Friessner and von Greiffenberg (the Plenipotentiary General of Wehrmacht in Hungary). Szálasi's realistic opinion was that in the long run Budapest could not be defended because Hitler had intervened in Hungarian affairs 'too late' and the only thing that could be done now was 'damage limitation'. During the next three months one million or so Budapestians would contribute to that 'damage limitation' with their own suffering.

30

Much to the amazement of people all over the world, Malinovsky was stopped at the gates and the Magyar capital did not fall. On 7 November the *New York Times* ran an article buried deep inside the paper:

> Fighting along the Eastern Front slackened generally today – the twenty-seventh anniversary of the Russian Revolution – with Moscow announcing only that 'there were no essential changes on the front' and that yesterday sixteen German tanks were knocked out in scattered local engagements.

The American newspaper was not the only one that pushed the struggle for Hungary to the back pages. By the end of the first week of November the communiqués from the Hungarian battlefield disappeared from the other leading world newspapers. The battle of Budapest was no longer headline news.

10

CRISIS MANAGEMENT

1

By the evening of 4 November it was already crystal clear to everyone in both camps that the Soviet offensive had shot its bolt. Not only would Budapest not fall, now all signs were pointing to a possible German counteroffensive somewhere in the flatland east or southeast of the capital. The Soviet commanders were experienced enough to foresee the looming danger on Shlemin's right flank and they knew that the time had come for preventive measures.

This new situation was tactically and strategically fraught with difficulty for the Soviets. The 7th Guards Army had managed to capture only Szolnok, while Tápióbicske was still in enemy hands. Thus the attack zone of the Front's left wing had become relatively narrow and the right flank of 46th Army remained unprotected. The configuration of the frontline now enabled Friessner to launch counter-attacks on the vulnerable flanks of Shlemin's mechanised and rifle formations, which were far extended towards Budapest. An immediate change of plan was necessary. Shtemenko recalls how the decision was taken to halt the head-on assault on Budapest and to begin an enveloping manoeuvre:

> By the evening of 3 November the 4th and 2nd Guards mechanised corps, commanded by V.I. Zhdanov and K.V. Sviridov, were within 10–15km of Budapest, in the south and southeast respectively.
>
> But with that, the advance of the Soviet troops came to an end. As our reconnaissance units reported, the enemy had taken advantage of the temporary halt of the 4th Ukrainian Front west of Uzhgorod [Ungvár] and near Chop [Csap], to transfer three panzer divisions from there to the battle zone of 46th Army. And we were soon made aware of this: our attacks in the relatively narrow zone beyond the Tisza met with resolute resistance. They were repeated, but got nowhere. As it turned out, the enemy's defences in this sector had been doubled and no one could guarantee they would not been increased even more. After all, the Budapest area was not isolated from the rest of the country or the other sectors of the front, hence the enemy was able to bring up his reserves to this area.
>
> At the General staff we were considering the options. The decision to strike beyond the Tisza had been made by the Supreme Commander personally, and no one would dare to cancel it or correct it. But we had to save the situation.
>
> The way out, as we saw it, was to expand the front considerably and increase the vigour of the offensive by Malinovsky's forces. Whereas according to Stalin's decision the offensive

was to be made chiefly by 46th Army on the front's left flank, the General Staff's thinking called for the forces of the centre also to increase pressure on the enemy and break through his defences. Thus while we the General Staff officers did not dispute the substance of the Supreme Commander's decision, we figured that it would be much more difficult for the enemy to organise a strong defence on a broad front than on a narrow one. Also, an offensive on a broad front would open up possibilities for taking Budapest not only with the forces of the front's left flank alone (the 46th Army) from the southwest, as had been planned earlier, but with the forces in the centre coming from the east and northeast. Under the circumstances this pincer movement would be more effective. Also, stepping up pressure in the middle of the 2nd Ukrainian Front's zone of attack would help Petrov's armies [the 4th Ukrainian Front] to break through the bottleneck at Csop and improve conditions for their advance.

Malinovsky agreed with the General Staff's suggestions – they coincided with his views – and said that the front's military council would support us vis-à-vis the Supreme Commander.

On 4 November the General Staff reported to the Stavka on its ideas. In so doing, we cited the suggestions of the 2nd Ukrainian Front's military council, which had just been sent to Moscow. Stalin did not object. He instructed us to issue a directive and to step up executions of the measures aimed at the capture of Budapest.[1]

The directive was signed by Stalin at 20:00 MT and was immediately cabled to Malinovsky's HQ:

The Stavka regards that the offensive toward Budapest, on a narrow front and using only two mechanised corps and a negligible quantity of infantry, may lead to unjustified losses and expose the forces advancing in this direction to a blow on their flank from the northeast.

Stemming from this, the Stavka orders:

1. Bring up more rapidly the Front's right wing (the 7th Guards, and the 53rd, 27th and 40th Armies) to the western bank of the Tisza river, so as to carry out an offensive on a broad front and crush the enemy's Budapest grouping with a blow by the Front's right wing from the north and northeast, combined with a blow by the Front's left wing (the 46th Army, and the 2nd and 4th Guards Mechanised Corps) from the south.

2. In order to accomplish this mission, the Pliev [Cavalry-Mechanised] Group, no later than 7 November, should strike towards the north from the region of Szolnok, roll back the enemy's defences on the Tisza river and bring the Front's right wing beyond the Tisza river.[2]

Malinovsky had actually already informed General Pliev that his troops would be going into battle again. At 17:00 MT he ordered him by the morning of 5 November to deploy his forces as follows:

•	4th Guards Cavalry Corps	Törökszentmiklós
•	6th Guards Cavalry Corps	at Somsich
•	23rd Tank Corps	to remain in its present assembly area at Karcag [3]

At that moment 23rd Tank Corps was down to just 59 tanks and SP guns and both cavalry corps were short of men, but the Soviet High Command was so determined to not lose the momentum and rejuvenate the offensive that it was ready to take certain risks. As General Shtemenko wrote after the war, 'Although Pliev had no infantry, Stalin gave this mission to his group since he had no other reserves available.'[4]

Less than four hours later Malinovsky and his staff were ready with the new battle plan. At midnight it was forwarded to frontline armies, which were given the following missions:

- 1. 46th Army: Temporarily to go over to the defensive along the Üllő–Andrássy–Rákócziliget–Taksony–Ráckeve line; only local attacks that could improve the tactical situation are allowed.
- 2nd and 4th Guards Mechanised Corps to be pulled out of combat and by the morning of 5 November 1944 to be assembled in the Alsónémedi–Inárcs–Ócsa–Sári area, to replenish and recuperate. The right-flanking rifle corps to continue their offensive with the mission by the end of 5 November to secure the Vecsés–Tápiósüly line.
- 2. 7th Guards Army: To attack more resolutely and by the morning of 6 November to reach the Jászapáti–Jászberény line.
- 3. The Pliev Group: By the morning of 6 November to cross the Tisza at Szolnok and assemble its troops in the Nagykőrös–Abony–Cegléd area, in readiness to attack in the direction of Jászapáti.
- 4. 40th, 27th and 53rd Armies: On the morning of 7 November to launch a resolute offensive, in accordance with the already sanctioned battle plans.[5]

Immediately upon receiving the order, 46th Army HQ issued the following instructions to the frontline formations:

- 37th Rifle Corps with 7th Artillery Division (less the 3rd Mortar Brigade): by the morning of 5 November to secure the Pánd–Bénye[6] line; one rifle division [the 320th] has to be kept in reserve.
- 10th Guards Rifle Corps with the 3rd Mortar Brigade (of 7th Artillery Division), 1st Battalion/45th Cannon-Artillery Brigade and 48th Guards Mortar Regiment: by the end of 5 November to secure the Bénye–Monor–Üllő line. The 86th and 49th Guards Rifle Divisions have to hand over their sectors [i.e. Gyál–Vecsés–Üllő] to the 23rd Rifle Corps and redeploy to the east.
- 23rd Rifle Corps with two battalions of the 45th Cannon-Artillery Brigade and 437th Anti-Tank Artillery Regiment: to switch over to the defensive along the Üllő–(southern limits of) Vecsés–(northern limits of) Gyál–Gyálpuszta–Taksony–(left bank of) Csepeli Dunaág–Tass line. The Taksony–Tass line has to be secured by one rifle division, while the rest of the designated frontline must be held with the other two rifle divisions. The takeover of the sectors of the 2nd and 4th Guards Mechanised Corps must be completed by the morning of 6 November.
- 2nd and 4th Guards Mechanised Corps have to hand over their sectors and assemble in the vicinity of Inárcs and Ócsa respectively.[7]

Both Malinovsky and Stalin had given up the idea of taking Budapest by a coup de main and had decided to try a pincer attack. The new plan called for a powerful blow delivered by the adjacent flanks of Shlemin's and Shumilov's armies, momentum would be maintained by a broad-front offensive conducted by Sviridov's and Zhdanov's armoured corps and the Pliev Cavalry-Mechanised Group. The only thing that the Marshal needed to put into practice his new battle plan was a couple of days to regroup his shock troops. But the German command had no intention of affording him such a luxury.

2

Malinovsky and the Soviet General Staff had every reason to worry about Shlemin's right flank, because German command was indeed preparing an offensive in that sector. In the evening of 3 November, during their regular phone conference, Lieutenant-General von Grolman,

Chief of Staff of Army Group South, ordered Lieutenant-Colonel Marcks, the 1st General Staff Officer of Armeegruppe Fretter-Pico, to pull the 13 Panzer and 'Feldherrnhalle' divisions out the 'Budapest bridgehead' and assemble them into a 'strong shock group' in the Monor–Üllő area. The mission of that group was, in cooperation with the forces defending the Pilis–Alberti line (1 and 23 Panzer-Divisions), to launch a powerful counteroffensive to the southwest. It was to be mounted 'on the following morning', before the arrival of the main Soviet forces, 'otherwise (if postponed) it will be too late, because the enemy infantry will already be there.'[8]

Major-General Gaedcke (the Chief of Staff of Armeegruppe Fretter-Pico), who joined the conversation a little later, did not agree with Friessner's staff. He was not against the attack, but emphasised the fact that the divisions that had to replace the 13th Panzer and the 'Feldherrnhalle' – the 8 and 22 SS-Cavalry-Divisions – were not fully deployed yet, most of their units were still en route. Gaedcke was firm in his intention to strengthen the security of the 'Budapest bridgehead' first and only then to attack Shlemin's right flank.[9]

The issue was decided not by von Grolman or by Friessner, but by Hitler himself. At 04:00 BT a directive arrived from the Operations Department of the General Staff, which ordered all combat-worthy forces in the Szolnok–Cegléd area to be assembled into a 'shock group' to slam the enemy's 'deep flank and rear', in the direction of Kecskemét.[10] Friessner and his staff, believed that the plan was not good enough to inflict the desired damage. At 10:15, during his phone conversation with Colonel von Bonin (the Chief of the Operations Department of the General Staff), von Grolman expressed the misgivings of the army group: 'The designated jump-off area is too distant from Budapest and since our armoured troops are very weak, it is unlikely that the counter-attack will force the Soviets to divert part of their forces engaged in the vicinity of the capital … On the other hand, if we mount an attack in the Pilis–Alberti area, we will engage both Soviet mechanised corps, as well as the 10th Guards Rifle Corps.' In his

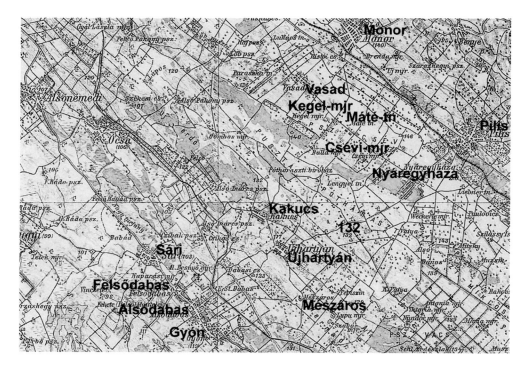

The area where the Germans launched their counterattacks on 5 and 6 November 1944.

opinion, the latter option was the best way to take some pressure off the 'Budapest bridgehead' and he literally begged von Bonin to permit it.[11]

Some 30 minutes later, von Bonin phoned back and informed the 5th General Staff Officer that the army group 'is being given a free hand to decide where to launch the panzer attack'.[12] For Friessner, who was impatient to close the growing gap south of Monor as quickly as possible, this was, of course, most welcome news. Shortly afterwards, at 11:05 BT, the HQ of the army group forwarded its decision to Gaedcke: the counterattack must be launched in the Pilis–Alberti sector only and nowhere else.[13]

The development of the situation since the morning, and especially the loss of Cegléd, apparently had made Fretter-Pico and his planners pessimistic about the prospects of the counteroffensive. When at 18:45 BT the Lieutenant-Colonel Marcks called the 5th General Staff Officer of Army Group South to fine-tune some details, there was no confidence in his voice:

> Tomorrow morning we will attack Pilis, but in view of the fact that the 13 Panzer-Division and Panzer-Grenadier Division 'Feldherrnhalle' are pinned down at Budapest, only weak tank units – the 1 and 23 Panzer-Division with just 15 tanks between them – will be able to take part in it.[14]

Hitler, undoubtedly, was also anxious. At 18:15 BT von Bonin informed Lieutenant-Colonel Schäfer, the 1st General Staff Officer of Army Group South, that 'the Führer is still thinking over whether the offensive should be launched in the Pilis area or farther to the south.' Schäfer replied that such an option was out of question.[15] Perhaps someone in Wolfschanze managed to persuade Hitler that the 'southern solution' would not bring the desired result, because at the end of the day it became clear that the counterblow would commence exactly where Army Group wanted.

3

The German attack on 5 November was planned and executed as a joint action of the left wing of Breith's III Panzer Corps and the right wing of Kirchner's LVII Panzer Corps. 1 Panzer-Division was the main player in this operation. Its mission was straightforward: to smash into the flank of the Soviet force trying to capture Budapest and cut its supply lines. For that purpose the division was reinforced with heavy artillery, the grenadier battalion of Panzer-Grenadier Division 'Feldherrnhalle', which was solely equipped with armoured halftracks (hereafter: SPW-Battalion 'Feldherrnhalle') and with the armoured battle group 'Fischer' (14 tanks and halftracks) from 23 Panzer-Division.

The attack of the 'oak leaf division' began at 06:00 BT, without waiting for the arrival of the SPW-Battalion 'Feldherrnhalle'.[16] The tanks and the panzer-grenadiers set out from Pilis and advanced westwards and southwestwards. They quickly cleared the terrain west of Alberti and established contact with 23 Panzer-Division, thereby closing the gap in that area. The Soviets were caught off-guard and reportedly lost ten guns and four heavy machine guns. Shortly afterwards the scouts reported long enemy motorised and horse-drawn columns moving down to Nyáregyháza from the northwest, as well as from Nyáregyháza to the east, toward Pilis.[17] Obviously, the Soviets were strengthening that sector, but the news did not discourage the Germans. This decision proved to be the right one and what began as a small-scale probing attack quickly turned into a daring panzer raid.

By midday units of 1st Panzer captured Nyáregyháza. Then the SPW-Battalion 'Feldherrnhalle' arrived and the German thrust intensified. The division left a small garrison in Nyáregyháza and the rest of the troops surged to the southwest. Another small blocking detachment was left at Hill 132 (halfway between Nyáregyháza and Újhartyán) to protect the southern flank against probable Soviet attacks from the south. Then the division turned to the

Friessner (left) and General Hermann Breith, commander of the III Panzer Corps, Budapest, November 1944. (Bundesarchiv)

Panther tanks of Panzer-Grenadier Division 'Feldherrnhalle' with panzer-grenadiers riding on them, Hungary, Autumn 1944. (Mirko Bayerl)

Volkswagen Schwimmwagen from SS-Reconnaissance Battalion 8 of 8 SS-Cavalry Division 'Florian Geyer' in the vicinity of Budapest, November 1944. Because of their excellent off-road capabilities, these light amphibious cars were extensively used by the reconnaissance detachments of the non-armoured German divisions during the later stages of the war. (Mirko Bayerl)

northwest and took Újhartyán.[18] Shortly afterwards the German spearheads reached the village of Alsódabas and began to fire on the Soviet supply traffic.[19]

Initially, Shlemin and his staff paid very little attention to the German counter-attack and it was even not mentioned in their regular daily reports to the 2nd Ukrainian Front. It was only at 20:00 when the unpleasant fact of the enemy penetration was officially announced for the first time by Shlemin's HQ: 'At 16:00 a group of more than 10 tanks advanced from the vicinity of Nyáregyháza towards Újhartyán.'[20] But this was something that Malinovsky already knew. There is no doubt the Marshal was infuriated; in the evening he sent the following accusatory order to Shlemin:

> You have been warned on several occasions about a gap between the divisions of the right wing, yet you took no definitive measures to liquidate these weaknesses in battle grouping of troops, to which I call your attention, for it was solely due to this that a group of tanks numbering up to 20 pieces passed through Nyáregyháza and reached the road at Örkény. The possibility is not excluded that this is a group of forward tanks of a more powerful enemy tank grouping.
>
> I ORDER YOU:
>
> 1. To use infantry with anti-tank means and to close this gap as well as the rest.
> 2. To destroy with forces of the 2nd Guards Mechanised Corps the enemy tanks that have broken through and to build by 12:00 on 6.11.44 a regular tactical grouping of infantry at the army's right flank and to continue the offensive aimed to reach the Tápiószőlős–Vecsés line.[21]

Shlemin took the warning seriously and reacted accordingly. By 6 November the following troops were rushed from all over the area towards the endangered zone:

- One regiment of the 4th Guards Rifle Division (from the army reserve).
- Two regiments of the 320th Rifle Division and one battalion of the 59th Guards Rifle Division (from the 37th Rifle Corps).
- 86th Guards Rifle Division (from the 10th Guards Rifle Corps).
- 22nd Anti-Tank Artillery Brigade (from the reserves of the 2nd Ukrainian Front).
- 2nd Guards Mechanised Corps.
- 4th Guards Mechanised Corps.
- A mobile obstacle detachment (an engineer platoon) with 450 anti-tank mines (from the engineer reserve).
- Five engineer-sapper battalions with anti-tank mines.

As one can see, this was quite a powerful force, a big bite for the Germans to swallow. But, as we already know, the objective of the Germans was not to defeat the force, but to divert it from Budapest. In this they succeeded; most of the formations mentioned just two days before had been trying to take the Hungarian capital.

The Soviets were not the only ones that were reinforcing the perimeter, the Germans were gradually bringing troops there. Whilst waiting for 13 Panzer-Division to regroup, Panzer-Grenadier Division 'Feldherrnhalle' launched some local actions in the Monor–Üllő area. Their aim was to improve the jump-off positions for the main offensive, gain information about the enemy dispositions, as well as to close some gaps in the Axis line southeast of Budapest. Thus in the morning of 5 November the armoured battle group of 'Feldherrnhalle' made a reconnaissance in force from Monor. Tanks and armoured halftracks with painted wolf-runes

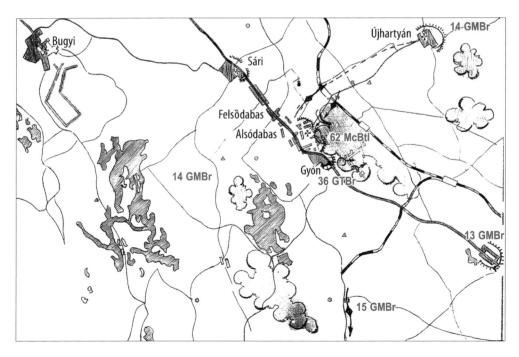

The actions of the 4th Guards Mechanised Corps on 5 and 6 November 1944.

on them advanced to the south, exploring the gap between the 49th and 109th Guards Rifle Divisions. Facing very little resistance, they reached the intersection near Máté tanya (hamlet), some 6km south of Monor. The German heavy artillery began to bombard the Soviet supply routes running through the area, adding more chaos to the already chaotic situation. By the end of the day, the armoured battle group fell back to its original jump-off position.[22] Its mission, however, could be considered a success: another weak gap in the overstretched Soviet eastern flank had just been revealed.

4

One of the first Soviet units that arrived at the crisis point was the 62nd Motorcycle Battalion of 4th Guards Mechanised Corps. The mission of the battalion, which had been reinforced with the 3rd Tank Battalion of 36th Guards Tank Brigade, was to occupy Alsódabas and Gyón and thus to prevent the enemy from cutting the corps' main supply route. At the same time the entire artillery of the corps (including both self-propelled regiments) was ordered deploy in the vicinity of Sári and take firing positions at the southeastern, southern and southwestern limits of the village. The task of this artillery grouping was to block any attempts by the Germans to advance farther to the northwest.[23]

Throughout the war Soviets developed and mastered the system of forward detachments, the primary mission of which was to spearhead the main mobile forces. The forward detachments, in turn, were spearheaded by small reconnaissance parties tasked with the quick seizure of key bridges and crossroads, scouting the terrain and providing up-to-date intelligence. This picture, which was taken in November 1944 near Budapest, shows a typical reconnaissance party: a M3 Scout Car, followed by a M3 halftrack and three M17 Multiple Gun Motor Carriages. The insignia on the vehicles (deer) suggests that they belonged to the 13th Guards Mechanised Brigade of the 4th Guards Mechanised Corps. (Author's Collection)

Meanwhile, on the evening of 5 November, Shlemin's biggest concern – the armoured battle group of 1 Panzer-Division – again raided the Soviet supply columns moving on the motorway east of Alsódabas.[24] The attempts of the panzers to enter the village were parried by the 62nd Motorcycle Battalion, which from 24:00 MT onwards was engaged in a constant firefight with the enemy. The Germans then attempted to bypass Alsódabas to the south but encountered fierce resistance at its southern and southwestern limits. The only damage they inflicted that night in the sector were up to eight trucks (of various Soviet units) that had been set on fire on the road south of Gyón.[25] The arrival of additional reinforcements allowed the Soviets to launch a counter-attack and by 08:00 MT the German armoured group ('more than 10 tanks') was finally pushed to the northeast, beyond the Kecskemét–Budapest railway line.[26]

The attempt of the German panzer group to bypass the Soviet stronghold (Sári–Alsódabas–Gyón) to the north was also unsuccessful. In the early hours of 6 November some its troops attacked from Újhartyán to the northwest, but south of Kakucs (north/northwest of Újhartyán) they ran into a 'strong anti-tank defence' that forced them to turn to the north.[27] In the forenoon the entire battle group of 1 Panzer-Division withdrew from the Újhartyán–Alsódabas area to the northeast and assembled southeast of Monor, where it was placed under the newly arrived 13 Panzer-Division.

With this, the first phase of the German counteroffensive was over. During the raid 1 Panzer-Division reportedly inflicted the following losses on the Soviets (captured or destroyed): 61 motor vehicles, 60 horse-drawn carts, 1 T-34 tank, 1 American-made armoured car, 2 20mm anti-aircraft guns, 2 88mm German Flak guns, 1 172mm [152mm] gun, 1 75mm [sic] anti-tank gun and 1 prime mover.[28] The raid forced Soviet command to divert away from Budapest most of its 'shock troops' and thus lifted the immediate threat to the Hungarian capital. This, undoubtedly, had a great psychological effect on both sides.

5

Throughout the first half of 6 November the remaining units of the hurriedly redeployed 4th Guards Mechanised Corps gradually began to arrive in the endangered sector. Much to their amazement, they found no enemy in front of them. The 13th Guards Mechanised Brigade reached the area of Örkény at around 12:10 MT and immediately sent out elements of its 1st and 3rd Rifle Battalions to clear the forest southeast of Gyón. The report that arrived from them was shocking: no contact! The same happened to 14th Guards Mechanised Brigade, which had arrived a little earlier. At 11:00 MT the 'Elephant Brigade' reached Újhartyán, but no combat followed, because it turned out that the Germans had already abandoned the place. Colonel Nikitin (brigade commander) even sent patrols to scout the perimeter as far as Mészáros (a small place to the southeast of Újhartyán), but again, nothing. The same thing happened to 15th Guards Mechanised Brigade, which in the morning went from Sári to Gyón without firing a single shot.[29]

The sudden cessation of enemy activity in the Újhartyán–Alsódabas on 6 November confused Soviet command. Most probably it convinced Shlemin that the Germans, fearing encirclement, had fallen back to their original jump-off positions. If this were so, he could not have been more wrong: having detected on the previous day that the Soviet front at Monor was weakly protected, the German Command was now building up forces there for another powerful counter-attack.

The daring raid of 1 Panzer-Division on Alsódabas and the subsequent retreat were, actually yet another successful implementation of 'hit-and-run' tactics, a technique the Germans had mastered to perfection. Now another example was in the making and this time much stronger forces would be involved: 13 Panzer-Division, reinforced with the SPW-Battalion

'Feldherrnhalle', the armoured battle group of 1 Panzer-Division, five Panther tanks of 23 Panzer-Division, four Pz IV/70 tank-destroyers of Panzer-Grenadier Division 'Feldherrnhalle', as well as some smaller armoured units.[30] Its mission was to attack from Monor to the north-west, towards Vecsés and in so doing, to encircle the Soviet forces defending the Üllő salient.[31]

The redeployment of 13th Panzer from Pestszentimre to Monor was completed by midday and its attack began immediately after that. Initially the German armour and infantry advanced from Monor to the southwest. Right from the outset, however, they encountered very fierce resistance ('much stronger than we expected', says Breith's report.). It was evident that their opponent (the bulk of the 109th Guards Rifle Division and 263rd Guards Rifle Regiment of the 86th Guards Rifle Division) was prepared for the onslaught. Throughout the afternoon the Soviets gave very little ground and by nightfall the attackers penetrated into the southern part of Vasad but were not able to advance beyond the Vasad–Kegel-major–Csévi-major line.[32]

The Soviet guardsmen not only defended their positions with great determination, but also used every opportunity to counter-attack. During the same afternoon the 109th Guards delivered a powerful blow to the left flank of 13th Panzer and thus forced General Schmidhuber to redirect most of its armour to the southeast. Immediately, a powerful 'shock group' was formed comprising the armoured battle group of 13 Panzer-Division, the SPW-Battalion 'Feldherrnhalle' and the armoured battle group of 1 Panzer-Division.[33] The 'shock group' was placed under Colonel Bradel, commander of Panzer-Grenadier Regiment 113.[34]

Bradel's men succeeded in eliminating the threat to their flank but at the cost of losing the momentum of the entire attack. The fiercest engagement took place south of the crossroads, somewhere southeast of Vasad. Five Panthers of 23rd Panzer, for instance, succeeded in gaining some 800m of ground, destroying five anti-tank guns, two mortars, eight heavy and five light machine guns. One of the Panthers was destroyed beyond repair.[35]

The 21-year-old Senior Sergeant Mirza Veliev from Azerbaijan, commander of one of the 45mm anti-tank guns of 309th Guards Rifle Regiment (109th Guards Rifle Division) achieved great things during the engagement with Bradel's panzers. When the rifle battalion to which his gun had been assigned was suddenly attacked by approximately 20 German panzers, Veliev's crew immediately engaged them, setting fire to the leading panzer. Shortly after, the crew was eliminated by artillery. Veliev, however, survived and continued to fight alone. Firing round after round into the advancing Germans, he reportedly put out of action three more tanks, an armoured half-track and destroyed a truck with enemy infantry. An enemy bullet ended his young life. For his remarkable bravery, on 24 March 1945 Veliev posthumously became a Hero of the Soviet Union.[36]

11

THE AFTERMATH

1

By the end of 6 November the advance of Shlemin's 46th Army was stopped everywhere. The first battle for Budapest was over. Many kilometres to the north, in *Wolfsschanze*, Adolf Hitler's Eastern Front military headquarters near Rastenburg, East Prussia, General Wenck reported with obvious satisfaction:

> My Führer, the Army Group South situation is still tense, especially in the region of Szolnok. In the Budapest area it has become more stable, primary because of yesterday's first advance of the panzer group. So far the group has thrust into a long column and caused quite a disaster, but during the night the group stayed behind because they want to act together with the 13th [Panzer-Division], which will come out of here tonight, and the 1st Panzer Division against these two tank corps [the 2nd and 4th Guards Mechanized Corps].[1]

It was three in the afternoon and even though Fretter-Pico's counter-attack was far from over, it was already evident to everyone in the German chain of command that it had achieved its primary goal: to prevent the Soviets from taking the Hungarian capital. There was one officer, however, who didn't share that outburst of optimism and considered it premature. His name was Richard Gehlen, Colonel, Chief of 'Foreign Armies East' intelligence-gathering section of the German General Staff and his reputation was that of a cunning fox.

In those first November days Gehlen was very busy preparing his regular monthly intelligence report to Hitler. The report in question landed on the desk of the Fuehrer on 10 November. As usual, his assessment of the overall military situation in the East was correct. Already in the opening lines of the document Gehlen attempted to warn the dictator about the intentions of the Soviets to divert the German operational reserves away from the main (central) sector of the Eastern Front by repeatedly attacking at the flanks:

> Independently from the current operations of the RA [Red Army] against the flanks (Hungary and Courland), the preparations for large-scale offensive operations against the centre of the German Front between the Carpathian Mountains and the Memel River are still in progress. It seems that they will soon come to an end.

> The original intentions of the enemy were obviously based on the following assumptions:

a) Political breakdown of Hungary and thereby the opportunity to destroy Army Group 'South' using only relatively small forces and then to thrust forward towards the 'Vienna Gate'. [...][2]

Gehlen then mentioned two other assumptions, related to the other sectors of *Ostfront* (the central part and Courland) and then continued, relating to the events in the south:

Because of the consolidation of the political situation in Hungary, the suppression of the rebellions in Warsaw and in Slovakia, the German defensive successes in the Battle of Debrecen, in the Warsaw–Narew area and in Courland, and finally, as a consequence of its heavy losses, the enemy was forced to delay considerably its planned operations and also to change the foreseen deployment of forces. The scale of the planned offensive operations, however, has basically not been altered. From the [Soviet] preparations we have observed, one can see two main operations that are unchanged and will begin soon:

1) <u>An offensive operation in the area of Hungary–Slovakia–southern Poland.</u> Its objective is to reach the 'Vienna Gate' and Moravia/Upper Silesia early by pushing forward from Hungary and from the sector of Army Group 'A', thereby bypassing the Carpathian Mountains in order to reach the area of Czechoslovakia/Austria. The basic idea behind this operation will be to gain the possibility of using south-east Germany and the politically unstable former Czechoslovakian areas as a platform for the final seizure of Central Europe.

2) <u>An offensive operation against Army Group Centre in the area of East and West Prussia.</u> Its objective is, by attacking from the area around and north of Warsaw (the Vistula–Narew front), and in cooperation with another offensive operation across the East Prussian eastern border, to capture the western part of East Prussia and the lower Vistula, to destroy the German forces in East Prussia and thus open the way to the northern German Plain.[3]

Colonel Gehlen then discussed in greater detail the situation on the central and northern sectors of the Eastern Front. The report in question was supplemented with an annexe, in which the likely intentions of the individual Soviet Fronts were covered in more detail. Regarding the Hungarian theatre of war Gehlen made the following assessment:

- The 3rd Ukrainian Front seemed to have two main missions: a) in cooperation with the Bulgarian forces to destroy the Army Group 'E' in Serbia – Macedonia, and b) to protect the left flank of the 2nd Ukrainian Front operations and in doing so to employ the bulk of its forces towards the gap between River Drava and Lake Balaton.
- The 2nd Ukrainian Front was believed to have the mission to assemble its main forces between the rivers Danube and Tisza and attack with them in the northerly direction. Subsequently, one task force would land on the western bank of the Danube (south of the Hungarian capital) and advance towards Székesfehérvár, while one mobile group would turn to the north and isolate Budapest from the west.
- The 4th Ukrainian Front would support the main thrust of the 2nd Ukrainian Front by attacking the northern flank of the Army Group 'South'.[4]

Gehlen also pointed clearly to the probable missions of the Soviet Fronts deployed in the centre:

- The 1st Ukrainian Front would seize the area from Crakow to Upper Silesia first and then Moravia.

- The 1st and 2nd Byelorussian Fronts would be given the mission of pushing out of the Vistula–Narew front, enveloping Warsaw from both sides, with the main thrust north of the Vistula in a northwesterly direction towards the lower Vistula with the aim of destroying the German forces in East Prussia.[5]

Needless to say, Gehlen's assessments proved to be spot on. Even though in his November report he did not yet foresee the depth of the objective of the Soviet central group of Fronts (the river Oder), he was correct in his prediction that the goal of the enemy attacks at the flanks was to divert the German armored reserves away from central sector. As we know, in the following months the Soviet offensives on the Eastern Front unfolded, more or less, as Gehlen had said they would.

2

Throughout the rest of November 1944 the German High Command continued to reject all Friessner's requests for reinforcements. Apparently, Hitler and his military planners kept believing that the Army Group South could contain the Russian onslaught with the forces at its disposal. But by the beginning of December 1944, the military situation in Hungary grew much worse: the 3rd Ukrainian Front crossed the Danube and approached Székesfehérvár and Nagykanizsa, thus endangering the precious oilfields in the vicinity of the latter; in the meantime the 2nd Ukrainian Front isolated Budapest from the east and succeeded in pushing the opposing Axis troops into the Mátra and Carpathian Mountains. Apart from the enemy military pressure, there was also a political pressure coming from Arrow Cross: the General Staff of *Honvédség* repeatedly hinted that after the fall of Budapest the Third Reich would be forced to shelter and feed waves of Magyar refugees, while Szálasi shared his deep frustrations with Hitler during his official visit on 4 December.

Around that time the opinion of the Fuehrer about the fighting capacity of the Army Group South plummeted. As we have seen, there were several reasons, one of which was that the *Honvédség* was disintegrating. After the battle at Kecskemét the decline of both numerical strength and fighting morale of the Hungarian Army was unstoppable. Although the majority of the Magyar senior officers were still openly pro-German, most of the troops did not want to die for any cause and began to desert in growing numbers. Nearly every day whole companies and even battalions surrendered to the Soviets and in a matter of just two months *Honvédség* simply melted away. On 10 November Friessner even submitted a special report to OKH saying that 'in its current state, the Hungarian Army is no longer willing to fight.'[6] Thus the Germans found themselves forced to move more and more troops to Hungary in order to plug up the gaps in the front line that had emerged.

From the end of November 1944 Hitler and Guderian began to send division after division to Hungary. In a matter of just three weeks, three panzer divisions, two cavalry brigades (of divisional size) and several smaller armoured units were transferred to the *Puszta*. The divisions and brigades, in particular, came from the Vistula front and East Prussia and thus the Soviet strategy of diverting German reserves away from the 'Berlin direction' finally began to bear fruit.

In Hungary, however, this powerful 'panzer armada' (Guderian's words) failed to turn the tables because it was employed in the worst possible way (after all, in terms of skills Friessner and Fretter-Pico were average commanders, at best) and on Christmas Day Budapest was encircled by the Soviets. About 48,000 German and 54,000 Hungarian troops, plus unknown numbers of other Hungarian personnel were trapped in the city and subsequently lost for good.[7] Friessner and Fretter-Pico were sacked on 22 December but the situation was already beyond repair.

In an attempt to lift the siege, Hitler and Guderian urgently sent more reinforcements to the Budapest area. By the beginning of January 1945, much to the horror of Gehlen and much to the satisfaction of the *Stavka*, five more divisions (three panzer and two infantry) were redeployed from the central sector of the Eastern Front to Hungary. The Germans used them to launch two violent relief attacks, both of them unsuccessful. In the meantime the Red Army finished its preparations for its enormous winter offensive in Poland and East Prussia and when between 12–15 January five Soviet fronts unleashed their onslaught, there were no enemy reserves standing on their way. Budapest fell on 13 February 1945 after months of very heavy fighting; these Soviet efforts paid off because at that moment the spearheads of the 1st Byelorussian Front had already firmly entrenched themselves on the western bank of the Oder. Berlin was less than 60km away. It would fall on 2 May. Munich, the ultimate goal of Stalin's southern pincer, however, would remain forever outside the reach of Malinovsky's armoured wedges. This hardly bothered Joseph Vissarionovich any longer – thanks to the Hungarian merry-go-round, the western border of his empire was now running along the River Elbe and the ridges of the Austrian Alps.

APPENDIX 1

COMMAND POSITIONS

1.1 SOVIET COMMAND POSITIONS, 29 OCTOBER–7 NOVEMBER 1944

2nd Ukrainian Front	Marshal Rodion Malinovsky
27th Army	Colonel-General Sergei Trofimenko
40th Army	Lieutenant-General Philip Zhmachenko
46th Army	Lieutenant-General Ivan Shlemin
53rd Army	Lieutenant-General Ivan Managarov
7th Guards Army	Colonel-General Mikhail Shumilov
6th Guards Tank Army	Colonel-General Andrei Kravchenko
1st Army (Rom)	Corps-General Nicolae Macici
4th Army (Rom)	Corps-General Gheorghe Avramescu
5th Air Army	Colonel-General Sergei Goryunov
23rd Rifle Corps	Major-General Mikhail Grigorovich
37th Rifle Corps	Major-General Fyodor Kolchuk
10th Guards Rifle Corps	Lieutenant-General Ivan Rubanyuk
24th Guards Rifle Corps	Major-General Peter Avdeenko
25th Guards Rifle Corps	Major-General (from 2 November 1944 Lieutenant-General) Gany Safiulin
27th Guards Rifle Corps	Major-General Evgeny Alekhin
31st Guards Rifle Corps	Major-General Sergei Bobruk
4th Guards Cavalry Corps	Lieutenant-General Issa Pliev
5th Guards Cavalry Corps	Lieutenant-General Sergei Gorshkov
6th Guards Cavalry Corps	Lieutenant-General Sergei Sokolov
IV Corps (Rom)	Divisional-General Nicolae Stoenescu
VII Corps (Rom)	Corps-General Nicolae Sova
23rd Tank Corps	Lieutenant-General Aleksei Akhmanov
5th Guards Tank Corps	Major-General Mikhail Saveliev
7th Mechanised Corps	Major-General Fyodor Katkov
2nd Guards Mechanised Corps	Lieutenant-General Karp Sviridov
4th Guards Mechanised Corps	Lieutenant-General Vladimir Zhdanov
9th Guards Mechanised Corps	Lieutenant-General Mikhail Volkov
3rd Guards Fighter Air Corps	Lieutenant-General Ivan Podgorny
3rd Guards Assault Air Corps	Lieutenant-General Vasily Stepichev
5th Assault Air Corps	Major-General Nikolai Kamanin
53rd Rifle Division	Colonel David Vasilevsky
99th Rifle Division	Major-General Alexander Saraev

227th Rifle Division	Major-General Georgy Preobrazhensky
297th Rifle Division	Colonel Andrei Kovtun-Stankevich
303rd Rifle Division	Major-General Konstantin Fedorovsky
316th Rifle Division	Colonel N. Korkin (till 30 October 1944); Colonel L. Voloshin
320th Rifle Division	Colonel Josif Burik
409th Rifle Division	Major-General Evstafy Grechanyi
4th Guards Rifle Division	Colonel Kuzma Parfenov
34th Guards Rifle Division	Colonel Gerasim Kuks
36th Guards Rifle Division	Major-General Georgy Lilenkov
40th Guards Rifle Division	Colonel Lev Bransburg
49th Guards Rifle Division	Major-General Vasily Margelov
59th Guards Rifle Division	Major-General Georgy Karamyshev
68th Guards Rifle Division	Major-General Ivan Nekrasov
72nd Guards Rifle Division	Major-General Anatoly Losev
81st Guards Rifle Division	Major-General Ivan Morozov
86th Guards Rifle Division	Major-General Vasily Sokolovsky
108th Guards Rifle Division	Major-General Sergei Dunaev
109th Guards Rifle Division	Colonel Ilya Baldynov
6th Guards Airborne Division	Major-General Mikhail Smirnov
7th Artillery Division	Major-General Ivan Bobrovnikov
16th Artillery Division	Colonel P. Yurko
2nd Infantry Division (Rom)	Brigadier-General Mihail Voicu
19th Infantry Division (Rom)	Lieutenant-General Mihail Lăcătuşu
9th Cavalry Division (Rom)	Lieutenant-General Dumitru Popescu (till 31 October 1944); Colonel Dumitru Neferu
279th Fighter Air Division	Colonel Vsevolod Blagoveschensky
331st Fighter Air Division	Colonel Ivan Semenenko
6th Guards Fighter Air Division	Colonel Josif Geibo
13th Guards Fighter Air Division	Colonel Ivan Taranenko
14th Guards Fighter Air Division	Colonel Alexei Yudakov
264th Assault Air Division	Colonel Evgeny Klobukov
4th Guards Assault Air Division	Colonel Valentin Saprykin
7th Guards Assault Air Division	Lieutenant-Colonel G. Shuteev
12th Guards Assault Air Division	Colonel Leonid Chizhikov
218th Bomber Air Division	Colonel Nikolai Romanov
312th Night Bomber Air Division	Colonel Vasily Chanpalov

Corps-General Nicolae Sova, commander of the VII Army Corps (Romanian).

1.2 GERMAN COMMAND POSITIONS, 29 OCTOBER–7 NOVEMBER 1944

Army Group South	Colonel-General Johannes Friessner
6.Army	General der Artillerie Maximilian Fretter-Pico
8.Army	General der Infanterie Otto Wöhler
Air Fleet 4	Colonel-General Otto Dessloch
III Panzer Corps	General der Panzertruppe Hermann Breith
IV Panzer Corps	General der Panzertruppe Ulrich Kleemann
LVII Panzer Corps	General der Panzertruppe Friedrich Kirchner
I Air Corps	Lieutenant-General Paul Deichmann
II Air Corps	General der Flieger Johannes Fink
Commanding General of Luftwaffe in Hungary	Lieutenant-General Kuno Heribert Fütterer
V Flak-Corps	General der Flakartillerie Otto-Wilhelm von Renz
46.Infantry Division	Lieutenant-General Erich Reuter
271.Volks-Grenadier Division	Colonel Martin Bieber
153.Field Training Division	Major-General Hermann Winkler
1.Panzer-Division	Major-General Eberhard Thunert
13.Panzer-Division	Major-General Gerhard Schmidhuber
23.Panzer-Division	Major-General Josef von Radowitz
24.Panzer Division	Colonel Gustav-Adolf von Nostitz–Wallwitz
Panzer-Grenadier Division 'Feldherrnhalle'	Colonel Günther Pape
4.SS-Police-Panzer-Grenadier Division	SS-Brigadenführer Fritz Schmedes
8.SS-Cavalry-Division 'Florian Geyer'	SS-Brigadenführer Joachim Rumohr
18.SS-Panzer-Grenadier Division 'Horst Wessel'	SS-Brigadenführer Wilhelm Trabandt
22.SS-Cavalry-Division 'Maria Theresia'	SS-Brigadenführer August Zehender
31.SS-Volunteer Grenadier Division	SS-Oberführer Gustav Lombard
15.Flak-Division	Major-General Theodor Herbert

1.3 HUNGARIAN COMMAND POSITIONS, 29 OCTOBER–9 NOVEMBER 1944

1.Army	Lieutenant-General Dezsö Lászlo
2.Army	Lieutenant-General Jenö Major
3.Army	Lieutenant-General József Heszlényi
I Corps	Lieutenant-General Iván Hindy
II Corps	Major-General István Kiss
VI Corps	Brigadier-General Miklós Nagyöszy
VII Corps	Lieutenant-General János Markóczy
VIII Corps	Major-General Belá Lengyel
10.Infantry Division	Brigadier-General István Kudriczy
12.Reserve Division/12.Infantry Division	Brigadier-General Ference Mikófalvy
20.Infantry Division	Brigadier-General Jenö Tömöry
23.Reserve Division/23.Infantry Division	Brigadier-General Ferenc Osztovics
5.Reserve Division	Brigadier-General László János Szábo
8.Reserve Division	Brigadier-General Bela Temesy
1.Armoured Division	Colonel Zoltán Schell
2.Armoured Division	Brigadier-General Zoltán Zsedényi
1.Huszar-Division	Major-General Mihály Ibrányi (till 4 November 1944); Colonel Attila Makay

APPENDIX 2

ORDERS OF BATTLE

2.1 ARMY GROUP SOUTH, 30/31 OCTOBER 1944

Assets: Plenipotentiary General of the German Armed Forces in Hungary; Commander of the rear area in Hungary (with subordinated 153.Field-Training Division).

Artillery: Light Topographic Detachment 611.

Engineers: Engineer Bridge-Building Battalion 699; 1.Company/Engineer Battalion 771; Light Assault Boat Companies 906 and 912; Engineer Bridge-Building Staff's Section 939; Bridge Columns 'B' (mot.) 13, 16, 138, 2./408 and 667; Heavy Tank Bridge Column (mot.) 842 (parts); Light Tank Bridge Column (mot.) 4; Bridge Columns 74 and 94; Engineer Depot Battalion 571.

Air Force: Air Fleet 4; 15.Anti-Aircraft Artillery Division.

Armeegruppe 'Wöhler' (the command of 8.Army)

1.Army (Hung)

III Army Corps (Hung): 6.Infantry Division (Hung), 2.Mountain Brigade (Hung), Group 'Shölze', 15.Infantry Division.

V Army Corps (Hung): 13.Infantry Division (Hung), 1.Mountain Brigade (Hung).

XVII Army Corps: 8.Jaeger Division, 24.Infantry Division (Hung), 16.Infantry Division (Hung).

Artillery: Arko 7 (Corps Artillery Command 7); 3.Battery/Artillery Observation Battalion (horse-drawn) 25.

Engineers: Engineer-Regiment-Staff 700; Engineer Battalion (part. mot.) 635.

XXIX Army Corps: 4.Mountain Division, 8.SS-Cavalry-Division, 2.Armoured Division (Hung), 13.Panzer-Division (in transit for Army Grouping Fretter-Pico), 3.Mountain Division, 46.Infantry Division, 2.Reserve Division (Hung).

Artillery: Arko 102 (Corps Artillery Command 102); Artillery-Regiment-Staff 781; Assault Gun Brigade 286; Assault Artillery Brigade 239; Artillery Battalions II./818 and III./818 (le.F.H./RSO); Artillery Battalion I./127 (s.F.H./mot.), 3.Battery/Artillery Observation Battalion (mot.) 13.

Engineers: Engineer-Regiment-Staff 681; Engineer Battalion (mount.) 74; Engineer Battalion (mot.) 52.

Armour: Anti-Tank Battalions 663 and 721 (sPak, mot Z.).

IX Army Corps (Hung): 9.Border-Guard Brigade (Hung), 27.Light-Division (Hung), Group 'Finta' [7.Reserve Division (Hung), 1.Mountain Reserve Brigade (Hung) and 2.Mountain Reserve Brigade (Hung)].

Engineers: Engineer Brigade (mot.) 52; Engineer Battalion (mot.) 666.

8.Army assets: Korück 558

Artillery: Harko 310 (Army Artillery Command 310); Anti-Aircraft Artillery Battalion (static) 289 (8.8m Flak); Artillery Observation Battalion (mot.) 13 (less 3.Battery); Artillery Observation Battalions (horse-drawn) 25 (less 3.Battery) and 40; Light Topographic Detachment 650.

Engineers: Engineer-Regiment-Staff 617; Engineer Bridge-Building Battalions 531, 577, 624; Engineer Bridge-Building Staff's Section 923; Bridge Columns 'B' (mot.) 1, 54, 297 and 603; Engineer Depot Battalion 591.

Armeegruppe Fretter-Pico (the command of 6.Army)

6.Army

Group 'Schmidt' (command of the LXXII Army Corps):
II Army Corps (Hung): remnants of 12.Reserve Division (Hung), 25.Infantry Division (Hung)
LXXII Army Corps: 76.Infantry Division.
Artillery: Arko 114 (Corps Artillery Command 114); Artillery Battalion 736 (21cm Mörser); Artillery Observation Battalion (mot.) 36.

IV Panzer Corps: 4.SS-Police-Panzer-Grenadier Division.
Artillery: Arko 404 (Corps Artillery Command 404); Artillery Battalion 809 (less 1. and 3.Batteries) (21cm Mörser); Artillery Battery 800 (17cm K/mot.); Artillery Observation Battalion (mot.) 32.

III Panzer Corps (command only; in transit from 8.Army):
Artillery: Arko 3 (Corps Artillery Command 3); Artillery-Regiment-Staffs 511 and 959; Assault Gun Brigades 228 and 325; Artillery Battalion I./77 (le.F.H./RSO); Artillery Battalion II./52 (s.F.H./mot.); Artillery Battalion 607 and 3.Battery/Artillery Battalion 809 (21cm Mörser).
Engineers: Engineer-Regiment-Staff 518.
Armour: Heavy Panzer Battalion 503 (Tiger); Anti-Tank Companies 1179, 1257 and 1335 (Hetzer); Anti-Tank Battalion (mot.) 662 (8.8cm sPak); Anti-Tank Battalion 661 (Hornisse).

6.Army reserves: VI Army Corps (Hung) (command only); Panzer-Grenadier Division 'Feldherrnhalle', 1.Panzer-Division, 22.SS-Cavalry-Division.

6.Army assets: Korück 593.
Artillery: Harko 306 (Army Artillery Command 306); Artillery Observation Battalion (mot.) 43; Light Topographic Detachment 638.
Engineers: Engineer Brigade 127; Engineer-Regiment-Staff 685; Engineer Battalions (mot.) 127 and 651; Engineer Battalions (part. mot.) 255 and 741; Engineer Bridge-Building Battalions (mot.) 21 and 552; Engineer Bridge-Building Staff Sections 921 and 927; Bridge Columns 'B' (mot.) 7, 8, 37, 50, 85, 129 and 651; Engineer Depot Battalion 541.

3.Army (Hung)

VIII Army Corps (Hung): 1.Huszar-Division (Hung), 8.Reserve Division (Hung), 20.Infantry Division (Hung), 5.Infantry Division (Hung).

LVII Panzer Corps: 24.Panzer-Division, 23.Panzer-Division, 1.Armoured Division (Hung).
Artillery: Arko 121 (Corps Artillery Command 121); Artillery Battalions 844 and III./140 (s.F.H./mot.); Artillery Observation Battalion (mot.) 29.
Engineers: Engineer-Regiment-Staff 678; Engineer Bridge-Building Battalion 646; Engineer Bridge-Building Staff's Section 925; Bridge Columns 'B' (mot.) 59, 110 and 663.

VII Army Corps (Hung): Group 'Szücs' (Hung), 10.Infantry Division (Hung), 23.Reserve Division (Hung).

2.Army (Hung)
IV Army Corps (Hung): 31.SS–Grenadier Division, Training Grenadier Regiment 44, Police
Regiment 6, SS–Tatar Brigade, River Brigade (Hung), Anti-Aircraft Brigade 'Matoltsy' (Hung).

2.2 LEFT WING OF THE 2ND UKRAINIAN FRONT, 31 OCTOBER 1944

46th Army
10th Guards Rifle Corps: 49th Guards Rifle Division, 86th Guards Rifle Division, 109th Guards Rifle
Division

31st Guards Rifle Corps: 34th Guards Rifle Division, 40th Guards Rifle Division

23rd Rifle Corps: 68th Guards Rifle Division, 99th Rifle Division, 316th Rifle Division.

37th Rifle Corps: 59th Guards Rifle Division, 108th Guards Rifle Division, 320th Rifle Division

2nd Guards Mechanised Corps: 4th, 5th and 6th Guards Mechanised Brigades; 37th Guards Tank
Brigade; 30th Guards Heavy Tank Regiment; 251st Guards and 1509th Self-Propelled Artillery
Regiments; 99th Guards Motorcycle Battalion; 524th Mortar Regiment; 408th Guards Mortar
Battalion; 159th Anti-Aircraft Artillery Regiment.

4th Guards Mechanised Corps: 13th, 14th and 15th Guards Mechanised Brigades; 36th Guards
Tank Brigade; 292nd Guards Self-Propelled Artillery Regiment; 352nd Guards Heavy Self-Propelled
Artillery Regiment; 62nd Motorcycle Battalion; 527th Mortar Regiment; 129th Guards Mortar
Battalion; 1512th Anti-Tank Artillery Regiment; 740th Anti-Aircraft Artillery Regiment.

46th Army assets:
Infantry: 4th Guards Rifle Division (Army reserve).
Artillery: 7th Artillery Division (9th Guards Canon-Artillery Brigade, 11th Light Artillery Brigade,
17th Canon-Artillery Brigade, 25th Howitzer-Artillery Brigade, 105th Super-Heavy Artillery
Brigade, 3rd Mortar Brigade); 45th Guards-Canon-Artillery Brigade; 92nd Corps Artillery
Regiment; 437th Anti-Tank Artillery Regiment; 462nd Mortar Regiment; 48th Guards Mortar
Regiment; 38th Anti-Aircraft Artillery Division.
Armour: 991st, 1505th and 1897th Self-Propelled Artillery Regiments.
Engineers: 51st Engineer Brigade.

7th Guards Army
24th Guards Rifle Corps: 72nd Guards Rifle Division, 81st Guards Rifle Division

25th Guards Rifle Corps: 36th Guards Rifle Division, 53rd Rifle Division, 297th Rifle Division

27th Guards Rifle Corps: 227th Rifle Division, 303rd Rifle Division

7th Guards Army assets:
Infantry: 409th Rifle Division; 6th Guards Airborne Division (in transit from the 53rd Army).
Artillery: 16th Artillery Division (49th Light Artillery Brigade, 61st Canon-Artillery Brigade, 52nd
Howitzer-Artillery Brigade, 90th Heavy-Howitzer-Artillery Brigade, 109th Super-Heavy Howitzer-
Artillery Brigade, 14th Mortar Brigade); 41st Guards-Canon-Artillery Brigade; 2nd and 11th
Anti-Tank Artillery Brigades; 115th Anti-Tank Artillery Regiment; 263rd, 290th and 493rd Mortar
Regiments; 302nd and 309th Guards Mortar Regiments; 5th Anti-Aircraft Artillery Division.
Engineers: 60th Engineer Brigade; 5th Mountain Engineer Brigade.

1st Army (Rom)
(operationally subordinated to the 7th Guards Army)
IV Army Corps: 2nd Infantry Division (Rom), 4th Infantry Division (Rom) (remnants only)

VII Army Corps: 19th Infantry Division (Rom), 9th Cavalry Division (Rom).

1st Army assets:
Artillery: 1st and 7th Artillery Regiments (Rom); 114th Anti-Tank Artillery Regiment (Soviet).

2.3 AXIS GROUND TROOPS IN HUNGARY AND NEIGHBORING AREAS, 5 NOVEMBER 1944

OKH Theatre of War

Army Group South
Army Group reserves: 18.SS-Panzer-Grenadier Division 'Horst Wessel' (arriving)

Armeegruppe 'Wöhler' [8.Army and 1.Army (Hung)]:
1.Army (Hung):
III Corps (Hung): 15.Infantry Division, 4.Mountain Division, 2.Mountain Brigade (Hung), 6.Infantry Division (Hung)
V Corps (Hung): 1.Mountain Brigade (Hung), 13.Infantry Division (Hung)
XVII Corps: 16.Infantry Division (Hung), 24.Infantry Division (Hung), 8.Jaeger Division

8.Army:
XXIX Corps: 3.Mountain Division, 2.Reserve Division (Hung)
IX Corps (Hung): Group 'Finta' [7.Reserve Division (Hung) (remnants), 1.Mountain Reserve Brigade (Hung), 2.Mountain Reserve Brigade (Hung), 9.Reserve Division (Hung)], 27.Light Division (Hung), 9.Border Guard Brigade (Hung)

Armeegruppe Fretter-Pico (command of 6.Army)
Army reserves: 3.Infantry Division (Hung), 153.Field Training Division, 12.Infantry Division (Hung)

Group 'General Kirchner' (command of LVII Panzer Corps):
LXXII Corps: 25.Infantry Division (Hung), 76.Infantry Division
IV Panzer Corps: 46.Infantry Division, 4.SS Police Panzer-Grenadier Division
VIII Corps (Hung): 5.Reserve Division (Hung), 20.Reserve Division (Hung) (remnants)
LVII Panzer Corps: 24.Panzer Division, 23.Panzer Division, 1.Panzer Division

Group 'General Breith' (command of III Panzer Corps): 8.SS-Cavalry-Division 'Florian Geyer', 1.Armoured Division (Hung), Panzer-Grenadier Division 'Feldherrnhalle', 13.Panzer-Division, 22.SS-Cavalry-Division 'Maria Theresia', 1.Huszar Division (Hung), 2.Armoured Division (Hung) (arriving)

2.Army (Hung):
Army reserves: command of II Corps (Hung)
VII Corps (Hung): 20.Infantry Division (Hung), 23.Reserve Division (Hung) (remnants)
IV Corps (Hung): 1.Assault Brigade (Hung), 31.SS-Volunteer-Grenadier Division

Commander of the German troops in Hungary: 23.SS Mountain Division 'Kama' (Croatian Nr 2) (forming), 277.Volks-Grenadier Division (forming and moving to the West), 326.Volks-Grenadier Division (forming)

OKW Theatre of War

Army Group F (Commander-in-Chief Southeast):
2.Panzer-Army: SS–Police Regiment 5, SS–Police-Mountain Regiment 18, Commander 'Syrmia' (Commandant of the Rear Area 582), Grenadier Brigade 92 (mot.) (remnants), Panzer-Grenadier Division 'Brandenburg', 1.Mountain Division + 117.Jaeger Division, 118.Jaeger Division

2.4 2ND UKRAINIAN FRONT, 7 NOVEMBER 1944

40th Army
II Army Corps (Rom): 8th, 11th and 21st Infantry Divisions (Rom); 1st Cavalry Division (Rom).
VI Army Corps (Rom): 3rd, 6th, 9th and 11th Infantry Divisions (Rom); 18th Mountain Division (Rom).
50th Rifle Corps: 38th and 232nd Rifle Divisions; 42nd Guards Rifle Division.
51st Rifle Corps: 38th, 133rd and 232nd Rifle Divisions.

40th Army assets:
Rifle Troops: 54th and 159th Fortified Regions 42nd Guards Rifle Division.
Artillery: 153rd Canon Artillery Brigade; 680th Anti-Tank Artillery Regiment; 10th Mortar Regiment (mule-borne); 97th Guards Mortar Regiment; 623rd Anti-Aircraft Artillery Regiment.

4th Army (Rom)
(operationally subordinated to the 40th Army)

27th Army
33rd Rifle Corps: 78th and 337th Rifle Divisions; 3rd Mountain Division (Rom).
104th Rifle Corps: 163rd Rifle Division; 4th Guards Airborne Division; 2nd Mountain Division (Rom).
35th Guards Rifle Corps: 202nd and 206th Rifle Divisions; 93rd Guards Rifle Division; 3rd Guards Airborne Division.

27th Army assets:
Armour: 25th Tank Regiment.
Artillery: 11th Artillery Division; 27th Canon Artillery Brigade; 30th Anti-Tank Artillery Brigade; 315th Anti-Tank Artillery Regiment; 480th and 492nd Mortar Regiments; 80th and 328th Guards Mortar Regiments; 11th Anti-Aircraft Artillery Division.

53rd Army
57th Rifle Corps: 203rd and 228th Rifle Divisions; 1st Guards Airborne Division.
49th Rifle Corps: 6th, 243rd and 375th Rifle Divisions; 110th Guards Rifle Division.

53rd Army assets:
Artillery: 5th Artillery Division; 152nd Canon Artillery Brigade; 1316th Anti-Tank Artillery Regiment; 461st Mortar Regiment; 17th Guards Mortar Regiment; 27th Anti-Aircraft Artillery Division.

7th Guards Army
24th Guards Rifle Corps: 72nd and 81st Guards Rifle Divisions.
27th Guards Rifle Corps: 227th, 303rd and 409th Rifle Divisions.
25th Guards Rifle Corps: 53rd and 297th Rifle Division; 36th Guards Rifle Division.
VII Army Corps (Rom): 2nd and 19th Infantry Divisions (Rom); 9th Cavalry Division (Rom); 1st and 7th Artillery Regiments (Rom).

7th Guards Army assets:

Rifle Troops: 6th Guards Airborne Division.
Armour: 27th Guards Tank Brigade.
Artillery: 16th Artillery Division; 41st Canon Artillery Brigade; 2nd and 34th Anti-Tank Artillery Brigades; 114th and 115th Anti-Tank Artillery Regiments; 263rd, 290th and 493rd Mortar Regiments; 302nd and 309th Guards Mortar Regiments; 5th and 26th Anti-Aircraft Artillery Divisions.

1st Army (Rom)

(operationally subordinated to the 7th Guards Army)

46th Army

37th Rifle Corps: 320th Rifle Division; 59th and 108th Guards Rifle Divisions.
10th Guards Rifle Corps: 49th, 86th and 109th Guards Rifle Divisions.
23rd Rifle Corps: 99th and 316th Rifle Divisions; 68th Guards Rifle Division.
31st Guards Rifle Corps: 34th and 40th Guards Rifle Divisions.
2nd Guards Mechanised Corps: 4th, 5th and 6th Guards Mechanised Brigades; 37th Guards Tank Brigade.
4thGuards Mechanised Corps: 13th, 14th and 15th Guards Mechanised Brigades; 36th Guards Tank Brigade.

46th Army assets:

Rifle Troops: 4th Guards Rifle Division (Army reserve).
Artillery: 7th Artillery Division; 45th Canon Artillery Brigade; 12th and 24th Anti-Tank Artillery Brigades; 437th Anti-Tank Artillery Regiment; 462nd Mortar Regiment; 47th and 48th Guards Mortar Regiments; 9th and 38th Anti-Aircraft Artillery Divisions.
Armour: 991st, 1505th and 1897th Self-Propelled Artillery Regiments.

6th Guards Tank Army

5th Guards Tank Corps: 20th, 21st and 22nd Guards Tank Brigades; 6th Guards Motorised Rifle Brigade.
9th Guards Mechanised Corps: 18th, 30th and 31st Guards Mechanised Brigades; 46th Guards Tank Brigade.

6th Guards Tank Army assets:

Artillery: 202nd Light Artillery Brigade; 301st and 1667th Anti-Tank Artillery Regiments; 454th and 458th Mortar Regiments; 57th Guards Mortar Regiment; 1696th and 1700th Anti-Aircraft Artillery Regiments.

Gorshkov Cavalry-Tank Group

(the command of the 5th Guards Cavalry Corps)
5th Guards Cavalry Corps: 11th and 12th Guards Cavalry Divisions; 63rd Cavalry Division.
7th Mechanised Corps: 16th, 63rd and 64th Mechanised Brigades; 41st Guards Tank Brigade.

Gorshkov Cavalry-Tank Group assets:

Artillery assigned to **5th Guards Cavalry Corps:** 150th Anti-Tank Artillery Regiment; 9th Guards Mortar Regiment; 585th Anti-Aircraft Artillery Regiment.
Artillery assigned to **7th Mechanised Corps:** 109th Anti-Tank Artillery Regiment; 614th Mortar Regiment; 1713th Anti-Aircraft Artillery Regiment.

Pliev Cavalry-Tank Group
(the command of the 4th Guards Cavalry Corps)
4th Guards Cavalry Corps: 9th and 10th Guards Cavalry Divisions; 30th Cavalry Division.
6th Guards Cavalry Corps: 8th and 13th Guards Cavalry Divisions; 8th Cavalry Division.
23rd Tank Corps: 3rd, 39th and 135th Tank Brigades; 56th Motorised Rifle Brigade.

Pliev Cavalry-Tank Group assets:
Artillery assigned to **23rd Tank Corps:** 11th Anti-Tank Artillery Brigade; 12th Guards Mortar
    Regiment; 225th and 255th Anti-Aircraft Artillery Regiments.
Artillery assigned to **6th Guards Cavalry Corps:** 142nd Anti-Tank Artillery Regiment; 11th Guards
    Mortar Regiment; 459th and 1732nd Anti-Aircraft Artillery Regiments.

Front Assets
Rifle Troops: 180th Rifle Division; 25th Guards Rifle Division; 1st Volunteer Infantry Division 'Tudor
    Vladimirescu' (Rom).
Artillery: 22nd and 31st Anti-Tank Artillery Brigades; 66th and 324th Guards Mortar Regiments; 30th
    Anti-Aircraft Artillery Division; 249th, 272nd and 1651st Anti-Aircraft Artillery Regiments.

2.5 ARMY GROUP SOUTH TROOP ASSIGNMENTS AND SUBORDINATIONS, 29 OCTOBER–6 NOVEMBER 1944

29 October 1944
3.Army (Hung) was subordinated to 6.Army and thus Armeegruppe Fretter-Pico was created
1.Panzer Division was subordinated to LVII Panzer Corps
3.Mountain-Division was subordinated to III Panzer Corps

30 October 1944
Group 'Budapest' [VI Army Corps (Hung), 22.SS-Cavalry-Division 'Maria Theresa' and Combat
    Commandant 'Budapest'] was subordinated to Armeegruppe Fretter-Pico
1.Armoured Division (Hung), 23.Panzer Division (with Heavy Panzer Battalion 503) and 24.Panzer
    Division were subordinated to LVII Panzer Corps
8.Reserve Division (Hung) was subordinated to LVII Panzer Corps
Panzer-Grenadier Division 'Feldherrnhalle' was subordinated to Armeegruppe Fretter-Pico
5.Reserve Division (Hung) was subordinated to VIII Army Corps (Hung)
II Army Corps (Hung), with the remnants of 4. and 12.Reserve Divisions (Hung), was subordinated to
    2.Army (Hung)
VII Army Corps (Hung) with Group 'Szücs' (Hung), 10.Infantry Division (Hung) and 23.Reserve
    Division (Hung) was subordinated to Armeegruppe Fretter-Pico
Group 'Finta' (Hung) was subordinated to IX Army Corps (Hung)
2.Armoured Division (Hung), 13.Panzer Division, 3.Mountain-Division, 46.Infantry Division and
    2.Reserve Division (Hung) were subordinated to XXIX Army Corps

31 October 1944
II Army Corps (Hung) was subordinated to Armeegruppe Fretter-Pico
1.Huszar Division (Hung) was subordinated to VII Army Corps (Hung)
20.Infantry Division (Hung) was subordinated to VIII Army Corps (Hung)
III Panzer Corps was subordinated Armeegruppe Fretter-Pico

1 November 1944

VII Army Corps (Hung) with 10.Infantry Division (Hung), 23.Reserve Division and 1.Huszar Division (Hung) was subordinated to III Panzer Corps

LVII Panzer Corps [1.Panzer Division, 23.Panzer Division, 24.Panzer Division and 1.Armoured Division (Hung)] was consolidated with VIII Army Corps (Hung) [5.Reserve Division (Hung), 8.Reserve Division (Hung) and 20.Infantry Division (Hung)] into Group 'Kirchner'

25.Infantry Division (Hung) was subordinated to 76.Infantry Division

II Army Corps (Hung) was subordinated to 2.Army (Hung)

Until the arrival of a SS-Corps headquarters, 22.SS-Cavalry-Division 'Maria Theresa' would be tactically subordinated to 8.SS-Cavalry-Division 'Floryan Geyer'

2 November 1944

18.SS-Panzer-Grenadier Division 'Horst Wessel' (Commander-in-Chief 'Slovakia') was ordered to transfer to Army Group South and upon its arrival to subordinate to it

VII Army Corps (Hung) [the remnants of 23.Reserve Division (Hung), 1.Armoured Division (Hung) and 1.Huszar Division (Hung)] and III Panzer Corps (22.SS-Cavalry-Division 'Maria Theresa', part of 13.Panzer Division, Panzer-Grenadier Division 'Feldherrnhalle' and 8.SS-Cavalry-Division 'Floryan Geyer') were consolidated into Panzer Group 'Breith'

4.SS-Police-Panzer-Grenadier Division was subordinated to IV Panzer Corps

25.Infantry Division (Hung) and 76.Infantry Division were subordinated to LXXII Army Corps

12.Reserve Division (Hung), which had absorbed the remnants of the 4.Infantry Division (Hung), was subordinated to Armeegruppe Fretter-Pico

4.Mountain-Division was subordinated to 1.Army (Hung)

3 November 1944

VII Army Corps (Hung) [10.Infantry Division (Hung) and the remnants of 23.Reserve Division (Hung)] was subordinated to 2.Army (Hung)

1.Armoured Division (Hung) was subordinated to Panzer-Grenadier Division 'Feldherrnhalle'

4 November 1944

Corps Group 'Budapest' was subordinated to III Panzer Corps

Grenadier Regiment 42 (46.Infantry Division) was subordinated to 24.Panzer Division

VIII Army Corps (Hung) and the headquarters of 20.Infantry Division (Hung) were placed at the disposal of 3.Army (Hung)

18.SS-Panzer-Grenadier Division 'Horst Wessel' was ordered to deploy in the Jászberény area and to subordinate to Armeegruppe Fretter-Pico

XVII Army Corps [8.Jaeger-Division, 16.Infantry Division (Hung) and 24.Infantry Division (Hung)] was subordinated to 1.Army (Hung)

5 November 1944

31.SS-Grenadier Division and the River Brigade (Hung) were subordinated to II Army Corps (Hung) [2.Army (Hung)]

271.Volks-Grenadier Division (Commander-in-Chief 'Slovakia') was ordered to transfer to Army Group South

VII Army Corps (Hung) [10.Infantry Division (Hung) and 271.Volks-Grendaier Division] was subordinated to Armeegruppe Fretter-Pico

Corps Group 'Budapest' was disbanded; Battle Commandant 'Budapest' and VI Army Corps (Hung) were subordinated to Panzer Group 'Breith'

46.Infantry Division was subordinated to LVII Panzer Corps

6 November 1944

The remnants of 23.Reserve Division (Hung) were subordinated to Group 'Kesseoe' [2.Army (Hung)]

The main body of 1.Panzer Division was subordinated to 13.Panzer Division

18.SS-Panzer-Grenadier Division 'Horst Wessel' was subordinated to IV Panzer Corps

76.Infantry Division, with the assigned 25.Infantry Division (Hung), was subordinated to IV Panzer Corps

24.Panzer Division was subordinated to IV Panzer Corps

The combat-capable elements of 2.Armoured Division (Hung) were subordinated to 24.Panzer Division

2.6 2ND UKRAINIAN FRONT TROOP ASSIGNMENTS AND SUBORDINATIONS, 29 OCTOBER–6 NOVEMBER 1944

29 October 1944

2nd Guards Mechanised Corps was subordinated to 46th Army

4th Guards Mechanised Corps was subordinated to 46th Army

23rd Rifle Corps was subordinated to 46th Army

24th Anti-Tank Artillery Brigade was subordinated to 46th Army

5th Mountain Engineer Brigade was subordinated to 46th Army

2nd Anti-Tank Artillery Brigade was ordered to detach from the 7th Guards Army and assemble in the vicinity of Karcag as Front reserve

34th Anti-Tank Artillery Brigade was ordered to detach from the Pliev Cavalry-Tank Group and assemble in the vicinity of Debrecen as Front reserve

27th Guards Tank Brigade was ordered to detach from the 27th Army and assemble at Mez túr as Front reserve to rest and refit.

30 October 1944

6th Guards Airborne Division was detached from the 53rd Army and subordinated to the 7th Guards Army

31 October 1944

5th Guards Cavalry Corps was ordered to detach from the Pliev Cavalry-Tank Group and assemble in the vicinity of Sáránd and Hosszú-Pályi as Front reserve

7th Mechanised Corps was ordered to pull off the frontline and assemble in the vicinity of Hajdúszoboszló as reserve of the Pliev Cavalry-Tank Group

35th Guards Rifle Corps (6th Guards Airborne Division, 93rd Guards Rifle Division and 180th Rifle Division) was ordered to pull off the frontline and assemble in the vicinity of Balmazújváros and Hajdúböszörmény as reserve of the 27th Army

18th Tank Corps was detached from the 6th Guards Tank Army and transferred to the 3rd Ukrainian Front

1 November 1944

51st Rifle Corps (38th Rifle Division and 42nd Guards Rifle Division) was detached from the 27th Army and subordinated to the 40th Army.

180th Rifle Division was ordered to detach from the 27th Army and assemble in the vicinity of Kisújszállás as Front reserve

27th Guards Tank Brigade was subordinated to 7th Guards Army

2 November 1944

7th Mechanised Corps and 5th Guards Cavalry Corps were detached from the Pliev Cavalry-Tank Group and placed directly under the command of the 2nd Ukrainian Front

5 November 1944

Gorshkov Cavalry-Mechanised Group was formed consisting of 5th Guards Cavalry Corps and 7th Mechanised Corps

2.7 GERMAN AUXILIARY STAFF ASSIGNED TO HUNGARIAN FORMATIONS, 28 OCTOBER 1944

DVSt 2	2.Army
DVSt 3	3.Army
DVSt 6	1.Army
DVK 14	VIII Corps
DVK 15	IV Corps
DVK 16	II Corps
DVK 17	IX Corps
DVK 21	VII Corps
DVK 23	VI Corps
DVK 25	V Corps
DVK 100	4.Reserve Division
DVK 102	9.Border-Guard Brigade
DVK 106	12.Reserve Division
DVK 114	1.Huszar Division
DVK 129	23.Infantry (Reserve) Division
DVK 130	1.Armoured Division
DVK 131	2.Reserve Division
DVK 134	8.Infantry (Reserve) Division
DVK 139	16.Infantry Division
DVK 140	13.Infantry Division
DVK 142	20.Infantry Division
DVK 145	24.Infantry Division
DVK 146	25.Infantry Division
DVK 147	27.Light Division
DVK 148	10.Infantry Division
DVK 149	2.Armoured Division
DVK 150	1.Mountain Brigade
DVK 151	2.Mountain Brigade
DVK 154	6.Infantry Division

APPENDIX 3

TROOP STRENGTHS

3.1 ARMY GROUP SOUTH, 27 OCTOBER 1944

Division	Infantry	Tanks				Assault Guns	Artillery Guns	Heavy AT Guns	Combat worth
		III	IV	V	VI				
1. Army (Hung)									
6. Infantry Division (Hung)	n/a	–	–	–	–	–	43	4	>IV
13. Infantry Division (Hung)	n/a	–	–	–	–	–	42	7	n/a
16. Infantry Division (Hung)	2000	–	–	–	–	–	33	8	III/IV
24. Infantry Division (Hung)	2000	–	–	–	–	–	28	10	IV
1. Mountain Brigade (Hung)	700	–	–	–	–	–	28	4	IV
2. Mountain Brigade (Hung)	700	–	–	–	–	–	21	4	>IV
8. Army									
15. Infantry Division	900	–	–	–	–	6	3	6	III
4. Mountain Division	3350	–	–	–	–	17	35	12	II
8. SS–Cavalry–Division	3060	–	–	–	–	10	37	19	II
3. Mountain Division	2000	–	–	–	–	5	35	10	III
8. Jaeger–Division	2100	–	–	–	–	3	41	20	I
2. Reserve Division (Hung)	n/a	–	–	–	–	–	8	4	IV
Group 'Finta': 7. Reserve Division (Hung) 1. Mountain Res. Brigade (Hung) 2. Mountain Res. Brigade (Hung)	2250	–	–	–	–	–	12	1	>IV
9. Reserve–Division (Hung)	n/a	–	–	–	–	–	12	1	n/a
9. Border–Guard Brigade (Hung)	n/a	–	–	–	–	–	4	–	>IV
27. Light Division (Hung)	1200	–	–	–	–	–	29	18	IV
6. Army									
24. Panzer–Division	1600	–	11	–	14	7	45	13	II
4. SS–Panzer–Grenadier Division	1100	–	–	–	30	8	41	18	II
Pz.G. Division 'Feldherrnhalle'	900	–	–	–	–	10	7	3	III

13.Panzer–Division	1100	1	–	6	–	1	14	2	II
23.Panzer–Division	850	2	–	2	–	28	30	9	II
1.Panzer–Division	1000	9	–	8	–	2	30	11	II
76.Infantry–Division	1900	–	–	–	–	2	13	2	III
4.Reserve Division (Hung)	Destroyed, the remnants were assigned to 12.Res.Div.								
12.Reserve Division (Hung)	1800	–	–	–	–	–	19	5	>IV
25.Infantry Division (Hung)	n/a	–	–	–	–	–	8	16	>IV
2.Armoured Division (Hung)	700	n/a				n/a	18	8	II/III
3.Army (Hung)									
5.Reserve Division (Hung)	n/a								
6.Reserve Division (Hung)	Destroyed, the remnants were assigned to 8.Res.Div.								
8.Reserve Division (Hung)	3300	–	–	–	–	–	26	15	>IV
10.Infantry Division (Hung)	800	–	–	–	–	–	12	9	–
20.Infantry Division (Hung)	1500	–	–	–	–	–	15	11	IV
23.Reserve Division (Hung)	3600	–	–	–	–	–	47	26	IV
1.Huszar–Division (Hung)	3700	Ca. 20 light tanks				n/a	30	15	II
1.Armoured Division (Hung)	700					n/a	7	2	III
Group 'Szücs' (Hung)	1800	–	–	–	–	–	8	3	IV

Notes
- The strength of the Hungarian divisions as per 25 October 1944.
- The mentioned figures by no means represent the combat strength of the whole army group; for example, the strength of the majority of the GHQ units at the disposal of the army group was not reported, as well as the ground units of the Luftwaffe and the Navy.
- The Tiger tanks (VI) reported by 24.Panzer and 4.SS-Police-Panzer-Grenadier Divisions belonged to the Heavy Panzer Battalion 503.

3.2 STRENGTH OF THE 2ND GUARDS MECHANISED CORPS, 29 OCTOBER 1944

Unit	Personnel				Motor vehicles				Motorcycles	Tanks		Self-propelled guns		Armoured personnel carriers
	Officers	NCO	Men	Total	Cars	Trucks	Special	Tractors		T-34-85	JS-2	SU-76	SU-85	
4th Guards Mechanised Brigade	370	1115	1992	3477	12	209	19	–	19	35	–	–	–	12
5th Guards Mechanised Brigade	371	1016	2134	3521	13	217	23	–	22	35	–	–	–	12
6th Guards Mechanised Brigade	368	988	2161	3517	13	209	21	–	23	35	–	–	–	12

Units														
37th Guards Tank Brigade	263	584	549	1396	5	105	17	3	13	65	–	–	–	3
30th Guards Heavy Tank Regiment	87	137	149	373	2	38	6	–	2	–	21	–	–	3
1509th Self-Propelled Artillery Regiment	54	107	61	222	1	24	–	–	5	–	–	21	–	–
251st Self-Propelled Artillery Regiment	60	139	110	309	2	39	2	–	3	–	–	–	21	–
99th Guards Motorcycle Battalion	48	189	224	461	2	13	2	–	98	10	–	–	–	12
524th Mortar Regiment	64	150	351	565	1	63	–	–	3	–	–	–	–	–
408th Guards Mortar Battalion	19	63	110	192	1	25	1	–	–	–	–	–	–	–
159th Anti-Aircraft Artillery Regiment	41	103	254	398	2	44	–	–	1	–	–	–	–	–
Corps' command and corps' units	320	399	895	1615	29	199	60	–	27	5	–	–	–	–
Total	2065	4990	8990	16045	83	1185	151	3	216	185	21	21	21	54

Units	BA-64 Armoured cars	M17 Anti-aircraft half-tracks	Rifles	PPSh sub-machine guns	Machine guns			Anti-tank rifles	Artillery guns				Mortars	
					7.62mm light	7.62mm heavy	12.7mm DShK		76mm	45mm	57mm	37mm AA	82mm	120mm
4th Guards Mechanised Brigade	8	–	1466	1301	113	45	10	88	11	8	4	–	30	6
5th Guards Mechanised Brigade	8	–	1469	1283	112	45	9	89	12	8	4	2	30	6
6th Guards Mechanised Brigade	8	–	1456	1303	113	45	10	99	12	8	4	–	30	6

Unit														
37th Guards Tank Brigade	–	–	351	446	22	4	9	18	4	–	–	–	6	–
30th Guards Heavy Tank Regiment	1	–	97	145	1	–	–	–	–	–	–	–	–	–
1509th Self-Propelled Artillery Regiment	1	–	83	27	–	–	–	–	–	–	–	–	–	–
251st Self-Propelled Artillery Regiment	1	–	105	97	–	–	–	–	–	–	–	–	–	–
99th Guards Motorcycle Battalion	7	–	91	183	18	–	–	–	–	–	4	–	4	–
524th Mortar Regiment	–	–	334	95	–	–	–	36	–	–	–	–	–	36
408th Guards Mortar Battalion	–	–	96	21	4	–	–	–	–	–	–	–	–	–
159th Anti-Aircraft Artillery Regiment	–	16	256	53	–	–	16	–	–	–	–	16	–	–
Corps' command and corps' units	10	–	776	159	4	–	–	–	–	–	–	–	–	–
Total	44	16	6580	5113	386	139	54	330	39	24	16	18	100	54

Unit	M-13 Katyusha	Radios
4th Guards Mechanised Brigade	–	30
5th Guards Mechanised Brigade	–	30
6th Guards Mechanised Brigade	–	31
37th Guards Tank Brigade	–	12
30th Guards Heavy Tank Regiment	–	4
1509th Self-Propelled Artillery Regiment	–	2
251st Self-Propelled Artillery Regiment	–	2
99th Guards Motorcycle Battalion	–	6
524th Mortar Regiment	–	12
408th Guards Mortar Battalion	8	6
159th Anti-Aircraft Artillery Regiment	–	9
Corps' command and corps' units	–	18
Total	8	163

3.3 STRENGTH OF 46TH ARMY, 1 NOVEMBER 1944

Units and Formations	Personnel (men/women)				Horses	Motor vehicles	Tractors, prime movers	Motorcycles	Rifles	Sub-machine guns	Machine-guns	Anti-tank rifles	Artillery Guns/Mortars	Self-propelled guns
	Officers	NCO	Enlisted men	Total										
Rifle Troops														
10 Guards Rifle Corps														
10 Guards Rifle Corps' staff and units	155/3	248/5	759/10	1163/19	173	100	3	5	800	120	12	10	–	–
49 Guards Rifle Division	737/13	1237/13	4052/44	6027/71	1765	171	2	4	2614	1088	276	94	61/61	–
86 Guards Rifle Division	769/21	1399/13	5092/3	7260/37	1856	105	–	–	3010	940	330	62	63/60	–
109 Guards Rifle Division	723/16	1157/20	3828/9	5708/45	1515	116	–	–	2254	914	232	53	64/59	–
Total	2384/53	4041/51	13731/66	20158/172	5309	492	5	9	8678	3062	850	219	188/180	–
31 Guards Rifle Corps														
31 Guards Rifle Corps' staff and units	136/5	177/9	516/19	833/37	109	80	–	5	320	213	–	–	–	–
34 Guards Rifle Division	803/22	1127/18	3556/32	5486/72	1232	149	35	–	2040	1108	211	40	46/59	–
40 Guards Rifle Division	841/15	1241/14	4904/31	6986/60	1752	158	–	–	3174	1515	293	55	61/69	–
Total	1780/42	2545/41	8976/82	13301/165	3093	387	35	5	5534	2836	504	95	107/128	–
37 Rifle Corps														
37 Rifle Corps' staff and units	133/3	172/12	511/25	817/41	117	84	–	–	308	112	–	–	–	–
59 Guards Rifle Division	699/20	963/27	5545/51	7207/98	1756	123	1	–	2558	902	187	24	62/57	–
108 Guards Rifle Division	799/17	1165/23	5456/17	7420/57	1415	163	–	–	2565	881	223	47	79/61	–
320 Rifle Division	703/25	1151/20	5363/3	7217/48	1929	137	–	–	2765	943	244	51	58/62	–
Total	2334/65	3451/82	16875/96	22661/244	5217	508	1	–	8196	2838	654	122	199/180	–
Army Reserve														
4 Guards Rifle Division	845/18	1193/18	4796/16	6834/52	1823	151	1	–	2863	1616	355	45	89/64	–
Blocking Detachments														
112 Blocking Detachment	9	39	142	190	10	5	–	–	28	113	10	–	–	–
115 Blocking Detachment	9	41	144	194	12	2	–	–	52	111	9	–	–	–
139 Blocking Detachment	9	41	147	197	75	3	–	–	71	108	9	–	–	–
Total	27	121	433	581	97	10	–	–	151	332	28	–	–	–

Penal Companies

84 Army Penal Company	10	24	152	186	24	-	-	-	110	40	-	2	-
127 Army Penal Company	9	19	196	224	9	-	-	-	210	44	14	-	-
206 Army Penal Company	5	23	188	216	39	-	-	-	131	17	10	-	-
206 'A' Army Penal Company	6	4	16	26	10	-	-	-	-	-	-	-	-
331 Army Penal Company	8	2	297	307	13	-	-	-	206	32	6	3	-
Penal companies total	38	72	849	959	95	-	-	-	657	133	30	5	-
Total	7408/178	11423/192	45660/260	64498/637	15634	1548	42	14	26079	10817	2421	486	583/559

Armoured Troops

991 Self-Propelled Artillery Regiment	50	80	77	207	-	31	-	3	90	33	-	-	14
1505 Self-Propelled Artillery Regiment	57	82	83	222	-	27	-	5	90	36	-	-	19
1897 Self-Propelled Artillery Regiment	56	104	62	222	-	27	-	-	56	19	-	-	21
Total	163	266	222	651	-	85	-	8	236	88	-	-	54

Artillery

7 Artillery Division

Divisional staff and units	119	142	440	701	-	128	3	-	105	103	-	-	-
11 Light Artillery Brigade	139	315/3	596	1050/3	-	70	88	-	140	172	-	6	45
25 Howitzer Artillery Brigade	224	488	1114	1826	-	87	101	-	677	176	-	40	76
17 Cannon Artillery Brigade	178/1	370/3	855/3	1403/7	-	71	34	-	721	215	6	24	34
9 Guards Cannon Artillery Brigade	174/1	348/4	884/3	1406/8	-	125	60	-	403	281	18	37	36
3 Mortar Brigade	193/3	372/4	899/2	1464/9	-	124	-	-	458	304	-	66	-/92
105 Super-Heavy Howitzer Artillery Brigade	120	207	705	1032	-	78	85	-	718	171	23	24	24
Total	1147/5	2242/14	5493/8	8882/27	-	683	371	-	3222	1422	47	197	215/92

Army Artillery

45 Cannon Artillery Brigade	135	385	873	1393	-	95	65	-	977	199	12	36	36
437 Anti-Tank Artillery Regiment	53	119	302	474	-	16	27	-	53	232	11	23	23
462 Mortar Regiment	65	140	303	596	-	30	15	-	250	164	-	25	-/29
92 Corps Artillery Regiment	65	180	355	600	38	22	20	1	223	44	10	-	26
Total	1465/5	3266/14	7326/8	12057/27	38	846	498	1	4725	2061	80	281	300/121

Anti-Aircraft Artillery

Staff and support units of 38 Anti-Aircraft Artillery Division	55/1	48/1	115/2	224/10	34	28	6	–	102	46	–	–	–	–
1401 Anti-Aircraft Artillery Regiment	40/1	124/2	298/1	462/4	20	13	21	–	259	56	4	–	16	–
1405 Anti-Aircraft Artillery Regiment	39	107/3	335	481/3	16	9	18	–	140	88	13	–	22	–
1409 Anti-Aircraft Artillery Regiment	43/1	134/2	306/1	483/4	19	13	19	–	172	75	13	–	24	–
1712 Anti-Aircraft Artillery Regiment	37/2	123/8	321	481/10	20	18	12	–	140	83	16	–	22	–
115 Aerial Surveillance Company	8/1	39/3	91/3	138/7	36	5	–	–	98	8	–	–	–	–
38 Anti-Aircraft Artillery Division total	222/6	575/19	1466/7	2269/38	145	86	76	–	911	356	46	–	84	–
Combat Troops Total	9258/9	15430/225	54674/275	79375/702	15817	2365	616	23	31951	13322	2547	767	967/680	54
Combat-Support Troops														
Signal troops	161/4	304/17	1253/59	1718/80	314	127	3	11	940	135	–	–	–	–
Engineer troops	138/15	119/16	912/39	1169/70	250	41	13	5	572	194	8	–	–	–
Motorised transport troops	82/4	120/1	669/15	871/20	–	307	12	9	318	–	–	–	–	–
Horse-drawn transport troops	8/2	28/1	176	212/3	336	–	–	–	131	8	–	–	–	–
Field HQ of 46 Army	377/4	29	4	456/50	–	–	–	–	–	30	–	–	–	–
HQ support units	44	143/2	304	491/2	39	142	4	4	188	103	9	9	–	–
SMERSH (Counterintelligence)	62	33	85	180	20	1	–	–	21	76	10	1	–	–
Combat Support Troops Total	1036/39	1083/45	4377/114	6542/244	1145	765	32	29	2725	893	73	31	–	–
Service and Support Troops Total	1072/256	966/286	4323/221	7139/1388	1139	324	2	7	2299	57	11	–	–	–
Replacement and Convalescent Troops Total	356	556	4719	5647/16	361	11	2	–	4867	307	128	4	10	–
Field Training Troops Total	40/2	5	7	291/20	15	2	–	–	104	31	14	2	–	–
452 Army Air Squadron Total	29	23	23	75	–	5	–	–	11	–	–	–	–	–
Miscellaneous troops Total	278/13	400/19	939/18	1811/211	336	58	–	–	737	308	48	27	–	–
46th Army Total	12069/499	19874/767	69062/628	W100880/2581	18813	3830	650	59	42694	14918	2821	831	977/680	54

Notes

- No breakdown is given for the signal, engineer, motorised and horse-drawn transport troops, HQ support troops, service and support troops (medical and veterinary units, bakeries, baggage trains, trophy-collection services, fuel depots, army's newspaper and print service, workshops and technical maintenance, goods and spare-parts stores, traffic control services, commandants offices, construction battalions), replacement and convalescent troops, miscellaneous troops (military censorship, military trade, commercial and financial services, NKVD troops).

- The following formations of 46th Army are not included in the table:

2nd Guards Mechanised Corps
4th Guards Mechanised Corps
The HQ of the 23rd Rifle Corps (subordinated on 29.10.1944) – 847 men
68th Guards Rifle Division (subordinated on 29.10.1944) – 6768 men
99th Rifle Division (subordinated on 29.10.1944) – 6525 men
316th Rifle Division (subordinated on 29.10.1944) – 7313 men
12th Anti-Tank Artillery Brigade (subordinated on 1.11.1944) – 1256 men
24th Anti-Tank Artillery Brigade (subordinated on 29.10.1944) – 1230 men
9th Anti-Aircraft Artillery Division (subordinated on 25.10.1944) – 2119 men
208th and 209th Horse-drawn Transport Companies (created on 25.10.1944) – 216 men

- The 112th, 115th and 139th Blocking Detachments were ordered to disband on 1.11.1944.

3.4 FIREPOWER OF THE COMBAT TROOPS OF 46TH ARMY, 1 NOVEMBER 1944

Units and Formations	Machine guns				Artillery guns								Mortars	
	7.62mm light	7.62mm heavy	12.7mm	12.7mm Anti-Aircraft	76mm Regimental	76mm Divisional	122mm Howitzer	152mm Gun-Howitzer	203mm Howitzer	45mm Anti-Tank	37mm Anti-Aircraft	85mm Anti-Aircraft	82mm	120mm
Rifle Troops														
10 Guards Rifle Corps														
10 Guards Rifle Corps' staff and units	12	–	–	–	–	–	–	–	–	–	–	–	–	–
49 Guards Rifle Division	145	113	18	–	9	27	9	–	–	16	–	–	49	12
86 Guards Rifle Division	192	120	–	18	8	26	8	–	–	21	–	–	50	10
109 Guards Rifle Division	141	78	13	–	10	26	8	–	–	21	–	–	47	12
Total	490	311	31	18	27	79	27	–	–	58	–	–	146	34
31 Guards Rifle Corps														
34 Guards Rifle Division	95	99	–	17	6	25	8	–	–	7	–	–	49	10
40 Guards Rifle Division	162	112	–	19	6	28	9	–	–	18	–	–	58	11
Total	257	211	–	36	12	53	17	–	–	25	–	–	107	21
37 Rifle Corps														
59 Guards Rifle Division	93	78	–	16	9	27	10	–	–	16	–	–	48	9
108 Guards Rifle Division	142	67	14	–	8	33	12	–	–	26	–	–	50	11
320 Rifle Division	150	81	13	–	8	28	4	–	–	18	–	–	51	11
Total	385	226	27	16	27	88	26	–	–	60	–	–	149	31
Army Reserve														
4 Guards Rifle Division	201	136	–	18	6	29	9	–	–	45	–	–	51	13
Blocking Detachments														
112 Blocking Detachment	7	3	–	–	–	–	–	–	–	–	–	–	–	–
115 Blocking Detachment	6	3	–	–	–	–	–	–	–	–	–	–	–	–
139 Blocking Detachment	9	–	–	–	–	–	–	–	–	–	–	–	–	–
Total	22	6	–	–	–	–	–	–	–	–	–	–	–	–
Penal Companies														
84 Army Penal Company	–	–	–	–	–	–	–	–	–	–	–	–	3	–
127 Army Penal Company	11	3	–	–	–	–	–	–	–	–	–	–	–	–
206 Army Penal Company	10	–	–	–	–	–	–	–	–	–	–	–	2	–
331 Army Penal Company	4	2	–	–	–	–	–	–	–	–	–	–	2	–
Total	25	5	–	–	–	–	–	–	–	–	–	–	7	–
Rifle Troops Total	1380	895	58	88	72	249	79	–	–	178	–	–	460	81

Artillery													
7 Artillery Division													
11 Light Artillery Brigade	–	–	–	–	–	45	–	–	–	–	–	–	–	–
25 Howitzer Artillery Brigade	–	–	–	–	–	–	76	–	–	–	–	–	–	–
17 Cannon Artillery Brigade	6	–	–	–	–	–	–	34	–	–	–	–	–	–
9 Guards Cannon Artillery Brigade	18	–	–	–	–	–	18	18	–	–	–	–	–	–
3 Mortar Brigade	–	–	–	–	–	–	–	–	–	–	–	–	–	92
105 Super-Heavy Howitzer Artillery Brigade	23	–	–	–	–	–	–	–	24	–	–	–	–	–
Total	47	–	–	–	–	45	94	52	24	–	–	–	–	92
Army Artillery													
45 Cannon Artillery Brigade	12	–	–	–	–	–	–	36	–	–	–	–	–	–
437 Anti-Tank Artillery Regiment	11	–	–	–	–	23	–	–	–	–	–	–	–	–
462 Mortar Regiment	–	–	–	–	–	–	–	–	–	–	–	–	–	–
92 Corps Artillery Regiment	10	–	–	–	–	15	11	–	–	–	–	–	–	29
Total	80	–	–	–	–	83	105	88	24	–	–	–	–	121
Anti-Aircraft Artillery													
1401 Anti-A. Artillery Regiment	–	–	4	–	–	–	–	–	–	–	–	16	–	–
1405 Anti-A. Artillery Regiment	–	–	13	–	–	–	–	–	–	–	22	–	–	–
1409 Anti-A. Artillery Regiment	–	–	13	–	–	–	–	–	–	–	24	–	–	–
1712 Anti-A. Artillery Regiment	–	–	16	–	–	–	–	–	–	–	22	–	–	–
38 Anti-Aircraft Artillery Division total	–	–	46	–	–	–	–	–	–	–	68	16	–	–
Combat Troops Total	1460	895	104	88	72	332	184	88	24	178	68	16	460	202

3.5 STRENGTH OF 4TH GUARDS MECHANISED CORPS, 1 NOVEMBER 1944

Personnel   13,403 men

Vehicles

Motor vehicles	1263
Motorcycles	41
Prime movers	33
Armoured personnel carriers and armoured cars	45
T-34 tanks	106
SU-85 self-propelled guns	3
ISU-122 self-propelled guns	15

Artillery

45mm anti-tank guns	25
57mm anti-tank guns	18
76mm guns	31
37mm anti-aircraft guns	20
25mm anti-aircraft guns	8
82mm mortars	93
120mm mortars	44
M–13 rocket launchers	7

Infantry Arms

Rifles	5337
PPSh sub-machine guns	4794
7.62mm light machine guns	381
7.62mm heavy machine guns	124
12.7mm DShK heavy machine guns	69
Anti-tank rifles	153

3.6 RATIO OF FORCES, 2ND UKRAINIAN FRONT (SOVIET VIEW), 1 NOVEMBER 1944

2nd Ukrainian Front	Quantity	Ratio	Quantity	Axis Forces
Troops	578,000	4:1	146,000	Troops
Divisions	68	2,4:1	28	Divisions and Brigades
Machine guns	16,100	2:1	8200	Machine guns
Guns (less anti-aircraft and anti-tank)	3900	4:1	960	Guns (less the anti-aircraft and the anti-tank ones)
Mortars (less the rocket launchers)	5400	4.5:1	1200	Mortars (less *Nebelwerfer*)
Tanks	525	2.5:1	220	Tanks
Self-propelled guns	185	1:1	150	Assault Guns
Aircraft	925	3:1	350	Aircraft

Notes
- The table is taken from the war diary of the 2nd Ukrainian Front for November 1944. The Soviet data is based on the strength reports as per 1 November 1944. It also does include the Romanian troops subordinate to the armies of the 2nd Ukrainian Front.
- The estimated strength of the Axis forces is based on an intelligence bulletin of 10 November 1944. The estimated number of the Axis aircraft is based on the intelligence report of the 2nd Ukrainian Front of 5 November 1944.
- The strength of the Soviet/Romanian troops does not include the personnel of the replacement regiments of the Front and the armies.

- The number of the Soviet divisions and brigades does not include the Soviet tank and mechanised corps and their brigades, or the Soviet artillery divisions and brigades.
- The number of the Axis divisions and brigades does not include the panzer-divisions, as well as the battle groups.
- Two Soviet fortified regions are counted as one division; six Axis border-guard battalions are also counted as one division. The decimated Axis divisions and brigades are counted as divisions and brigades
- The non-operational tanks, guns, self-propelled guns and aircraft are not included in the above figures.

3.7 RATIO OF FORCES, ARMY GROUP SOUTH SECTOR (GERMAN VIEW), 1 NOVEMBER 1944

Army Group South	Quantity	Ratio	Quantity	Soviet Forces
Troops	440,000★	1:2,3	1,000,000★★	Troops
Artillery guns	400	1:14,75	5900	Artillery guns
Tanks and assault guns	500	1:2,5	1100	Tanks and assault guns

Notes

- The table is taken from the *Fremde Heere Ost* strength report, 1 November 1944.
- The artillery guns figures don't include the anti-tank and anti-aircraft guns, the infantry guns and mortars.

★ Including 110,000 Hugarians
★★ Including 100,000 Romanians

3.8 GERMAN ARMOURED AND MOBILE FORCES SUBORDINATE TO ARMEEGRUPPE FRETTER–PICO, 1 NOVEMBER 1944

Division		1.Pz-Div	13.Pz-Div	23.Pz-Div	24.Pz-Div	PGD FHH	H.Pz-Btn 503	4.SS-Pol-PGD	8.SS-Cav-Div	22.SS-Cav-Div
Ration strength		13,355	8426	10,793	11,500	c.10,700	937	c.14,000	c.14,000	c.13,000
Tanks	Pz III	3 (1)	2 (1)	-	4 (2)	-	4 (2)	2 (1)	-	-
	Pz IV	25 (5)	3 (3)	5 (1)	34 (12)	-	34 (12)	-	-	-
	Pz V	28 (3)	11 (2)	27 (9)	-	12 (7)	-	-	-	-
	Pz VI	-	-	-	-	-	-	-	-	-
	Flak-Pz IV	-	-	-	-	4 (3)	-	-	-	-
Assault Guns		4 (2)	-	12 (10)	14 (4)	19 (15)	-	27 (12)	-	-
Tank Destroyers		4 (0)	-	17 (16)	-	6 (2)	-	-	7	5
Armoured Vehicles		117 (89)	137 (110)	98 (75)	104 (70)	151 (118)	6 (3)	9 (9)	n/a	n/a
Heavy Anti-Tank Guns		18	4 (2)	54 (46)	12 (10)	9	-	22	10	10
Artillery Guns		43	28 (24)	49 (47)	35 (23)	27 (25)	-	38	c.40	c.30

Notes

- The operational vehicles/weapons are given in brackets.
- On 3 November 1944 23.Panzer Division received 17 Pz IV from the Armed Forces Ordnance Depot.

3.9 STATUS REPORT OF THE DIVISIONS OF ARMEEGRUPPE FRETTER-PICO AND 2.ARMY (HUNG), 4 NOVEMBER 1944

Armeegruppe Fretter-Pico

76.Infantry Division

Infantry: 1 strong battalion; 3 medium-strong battalions; 2 average battalions; 1 weak field-replacement battalion
Subordinated: 4 exhausted ad-hoc units; 1 weak exhausted ad-hoc unit
Tanks and AT guns: 6 heavy AT guns
Artillery: 4 light batteries
Degree of mobility: motorised: 70 per cent; horse-drawn: 75 per cent
Combat worth: IV

IV Panzer Corps

4.SS-Police-Panzer-Grenadier Division

Infantry: 2 medium-strong battalions; 3 average battalions; 1 weak battalion
Tanks and AT guns: 16 heavy AT guns; 12 StuG
Artillery: 6 light and 4 heavy batteries
Degree of mobility: motorised: 70 per cent
Combat worth: II

LVII Panzer Corps

1.Panzer-Division

Infantry: 1 medium-strong battalion; 2 weak battalions; 1 exhausted battalion; 1 weak field-replacement battalion
Subordinated: 1 battalion (from Panzer-Grenadier Division 'Feldherrnhalle')
Tanks and AT guns: 8 heavy AT guns; 5 Pz IV, 1 Pz V, 2 StuG
Artillery: 3 light and 6 heavy batteries
Degree of mobility: motorised: 50 per cent
Combat worth: II

46.Infantry Division

Infantry: 1 medium-strong battalion; 2 average battalions; 1 field-replacement battalion (the cadre personnel only)
Detached: 1 battalion (to 24.Panzer Division)
Tanks and AT guns: 21 heavy AT guns; 6 StuG
Artillery: 10 light and 2 heavy batteries
Degree of mobility: motorised: 93 per cent; horse-drawn: 62 per cent
Combat worth: III

24.Panzer-Division

Infantry: 2 weak battalions; 2 weak battalions; exhausted; 1 average field-replacement battalion
Subordinated: 1 battalion (from 46.Infantry Division)
Tanks and AT guns: 6 heavy AT guns; 7 Pz IV, 2 StuG
Artillery: 2 light and 3 heavy batteries
Degree of mobility: motorised: 30 per cent
Combat worth: II

23.Panzer-Division
Infantry: 4 average battalions; 1 strong field-replacement battalion
Tanks and AT guns: 21 heavy AT guns; 3 Pz IV, 2 PzV, 26 StuG
Artillery: 4 light and 4 heavy batteries
Degree of mobility: motorised: 40 per cent
Combat worth: II

Panzer Group 'Breith' (III Panzer Corps)
22.SS–Cavalry–Division 'Maria Theresia'
Information not available

8.SS–Cavalry–Division 'Florian Geyer'
Infantry: 3 medium-strong cavalry regiments; 1 strong field-replacement battalion
Tanks and AT guns: 10 heavy AT guns; 7 StuG
Artillery: 9 light and 1 heavy batteries
Degree of mobility: motorised: 40 per cent; horse-drawn: 75 per cent
Combat worth: II

Panzer-Grenadier Division 'Feldherrnhalle'
Infantry: 1 strong battalion; 1 medium-strong battalion; 1 field-replacement battalion
   Detached: 1 battalion (to 1.Panzer-Division)
Tanks and AT guns: 8 heavy AT guns; 3 Flak-Pz IV, 5 PzV, 13 StuG
Artillery: 6 heavy batteries
Degree of mobility: motorised: 70 per cent
Combat worth: II

1.Armoured Division (Hung) (subordinated to the Panzer-Grenadier Division 'Feldherrnhalle')
Infantry: 2 battalions; 1 armoured reconnaissance battalion; 1 armoured battalion
   Total infantry combat strength: 2032 infantrymen
Tanks and AT guns: 4 heavy AT guns; 7 Turan 40, 3 Turan 75, 3 Toldi 40, 6 Nimrod
Artillery: 5 light batteries (10.5 cm)
Degree of mobility: motorised: 20 per cent
Combat worth: IV

13.Panzer-Division
Infantry: 1.medium-strong battalion; 3 average battalions
Tanks and AT guns: 2 heavy AT guns; 4 Pz IV, 5 PzV
Artillery: 3 light and 2 heavy batteries
Degree of mobility: motorised: 70 per cent; horse-drawn: 100 per cent
Combat worth: II

12.Reserve Division (Hung)
Infantry: 2 medium-strong battalions; 4 average battalions
Tanks and AT guns: 5 heavy AT guns
Artillery: 5 light batteries
Degree of mobility: motorised: 100 per cent; horse-drawn: 100 per cent
Combat worth: IV

1.Huszar Division (Hung)

Infantry: 3 average battalions; 1 weak battalion; 1 exhausted battalion; 1 average bicycle battalion
    Subordinated: 2 medium-strong and 1 average Hungarian Huszar battalions
    Total infantry combat strength: 1750 infantrymen
Tanks and AT guns: 11 heavy AT guns
    Subordinated: 3 heavy AT guns [from 6.Infantry Division (Hung)]
Artillery: 8 light batteries
    Subordinated: 6 light batteries [from Division '*Szent László*' (Hung)]
Degree of mobility: motorised: 45 per cent; horse-drawn: 70 per cent
Combat worth: IV

2.Army (Hung)

VII Army Corps (Hung)

10.Infantry Division (Hung)

Infantry: 6 strong battalions; 2 medium-strong battalions; 1 average battalion; 1 strong engineer battalion
    Detached: 1 battalion (to bridgehead Csap); 1 battalion (to bridgehead Dunaföldvar)
Tanks and AT guns: 6 heavy AT guns
Artillery: 5 light and 2 heavy batteries; 2 heavy mortar batteries
    Detached: 3 light and 2 heavy batteries; 1 heavy mortar battery (to bridgehead Dunaföldvar)
Degree of mobility: motorised: 50 per cent; horse-drawn: 65 per cent
Combat worth: IV

31.SS-Voluntary Grenadier Division

Infantry: 4 strong battalions; 1 average field-replacement battalion
    Subordinated: 4 strong battalions (from Field-Reserve-and-Training Regiment 44)
    Total infantry combat strength: 3300 infantrymen
Tanks and AT guns: 8 heavy AT guns
Artillery: 2 light batteries
Degree of mobility: horse-drawn: 30 per cent
Combat worth: IV

3.10 STRENGTH OF THE ARMOURED DIVISIONS OF ARMEEGRUPPE FRETTER PICO AT THE BEGINNING OF NOVEMBER 1944

Troops/Weapons/Equipment	1.Panzer-Division (31.10.1944)	13.Panzer-Division (6.11.1944)	23.Panzer-Division (7.11.1944)	24.Panzer-Division (7.11.1944)	Panzer-Grenadier Division 'FH' (3.11.1944)	4.SS-Polizei-Panzer-Grenadier Division (8.11.1944)
Personnel	13,626	9350	13,484	11,197	n/a	n/a
Tanks						
Pz III	–	1 (0)	–	–	–	–
Pz IV	25 (5)	1 (0)	7 (1)	20 (7)	–	–
Pz IV/70 (A)	–	–	–	11 (3)	–	–
Pz IV/70 (V)	–	4 (3)	–	–	6 (2)	–
Pz V	25 (2)	14 (2)	37 (6)	–	12 (7)	–
Command tanks						
Pz. Bef. Wg. III	3 (1)	2 (0)	1 (1)	2 (1)	–	2 (1)
Pz. Bef. Wg. IV	–	1 (1)	1 (0)	–	–	–
Pz. Bef. Wg.V	3 (1)	2 (0)	1 (0)	–	–	–
Anti-aircraft tanks						
Flak-Pz IV Moebelwgen	–	3 (2)	–	–	4 (3)	–
Artillery obseravtion tanks						
Pz. Beob. Wg. III	6 (4)	–	3 (1)	1 (1)	3 (2)	–
Pz. Beob. Wg. IV	–	1 (1)	2 (2)	–	–	–
Armoured recovery vehicles						
Berge-Pz III	–	–	1 (1)	–	–	–
Berge-Pz IV	2 (1)	–	–	–	–	–
Berge-Pz V (Bergepanther)	6 (1)	1 (1)	6 (2)	–	2 (0)	–
Tank destroyers						
Panzerjager IV	–	–	20 (15)	–	–	–
Nashorn	4 (0)	–	–	–	–	–
Assault guns						
StuG III	4 (2)	–	13 (1)	12 (0)	19 (15)	–
StuG IV	–	–	–	–	–	27 (12)
Self-propelled guns						
Grille	7	6	5	10	–	–
Wespe	–	–	14 (7)	–	1 (0)	–
Hummel	18 (12)	8 (7)	6 (4)	6 (2)	10 (9)	–
Ammunition carriers						
MunTräger II	1 (0)	1 (0)	–	1 (1)	–	–
MunTräger IV	6 (4)	3 (3)	2 (1)	2 (0)	2 (0)	–
Armoured cars						
le. Pz.Späh–Wg	4 (3)	2 (2)	10 (8)	2 (1)	–	–
s. Pz.Späh–Wg	4 (1)	6 (6)	2 (1)	3 (2)	–	–

Armoured personnel carriers						
le. SPW	20 (15)	43 (43)	57 (35)	50 (26)	37 (31)	–
m. SPW	83 (66)	111 (111)	32 (23)	56 (28)	107 (85)	9 (9)
Motorcycles						
Light motorcycles	120	90	74	189	103	273
Motorcycles with sidecars	74	33	133	59	39	254
Tracked motorcycles	6	17	14	10	9	–
Motor vehicles						
Light passenger cars	50	39	88	30	63	451
Medium passenger cars	24	47	84	112	108	451
Heavy passenger cars	49	2	6	7	5	3
Light trucks	25	129	115	67	8	106
Medium trucks	260	358	420	347	199	1408
Heavy trucks	20	77	86	41	67	154
Cross–country vehicles						
Light passenger cars	159	101	177	91	410	229
Medium passenger cars	48	59	44	66	24	283
Heavy passenger cars	44	7	56	–	1	–
Light trucks	144	47	6	66	89	–
Medium trucks	137	52	100	61	72	139
Heavy trucks	34	9	10	11	52	13
Crane recovery vehicles						
Kfz 100 medium trucks	1	1	1	1	–	1
SdKfz 9/1 tractors	1	2	–	–	–	–
Halftracks and tractors						
SdKfz 10 (1 t halftrack)	35	17	39	31	9	45
SdKfz 11 (3 t halftrack)	25	26	38	21	13	6
SdKfz 6 (5 t halftrack)	18	7	10	1	–	–
SdKfz 7 (8 t halftrack)	27	25	20	24	41	13
SdKfz 8 (12 t halftrack)	2	4	5	–	4	2
SdKfz 9 (18 t halftrack)	7	10	4	7	7	–
Maultier (2 t halftrack)	71	35	67	–	80	43
Maultier (3 t halftrack)	–	–	–	86	–	–
Maultier (4.5 t halftrack)	–	–	29	–	–	–
RSO tractors	2	–	6	9	–	–
Firearms						
Rifles	6048	4046	7910	7200	6530	10,180
Sub-machine guns	689	570	860	917	369	1224
StG 44 assault rifles	8	82	6	–	–	–
Machine guns	507	239	495	521	328	827
Heavy machine guns	29	8	55	21	27	80
Heavy infantry weapons						
8cm medium mortars	29	24	49	28	33	84
12cm heavy mortars	6	8	21	7	15	–
7.5cm light infantry guns	8	8	16	7	–	26
15cm heavy infantry guns	–	–	4	–	6	8

Anti-aircraft guns						
15mm Drilling	–	31	–	–	37	–
2cm light Flak	21	3	39	17	16	30
2cm Vierling	1	–	6	4	3	7
3.7cm medium Flak	–	–	–	2	10	5
3.7cm Flakzwilling	–	–	–	–	3	–
8.8cm heavy Flak	4	2	6	4	12	2
Artillery guns						
10.5cm light howitzers	12	9	12	9	1	34
15cm heavy howitzers	28	2	11	6	12	–
10cm cannons	3	4	–	3	4	4
Anti-tank guns						
7.5cm heavy anti-tank guns	16	4	27	13	9	22

Notes
- The number of the operational vehicles is given in brackets
- In some instances the numbers of some of the weapons include also those installed on a self-propelled chassis

APPENDIX 4

ARMOUR STRENGTHS

4.1 TANK INVENTORY OF THE 2ND UKRAINIAN FRONT, 29 OCTOBER 1944, 06:00

Unit		Type								
		T-34	M4-A2	T-70	JS-2	Mk III	Mk IX	SU-76	SU-85	Total
6 G. Tank Army	5 G. Tank Corps	21	–	–	–	–	–	–	–	21
	9 G. Mech. Corps	–	12	–	–	–	–	–	2	14
	Other units	3	–	–	6	–	3	–	–	12
Pliev Group	4 G. Cavalry Corps	35	–	–	–	–	–	20	–	55
	5 G. Cavalry Corps	–	8	–	–	–	–	–	–	8
	6 G. Cavalry Corps	30	–	2	–	2	–	14	3	51
	23 Tank Corps	9	–	–	–	–	–	–	2	11
	7 Mech. Corps	29	–	–	4	–	–	2	16	51
46 Army	2 G. Mech. Corps	181	–	–	21	–	–	21	21	244
	991 S.-P. Art. Reg.	–	–	–	–	–	–	14	–	14
	1505 S.-P. Art. Reg.	–	–	–	–	–	–	18	–	18
	1897 S.-P. Art. Reg.	–	–	–	–	–	–	21	–	21
27 Army	25 Tank Regiment	3	–	–	–	–	–	–	1	4
	27 G. Tank Brigade	2	–	–	–	–	–	1	–	3
–	18 Tank Corps	14	–	–	–	–	–	–	4	18
Total		327	20	2	31	2	3	111	49	545

Notes
- Non-operational machines are not shown
- 4 G. Cavalry Corps figures: as per 19 October
- 6 G. Cavalry Corps figures: as per 25 October
- 7 Mechanised Corps figures: as per 28 October

4.2 ARMOURED INVENTORY OF ARMY GROUP SOUTH, 31 OCTOBER 1944

	Pz III	Pz IV	Pz V	Pz VI	StuG	le.SPW	m.SPW	Pz.Sp. Wg.	Pz.Fu. Wg	Pak (Sf.)	Art (Sf.)
operational	14	50	27	18	119	168	325	22	9	37	68
in repair	13	70	73	27	80	44	95	12	2	35	29
in transit	–	31	–	–	38	1	42	1	–	79	8
total	27	151	100	45	237	213	462	35	11	151	105

Notes

- Pz III (Panzer III, Panzerkampfwagen III)   medium tank
- Pz IV (Panzer IV, Panzerkampfwagen IV)   medium tank
- Pz V (Panzer V, Panzerkampfwagen V)   medium tank
- Pz VI (Panzer VI, Panzerkampfwagen VI)   heavy tank
- StuG (Sturmgeschütz)   assault gun
- le.SPW (leichte Schützenpanzerwagen)   light armoured half-track
- m.SPW (mittlere Schützenpanzerwagen)   medium armoured half-track
- Pz.Sp.Wg (Panzerspähwagen)   wheeled armoured car
- Pz.Fu.Wg (Panzerfunkwagen)   armoured radio vehicle
- Pak (Sf.)   self-propelled anti-tank gun (including fully armoured tank destroyers)
- Art (Sf.)   self-propelled artillery vehicle

4.3 PANZER INVENTORY OF ARMEEGRUPPE FRETTER-PICO, 1 NOVEMBER 1944

unit/model	Pz III	Pz IV	Pz V	Pz VI	StuG	JgPz IV	JgPz 38	7.5cm Pak (Sf)	8.8cm Pak (Sf)	Toldi	Turan 40	Turan 75	Nimrod	7.5cm Pak 40	8.8cm Pak 43
1.Pz-Div	1/-/2	6/9/8	8/7/15	–	2/3/-	–	–	8/2/-	–	–	–	–	–	4/4/-	–
AT Comp 1179 (with 1.Pz-Div)	–	–	–	–	–	–	2/1/2	–	–	–	–	–	–	–	–
AT Comp 1257 (with 1.Pz-Div)	–	–	–	–	–	–	5/-/2	–	–	–	–	–	–	–	–
AT Btn 661 (with 1.Pz-Div)	–	–	–	–	–	–	–	–	3/-/-	–	–	–	–	–	–
AT Btn 662 (with 1.Pz-Div)	–	–	–	–	–	–	–	–	–	–	–	–	–	–	13/-/-
13.Pz-Div	1/1/-	5/-/4	2/9/2	–	–	5/-/-	–	3/-/3	–	–	–	–	–	3/-/-	–
23.Pz-Div	–	2/3/5	5/?/?	–	9/-/-	11/-/-	–	–	–	–	–	–	–	14/3/2	–
H.Pz-Btn 503 (with 23.Pz-Div)	–	–	–	21/9/12	–	–	–	–	–	–	–	–	–	–	–
24.Pz-Div	–	11/-/-	–	–	7/-/-	–	–	–	–	–	–	–	–	13/-/-	–
PzGDiv FHH	–	–	2/1/12	–	10/2/8	–	–	–	–	–	–	–	–	7/-/-	–
4.SS-Pol-PzGDiv	–	–	–	–	10/16/6	9/1/-	–	–	–	–	–	–	–	22/2/1	–
AT Btn 128 (with 4.SS-Pol-PzGDiv)	–	–	–	–	–	–	4/1/-	–	–	–	–	–	–	–	–
76.Inf-Div	–	–	–	–	–	–	–	–	–	–	–	–	–	5/-/-	–
As.Gun-Brig 325 (with 76.Inf-Div)	–	–	–	–	18/5/3	–	–	–	–	–	–	–	–	–	–
As.Gun-Brig 228	–	–	–	–	12/10/3	–	–	–	–	–	–	–	–	–	–
AT Comp 1176	–	–	–	–	–	–	–	–	–	–	–	–	–	–	–
1.Arm.Div (Hun.)	–	–	–	–	–	–	–	–	–	–	6/-/-	3/-/-	5/-/-	2/-/-	–
As.Gun-Btn 7 (Hun.) (with 1.Arm.Div (Hun.))	–	–	–	–	7/6/6	–	–	–	–	10/1/3	4/5/11	1/3/1	4/6/7	–	–
2.Arm.Div (Hun.)	2/-/2	4/5/15	–	–	–	–	–	–	–	–	–	–	–	8/-/4	–
1.Hus.Div (Hun.)	–	–	–	–	–	–	–	–	–	–	–	–	–	16/-/-	–
10.Inf-Div (Hun.)	–	–	–	–	–	–	–	–	–	–	–	–	–	9/1/-	–
12.Inf-Div (Hun.)	–	–	–	–	–	–	–	–	–	–	–	–	–	5/-/-	–
20.Inf-Div (Hun.)	–	–	–	–	–	–	–	–	–	–	–	–	–	8/3/-	–
25.Inf-Div (Hun.)	–	–	–	–	5/-/-	–	–	–	–	–	–	–	–	7/-/-	–

4.4 PANZER INVENTORY OF ARMEEGRUPPE FRETTER–PICO, 3 NOVEMBER 1944

unit/model	8.8cm Pak 43	7.5cm Pak 40	Nimrod	Turan 75	Turan 40	Toldi	8.8cm Pak (Sf)	7.5cm Pak (Sf)	JgPz 38	JgPz IV	StuG	Pz VI	Pz V	Pz IV	Pz III
1.Pz-Div	–	4/4/–	–	–	–	–	–	7/2/1	–	–	3/2/–	–	11/7/12	7/9/7	1/–/2
13.Pz-Div	–	3/–/–	–	–	–	–	–	–	–	–	2/3/–	–	2/9/2	5/–/4	1/1/–
AT Btn 661 (with 13.Pz-Div)	–	–	–	–	–	–	3/–/–	–	–	–	–	–	–	–	–
AT Comp 1179 and 1257 (with 13.Pz-Div)	–	–	–	–	–	–	–	–	6/1/5	–	–	–	–	–	–
SS-AT Btn 8 (with 13.Pz-Div)	–	–	–	–	–	–	–	–	–	–	–	–	–	–	–
23.Pz-Div	–	3/–/–	–	–	–	–	–	3/–/3	–	–	6/–/–	–	7/15/5	2/2/2	–
AT Btn 662 (with 23.Pz-Div)	11/–/–	15/2/2	–	–	–	–	–	–	–	16/3/2	–	–	–	–	–
24.Pz-Div	–	–	–	–	–	–	–	–	–	–	1/?/?	–	–	8/–/–	–
PzGDiv FHH	–	13/–/–	–	–	–	–	–	–	–	–	10/2/8	–	2/1/12	4/–/–	–
4.SS-Pol-PzGDiv	–	7/–/–	–	–	–	–	–	–	–	–	9/13/7	–	–	–	–
As.Gun-Brig 228 (with 4.SS-Pol-PzGDiv)	–	18/6/1	–	–	–	–	–	–	–	–	8/10/4	–	–	–	–
As.Gun-Brig 325 (with 4.SS-Pol-PzGDiv)	–	–	–	–	–	–	–	–	–	–	13/8/6	–	–	–	–
76.Inf-Div	–	12/–/–	–	–	–	–	–	–	–	–	–	–	–	–	–
H.Pz-Btn 503	–	–	–	–	–	–	–	–	–	–	–	10/?/?	–	–	–
AT Btn 662	3/–/–	2/–/–	5/–/–	3/–/–	6/–/–	–	–	–	–	–	–	–	–	–	–
1.Arm.Div (Hun.)	–	–	4/6/7	1/3/1	4/5/11	10/1/3	–	–	–	–	–	–	–	4/5/15	–
As.Gun-Btn 7 (Hun.) (with 1.Arm.Div (Hun.))	–	–	–	–	–	–	–	–	–	–	3/8/8	–	–	–	–
2.Arm.Div (Hun.)	–	8/–/4	–	–	–	–	–	–	–	–	–	–	2/–/2	–	–
1.Hus.Div (Hun.)	–	15/–/–	–	–	–	–	–	–	–	–	–	–	–	–	–
20.Inf-Div (Hun.)	–	8/3/–	–	–	–	–	–	–	–	–	–	–	–	–	–

4.5 PANZER INVENTORY OF ARMEEGRUPPE FRETTER-PICO, 4 NOVEMBER 1944

unit/model	Pz III	Pz IV	Pz V	Pz VI	StuG	JgPz IV	JgPz 38	7.5cm Pak (Sf)	8.8cm Pak (Sf)	Toldi	Turan 40	Turan 75	Nimrod	7.5cm Pak 40	8.8cm Pak 43
1.Pz-Div	1/-/2	6/10/7	4/9/17	-	2/3/-	-	-	7/2/-	-	-	-	-	-	4/4/-	-
13.Pz-Div	1/1/-	5/-/4	5/7/1	-	-	-/4/-	-	-	-	-	-	-	-	2/-/-	-
4./AT Btn 661 (with 13.Pz-Div)	-	-	-	-	-	-	-	-	2/1/-	-	-	-	-	-	-
AT Comp 1179 (with 13.Pz-Div)	-	-	-	-	-	-	2/1/2	-	-	-	-	-	-	-	-
AT Comp 1257 (with 13.Pz-Div)	-	-	-	-	-	-	4/2/2	-	-	-	-	-	-	-	-
23.Pz-Div	-	1/3/2	3/17/7	-	4/-/-	16/3/2	-	3/-/3	-	-	-	-	-	15/2/2	-
AT Btn 662 (with 23.Pz-Div)	-	-	-	-	-	-	-	-	-	-	-	-	-	-	11/-/-
24.Pz-Div	-	10/-/-	-	-	4/-/-	-	-	-	-	-	-	-	-	-	-
PzGDiv FHH	-	4/-/-	-	-	15/2/-	-	-	-	-	-	-	-	-	6/-/-	-
4.SS-Pol-PzGDiv	-	-	2/1/12	-	10/12/7	-	-	-	-	-	-	-	-	7/-/-	-
8.SS-Cav-Div	-	-	-	-	-	-	6/6/11	-	-	-	-	-	-	16/8/1	-
76.Inf-Div	-	-	-	-	-	-	-	-	-	-	-	-	-	10/-/-	-
As.Gun-Brig 228	-	-	-	-	8/10/4	-	-	-	-	-	-	-	-	12/-/-	-
As.Gun-Brig 325	-	-	-	-	15/6/6	-	-	-	-	-	-	-	-	-	-
H.Pz-Btn 503	-	-	-	n/a	-	-	-	-	-	-	-	-	-	-	3/-/-
AT Comp 1179	-	-	-	-	-	-	2/1/2	-	-	-	-	-	-	12/-/-	-
AT Comp 1257	-	-	-	-	-	-	4/2/2	-	-	-	-	-	-	-	-
1.Arm.Div (Hun.)	-	-	-	-	-	-	-	-	-	-	6/-/-	3/-/-	5/-/-	2/-/-	-
As.Gun-Btn 7 (Hun.) (with 1.Arm.Div (Hun.))	-	-	-	-	3/8/8	-	-	-	-	-	-	-	-	-	-
2.Arm.Div (Hun.)	-	4/5/15	-	-	-	-	-	-	-	10/1/3	4/5/11	1/3/1	4/6/7	8/-/4	-
1.Hus.Div (Hun.)	-	-	-	-	-	-	-	-	-	-	-	-	-	15/-/-	-
20.Inf-Div (Hun.)	-	-	-	-	-	-	-	-	-	-	-	-	-	8/3/-	-

4.6 PANZER INVENTORY OF ARMEEGRUPPE FRETTER-PICO, 5 NOVEMBER 1944

unit/model	8.8cm Pak 43	7.5cm Pak 40	Nimrod	Turan 75	Turan 40	Toldi	8.8cm Pak (Sf)	7.5cm Pak (Sf)	JgPz 38	JgPz IV	StuG	Pz VI	Pz V	Pz IV	Pz III
1.Pz-Div	–	4/4/–	–	–	–	–	–	4/3/1	–	–	2/2/–	–	11/7/12	8/8/9	2/–/2
13.Pz-Div	–	1/–/–	–	–	–	–	–	–	–	–/2/2	–	–	6/5/2	7/2/4	1/–/1
4./AT Btn 661 (with 13.Pz-Div)	–	–	–	–	–	–	2/1/–	–	–	–	–	–	–	–	–
AT Comp 1179 and 1257 (with 13.Pz-Div)	–	–	–	–	–	–	–	–	3/5/4	–	–	–	–	–	–
23.Pz-Div	–	18/1/–	–	–	–	–	–	3/–/3	–	16/3/2	4/–/–	–	2/17/8	3/1/2	–
24.Pz-Div	–	6/–/–	–	–	–	–	–	–	–	–	2/–/–	–	7/–/–	7/–/–	–
PzGDiv FHH	–	8/–/–	–	–	–	–	–	–	–	–	8/7/3	–	n/a	–	–
4.SS-Pol-PzGDiv	–	17/2/2	–	–	–	–	–	–	–	–	12/11/9	–	–	–	–
As.Gun-Brig 228 (with 4.SS-Pol-PzGDiv)	–	–	–	–	–	–	–	–	–	–	9/13/4	–	–	–	–
As.Gun-Brig 325 (with 4.SS-Pol-PzGDiv)	–	–	–	–	–	–	–	–	–	–	15/11/1	–	–	–	–
8.SS-Cav-Div	–	15/4/2	–	–	–	–	–	–	7/5/11	–	–	–	–	–	–
22.SS-Cav-Div	–	16/–/2	–	–	–	–	–	–	7/–/–	–	–	–	–	–	–
76.Inf-Div	–	12/–/–	–	–	–	–	–	–	–	–	–	n/a	–	–	–
H.Pz-Btn 503	–	–	–	–	–	–	–	–	–	–	–	n/a	–	–	–
AT Btn 662	14/–/–	–	–	–	–	–	–	–	–	–	–	–	–	–	–
1.Arm.Div (Hun.)	–	2/–/–	5/–/–	3/–/–	6/–/–	–	–	–	–	–	–/4/11	–	2/–/2	4/5/15	–
As.Gun-Btn 7 (Hun.) (with 1.Arm.Div (Hun.))	–	–	–	–	–	–	–	–	–	–	–	–	–	–	–
2.Arm.Div (Hun.)	–	8/–/4	4/6/7	1/3/1	4/5/11	10/1/3	–	–	–	–	–	–	–	–	–
1.Hus.Div (Hun.)	–	15/–/–	–	–	–	–	–	–	–	–	–	–	–	–	–
20.Inf-Div (Hun.)	–	8/3/–	–	–	–	–	–	–	–	–	–	–	–	–	–

4.7 ARMOURED VEHICLE ROSTER OF THE 2ND UKRAINIAN FRONT, 5 NOVEMBER 1944

Unit		T-34	M4-A2	JS-2	T-70	Mk III	Mk IX	SU-76	SU-85	ISU-122	Total
6 GTA	5 GTC	51	–	–	–	–	–	–	–	–	51
	9 GMC	–	21	–	–	–	30	1	1	–	53
	49 GHTR	–	–	6	–	–	–	–	–	–	6
	1462 SPAR	–	–	–	–	–	–	–	6	–	6
	4 MCR	–	–	–	–	–	1	–	–	–	1
	76 SR	3	–	–	–	–	–	–	–	–	3
	248 TTBn	2	–	–	3	–	–	1	1	–	7
	Total	56	21	6	3	–	31	2	8	–	126
23 TC	Corps' Brigades	58	–	–	–	–	–	–	–	–	58
	1443 SPAR	–	–	–	–	–	–	–	1	–	1
	Total	58	–	–	–	–	–	–	1	–	59
7 MC	Corps' Brigades	49	–	–	–	–	–	–	–	–	49
	78 GHTR	–	–	9	–	–	–	–	–	–	9
	1289 SPAR	–	–	–	–	–	–	3	–	–	3
	1440 SPAR	–	–	–	–	–	–	–	19	–	19
	Total	49	–	9	–	–	–	3	19	–	81
2 GMC	Corps' Brigades	118	–	–	–	–	–	–	–	–	49
	30 GHTR	–	–	18	–	–	–	–	–	–	9
	1509 SPAR	–	–	–	–	–	–	18	–	–	3
	251 GSPAR	–	–	–	–	–	–	–	16	–	19
	Total	118	–	18	–	–	–	18	16	–	170
4 GMC	Corps' Brigades	80	–	–	–	–	–	–	–	–	80
	292 GSPAR	–	–	–	–	–	–	–	7	–	7
	352 GHSPAR	–	–	–	–	–	–	–	–	12	12
	Total	80	–	–	–	–	–	–	7	12	99
4 GCC	128 ITR (9 GCD)	2	–	–	–	–	–	–	–	–	2
	134 ITR (10 GCD)	4	–	–	–	–	–	–	–	–	4
	151 ITR (30 CD)	12	–	–	–	–	–	–	–	–	12
	1815 SPAR	–	–	–	–	–	–	10	–	–	10
	Total	18	–	–	–	–	–	10	–	–	28
5 GCC	54 ITR (12 GCD)	–	–	–	–	–	–	–	–	–	–
	60 ITR (63 CD)	–	1	–	–	–	–	–	–	–	1
	71 ITR (11 GCD)	–	3	–	–	–	–	–	–	–	3
	1896 SPAR	–	–	–	–	–	–	–	–	–	–
	Total	–	4	–	–	–	–	–	–	–	4

6 GCC	136 ITR (8 GCD)	7	–	–	1	–	–	4	1	–	13
	154 ITR (8 CD)	4	–	–	–	1	–	4	–	–	9
	250 ITR (13 GCD)	2	–	–	1	–	–	2	1	–	6
	1813 SPAR	–	–	–	–	–	–	21	1	–	22
	Total	13	–	–	2	1	–	31	3	–	50
27 A	25 ITR	4	–	–	–	–	–	–	–	–	4
7 GA	27 GTB	41	–	–	–	–	–	4	15	–	60
46 A	991 SPAR	–	–	–	–	–	–	13	–	–	21
	1505 SPAR							17			
	1897 SPAR							21			
	Total	–	–	–	–	–	–	51	–	–	51
2 UF	Total	437	25	33	5	1	31	119	69	12	732

Abbreviations

A	Army
CD	Cavalry Division
GA	Guards Army
GCC	Guards Cavalry Corps
GCD	Guards Cavalry Division
GHSPAR	Heavy Self-Propelled Artillery Regiment
GHTR	Guards Heavy Tank Regiment
GMC	Guards Mechanised Corps
GSPAR	Heavy Self-Propelled Artillery Regiment
GTA	Guards Tank Army
GTB	Guards Tank Brigade
GTC	Guards Tank Corps
HQ	Headquarters
ITR	Independent Tank Regiment
MC	Mechanised Corps
MCR	Motorcycle Regiment
SPAR	Self-Propelled Artillery Regiment
SR	Signals Regiment
TC	Tank Corps
TTBn	Training Tank Battalion
UF	Ukrainian Front

Notes

The following three units of the 6th Guards Tank Army are not included in the table since on that day they did not have any armoured vehicles left:

- 6th Self-Propelled Artillery Brigade (SU-76)
- 364th Guards Heavy Self-Propelled Artillery Regiment (ISU-122)
- 375th Guards Heavy Self-Propelled Artillery Regiment (ISU-152)

4.8 PANZER INVENTORY OF ARMEEGRUPPE FRETTER-PICO, 6 NOVEMBER 1944

unit/model	Pz III	Pz IV	Pz V	Pz VI	StuG	JgPz IV	JgPz 38	7.5cm Pak (Sf)	8.8cm Pak (Sf)	7.5cm Pak 40	8.8cm Pak 43
1.Pz-Div	2/-/2	8/8/9	2/8/17	–	2/2/-	–	–	4/3/1	–	4/4/-	–
13.Pz-Div	1/-/1	7/2/4	5/6/2	–	1/1/2	–	–	–	–	2/-/-	–
4./AT Btn 661 (with 13.Pz-Div)	–	–	–	–	–	–	–	2/1/-	–	–	–
AT Comp 1179 and 1257 (with 13.Pz-Div)	–	–	–	–	–	–	3/5/4	–	–	–	–
23.Pz-Div	–	3/1/2	2/17/8	–	4/-/-	16/3/2	–	3/-/3	–	18/1/-	–
24.Pz-Div	–	7/-/-	–	–	2/-/-	–	–	–	–	6/-/-	–
PzGDiv FHH	–	–	n/a	–	8/7/3	–	–	–	–	8/-/-	–
4.SS-Pol-PzGDiv	–	–	–	–	13/11/9	–	–	–	–	17/4/1	–
As.Gun-Brig 228 (with 4.SS-Pol-PzGDiv)	–	–	–	–	8/14/4	–	–	–	–	–	
As.Gun-Brig 325 (with 4.SS-Pol-PzGDiv)	–	–	–	–	18/8/1	–	–	–	–	–	–
8.SS-Cav-Div	–	–	–	–	–	–	5/6/12	–	–	15/4/2	–
22.SS-Cav-Div	–	–	–	–	–	–	5/-/-	–	–	16/2/-	–
76.Inf-Div	–	–	–	–	–	–	–	–	–	15/-/-	–
H.Pz-Btn 503	–	–	–	n/a	–	–	–	–	–	–	–
AT Btn 662	–	–	–	–	–	–	–	–	–	–	14/-/-

4.9 TANK INVENTORY OF THE 2ND UKRAINIAN FRONT, 7 NOVEMBER 1944, 06:00

Unit		T-34	M4-A2	T-70	JS-2	Mk IX	SU-76	SU-85	ISU-122	Total
6 G. Tank Army	5 G. Tank Corps	66	–	–	–	–	–	–	–	66
	9 G. Mech. Corps	–	14	–	–	30	2	2	–	48
	Other units	3	–	–	6	1	–	–	–	10
Pliev Group	4 G. Cavalry Corps	29	–	–	–	–	10	–	–	39
	6 G. Cavalry Corps	13	–	5	–	1*	31	2	–	52
	23 Tank Corps	102	–	–	–	–	–	–	–	102
Gorshkov Group	5 G. Cavalry Corps	–	3	–	–	8	–	–	–	11
	7 Mech. Corps	44	–	–	9	–	3	18	–	74
46 Army	2 G. Mech. Corps	90	–	–	11	–	8	14	–	123
	4 G. Mech. Corps	82	–	–	–	–	–	8	9	99
	991 S.-P. Art. Reg.	–	–	–	–	–	13	–	–	13
	1505 S.-P. Art. Reg.	–	–	–	–	–	18	–	–	18
	1897 S.-P. Art. Reg.	–	–	–	–	–	18	–	–	18
27 Army	25 Tank Regiment	4	–	–	–	–	–	–	–	4
7 G. Army	27 G. Tank Brigade	16	–	–	–	–	2	5	–	23
2 Ukrainian Front Total		449	17	5	26	40	105	49	9	700

Notes
- Non-operational machines are not given
- 5 G. Cavalry Corps as per 5 November
- 6 G. Cavalry Corps as per 30 October
- 27 G. Tank Brigade as per 5 November

★ Mk III tank

4.10 PANZER INVENTORY OF ARMEEGRUPPE FRETTER-PICO, 7 NOVEMBER 1944

unit/model	Pz III	Pz IV	Pz V	Pz VI	StuG	JgPz IV	JgPz 38	7.5cm Pak (Sf)	8.8cm Pak (Sf)	7.5cm Pak 40	8.8cm Pak 43
1.Pz-Div	1/1/2	4/10/11	11/7/12	-	2/2/-	-	-	6/1/1	-	4/4/-	-
13.Pz-Div	1/-/1	7/2/4	5/6/2	-	-	1/1/2	-	-	-	2/-/-	-
4./AT Btn 661 (with 13.Pz-Div)	-	-	-	-	-	-	-	-	1/2/-	-	-
AT Comp 1179 and 1257 (with 13.Pz-Div)	-	-	-	-	-	-	2/6/4	-	-	-	-
23.Pz-Div	-	2/2/2	7/12/8	-	3/-/-	16/3/2	-	3/-/3	-	16/2/1	-
24.Pz-Div	-	10/-/-	-	-	-	-	-	-	-	6/-/-	-
PzGDiv FHH	-	-	3/5/4	-	11/5/7	-	-	-	-	8/-/-	-
4.SS-Pol-PzGDiv	-	-	-	-	14/11/8	-	-	-	-	17/4/1	-
As.Gun-Brig 228 and 325 (with 4.SS-Pol-PzGDiv)	-	-	-	-	30/17/6	-	-	-	-	-	-
8.SS-Cav-Div	-	-	-	-	-	-	3/7/13	-	-	18/1/2	-
22.SS-Cav-Div	-	-	-	-	-	-	4/1/2	-	-	16/2/-	-
46.Inf-Div	-	-	-	-	4/-/-	-	-	-	-	15/-/-	-
76.Inf-Div	-	-	-	-	-	-	-	-	-	15/-/-	-
H.Pz-Btn 503	-	-	-	12/-/30	-	-	-	-	-	-	-
AT Btn 662	-	-	-	-	-	-	-	-	-	-	13/-/-
AT Btn 721	-	-	-	-	-	-	-	-	-	23/-/4	-

APPENDIX 5

LOSSES

5.1 NON-OPERATIONAL ARMOUR (AS PER 5 NOVEMBER) AND LOSSES OF 46TH ARMY AND 7TH GUARDS ARMY, 29 OCTOBER–5 NOVEMBER 1944

Army	Formation/Unit	Type	in short term repair	in long term repair	write-offs
46th Army	2nd Guards Mechanised Corps	T-34	22	10	35
		JS-2	1	1	1
		SU-76	–	–	3
		SU-85	3	2	–
	4th Guards Mechanised Corps	T-34	26	2	9
		SU-85	7	–	–
		ISU-122	6	–	–
	991st Self-Propelled Artillery Regiment	SU-76	–	1	7*
	1505th Self-Propelled Artillery Regiment	SU-76	–	1	3*
	1897th Self-Propelled Artillery Regiment	SU-76	–	–	
7th G. Army	27th Guards Tank Brigade	T-34	5	17	–
		SU-76	–	2	2**
		SU-85	1	–	–

* Most probably pertain to an earlier period.
** Pertain to an earlier period.

5.2 NON-OPERATIONAL ARMOUR (AS PER 10 NOVEMBER) AND LOSSES OF 46TH ARMY AND 7TH GUARDS ARMY, 29 OCTOBER–10 NOVEMBER 1944

Army	Formation/Unit	Type	In short-term repair	In long-term repair	Total write-offs
46th Army	2nd Guards Mechanised Corps	T-34	16	21	48
		JS-2	3	4	3
		SU-76	–	–	14
		SU-85	–	–	5
	4th Guards Mechanised Corps	T-34	23	5	5
		SU-85	6	–	–
		ISU-122	6	–	1
	991st Self-Propelled Artillery Regiment	SU-76	–	1	9*
	1505th Self-Propelled Artillery Regiment	SU-76	–	1	2*
	1897th Self-Propelled Artillery Regiment	SU-76	1	–	*3
7th G. Army	27th Guards Tank Brigade	T-34	27	8	10
		SU-76	–	1	–
		SU-85	9	–	–

* Partly pertains to an earlier period.

5.3 LOSSES OF THE 2ND GUARDS MECHANISED CORPS, 29 OCTOBER–6 NOVEMBER 1944

Personnel Killed
89 officers
237 NCOs
379 enlisted men

Personnel Wounded
165 officers
523 NCOs
965 enlisted men

Weapons and Equipment Write-offs
3 JS-2 tanks
46 T-34 tanks
14 SU-76 self-propelled guns
5 SU-85 self-propelled guns
6 armoured personnel carriers
8 BA-64 armoured cars
5 M17 anti-aircraft halftracks
107 motor vehicles
23 motorcycles
12 radios

3 Po-2 aircraft
208 rifles
343 PPSh submachine guns
28 DP light machine guns
20 heavy machine guns
7 82mm mortars
11 120mm mortars
1 37mm anti-aircraft gun
5 45mm anti-tank guns
17 anti-tank rifles

Weapons and Equipment Damaged
5 JS-2 tanks
11 T-34 tanks
1 SU-85 self-propelled gun
8 motor vehicles

5.4 LOSSES OF 4TH GUARDS MECHANISED CORPS, 1–8 NOVEMBER 1944

Personnel Killed and Wounded
299 officers, NCO and enlisted men

Weapons and Equipment Write-offs
11 T-34 tanks
1 ISU-122 self-propelled gun
3 M3-A1 armoured personnel carriers
1 M17 anti-aircraft halftracks
4 BA-64 armoured cars
58 trucks
1 special motor vehicle
18 artillery prime movers
4 artillery guns
5 mortars

APPENDIX 6

CLAIMS

6.1 CLAIMS OF 2ND GUARDS MECHANISED CORPS (DAMAGE DONE TO THE ENEMY), 29 OCTOBER–6 NOVEMBER 1944

Enemy Troops Captured
1718 officers and men

Enemy Troops Killed and Wounded
6678 officers and men

Weapons and Equipment Captured
1 self-propelled gun
2 armoured personnel carriers
4 armoured cars
3 radios
342 motor vehicles
2 tractors
185 rifles
110 sub-machine guns
10 light machine guns
4 heavy machine guns
24 artillery guns of various calibres
26 motorcycles
80 bicycles
2 locomotives
3 military stores
240 horses

Weapons and Equipment Destroyed
140 tanks
19 self-propelled guns
11 armoured personnel carriers
45 armoured cars
22 aircraft

28 radios
479 motor vehicles
12 tractors
317 rifles
982 submachine guns
162 light machine guns
226 heavy machine guns
41 mortars
165 artillery guns of various calibres
92 motorcycles
1 locomotive
10 railway flatcars loaded with goods
1 ammunition dump
2 stores with various goods
492 horses
115 horse-drawn carts loaded with various goods

6.2 CLAIMS OF 4TH GUARDS MECHANISED CORPS (DAMAGE DONE TO THE ENEMY), 1–6 NOVEMBER 1944

Enemy Troops Captured
758 officers and men

Enemy Troops Killed and Wounded
2830 officers and men

Weapons and Equipment Captured
2 tanks
1 self-propelled gun
110 motor vehicles
23 artillery guns of various calibres
3 railway trains
1 ambulance railway train
9 aircraft
14 military stores

Weapons and Equipment Destroyed
10 tanks
7 self-propelled guns
137 motor vehicles
97 machine guns
36 mortars
39 artillery guns of various calibres
1 aircraft
246 horse-drawn carts

6.3 CLAIMS OF 46TH ARMY (DAMAGE DONE TO THE ENEMY), 29 OCTOBER–7 NOVEMBER 1944

29 October 1944

During the day the units of the army destroyed more than 500 enemy officers and men, up to 300 were taken prisoner. The army artillery reportedly destroyed an ammunition train at the Mohács railway station (on the western bank of the Danube).

30 October 1944

During the day the units of the army destroyed more than 1000 enemy officers and men, 23 tanks and 2 armoured personnel carriers. 6 enemy aircraft were reportedly shot down. More than 1300 Axis troops were taken prisoner, including a group of staff officers of the Hungarian 23.Infantry-Division.

31 October 1944

During the day the units of the army destroyed up to 1000 enemy troops, another 800 were taken prisoner (including 2 enlisted men of the German 24.Panzer-Division).

1 November 1944

During the day the units of the army destroyed more than 2600 enemy officers and men, 48 tanks and self-propelled guns, 4 armoured personnel carriers, 40 motor vehicles, 240 horse-drawn carts loaded with various goods, 23 artillery guns, 22 mortars and 40 machine guns. 1124 Axis troops were taken prisoner. The following booty was captured: 24 artillery guns, 19 machine guns, 350 rifles and 11 motor vehicles.

2 November 1944

During the day the units of the army destroyed 600 enemy officers and men and 3 tanks. 14 Axis motor vehicles were reportedly knocked-out. More than 150 Axis troops were taken prisoner, including a captain of the German 1.Panzer-Division who was captured in the vicinity of Örkény. The following booty was captured: 24 artillery guns, 19 machine guns, 350 rifles and 11 motor vehicles.

3 November 1944

During the day the units of the army destroyed more than 600 enemy officers and men. 2 enemy aircraft were reportedly shot down. 600 Axis troops were taken prisoner. The following booty was captured: 25 artillery guns of various calibres, 2 self-propelled guns and 2 prime movers.

4 November 1944

During the day the units of the army destroyed more than 1000 enemy officers and men; another 1000 were taken prisoner. 3 tanks and 13 armoured personnel carriers were reportedly knocked out.

5 November 1944

During the day the units of the army destroyed more than 200 enemy officers and men; another 375 were taken prisoner. (Some of them, who were captured in the Vecsés area, belonged to an independent Hungarian police battalion.)

6 November 1944

During the day the units of the army destroyed more than 300 enemy officers and men; another 35 were taken prisoner. 8 Axis tanks were reportedly knocked out or destroyed.

7 November 1944

During the day the units of the army destroyed more up to 300 enemy officers and men. 45 Axis troops were taken prisoner, among them were members of the German 13. and 23.Panzer-Divisions and the Hungarian 1.Armoured and 1.Huszar-Divisions.

6.4 CLAIMS OF ARMEEGRUPPE FRETTER-PICO (DAMAGE DONE TO THE ENEMY) IN THE AREA OF KECSKEMET–BUDAPEST–SZOLNOK, 29 OCTOBER–9 NOVEMBER 1944

Enemy Troops Captured
806 POWs
10 deserters

Enemy Troops Killed and Wounded
2173 verified enemy killed
3560 estimated enemy killed

Weapons and Equipment Captured or Destroyed
137 tanks
2 operational tanks
2 tanks (captured)
2 self-propelled guns
5 armoured cars
51 artillery guns
84 anti-tank guns
4 anti-aircraft guns
34 mortars
193 machine guns
45 anti-tank rifles
107 sub-machine guns
4 aircraft
68 motor vehicles
60 horse-drawn carts
26 assault boats

APPENDIX 7

AIR WAR

7.1 STRENGTH OF THE GERMAN COMBAT AIR UNITS OF AIR FLEET 4, 31 OCTOBER 1944

Unit	Aircraft											
	Bf 109 G	FW 190F-8	FW 190G-8	Ju 87 D	Ju 87 G2	Hs 129 B2	He 111 H	Ju 88	Ju 188	Go 145	Ar 66	Total
II./JG 51	33	–	–	–	–	–	–	–	–	–	–	33
II./JG 52	28	–	–	–	–	–	–	–	–	–	–	28
I./JG 53	24	–	–	–	–	–	–	–	–	–	–	24
II./NJG 100	–	–	–	–	–	–	–	21	–	–	–	21
Stab/SG 2	–	5	–	–	1	–	–	–	–	–	–	6
I./SG 2	–	22	–	–	–	–	–	–	–	–	–	22
II./SG 2	–	22	1	–	–	–	–	–	–	–	–	23
III./SG 2	–	–	–	26	–	–	–	–	–	–	–	26
10.(Pz)/SG 2	–	–	–	4	12	–	–	–	–	–	–	16
14.(Pz)/SG 9	–	–	–	–	–	9	–	–	–	–	–	9
Stab/SG 10	–	3	–	–	–	–	–	–	–	–	–	3
I./SG 10	–	25	–	–	–	–	–	–	–	–	–	25
II./SG 10	–	20	–	–	–	–	–	–	–	–	–	20
III./SG 10	–	23	–	–	–	–	–	–	–	–	–	23
Stab/KG 4	–	–	–	–	–	–	1	–	–	–	–	1
I./KG 4	–	–	–	–	–	–	30	–	–	–	–	30
II./KG 4	–	–	–	–	–	–	32	–	–	–	–	32
4./NSGr 2	–	–	–	9	–	–	–	–	–	–	–	9
NSGr 5	–	–	–	21	–	–	–	–	–	22	2	45
NSGr 10	–	–	–	25	–	–	–	–	–	–	–	25
2./NAGr 12	9	–	–	–	–	–	–	–	–	–	–	9
NAGr 14	23	–	–	–	–	–	–	–	–	–	–	23
3.(F)/AGr 121	–	–	–	–	–	–	–	1	9	–	–	10
Total	117	120	1	85	13	9	63	22	9	22	2	463

7.2 STRENGTH OF THE HUNGARIAN 102 AIR BRIGADE, 31 OCTOBER 1944

Unit	Aircraft						
	Bf 109	Fw 190 F-8	Fw 190 G-8	Me 210	Ju 88	Fw 189	Total
101/1. Fighter Squadron	11	-	-	-	-	-	11
101/2. Fighter Squadron	11	-	-	-	-	-	11
102/1. 'Fast' Bomber Squadron	-	-	-	12	-	-	12
102/2. 'Fast' Bomber Squadron	-	-	-	11	-	-	11
102/1. Ground Attack Squadron	-	16	1	-	-	-	17
102. Short-Range Reconnaissance Squadron	-	-	-	-	4	-	4
102. Long-Range Reconnaissance Squadron	-	-	-	-	-	4	4
Total	22	16	1	23	4	4	70

7.3 DEPLOYMENT OF 5TH AIR ARMY AIR UNITS, 1 NOVEMBER 1944

Corps	Division	Regiments	Aircraft	Air Base
3rd GAAC	7th GAAD	130, 131, 132	Il-2	Kisszénás, Szarvas
	12th GAAD	187, 188, 189	Il-2	Pitvaros, Mezőhegyes, Nagylak
	279th FAD	92, 192, 486	La-5	Szarvas, Tótkomlós
5th AAC	4th GAAD	90, 91, 92	Il-2	Nagyvárad, Toboliu
	264th AAD	235, 451, 809	Il-2	Nagyvárad, Debrecen
	331st FAD	122, 179, 513	Yak-1 and 9	Debrecen, Toboliu
3rd GFAC	6th GFAD	149, 150, 151	Yak	Mezőhegyes, Túrkeve
	13th GFAD	177, 178, 179	La-5, Yak	n/a
	14th GFAD	31, 73, 85	La-5	Gyoma, Szőrös
218th BAD		48, 452, 453	A-20 'Boston'	Arad, Sfânta Ana, Tornya
312th NBAD		392, 930, 992	Po-2	Szeghalom, Körösladány
511th IRAR			Pe-2	n/a
207th IACAR			Il-2, Yak, Po-2	Arad

Abbreviations

AAD	Assault Air Division
BAD	Bomber Air Division
FAD	Fighter Air Division
GAAC	Guards Assault Air Corps
GAAD	Guards Assault Air Division
GAAC	Guards Fighter Air Corps
GFAD	Guards Fighter Air Division
IACAR	Independent Artillery-Correction Air Regiment
IRAR	Independent Reconnaissance Air Regiment
NBAD	Night Bomber Air Division

7.4 COMBAT STRENGTH OF 5TH AIR ARMY, 4 NOVEMBER 1944

Formation/Unit	Aircraft						
	La-5	Yak-1,9	Il-2	A-20	Pe-2	Po-2	Total
3rd Guards Assault Air Corps	45	–	153	–	–	–	198
5th Assault Air Corps	–	83	125	–	–	–	208
3rd Guards Fighter Air Corps	35	161	–	–	–	–	196
218th Bomber Air Division	–	–	–	78	–	–	78
312th Night Bomber Air Division	–	–	–	–	–	57	57
511th Reconnaissance Air Regiment	–	–	–	–	21	–	21
207th Artillery-Correction Air Regiment	–	5	13	–	–	3	21
Total	80	249	291	78	21	60	779

7.5 THE AIR WAR, 29 OCTOBER–7 NOVEMBER 1944

29 October 1944

5th Air Army

A total of 327 sorties were flown, 116 of which were for close air support at Kecskemét and Nagykőrös, as well at Nyíregyháza and Újfehértó. The Army also conducted 35 reconnaissance, 88 escort and 9 'free hunt' missions and flew 79 sorties on the protection of the ground troops.

Air Fleet 4

The focal point of the enemy aerial activity was the sector of the 3.Army (Hung). The Axis air-force was engaged in the area of Tiszafüred as well as in performing of reconnaissance missions.

Axis Fighter Claims

• Captain Heinrich Sturm (5./JG 52) – 1 La-5 and 1 Il-2

30 October 1944

5th Air Army

A total of 406 sorties were undertaken: 106 of which were close air support sorties against enemy troop concentrations at Nagykőrös and Cegléd, as well at Nyíregyháza and Rakamaz. The Army also carried out 59 reconnaissance, 91 escort and 14 'free hunt' missions and flew 136 sorties for the protection of the ground troops. 347 of these sorties were carried out in the Budapest direction, while the remaining 59 were in the direction of Nyíregyháza.

9 air fights took place, in which 13 enemy aircraft were shot down.

Soviet Fighter Claims

• Captain Sergey Dynda (149th GFAR) – 1 Bf 109, southeast of Szolnok
• Senior-Lieutenant Vasily Torubalko (151st GFAR) – 1 Bf 109, south of Tiha-Tyrda [sic]
• Senior-Lieutenant Ivan Egorov (129th FAR) – 1 Fw 190, at Tiszaföldvár
• Lieutenant Ivan Nikolaev (85th GFAR) – 1 Ju 87, west of Kecskemét
• Major Aleksey Reshetov (31st GFAR) – 2 Fw 190, at Kecskemét
• Senior-Lieutenant Nikolai Smirnov (192nd FAR) – 1 Bf 109, southeast of Kecskemét

Air Fleet 4

The focal point of the Axis aerial activity was the Kecskemét area, but strong air units were engaged in the Ungvár also. 5 tanks, 1 armoured car, 60 trucks and 20 horse-drawn wagons were destroyed, while at Ungvár 8 enemy aircraft were shot down. During the night of 29/30 October friendly night-ground-attack aircraft attacked the enemy airfield at Debrecen.

Axis Fighter Claims
- Corporal Wagner (5./JG 52) – 1 Boston Mk III
- Lieutenant Peter Düttmann (6./JG 52) – 2 MiG-3 [sic]

31 October 1944

5th Air Army

A total of 684 sorties were flown, 240 of which were ground-attack sorties against enemy troops at Szolnok, Nagykőrös, Kiskőrös and in the area of Gyöngyös. The Army also flew 187 sorties on the protection of the ground troops and conducted 131 escort, 32 reconnaissance and 36 bomber missions. 8 sorties were flown against enemy airfields.

18 air fights took place, in which 12 enemy aircraft were shot down.

The army's own losses were: 2 aircraft shot down by the enemy anti-aircraft artillery; 10 aircraft failed to return from mission.

Soviet Fighter Claims
- Senior-Lieutenant Nikolai Vydrigan (31st GFAR) – 1 Fw 190, south of Lajosmizse
- Major Aleksey Reshetov (31st GFAR) – 1 Fw 190, west of Kecskemét
- Senior-Lieutenant Valentin Shapiro (31st GFAR) – 1 Fw 190, at Kecskemét
- Lieutenant Pavel Morduhovich (177th GFAR) – 1 Fw 190, north of Kerekegyháza
- Captain Konstantin Piunov (177th GFAR) – 1 Bf 109, west of Nagykőrös
- Major Evgeny Chistyakov (73rd GFAR) – 1 Fw 190, west of Nagykőrös

Air Fleet 4

The focal point of the enemy aerial activity was the Kecskemét area and the areas of Tokaj and Miskolc. The focal point of the Axis aerial activity was the area of Kecskemét too. 10 tanks, 50 motor vehicles, 20 horse-drawn wagons and a considerable number of anti-aircraft guns were destroyed; 12 enemy aircraft were shot down.

Strong groups of Axis ground-attack planes assaulted the enemy troop concentrations northwest of Kiskunhalas.

Axis Fighter Claims
- Non-commissioned officer Eugen Lörcher (5./SG 2) – 1 Il-2
- Captain Heinrich Sturm (5./JG 52) – 2 La-5 and 2 Il-2
- Lieutenant Peter Düttmann (6./JG 52) – 3 Il-2
- Captain Erich Hartmann (7./JG 52) – 1 Yak-7 [sic]
- Lieutenant Heinz Ewald (7./JG 52) – 1 La-5 and 1 Il-2

1 November 1944

5th Air Army

The Army supported the ground forces of the Front with bomber and assault air strikes against the enemy troop concentrations in the areas of Nagykőrös, Cegléd, Abony and Alberti, and covered them from the air with fighters, as well as performed reconnaissance missions. A total of 530 sorties were conducted: 260 on close support missions and bombing, 16 on reconnaissance, 136 on the protection of the ground troops and 118 on fighter escort missions.

14 air fights took place, in which 17 enemy aircraft were shot down.

Soviet Fighter Claims
- Lieutenant Leonid Andreev (122nd FAR) – 1 Fw 190, at Sereg [sic]
- Lieutenant Izmail Rulev (85th GFAR) – 2 Fw 190, northeast of Lajosmizse
- Lieutenant Mikhail Gamsheev (85th GFAR) – 1 Fw 190, east of Kovacsmanor [sic] (Kovács-major?)
- Lieutenant Nikolai Minin (85th GFAR) – 1 Fw 190, at Kovacsmanor [sic] (Kovács-major?)
- Senior-Lieutenant Vladimir Lyusin (85th GFAR) – 1 Fw 190, northwest of Nagyk rös
- Major Mikhail Zuev (73rd GFAR) – 1 Bf 109, southeast of Kyoros [sic] (Nagyk rös?)
- Major Victor Maltsev (177th GFAR) – 1 Fw 190, at Cegléd
- Lieutenant Boris Ushakov (177th GFAR) – 1 Bf 109, at Tertely [sic]
- Lieutenant Naum Rabinovich (513th FAR) – 1 Fw 190, southwest of Cegléd

Air Fleet 4
Increased enemy air activity in the sector of Armeegruppe Fretter-Pico and in the areas of Tokaj and Miskolc.

The focal point of the Axis aerial activity was the area between the Danube and Tisza. In the vicinity of Kecskemét and west of the town a considerable number of tanks and motor vehicles were destroyed or damaged.

A total of 243 Axis aircraft (156 bombers, 46 fighters, 30 reconnaissance airplanes and 11 tank-killing airplanes) of the I Air Corps took part in combat missions. Direct hits on tanks, motor vehicles and troop positions were reported. The pilots of the corps claimed 22 lorries, 3 passenger cars, 8 horse-drawn carts and 3 anti-tank guns. 9 tanks were destroyed, 3 more tanks were probably destroyed too. Another tank was reportedly knocked out. The tank-killing airplanes destroyed 4 tanks and 2 armoured cars. 17 enemy aircraft were shot down, while friendly losses amounted to 6 aircraft.

In the night of 31 October/1 November the Axis aircraft twice attacked the railway station of Arad.

Axis Fighter Claims
- Sergeant-major Schneider (II./SG 2) – 1 La-5, northeast of Kecskemét
- Lieutenant Friedrich Haas (5./JG 52) – 1 Yak-9
- Lieutenant Peter Düttmann (6./JG 52) – 4 Yak-9
- Captain Erich Hartmann (7./JG 52) – 1 La-5
- Lieutenant Heinz Ewald (7./JG 52) – 2 Yak-7 [sic]
- Non-commissioned officer Gelin (7./JG 52) – 1 Il-2
- Non-commissioned officer Pitzl (7./JG 52) – 1 La-5
- Lieutenant István Kálmán (102/1. FS) – 1 Boston Mk III, near Cegléd
- 1st Lieutenant Ferenc Málnássy (102/2. FS) – 1 Boston Mk III, near Cegléd
- Captain László Pottyondy (102/2. FS) – 1 La-5, near Cegléd

2 November 1944

5th Air Army
The Army flew a total of 543 sorties as follows: 59 bomber missions; 202 ground-attack sorties against enemy troops at Nagyk rös, Cegléd, Abony and Alberti; 136 sorties on the protection of the ground troops; 118 escort sorties, while the rest were reconnaissance, 'free hunt' and interception missions.

6 air fights took place, in which 10 enemy aircraft were shot down.

14 enemy aircraft were destroyed or damaged on the Tápiószentmárton airfield.

Soviet Fighter Claims
- Junior-Lieutenant Fotii Morozov (31st GFAR) – 1 Ju 87, south of Monor [sic]
- Senior-Lieutenant Nikolai Smirnov (192nd FAR) – 1 Bf 109, southwest of Cegléd
- Senior-Lieutenant Nikolai Smirnov (192nd FAR) – ½ Bf 109 (a shared victory), northeast of Kecskemét

Air Fleet 4

There was strong activity of the enemy fighter and close support aircraft in the area southeast of Budapest. The actions of the air units of the I Air Corps were considerably hampered by the bad weather, miserable condition of the airfields, as well as by the very strong enemy fighter opposition and anti-aircraft fire. The attacks of the Axis bombers were directed predominantly against the Soviet spearheads, as well as the troop concentrations east of Budapest. It was in that area where most of the air battles with enemy fighters took place.

In the course of the day the I Air Corps supported the defensive and offensive battles of Armeegruppe Fretter-Pico with good effect. A total of 147 Axis aircraft (109 bombers, 26 fighters, and 12 reconnaissance airplanes) participated in combat missions. The Axis pilots shot down 5 enemy planes without any losses of their own. 2 Soviet tanks were destroyed too.

3 Fw 190 were damaged during the Soviet air raid against the Tápiószentmárton airfield.

During the night of 1/2 November the 15 Axis night bombers attacked the Békéscsaba railway station, where they supposedly managed to destroy 1 ammunition and 2 fuel trains. In the course of the same night another 37 Axis bombers attacked Soviet transport columns in the areas of Kecskemét and Kiskunfélegyháza, as well as the river crossing at Vecseny [sic]. As result of these attacks numerous small explosions and fires erupted on the ground.

Axis Fighter Claims

- 1st Lieutenant György Bánlaki (102/4. FS) – 1 Il-2, southeast of Cegléd
- Sergeant Lajos Molnár (102/4. FS) – 1 La-5, southeast of Cegléd

3 November 1944

5th Air Army

Due to the bad weather the army flew only 38 sorties on that day.

Air Fleet 4

Due to the bad weather the Axis air activity was very weak.

Axis Fighter Claims

- 1st Lieutenant Béla Füleki (101/4. FS) – 1 Il-2, near Tiszasqly [sic]
- Ensign Mihály Sziráki (101/4. FS) – 1 Il-2, near Tiszasqly [sic]

4 November 1944

5th Air Army

A total of 185 missions were flown, 82 of which were ground-attack sorties against enemy troops in Budapest and in the areas of Jászkisér, Bessenszeg and Heves. The Army also conducted 42 escort and 9 reconnaissance missions, and flew 52 sorties on the protection of the ground troops.

5 air fights took place, in which 5 enemy aircraft were shot down.

Soviet Fighter Claims

- Senior-Lieutenant Vladimir Ananyev (85th GFAR) – 1 Fw 190, south of Kabonya [sic] (Kőbánya?)
- Senior-Lieutenant Sergey Konovalov (150th GFAR) – 1 Fw 190, at Sorok [sic] (Soroksár?)
- Major Aleksey Reshetov (31st GFAR) – 1 Ju 88, west of Budyon [sic] (Bugyi?)
- Captain Victor Ryazankin (149th GFAR) – 2 Fw 190, south of Kecskemét

Air Fleet 4

Due to the bad weather the enemy aerial activity was low. The friendly aircraft supported the defensive and offensive battles of Armeegruppe Fretter-Pico. 3 enemy aircraft were shot down.

Axis Fighter Claims
- Major Ernst Dülberg (Stab/JG 76) – 1 Yak-9, southwest of Pilis

5 November 1944

5th Air Army

The Army flew a total of 374 sorties as follows: 150 ground attack , 15 reconnaissance, 79 escort and 130 sorties on the protection of the ground troops.

Soviet Fighter Claims
- Lieutenant Leonid Kochergin (151st GFAR) – 1 Bf 109, south of Kossuth Ferenc

Air Fleet 4

The focal point of the enemy aerial activity was the Cegléd–Szolnok area. The aircraft were used against the enemy deployment areas and attack columns on the right flank of Armeegruppe Fretter-Pico.

The focal point of the air attacks was the area southeast of Budapest. 5 tanks, 1 motor vehicle, 4 horse-drawn carts and 1 quad anti-aircraft machine gun were destroyed. Only part of the serviceable friendly aircraft took part in the operations; the rest were grounded due to the bad condition of the airfields. A total of 108 Axis aircraft (94 bombers and 14 reconnaissance airplanes) participated in combat missions. They sustained no losses during the day.

In the course of the night the Axis aircraft attacked the Békéscsaba railway station.

6 November 1944

5th Air Army

The army flew a total of 252 sorties, 115 of which were ground-attack sorties against enemy troops at Tápiószele, Újszász, Tápiógyörgye and Tiszaszőlős. The Army also flew 66 sorties on the protection of the ground troops and conducted 21 reconnaissance and 50 escort missions.

1 air fight took place, in which 3 enemy aircraft were shot down.

Soviet Fighter Claims
- Major Shalva Kiriya (151st GFAR) – 1 Hs 129, north of Lajosmizse
- Senior-Lieutenant Dmitry Menshikov (151st GFAR) – 1 Bf 109, north of Lajosmizse
- Senior-Lieutenant Nikolai Smirnov (192nd FAR) – ½ Fw 190 (a shared victory), southwest of the Bugatsi Puszta airfield [sic] (Bugacpuszta?)

Air Fleet 4

The focal point of the enemy aerial activity was the Cegléd–Szolnok area. The German Luftwaffe units and the Hungarian fast ground attack aircraft were engaged in the area southeast of Budapest, between Cegléd–Kecskemét, as well as in support of the attack of the 13.Panzer-Division. 2 tanks were shot up and 60 trucks were destroyed.

Strong enemy fighter activity and concentrated anti-aircraft artillery fire, especially in the area southeast of Budapest, considerably hampered the actions of the friendly bomber aircraft. The number of the sorties flown by the reconnaissance airplanes was limited due to the bad weather.

In the night of 5/6 November the Axis aircraft bombed the Arad railway station.

7 November 1944

5th Air Army

A total of 528 sorties were flown, 82 of which were ground-attack missions against enemy troops in the areas of Poroszló, Tiszanána, Kemle (???), Jászapáti, Füzesabony, Jászladány, Újszász and Budapest. The Army also conducted 25 reconnaissance and 145 escort missions and flew 126 sorties on the protection of the ground troops.

5 air fights took place, in which 3 enemy aircraft were shot down.

Soviet Fighter Claims

- Senior-Lieutenant Nikolai Davydov (149th GFAR) – 1 Bf 109, northeast of Pestszentimre
- Senior-Lieutenant Nikolai Kireev (150th GFAR) – 1 Fw 190, northwest of Lajosmizse

Air Fleet 4

Aggravation of the Axis air actions southeast of Budapest because of the increasing enemy fighter activity and anti-aircraft artillery fire.

Lively enemy aerial activity over the area of the IX Army Corps (Hung).

3 enemy pontoons were destroyed at Apatin.

Axis Fighter Claims

- Sergeant-major Braun (1./NAGr 14) – 1 Po-2
- Senior-Lieutenant Pohl (1./SG 10) – 1 Yak-9
- Lieutenant Peter Düttmann (6./JG 52) – 1 Yak-9
- Captain Erich Hartmann (7./JG 52) – 1 Yak-7 [sic]

APPENDIX 8

WAR CRIMES

8.1 SOVIET LOOTING

To: the troops of the 2nd Ukrainian Front
2.10.44
Order No.00152

In recent times, cases were observed when there was no due military order during occupation of settlements by troops, staffs of divisions, corps, armies and Front headquarters' departments.
Guard service is not properly organised. Privates, sergeants, and – in a number of cases – officers, taking advantage of absence of inhabitants, are engaged in, putting it bluntly, marauding: they break into cellars, take wine, and steal goods from houses.
All these actions have a corrupting effect on troops and embitter the population against the Red Army.

I order:

1. Under personal responsibility of commanders of units, divisions, corps, commanding generals of armies and chiefs of the front headquarters' departments to eliminate the aforementioned cases and establish firm order when stationing troops and staffs in settlements.

2. To establish a guard of property and warehouses and a patrol of settlements. Those who were seen engaged in marauding are to be court-martialled severely and subject to punishments including death by shooting.

3. Military prosecutors are to immediately investigate on the spot all cases of marauding for court-martialing by the Military Tribunal.

4. This order is to be read to all the personnel and destroyed after that.

Signed: Malinovsky Susaikov Zakharov

8.2 ROMANIAN CRIMES

To: the Military Councils of the 7th Guards, 27th and 53rd Armies

CC: to the Military Councils of the 40th, 46th and 6th Tank Armies
To the Head of the Political Administration of the Front
To the Military Prosecutor of the Front
To the Head of the Rear Services of the Front

The Front Military Council has been made aware of a number of occasions when Romanian units break into, ransack and plunder private properties of people from Transylvania and Hungary, pick out the last remaining household goods, rape women and children, abuse the locals in various ways. Those facts bring about negative reactions in the local population.

Romanian units should fight, not engage in banditry; their unacceptable behaviour in the territories of Transylvania and Hungary evokes feelings and moods against the Red Army that are not politically advantageous.

In order to eradicate the habit of looting from the Romanian troops, the Military Council orders the Army Military Councils immediately to take the respective measures and issue a special order to the commanders of the Romanian divisions, requiring that they, in turn, should take all the necessary measures immediately to stop cases of banditry and make sure that all such cases are investigated locally and those found guilty tried and punished severely.

Military Councils should immediately report those cases to the Military Council of the Front. Special control should be established at the checkpoints over the goods transported by any of the Romanian vehicles.

If it is proved that the transported goods have been taken from the population, the checkpoint staff should confiscate all goods with no relation to military property and an inventory should be made with a report attached to it.

A report about the measures taken should be submitted by 20.10.44

Signed: Malinovsky Susaikov Zakharov

14.10.44
No. 17563/Sh

8.3 SOVIET RAPES

No.00685/op
30 October 1944

The enemy should be beaten and annihilated with the utmost hatred, but the civilian population should be treated with justice, and in no cases are pillage, marauding and violence to be tolerated.
However, I receive reports on cases of marauding and raping women, especially by the units of the Kuban and Don Cossacks and cavalrymen.
They have apparently forgotten that they bear the great name of Red Army warriors, who are known for their exceptional discipline, great firmness in battle, but also along with it – a just attitude to the civilian population.

I order:

The military prosecutor of the Front is urgently to investigate cases of rape of women and those guilty of these disgraceful acts, and also the commanders tolerating them, are to be court-martialled by the Military Tribunal.

All generals and officers must read this order in front of the ranks and must explain to NCOs and enlisted personnel that from now on all cases of raping women will be treated as a crime utterly disgracing the Red Army, and those found guilty will be sentenced to DEATH BY SHOOTING.

The military prosecutor of the Front and the chairman of the Tribunal are to be informed of these crimes no later than 48 hours after immediate execution of sentences and with simultaneous dispatch of reports to the native homes of the criminals, villages or collective farms.

Report to me on acquainting the troops with this order.

Signed: Malinovsky Susaikov Zakharov

8.4 GERMAN LOOTING

Communication of the Minister of the Interior in Szálasi Government to the Minister of Foreign Affairs concerning the outrages committed by the German Soldiery

The extension of the theatre of war to the administrative boundaries of Greater Budapest and the possibility of the provisional Russian occupation of Budapest have aroused a feeling of increasing fear and uncertainty in the inhabitants, not only in Budapest but also of the areas unoccupied by the enemy. To overcome this feeling of fear and uncertainty the government has done and will do everything possible.
It is, however, beyond doubt that any propaganda in this direction can only be effective if the psychological consolidation of the masses is not harmfully shaken by such events, the news of which spreads among the general public like wildfire, and which are also exceptionally suited to the specific aims of enemy propaganda.

It has to be taken into account that the judgment of the masses is not the result of speculation, but of sentiments based on facts, and is therefore unshakable as far the masses are concerned. In addition to strengthening propaganda, it therefore seems necessary to remove, as far as possible, all those harmful circumstances which influence the judgment of public opinion in a direction contrary to the interests of the war effort and the life and death struggle of our nation.

Violent actions which members of the German armed forces perpetrate against Hungarian citizens or against their property are such circumstances.

In what follows I inform the Minister of Foreign Affairs of cases which have been objected to from amongst the reports I have recently received.

According to the report of the local gendarmerie, the population around Gödöllő does not obey the calls for evacuation partially because the retreating German armies everywhere break into homes and shops, and carry off whatever can be moved (carpets, furniture, clothes, beverages, food and other goods).
At Aszód they broke open and looted the Jewish shops which had been closed and those private dwellings which had been left by the inhabitants. At Vác they seized the slaughterhouse and the butcher-shops, slaughtered the cattle and pig stock to be found there, processing them and taking them to Germany.
On the Gödöllő-Budapest road the Germans take away cars, horses, carriages throwing their owners off them.

At Pécel they looted the villa of Colonel Marton, a knight of rank. They carry off the animal stock, the cereals and the farm equipment from the estates.

In the village of Vecsés they robbed the co-operative shop. In this not only the German soldiery but the scum of the village population also took part.

As recounted by refugees arriving from the direction of Vecsés, the Germans enter dwellings even when the inhabitants are present, and use violence to take away the clothing and food found there.

In the village of Vecsés the German soldiers carried off the produce and animals of the farmers in full view of the patrolling gendarmerie.

The German soldiery drove away approximately 482 head of cattle owned by Hungarian Sugar Industries in the Aszód gendarmerie district, declaring that since they were the property of the Hungarian state, they were at the disposal of German military command.

At Rákosliget the German soldiery in several places even defiled the dwellings broken open by them.

Violence and looting committed by the Germans are the order of the day and occur so frequently that the security bodies cannot prevent them on account of their greatly reduced numbers.

Public opinion is slowly absorbing this news and the anti-German mood is spreading and increasing. The spread of this mood in the masses may have alarming consequences if measures are not taken in time to prevent acts of violence.

In view of this, I respectfully request the Minister of Foreign Affairs to urge the competent German authorities as quickly and successfully as possible to stop these irregularities so that the already perturbed mood of the general public should not be intensified, because the spread of this news through wide circles of society and the rise of a possible uniform anti-German sentiment may cause serious difficulties from the point of view of the fate of our country and the interests of the war effort.

Budapest, 16 November 1944

APPENDIX 9

DOCUMENTS

9.1 SOVIET REPRESENTATION TO THE HEAD OF THE HUNGARIAN PEACE DELEGATION IN MOSCOW

The Hungarian delegate sent from Budapest to Szeged – the truce envoy, Col. Utasi Laurend [Lóránd Utasi] – is an absolutely uninformed person and hence could not engage in talks with representatives of the Soviet command on matters of the Hungarian Government's compliance with the preliminary conditions for an armistice.

The Hungarian Government had requested the Soviet Government to hold up the advance towards Budapest so that the Hungarian Government might withdraw its forces from that sector and send them to Budapest.

The Soviet Government complied with this request from the Hungarian Government. But the latter not only failed to withdraw its forces from the Tisza river and send them to Budapest but stepped up their activity, especially in the vicinity of Szolnok.

The facts cited above indicate that the Hungarian Government has apparently chosen not to fulfil those pre-armistice conditions that it pledged itself to fulfil.

Such being the case, the Supreme Command of the Soviet Forces demands of the Hungarian Government that within 48 hours of receipt of this representation it fulfil the prearmistice conditions that it pledged itself to fulfil, and most urgently:

1. To break off all relations with the Germans and initiate military actions against their forces;
2. To proceed to the withdrawal of Hungarian forces from Romania, Yugoslavia, and Czechoslovakia;
3. By 08:00 on 16 October, via the link used earlier (i.e., via Szeged), to provide the representatives of the Soviet command with full information on the disposition of the Hungarian and German forces, and at the same time to report to the aforementioned Soviet representatives on the progress in fulfilling the prearmistice conditions.

By the authority of the Supreme Command of the Soviet Forces:

Army-General Antonov, Deputy Chief of the General Staff of the Red Army.

14 October 1944, 19:25 hours

9.2 ORDER OF THE COMMANDER OF THE 4TH UKRAINIAN FRONT CONCERNING THE TREATMENT OF HUNGARIAN OFFICERS AND SOLDIERS JOINING THE RED ARMY

The commander of the 1st Hungarian Army, Colonel-General Béla Dálnoki Miklós, a knight of rank, together with his staff, has come over to the side of the Red Army in order to organise the common struggle against the Germans. In the last few days 5785 Hungarian officers and soldiers have come over to the side of the Red Army, partly in organised platoons and companies, partly in groups and individually.

In connection with the Hungarian officers and soldiers who voluntarily cross the frontline, I hereby order:

1. To the commander of every military formation that he enlighten the Red Army soldiers that the soldiers, officers and generals coming over to our side, whether they come in organised detachments, by groups or individually, whether armed or unarmed, are adherents to the immediate cessation of the war against the red Army. Consequently, these members of the Hungarian army must be received in friendship, and they must at once be escorted from the danger zone to a safe place.

2. The Germans must be prevented by all available military means from obstructing Hungarian soldiers, officers and generals in crossing the frontline.

3. Everyone who comes over voluntarily to the side of the Red Army must be given a certificate showing that he has stopped fighting against the Russians and has crossed the frontline.

4. Those who come over voluntarily must be separated from the prisoners of war, and must be ensured better quarters and provisions than the POWs.

5. Every night at 24 hours I must be given a report of the number of the Hungarian army members who have come over voluntarily (how many officers and how many soldiers), and what army formations. Those officers who are battalion commanders or have still higher commands must be reported by telegraph to the command of the 1st Hónved Army.

The Commander of the 4th Ukrainian Front Colonel-General Ivan Petrov
[20 October 1944]

9.3 APPEAL OF THE RED ARMY'S COMMAND TO THE POPULATION OF THE LIBERATED TERRITORY OF HUNGARY

Hungarians!

In pursuit of the enemy, detachments of the Red Army have set foot on Hungarian soil.

As the Red Army sets foot on Hungarian territory, it is not led by the aim to occupy any part of it or to change Hungary's present social order.

The entry of the Soviet detachments into the territory of Hungary has been made inevitable solely by military necessity, because German detachments and the armed forces of Hungary allied to Germany continue to resist.

The Red Army is carrying out the order of its Supreme Command to pursue the enemy forces until they are completely defeated and lay down their arms.

The Hitlerite bandits and their Hungarian hirelings terrorise you over the entry of the Red Army into Hungary. You have no reason at all to be afraid! The Read Army does not come to Hungary as a conqueror but as the liberator of the Hungarian people from the German fascist yoke.

The Red Army has no other aim than to smash the enemy German army, and to wipe out the rule of Hitler's Germany in the countries subjugated by her.

The Soviet military authorities do not intend to change Hungary's present social order and to introduce their own regime in the territories occupied by them.

The private property of citizens shall remain untouched, and comes under the protection of the Soviet military authorities.

The local authorities and all organs of local self-government, which were operating before the entry of the Red Army, should remain in their places.

Citizens!
The Command of the Red Army calls on you to remain claim, keep order, and comply strictly with the decrees issued by the Soviet military authorities which are being issued in the light of the conditions of war.
Remain in your places and continue your peaceful work!
See to it that the operation of the industrial, commercial, municipal and other works, as well as that of the authorities, goes on undisturbed!
Workers and artisans! You can continue your work in the factories and workshops without fear!
Traders and contractors! Go about your business without misgivings!
Officials! Ensure the undisturbed operation of all offices and branches of administration!
Churchmen and believers can carry out their religious ceremonies without any hindrance.

Hungarians!
Hitler's Germany has lost the war. The German fascist army is in a hopeless position and faces collapse.
Help the Red Army in everything! By doing so you hasten the destruction of the German fascist army. And by doing so you bring nearer the hour when the war on Hungarian soil will end and we will finally drive the German bandits from your country.

The Command of the Red Army

[27 October 1944]

9.4 AFTER ACTION REPORT OF HEAVY-PANZER BATTALION 503

s.Panzer-Abteilung 503 Abt.Ia 371/44 geh.   <u>Experience Report</u> Abt.Gef.St., den 25.11.44

The battalion entrained for Hungary starting on 9 October 1944, in order to complete its reconstitution in the area of Budapest. The government crisis made it necessary to employ the battalion for the occupation of the [Buda] castle, which action, even though almost exclusively a demonstration, proved to be a success. The exacerbation of the situation east of the Tisza and at Debrecen required an immediate deployment. The panzer elements were unloaded in the vicinity of Szolnok, but due to the shortage of *Ssymswagen*,[1] they had to be transported by a shuttle train and not all of them arrived on time in the assembly area. Those that were unloaded marched off immediately to the assembly area in order to launch an attack several hours later. The tanks that arrived on the next day were assembled into a separate battle group and attached to another division, so the battalion went into action in two battle groups, with different divisions on different days, with the intention of reassembling once a breakthrough into the enemy's rear area was achieved. Both battle groups were extraordinary successful. From 19 October until the reassembly [of the battalion] on 23 October, 120 anti-tank guns and 19 artillery guns were destroyed. The very tough and determined enemy (a penal battalion) was shattered by an energetic charge, rearward communications were brought into complete confusion by destroying [supply] columns and a transport train, which forced the Russian 6th [Guards Tank] Army to pull out of the Debrecen area. The entire stretch of about 250km that was covered in this action was achieved without significant mechanical breakdowns. In these battles the Tiger II proved itself to be both very well-armoured and mechanically reliable. It was not exceptional that vehicles [tanks] that were hit up to 20 times were still operational.
The action that followed was limited to small missions, especially counter-attacks with weak infantry forces against the enemy who crossed over the Tisza northeast of Szolnok. Although on a small scale, they proved to be successful and caused the Russians to forbid their units from carrying out any major actions where Tigers were deployed.

During those weeks, and continuing up to today, the battalion was not given time to perform mainte-nance despite the urgent requests that were continually being made. This was partially due to the situation, but also partially due to the lack of understanding of higher command echelons, who [always] asked just two questions: 'How many are operational?' and 'How many will be repaired in the next few days?' In spite of this, up to 30 October on average 25 to 30 tanks were operational every day.

On 31 October the battalion rolled to a new assignment in the area of Kecskemét, which was, under LVII Panzer Corps, to intercept the Russian wedges advancing on Budapest. In very difficult, particularly swampy terrain, that was unsuitable for tanks, damage began to occur, especially to drive sprockets, tracks, track tension adjusters and engine cooling fans, and within a few days, due to a shortage of spare parts, which had been ordered on time but not delivered on time and then only partially, the bulk of the bat-talion was non-combatant due to mechanical breakdowns.

As a result of the lack of towing vehicles, the battalion was faced with the decision of either blowing up the broken-down tanks beyond the main battle line or recovering them with Tigers that were still operational. Naturally, this resulted in mechanical breakdowns to the vehicles used to tow the others out. Thanks to the timely and advanced preparations for loading the tanks on the rail [cars] that had been made in the very last moment, the battalion barely avoided losing a considerable number of tanks …

The [previous] experience that the Russians use to build up strong anti-tank gun positions directly behind their forward combat elements was proven again. Fortunately, the employment of the American 9.2 and conical bore (7.5 reduced to 5.7 [cm]) anti-tank guns[2] has led to only two total write-offs. These weapons can also penetrate the gun mantlet at ranges under 600m. Penetrations of the rear of the turret cause the ammunition stored there to explode and usually lead to the total destruction of the vehicle.

In tank-versus-tank combat, the 8.8 [cm] Kw.K.43 gun is effective in destroying all of the types of enemy tanks, including Stalin, at ranges up to 1500m. Under favourable conditions, the T 34 and T 43 tanks[3] can also be knocked out at ranges up to 3000m. Very often, as [previously experienced] in the West [with Allied tanks], it was often observed that the Russian tanks decline to fight Tigers or turn and flee after their first tank is knocked out. The same applies to the [Russian] assault guns as well as to the Stalin [tanks]. Kills at over 1500m have not yet occurred.

In summary, it can be said that the Tiger II has proven itself in every way and is a weapon that is feared by the enemy; when correctly employed tactically, the concentrated Tiger unit will always bring success, but the higher command echelons did not perceive the technical and tactical importance of a Tiger-Battalion.

[Fromme]
Captain and battalion commander

1   SSyms-Wagen: a series of special heavy-load-capacity railroad cars.
2   The original text says (in German): '*Der Einsatz amerik. 9,2 und konischer Pak (7,5 auf 5,7)*' … The anti-tank guns in question were most probably the Soviet 57mm ZiS-2. They used ammunition that had been originally developed for 76mm ZiS-3, only its neck diameter was reduced from 76 to 57mm, while the powder charge remained the same. The American gun was most probably the 90mm M1/M2 anti-aircraft gun, which was often employed against tanks. In October-November 1944, however, there were no American-made guns in the inventory of the 2nd Ukrainian Front. Therefore, here the reference is most probably to the experience that the battalion had gained while fighting against the Allied troops in Normandy during the summer.
3   These were the usual German designations for the T-34-76 and T-34-85 tanks.

NOTES

Chapter 1

1 C. Wilmot, *The Struggle for Europe*, Wordsworth, Ware, 1997, pp.560–561. For details see P. Schramm, *Kriegstagebuch des Oberkommandos der Wehrmacht*, Vol.IV/1, pp.432–435.

2 On 21 October 1944 Keitel indicated a requirement of 17,000m³ of fuel, which were to be provided by the end of November. Schramm, op cit, pp.434–435.

3 Report by the Joint Intelligence Sub-Committee on the Effects of Allied Attacks on the Enemy Oil Situation in Europe, 30 October 1944. Reproduced in C. Webster and N. Frankland, *The Strategic Bomber Offensive Against Germany* Vol.IV, Her Majesty's Stationery Office, London, 1961, pp.293–297.

4 Bundesarchiv/Militaerarchiv, Freiburg (Hereafter cited as BA-MA), RH10/312 and RH10/321.

5 By that time the German reserve pilots were receiving only 200 flying training hours, whilst their British and American opponents were getting 360 and 400 hours of practical flying before being dispatched to the combat units. K. Gundelach, 'Der alliierte Luftkrieg gegen die deutsche Flugtribstoffversorgung'. *Wehrwissenschaftliche Rundschau* (hereafter cited as WWR), 1963, No.12, p.701.

6 Wilmot, op cit, p.551.

7 Record of interrogation of Albert Speer, 18 July 1945. Reproduced in Webster and Frankland, op cit, Vol.IV, p.385. For details on the fuel shortages, decline in the production of aviation fuel and the overall effect of the Allied bombing raids see Gundelach, op. cit.

8 Report of 30 August 1944. Reproduced in Webster and Frankland, op cit, Vol.IV, pp.330–333.

9 Gundelach, op cit, p.699, cit. Albert Speer, Nr. 686/44 g. Res. (geheime Reichssache Berlin, 5 September 1944.

10 Wilmot, op cit, p.552.

11 Ibid.

12 Ibid.

13 Report of 5 October 1944. Reproduced in Webster and Frankland, op cit, Vol.IV, pp.333–335.

14 L. Srágli, 'American Capital and the Hungarian Oil Industry', *Hungarian Quarterly*, Vol.XLII, No.162, Summer 2001.

15 M. Fenyo, *Hitler, Horthy and Hungary*, Yale University Press, New Haven, 1972, p.214, cit. *Der Aussenhandel Ungarns 1941–1943* by the Statistisches Reichsamt, November 1944, NA Microcopy T-84, roll 135, 1438207.

16 Report by the Joint Intelligence Sub-Committee on the Effects of Allied Attacks on the Enemy Oil Situation in Europe, 30 October 1944. Reproduced in Webstwer and Frankland, op cit, Vol.IV, pp.293–297.

17 Record of interrogation of Albert Speer, 18 July 1945. Reproduced in Webstwer and Frankland, op cit, Vol.IV, p.386.

18 M. Minasyan, *Osvobozhdenie narodov Yugovostochnoi Evropy*, Voenizdat, Moscow, 1967, p.29.

19 M. Horthy, *Memoirs*, Safety Harbor, Simon Publications, 2000, p.274.

20 Hitler expressed his contempt for the Magyars many times. Some of his comments can be found in the transcriptions of various conferences. 'Even in Hungary, National Socialism could not be exported. In the mass the Hungarian is as lazy as the Russian. He's by nature a man of the steppe.' (17 September 1941, reproduced in H. Trevor-Roper, *Hitler's Table Talk, 1941–1944*, Enigma Books, New York, 2000, p.33.); 'The Hungarians have always been *poseurs*. In war they are like the British and the Poles; war to them is an affair which concerns the government and to which they go like oxen to the slaughter. They all wear swords, but have none of the earnest chivalry which the bearing of the sword should imply.' (22 August 1942, reproduced in Trevor-Roper, op. cit, p.654.); 'We shouldn't be surprised by the Hungarians. When we have such idiots or criminals with us, who say that even if the Russians come in we'll make peace, but if we have the Russians to ourselves not much can happen to us – so what right to do we have to complain when some Hungarian idiot or magnate says, "We'll let ourselves be occupied the British; they will have an interest in making sure that we aren't absorbed, so everything will be fine".' (31 July 1944, reproduced in H. Heiber and D. Glantz, *Hitler and His Generals*, Enigma Books, New York, 2003, pp.448–449.)

21 G. Lakatos. *As I Saw It*, Universe Publishing Company, Englewood, 1993, p.112.

22 Lakatos, op cit, p.109.

23 Meeting of the Fuhrer with Colonel-General Jodl, 31 July 1944. Conference transcription. Reproduced in Heiber and Glantz, op cit, pp.444–463.

24 D. Irving, *Hitler's War and The War Path*, Focal Point Publications, London, 2000, p.732.

25 GenStdH, Gruppe Planung, Nr I/013408/44g.K. 15.9.1944. National Archives Records Administration Microfilm Series T78, roll 413, frame 6381962. (Hereafter cited as NARA T78/413/6381962.)

26 Record of interrogation of Albert Speer, 30 May 1945. Reproduced in Webster and Frankland, op cit, Vol.IV, p.373.

27 Ibid.

28 Irving, op cit, p.732.

Chapter 2

1 Field-Marshal Harold Alexander, the commander of the Allied 15th Army Group.

2 W. Churchill, *The Second World War*, Vol.VI, Cassel and Co, London, 1954, p.131.

3 J. Ehrman, *Grand Strategy* Vol.V, Her Majesty's Stationery Office, London, 1956, p.510.

4 Churchill, op cit, p.137.

5 Ibid, pp.139–140. The report is reproduced only partially.

6 Ibid, p.140.

7 Field-Marshal Albert Kesselring, the Commander-in-Chief of the German forces in Italy.

8 Personal and Secret Message to Marshal Stalin from the United States Government and His Majesty's Government. Reproduced in S. Richardson, *The Secret History of the World War II*, Richardson and Sterman, NY, 1986, pp.201–202.

9 Letter of Molotov to the British Ambassador in Moscow, 26 September 1944. Reproduced in V. Zolotarev, *Velikaia Otechestvennaia Voina* Vol.14(3–2), Terra, Moscow, 1999), p.217.

10 TASS announcement, 29 September 1944. Reproduced in P. Zhilin, et al. (eds), *Osvoboditelnaya missia Sovetskih Vooruzennyh sil v Evrope vo Vtoroi Mirovoi Voine* (Hereafter cited as P. Zhilin, OMSVSVEVMV), Voenizdat, Moscow, 1985, p.162.

11 Surprisingly, Churchill did not inform Stalin in advance about the reason for his visit. This is confirmed by the message Stalin sent on 8 October to Roosevelt: 'I don't know what points Mr Churchill and Mr Eden want to discuss in Moscow. Neither of them has said anything to me so far. In a message, Mr Churchill expressed the wish to come to Moscow if it was all right with me. I agreed, of course.' (Secret and Personal from Premier J.V. Stalin to the President, Mr F. Roosevel; reproduced in Richardson, op cit, pp.204–205.)

12 Ehrman, op cit, Vol.VI, p.47.

13 Ibid, pp.47–48.

14 J. Erickson. *The Road to Berlin*, Weidenfeld and Nicolson, London, 1983, p.337, cit. M. Djilas, *Conversations with Stalin*.

15 Ibid, p.382.

16 Ibid, p.344. cit. M. Djilas, *Conversations with Stalin*.

17 Army-General Anton Antonov, Deputy Chief of the Soviet General Staff.

18 According to the logbook of Stalin's Kremlin cabinet, the meeting was held on 4 October 1944 from 21:45 to 22:45. See Y. Gorkov, *Kreml. Stavka. Genshtab.*, Tver, 1995, p.195. (The logbook is reproduced in the Appendix of Gorkov's book.)

19 S. Shtemenko, *The Last Six Months*, Doubleday, Garden City, 1977, pp.257–258.

20 G. Gorodetsky, *Rokovoi samoobman*, ROSSPEN, Moscow, p.336, cit. a letter of General Liashchenko to Lev Bezimensky.

21 Marshal V. Sokolovsky wrote the following regarding the pros and cons of the Stavka representatives: 'The Representative of the Supreme High Command [Stavka] helped the command of Army Groups [Fronts] to carry out the plans of the Supreme High Command, to make decisions depending on the role and place of Army Group in a given operation, and also to solve on-the-spot problems concerning operational and strategic cooperation. However, there were substantial shortcomings in the work of these representatives, mainly when they substituted for Army Group troop commanders and restrained the latter's initiative, and also when preferential reinforcement of troops and supply materials was given to one Army Group at the expense of others on the insistence of a representative.' (S. Bialer, *Stalin and his Generals*, Westview Press, Boulder and London, 1984, pp.596–597, cit. V. Sokolovsky, *Military Strategy*, Praeger, New York, 1963, p.365.)

22 Timoshenko received his appointment on 3 May 1944. On 16 September 1944 the area of his responsibilities was shifted to the north; he became Stavka representative to the 2nd and 4th Ukrainian Fronts while the 3rd Ukrainian was released from his control. Stavka directive #220216. *Tsentralnyi Arhiv Ministerstva Oborony*, fund 148a, inventory 3763, file 167, p.48. (Hereafter cited as TsAMO, fu.148a, inv.3763, f.167, p.48.) Reproduced in Zolotarev, op cit, Vol.16 (5–4), p.145. On 21 January 1945 his control was reversed. (Stavka directive. TsAMO, fu.132-A, inv.2642, f.49, p.13, reproduced in Zolotarev, op cit, Vol.14, p.356.)

23 Portugalsky et al., op cit, pp.309–310.

24 See Telegram Nr. VI, 11 October 1944, 00:30, partially reproduced in C.A. Macartney, *Ungarns Weg aus dem Zweiten Weltkrieg*, Vierteiljahrhefte für Zeitgeschichte, 1966/1, p.91. See also I. Elvedi, *Debretsenskaya operatsia i Sovetsko-Vengerskie peregovory o peremirii*, Voenno-Istoricheskii Zhurnal (hereafter cited as VIZh), 1973, No.9, p.104.

25 During the Second World War every activity in the Red Army (i.e. transmitting and delivering of reports, issuing of orders, submitting of directives, etc.), no matter the place or the time zone, was synchronised with Moscow time (MT). In the German Army, everything was synchronised with Berlin time (BT = CET). As by 1930 most countries had adopted hourly time zones, it can be assumed that during the war the hour difference between Berlin time (CET) and Moscow time was the same as today.

26 War diary of 2nd Ukrainian Front, order No. 00635, 11.10.1944. TsAMO, fu.240, inv.2779, f.1190, p.51. See also Elvedi, op cit, p.104.

27 Stavka (Stavka *Verkhovnogo Glavnokomandovaniya*) The HQ of the Supreme Main Command of the Armed Forces of the Soviet Union.

28 The terms were: 1) Immediate withdrawal of the Hungarian troops from the Tisza to Budapest and for some of them to attack the German forces at Szolnok. 2) After establishing contact with the Red Army the Hungarians should undertake actions against the Germans. 3) By 08:00 MT on 16 October full information on the disposition of the Axis forces should be delivered to Szeged. The document is reproduced in full in Shtemenko, *The Last Six Months*, p.250.

29 Report #00641. TsAMO, fu.240, inv.3131, f.142, pp.118–121, reproduced in Zolotarev, op cit, Vol.16 (5–4), pp.306–307.

30 Shtemenko, *The Last Six Months*, p.251. See the full text in Appendix 9.

31 Minasyan, op cit, pp.287–288, cit. TsAMO, fu.240, inv.73765, f.41/g, p.93. Minasyan emphasises that this order had a direct relevance to events in Budapest. There is no doubt that it was issued at the insistence of Stalin himself.

32 G. Baross, *Hungary and Hitler*, University of Southern California, Los Angeles, 1964, pp.85–90.

33 Mekhlis telegram to Stalin, 17.10.1944. TsAMO, fu.23, inv.14753, f.4, pp.93–104, reproduced in Zolotarev, op cit, Vol.14, pp.299–301.

34 According to the order of the commander of the 4th Ukrainian Front dated 20 October 1944, 'during recent days' 5785 Hungarian officers and men had come over to the Soviets in groups or alone (see B.

Esti, *The Liberation of Hungary 1944–1945*, Korvina, Budapest, 1975, p.37). See the full text in the Appendix.

35 Baross, op cit, pp.85–90.

36 Shtemenko says that the meeting was held on 24 October. (Shtemenko, *The Last Six Months*, p.255) Nevertheless, according to the logbook of Stalin's Kremlin cabinet it took place on the night of 23/24 October 1944 from 22:30 to 1:45. See Gorkov, op cit, p.195.

37 Stavka directive #220249. TsAMO, fu.148a, inv.3763, f.167, p.85, reproduced in Zolotarev, op cit, Vol.16(5-4), p.162.

38 Churchill, op cit, p.198.

39 O. Rzhevsky, *Stalin i Churchill*, Moscow, Nauka, 2004, p.435.

40 Churchill, op cit, p.200. Churchill did not yet know that Stalin would annex Ruthenia (a region of western Ukraine south of the Carpathians) and unite it with Soviet Ukraine. This area was inhabited mainly by Rusyns, who ethnically and linguistically did not differ from the Ukrainians. Nominally it was a Czechoslovakian territory, but in March 1939 it was re-annexed by the Hungarian Kingdom. It was completely cleared of Axis forces by the beginning of November 1944 and shortly thereafter (on 19 November) the meeting of local communists issued a resolution requesting separation of Ruthenia from Czechoslovakia and incorporation into the Soviet Ukraine. On 26 November the Congress of National Committees of Carpatho-Ukraine 'unanimously accepted' the 'resolution' of the communists and a delegation was sent to Moscow to discuss the union. The Czechoslovakian government succumbed to the pressure of the Czech and Slovakian communists, agreed to cede Ruthenia to the Soviet Union and a treaty was signed in June 1945.

41 Conference transcription, 14 October 1944. (The text is not directly quoted, but rather a description of what was said.) Reproduced in Rzhevsky, op cit, pp.459–466.

42 Ibid.

43 Churchill, op cit, pp.195–196.

44 Ehrman, op cit, pp.48–49.

45 Ibid, pp.106–107.

46 Shtemenko, *The Last Six Months*, p.258.

47 Ehrman, op cit, Vol.VI, pp.50–51.

48 Ibid.

49 Allied Forces Headquarters.

50 Ehrman, op cit, Vol.VI, p.382.

51 NKVD report, 20 October 1944. Reproduced in N. Patrushev et al. (eds), *Organy gosudarstvennoi bezopasnosti SSSR v Velikoi Otechestvenoi Voine*, Vol.5/2, Kuchkovo pole, Moscow, 2007, pp.483–485.

52 *Antifašističko Veće Narodnog Oslobođenja Jugoslavije* (Anti-Fascist Council of National Liberation of Yugoslavia)

53 Shtemenko, *The Last Six Months*, pp.258–259.

Chapter 3

1 Full title: Arrow Cross Hungarianist Movement or *Nyilaskeresztes Párt Hungarista Mozgalom*.

2 N. Nagy-Talavera, *The Green Shirts and the Others*, Hoover Institution Press, Stanford, 1970, p.230.

3 R. Braham, *The Politics of Genocide*, Vol.2, Columbia University Press, New York, 1981, p.830.

4 Ibid, p.832.

5 Ibid, p.830.

6 E. Szép, *The Smell of Humans*, Central European University Press, Budapest, 1994, p.158.

7 P. Gosztony, 'Fortress Budapest', *Hungarian Quarterly*, Vol.XXXIX, No. 151, Autumn 1998, cit. personal communication with Veesenmayer in Darmstad in 1961.

8 H. Guderian, *Panzer Leader*, Macdonald Futura, London, 1980, p.379.

9 A. Handler, *A Man for All Connections*, Praeger, Westport, 1996, p.87.

10 Ibid, p.88, footnote 7, cit. E. Karsai and L. Karsai, *A Szálasi per*, Magveto, Budapest, 1987, pp.662–663.

11 Ibid, p.87, footnote 3, cit. postwar interview of Vessenmayer quoted in P. Gosztony, *Légiveszéy, Budapest!* Nepszava, Budapest, 1989, pp.90–91.

12 Ibid, cit. S. Orbán and I. Vida, *Serédi Jusztinián hercegprímás feljegyzései 1941–1944*, Zrínyi, Budapest, 1990, p.114.

13 Ibid, p.88, footnote 7, cit. E. Karsai and L. Karsai, *A Szálasi per*, Magveto, Budapest, 1987, pp.662–663.

14 C.A. Macartney, *October Fifteenth*, Vol.2, University Press, Edinburgh, 1957, p.443.

15 Ibid.

16 A. Puskas, *Vengria v gody Vtoroi Mirovoi Voiny*, Nauka, Moscow, 1966, p.457, cit. J. Gazsi, *Adatok és dokumentumok a Szálasi-hadsereg történetéhez*, HK, 1960, 2 sz., 227.old.

17 A. Handler, op cit, p.86.

18 A. Puskas, op cit, p.456, cit. BMI, V-55184/1, 15.1.

19 Macartney, *October Fifteenth*, Vol.2, pp.448–449.

20 N. Nagy-Talavera, op cit, p.231.

21 A. Handler, op cit, p.96.

22 J. Hoensch, *A History of Modern Hungary 1867–1994*, Pearson, London, 1996, p.159.

23 Macartney, *October Fifteenth*, Vol.2, p.448.

24 Cecil D. Eby, *Hungary at War*, The Pennsylvania State University Press, University Park, 1998, p.51, cit. an interview with György Hanh, 16 May 1989.

25 Fenyo, op cit, p.215, cit. Telegram from German Military attaché to OKW Wehrmachtführungsstab, 24 Aug. 1944, NA Microcopy T-77, roll 883, 5631668–69.

26 Ibid, p.216, cit. Telegram from Vessenmayer to Berlin, 29 Sep. 1944, NA Microcopy T-120, roll 2721, E420965.

27 R. Hilberg, *The Destruction of the European Jews*, Vol.2, Holmes and Meier, New York, 1985, p.855.

28 I. Pintér and L. Szabó, *Criminals at Large*, Pannonia Press, Budapest, 1961, pp.50–51.

29 Hilberg, op cit, p.857, cit. Vessenmayer's message to Foreign Office, 18 Oct. 1944, NG-5570.

30 Ibid, cit. Ribbentrop's message to Vessenmayer, 20 Oct. 1944, NG-4986.

31 Szép, op cit, pp.63–64.

32 Nagy-Talavera, op cit, p.230.

33 Ibid.

34 Hilberg, op cit, p.857, Vessenmayer's message to Foreign Office, 26 Oct. 1944, NG-5570.

35 Braham, op cit, Vol.2, p.839.

36 P. Pierik, *Hungary 1944–1945: The Forgotten Tragedy*, Aspekt, Nieuwegein, 1998, pp 92–93.

37 Hilberg, op cit, Vol.2, p.857, cit. Vessenmayer's message to Foreign Office, 13 Nov. 1944, NG-5570.

38 Macartney, op cit, Vol.2, p.449, cit. *Black Book*, pp.364 ff.

39 Braham, op cit, Vol.2, p.846.

40 Ibid, p.850.

41 Handler, op cit, pp.96–101.

42 Lakatos, op cit, p.200.

43 L. Veress, *Clear the Line*, Prospero Publications, Cleveland, 1995, p.290.

44 S. Márai, 'Journal', *Hungarian Quarterly*, Vol.XLIV, No. 171, Autumn 2003.

45 The ethnic Germans arrived in Hungary mainly in the eighteenh century, when the Habsburgs carried out a systematic operation (known as *Impopulatio*), the purpose of which was the settlement of the empty territories that had been devastated during Turkish rule. The main receiving areas for the German flood were Banat and the sparsely populated lands of South Hungary and around lake Balaton. By 1848 three quarters of the residents of Budapest and Pécs were German-speaking. After the achievement of formal independence from Vienna in 1867, Hungary initiated a process of Magyarisation, during which a considerable number of the Germans had changed their names and joined the ranks of the Magyars. Over 20 years (1880–1900) the number of the people that giving Hungarian as their mother tongue rose by about 2.2 million (C.A. Macartney, *Hungary: A Short History*, University Press, Edinburgh, 1962, p.100). The 'old' German burghers of the towns and the German peasantry wanted to ensure better perspectives for their offspring. The Magyarisation of the Germans had very important sociological consequences. Many of these 'new Magyars' became part of the expanding middle class and soon occupied key posts in the administration, armed forces, the Church, as well as in some ministries. In some organisations they even outnumbered their Hungarian counterparts. On the other hand, a great number of 'Swabs' resisted assimilation and among them grew a common belief that the German genetic stock was superior to the Hungarian. In 1920 the ethnic Germans numbered 551,600 (Baross, op cit, p.109). In the 1930s *Volksdeutsche* embraced Hitler's declaration that there was no difference between Germans of the Reich and those living abroad, and that both groups were to serve the cause of Germany.

46 According to the official figures of the *Volksdeutsche* Association, some 10 per cent of the ethnic Germans played a leading role in the *Volksbund* or were actual members of the SS; 28 per cent belonged to the *Volksbund* or to the *Hitlerjugend*; 32 per cent supported the *Volksbund* and 30 per cent played no role in any of its organisations. Of the latter group, 28 per cent were neutral and only 2 per cent were actively opposed to the *Volksbund*. Braham, op cit, Vol.1, p.159, cit. Dezsõ Sulyok, *A magyar tragédia*, Newark, NJ, 1954, p.205.

47 Baross, op cit, p.111.

48 Full title: *Volksbund der Deutschen in Ungarn* (People's Association of Germans in Hungary).

49 J. Hajdu and B. Tóth, *The 'Volksbund' in Hungary*, Pannonia Press, Budapest, 1962, p.67.

50 A. Polcz, *One Woman in the War: Hungary, 1944–1945*, Central European University Press, Budapest, 2002, p.66.

51 Ibid, p.63.

Chapter 4

1 From 8 to 11 January 1941 the Soviet General Staff conducted an operational level map exercise, which was attended by Stalin himself. Amongst the players was Zhukov, who led the 'Easterners' (i.e. the Soviets). First the 'Easterners' successfully repulsed the invasion of the 'Westerners' (Germans), 'South-westerners' (Hungarians) and 'Southerners' (Romanians) against Ukraine, and drove them back beyond the Carpathians. The war game proved to be in many ways to be true to what really happened in 1944: the Southern Front of the invaders was encircled and destroyed in Bessarabia, while the Western one was defeated in the area of Lvov. Then the 'Easterners' mounted a general offensive towards Budapest, advancing through the Carpathian passes in the direction of Csap and Nyíregyháza. The exercise was stopped once the 'Easterners' reached the outskirts of Budapest. For details see B. Sokolov, *Neizvestnyi Zhukov: portret bez retushi*, Minsk, Rodiola-plus, 2000, pp.196–198.

2 General Staff orders #204651 (for the 38 A) and 204670 (for the 4 UF) dated 2 and 3 September 1944 respectively. TsAMO, fu.48a, inv.3410, f.14, pp.48 and 71, reproduced in Zolotarev, op cit, Vol.23(12-4), pp.403 and 407 respectively.

3 Stavka directive #220215. TsAMO, fu.148a, inv.3763, f.167, pp.45–47, reproduced in Zolotarev, op cit, Vol.16(5-4), pp.144–145.

4 Minasyan, op cit, pp.265–266.

5 Stavka directive #220239. TsAMO, fu.148a, inv.3763, f.167, p.75, reproduced in Zolotarev, op cit, Vol.16(5-4), 1999, pp.157–158.

6 General Staff order #296825. TsAMO, fu.48a, inv.3410, f.14, pp.457–458, reproduced in Zolotarev, op cit, Vol.23(12-4), p.478.

7 General Staff order #296943. TsAMO, fu.48a, inv.3410, f.14, p.499.), reproduced in Zolotarev, op cit, Vol.23(12-4), p.483.

8 War diary of 2nd Ukrainian Front, 8.10.1944.. TsAMO, fu.240, inv.2779, f.1190, p.38.

9 Report #00641. TsAMO, fu.240, inv.3131, f.142, pp.118–121, reproduced in Zolotarev, op cit, Vol.16(5-4), pp.306–307.

10 War diary of 2nd Ukrainian Front, order No. 00644, 16.10.1944. TsAMO, fu.240, inv.2779, f.1190, p.78. See also Minasyan, op cit, pp.287–288.

11 War diary of 2nd Ukrainian Front, order No. 00648, 17.10.1944. TsAMO, fu.240, inv.2779, f.1190, p.85.

12 Stavka directive #220243. TsAMO, fu.148a, inv.3763, f.167, p.81, reproduced in Zolotarev, op cit, Vol.16(5-4), p.160.

13 Stavka directive #220244. TsAMO, fu.148a, inv.3763, f.167, p.82, reproduced in Zolotarev, op cit, Vol.16(5-4), p.160.

14 Stavka directive #220241. TsAMO, fu.148a, inv.3763, f.167, p.77, reproduced in Zolotarev, op cit, Vol.16(5-4), p.158.

15 S. Shtemenko, 'The Soviet General Staff at war', Vol.2, Progress Publishers, Moscow, 1986, p.222.

16 Stavka directive #220244. TsAMO, fu.148a, inv.3763, f.167, p.82, reproduced in Zolotarev, op cit, Vol.16(5-4), p.160.

17 War diary of 2nd Ukrainian Front, orders No. 00650 (19.10.1944), No. 00652 (20.10.1944), No. 00654 (20.10.1944), No. 00656 (21.10.1944) and No. 00665 (21.10.1944). TsAMO, fu.240, inv.2779, f.1190, pp.91–93, 97–98 and 108–110.

18 War diary of 2nd Ukrainian Front, order No. 00654, 20.10.1944. TsAMO, fu.240, inv.2779, f.1190, pp.97–98.

19 G. Abrosimov et al., 'Gvardeiskii Nikolaevsko-Budapeshtenskii', Moscow, Voenizdat, 1978, p.118.

20 Stavka directive #220247. TsAMO, fu.148a, inv.3763, f.167, p.84, reproduced in Zolotarev, op cit, Vol.16 (5–4), p.161. Vršac is a town located northeast of Belgrade, in the southern part of the Banat region, not far from the Yugoslavian-Romanian border.

21 War diary of 2nd Ukrainian Front, order No. 00655, 21.10.1944. TsAMO, fu.240, inv.2779, f.1190, pp.111–112. Szentes is a town in southeastern Hungary and is situated northeast of Szeged.

22 Some publications by western authors tend to describe the defeat sustained by Pliev's troops at Nyíregyháza as a catastrophe. Often they claim that the Soviets lost 25,000 men and 632 tanks. These figures were, in fact, the German claims for the entire period of the Battle of Debrecen, i.e. 6–28 October 1944 (see NARA T311/159/7209574). Pliev's losses at Nyíregyháza were actually moderate: according to the official German records, from 25 October until the moment when the Nyíregyháza pocket was cleared (the morning of 28 October), they amounted to 32 artillery pieces, 48 anti-tank guns, 70 heavy machine guns, 171 light machine guns, 11 mortars, 70 anti-tank rifles, 1 anti-aircraft gun, 150 motor vehicles, 400 horses and 150 POWs. 1150 bodies were counted on the battlefield and 18 tanks were knocked out. (See HGr Süd, Ia Morgenmeldung, 28.10.1944, NARA T311/158/7200462.)

23 Report of 37th Rifle Corps for October 1944. TsAMO, fu.37SK, inv.1, f.21, pp.68–69.

24 S. Shtemenko, *Kak planirovalas posledniaia kampania po razgromu Gitlerovskoi Germanii*, VIZh, 1965, No.5, p.58.

25 Shtemenko, *The Last Six Months*, pp.255–256.

26 Ibid, p.256.

Chapter 5

1 Stavka directive #220251. TsAMO, fu.148a, inv.3763, f.167, p.87, reproduced in Zolotarev, op cit, Vol.16(5-4), p.161.

2 Hans Friessner, the former commander of Army Group South, claims in his memoirs that in the last week of October Malinovsky, who was eager to capture Budapest for the anniversary of the Bolshevik coup, had appealed to his troops: 'Comrades, exert yourselves so that we can lay the Hungarian capital at the feet of the great Stalin! Fame and rewards await you; if you fail I fear for your health.' (H. Friessner, *Verratene Schlachten*, Hamburg, Holsten Verlag, 1956, p.164) SS-Obergruppenführer Pfeffer-Wildenbruch, the ex-commander of the Budapest garrison, made a similar statement to Hungarian exile historian Peter Gosztony (P. Gosztony, *Der Kampf um Budapest 1944/45*, WWR, 1963, No.10, p.582, cit. *persönaliche Miitelung an den Verfasser*). Of course, no such orders had been ever issued by the leadership of 2nd Ukrainian Front.

3 R. Malinovsky, *Budapesht–Vena–Praga*, Nauka, Moscow, 1965, pp.81–82 (translation as per John Erickson, *The Road to Berlin*, Weidenfeld and Nicolson, London, 1983, p.396). Malinovsky gives no source for this conversation. In his detailed study of the Soviet campaign in the Southeast Europe, Minasyan, who has utilised all available sources, indirectly confessed that he was not able to locate the transcript in the archives. (Minasyan, op cit, p.315, footnote 1.)

4 Ibid, pp.82–83.

5 According to the 1989 Russian edition of Shtemenko's memoirs, the telegram was dated 28 October. (S. Shtemenko, *Generalnyi Shtab v gody voiny*, Vol.2. Voenizdat, Moscow, 1989, p.417.)

6 Shtemenko, *The Last Six Months*, pp.260–261. It is very difficult to say whether Shtemenko is telling the truth or not, because the logbook of the Kremlin shows that no visits were paid to the dictator on 28 October 1944 so Shtemenko probably had not been there on that day (however, it is certain that Stalin was briefed daily by the General Staff's representatives). The logbook does record that a meeting took place on the night of 27/28 October 1944 from 23:00 MT to 01:00 MT, in which Antonov, Shtemenko and Army-General Khrulev (Commander in Chief Red Army's Rear Services) were present (Khrulev arrived at 23:10 MT). The situation in Hungary was undoubtedly discussed. After they left, Stalin received Tolbukhin. Their meeting lasted from 01:00 MT to 01:45 MT (see Gorkov, op cit, p.195). According to Shtemenko, Tolbukhin already (i.e. before reporting to Stalin) had discussed the situation in Hungary with the General Staff and was well aware about the 'general plan' for the 'actions in the region of Budapest'. (See the following chapter.)

7 According to the records of the Soviet High Command, from 20–30 October Hungarian 1 Army had lost 14,390 men killed and wounded while another 19,924 were taken prisoner. Puskas, op cit, cit. TsAMO, fu.32, inv.11306, f.573, p.26.

8 See Chapter 2, footnote 37.

9 War diary of 2nd Ukrainian Front, entries for 25–28.10.1944. TsAMO, fu.240, inv.2779, f.1190, pp.130, 137, 141 and 145.

10 Shtemenko, *Kak planirovalas posledniaia kampania po razgromu Gitlerovskoi Germanii*, VIZh, 1965, No.5, pp.56–72.

11 Ibid, pp.57–59.

12 The article was incorporated almost intact in the chapter dealing with the final battles in Poland and Germany (see S. Shtemenko, *Generalnyi Shtab v gody voiny*, Vol.1, Voenizdat, Moscow, 1989, Chapter 14). It is probable that Shtemenko simply missed this contradiction.

13 Shtemenko, *The Last Six Months*, pp.256–257.

14 M. Zakharov, *Budapeshtenskaya Operatsiya*, in A.M. Samsonov (ed), *Osvobozhdenie Vengrii ot Fashizma*, Nauka, Moscow, 1965, p.30.

15 Ibid, p.31.

16 S.P. Platonov et al. (eds), *Operatsii Sovetskih vooruzhennyh sil*, Vol.3, Voenizdat, Moscow, 1958, pp.597–599.

17 *Istoria Velikoi Otechestvenoi Voiny Sovetskogo Soiuza 1941–1945*, Vol.4, Voenizdat, Moscow, 1963, p.390.

18 M. Malakhov, *Osvobozhdenie Vengrii i Vostochnoi Avstrii*, Voenizdat, Moscow, 1965, p.66.

19 Minasyan, op cit, pp.315–316.

20 V. Golubovich, *Marshal R.Y. Malinovsky*, Voenizdat, Moscow, 1983, p.153.

21 I. Shlemin, *Osvobozhdenie Vengrii*, Voennyi Vestnik, 1964, No.12, p.7.

22 M. Shumilov, *Budapeshtenskaya Operatsiya*, Voennyi Vestnik, 1969, No.12., p.16.

23 I. Pliev, *Dorogami Voiny*, Kniga, Moscow, 1985, pp.131–132.

24 War diary of 2nd Ukrainian Front, order No. 00662, 25.10.1944. TsAMO, fu.240, inv.2779, f.1190, pp.130–131.

25 After-action report of the 2nd Guards Mechanised Corps. TsAMO, fu.3426, inv.1, f.36, p.1.

26 War diary of 2nd Ukrainian Front, 28.10.1944. TsAMO, fu.240, inv.2779, f.1190, p.148.

27 Experience report of the 37th Rifle Corps for October 1944. TsAMO, fu.37SK, inv.1, f.21, p.69.

28 I. Kosenko, *Zvezda za gorod Budapesht*, Rossiiskoe Voennoe Obozrenie, 2005, No.3.

29 M. Zakharov, *Marshal Sovetskogo Soyuza Rodion Malinovsky* in A. Kiselev (ed), *Polkovodtsy i voenachal'niki Velikoi Otechestvenoi*, Vol.1, Molodaya gvardia, Moscow, 1971, p.247.

Chapter 6

1 D. Glantz and J. House, *When Titans Clashed*, University Press of Kansas, Lawrence, 1995, p.299.

2 The report gives the following breakdown: approximately 300 tanks had been lost as total write-offs, 590 had been sent to the tank factories in the homeland for refurbishing, while another 117 were being loaded on the trains for shipment to the factories. In addition, 222 tanks were undergoing short-term repair in the workshops of the Front. War diary of 2nd Ukrainian Front, Report to Stavka, No.17998–18000, 20.10.1944. TsAMO, fu.240, inv.2779, f.1190, pp.102–103.

3 In addition to those 300 en route to the front, Malinovsky requested 679 T-34, 79 'Lend-Lease tanks', 34 JS-2, 120 SU-76s, 93 SU-85s and 42 ISU-122s. The documents available to the author do not show how many tanks were issued to the 2nd Ukrainian Front as a result of this request, but it is clear that in reality only a fraction of the demanded armoured vehicles reached Malinovsky's troops by the end of the year.

4 Minasyan, op cit, p.314. Minasyan's calculations are based on the tank situation report from 29 October and the strength reports of 2nd and 4th Guards Mechanised Corps.

5 See the report of the commander of the armoured and mechanised troops of 7th Guards Army of 30 September 1944 (TsAMO, fu.341, inv.5312, f.685, pp.1–4, reproduced in Zolotarev, op cit, Vol.14, pp.55–57) regarding the successful actions of the Romanian Tank Regiment. See also the report of the HQ of 27th Army of 23 October 1944 (TsAMO, fu.240, inv.2769, f.148, pp.257–258, reproduced in Zolotarev, op cit, Vol.14, pp.65–66) complimenting the brilliant performance of the command of the 4th Army, the command of VI Army Corps, the Mountain Corps (with 2nd, 3rd and 18th Mountain Divisions), the 3rd and 20th Infantry Divisions.

6 See the report of the HQ of 46th Army of 2 October 1944 (TsAMO, fu.240, inv.2779, f.954, pp.18–19, reproduced in Zolotarev, op cit,Vol.14, p.59), which reveals how badly armed and equipped the infantry divisions (2nd, 4th, 5th and 15th) of the IV Army Corps were.

7 See the report of Colonel Nikiforov to the military council of the 40th Army dated 28 December 1944 (TsAMO, fu.395, inv.9134, f.12, pp.2–6, reproduced in Zolotarev, op cit,Vol.14, pp.70–73). The formations that were heavily criticised by Nikiforov were the 3rd, 9th and 20th Infantry Divisions, as well as the command of the VI Army Corps.

8 Ibid.

9 War diary of 2nd Ukrainian Front, order No. 00666, 25.10.1944. TsAMO, fu.240, inv.2779, f.1190, p.132.

10 A. Drabkin (ed), *Ya dralsya s Panzerwaffe*, Eksmo, Moscow, 2007, pp.340, 343.

11 Tarassuk in D. Glantz, *1986 Art of War Symposium*, US Army War College, Carlisle, 1986, p.720.

12 M. Axworthy, *Third Axis, Fourth Ally*, Arms and Armour Press, London, 1995, p.202.

13 War diary of 2nd Ukrainian Front, order No. 17563, 14.10.1944. TsAMO, fu.240, inv.2779, f.1190, pp.69–70. See the full text of the order in Appendix 8.

14 I. Konev, *Za osvobozhdenie Chehoslovakii*,Voenizdat, Moscow, 1965, pp.113–114.

15 The ammunition sets (*boekomplekts*) correspond with the number of rounds, which were carried in the individual tank or other vehicle, or for each artillery piece (or other weapon). By the beginning of 1945 the requirements ranged from 3 to 10 *boekomplekts* per tank or artillery piece and 1.5–2.5 for every infantryman. 'Fill' (*zapravka*) signifies the quantity of liquid fuel carried in the internal and external fuel tanks of every individual armoured- or soft-skinned vehicle. The basic requirements set for the Soviet January 1945 offensive in Poland were 4 to 4.5 fills per vehicle and they fell far short of consumption. See C. Duffy, *Red Storm on the Reich*, Da Capo Press, New York, 1993, p.329.

16 M. Zakharov, *Osvobozhdenie yugo-vostochnoi i tsentral'noi Evropy voiskami 2-go i 3-go Ukrainskih frontov 1944–1945*, Moscow, Nauka, 1970, p.296.

17 War diary of 2nd Ukrainian Front, Report to Stalin, No.17357, 12.10.1944. TsAMO, fu.240, inv.2779, f.1190, p.62. The Front requested permission to establish 11 horse-drawn transport battalions, but in reply, Stavka sanctioned the creation of company-sized units only.

18 War diary of 2nd Ukrainian Front, Report to the General Staff, No.17356, 12.10.1944. TsAMO, fu.240, inv.2779, f.1190, pp.61–62. The report cites six instances of sabotage that had taken place on the territory of Romania between 6 September and 7 October 1944.

19 By the beginning of the Debrecen operation in the rail stations in Moldova there were 1280 train cars with ammunition, 500 tanks and other heavy weapons still waiting to be transported to Hungary. Zakharov, *Osvobozhdenie yugo-vostochnoi i tsentral'noi Evropy voiskami 2-go i 3-go Ukrainskih frontov 1944–1945*, p.296.

20 War diary of 2nd Ukrainian Front, Report to the General Staff, No.17898, 19.10.1944. TsAMO, fu.240, inv.2779, f.1190, p.96.

21 War diary of 2nd Ukrainian Front, Report to Stavka, No.17897, 19.10.1944. TsAMO, fu.240, inv.2779, f.1190, pp.95–96. According to the document, the Front, in October alone, needed the following additional quantities of ammunition: 10,000 rounds for the 76mm regimental guns; 150,000 rounds for the 76mm divisional guns; and 50,000 rounds for the 122mm divisional howitzers.

22 Y. Kapilevich and B. Potulov, *Nekotorye voprosy organizatsii medicinskogo obespecheniya voisk 2-go i 3-go Ukrainskih frontov v Budapeshtenskoi operatsii*, Voenno-Meditsinskii Zhurnal, 1965, No.2, p.12.

23 Shtemenko, *The Last Six Months*, pp.257.

24 *Politruk* is an abbreviated designation of *politicheskii rukovoditel* (political leader), an officer appointed by the Soviet Communist Party to oversee a unit of the Red Army. After 1943 the political officers were no longer called *politruks* but *zampolits*, which is an abbreviation for *zamestitel komandira po politicheskoi rabote* (deputy of the commander for political work). This change reflected a change in the level of authority: the *zampolit* had no right to interfere with the operational orders of the unit's commander.

25 G. Temkin, *My Just War*, Presidio, Novato, 1998, pp.193–194.

26 Pusztaföldvár, Orosháza, Battonya, etc. (Minasyan, op cit, p.303.)

27 The archives of the 2nd Ukrainian Front hold information about an article that appeared in some of the Hungarian newspapers (from the first half of October 1944), which stated that Soviets had offered the following preliminary armistice conditions: 1) All Hungarian officers, gendarmes and police-

men should be deported to Siberia; 2) Hungary should give the Soviet Union 2 million workers for labour in Siberia; 3) Hungarian youth should be placed at the disposal of the Soviet authorities; 4) All churches should be destroyed and private property confiscated; 5) Hungary should pay 10 billion *pengo*. (Minasyan, op cit, pp.302–303)

28 Contrary to popular belief in the West, acts of rape and looting were never officially encouraged in the Red Army; it was just the other way around: strict orders had been issued on the behaviour of the troops. In October 1944 alone, the HQ of the 2nd Ukrainian Front issued four such orders. (Three of these orders are reproduced in the Appendix.) See the war diary of 2nd Ukrainian Front, TsAMO, fu.240, inv.2779, f.1190, pp.11–12, 57–58, 69–70 and 156–157.

29 G. Chukhrai, *Moya voina*, Algoritm, Moscow, 2001, pp.256–257.

30 Decree of the National Defence Committee in connection with the entry of the Red Army on the territory of Hungary. TsAMO, fu.243, inv.2914, f.215, p.44–47, reproduced in Zolotarev, op cit, Vol.14, pp.307–309.

31 Appeal of the Red Army's Command to the population of the liberated territory of Hungary. Reproduced in Zhilin, OMSVSVEVMV, pp.229–230. See the full text of the appeal in the Appendix.

32 Decree of the National Defence Committee in connection with the entry of the Red Army into Hungarian territory. TsAMO, fu.243, inv.2914, f.215, p.44–47, reproduced in Zolotarev, op cit, Vol.14, pp.307–309.

33 *Velikaya Otechestvennaya Voina 1941–1945*, Vol.3, Moscow, Nauka, 1999, p.135.

34 HGr Süd Ia Nr 186/44 g.K. Chef., 15.11.1944. NARA T311/159/7210238-7210248.

35 Minasyan, op cit, p.306. As already mentioned, I have included some of those orders found in the war diary of 2nd Ukrainian Front in the Appendix.

36 Tarassuk, *Views of a Red Army Soldier* in Glantz, op cit, p.57.

37 Combat diary of Army Group South, 24 October 1944. (Hereafter cited as KTB HGr Süd Ia, 24.10.1944) NARA T311/158/7209243.

38 KTB HGr Süd Ia, 25.10.1944. NARA T311/158/7209255.

39 KTB HGr Süd Ia, 26.10.1944. NARA T311/158/7209266.

40 KTB HGr Süd Ia, 26.10.1944. NARA T311/158/7209268.

41 KTB HGr Süd Ia, 27.10.1944. NARA T311/158/7209280.

42 KTB HGr Süd Ia, 25.10.1944. NARA T311/158/7209256.

43 HGr Süd Ia, Nr 4185/44g.K. 26.10.1944. NARA T311/159/7209492.

44 KTB HGr Süd Ia, 27.10.1944. NARA T311/158/7209282-7209283. See, as well, HGr Süd Ia, Nr 5174/44 Geh. 27.10.1944 that orders 1 and 13 Panzer-Divisions to deploy in the vicinity of Hajdúdorog–Hajdúnánás (southeast of Miskolc) to prevent an attack of the 6th Guards Tank Army from that area. (NARA T311/159/7209531)

45 KTB HGr Süd Ia, 28.10.1944. NARA T311/158/7209293.

46 Ibid.

47 KTB HGr Süd Ia, 27.10.1944. NARA T311/158/7209281. See, as well, HGr Süd Ia, Nr 4207/44 g.K. 28.10.1944. NARA T311/159/7209514-7209516.

48 H. Gaedcke, *Translation of the Taped Conversation with General Heinz Gaedcke, 13 April 1979*, Battele, Columbus, 1979, pp.23–24.

49 Ibid, pp.29–30.

50 Phone conversation between Friessner and Guderian, 27.10.1944, 21:55. KTB Ia HGr Süd, NARA T311/158/7209280.

51 KTB HGr Süd Ia, 28.10.1944. NARA T311/158/7209292. Another document – HGr Süd Ia, Nr 4216/44 g. Kdos. 28.10.1944 – gives a more precise picture of these losses. According to it, between 1 September and 23 October 1944 the divisions in question had lost 19,282 men killed, wounded and missing. During the same period they received 8669 replacements. The document stresses the need for the urgent delivery of at least 23,000 replacements. NARA T311/159/7209557.

52 Artillery Battalions I/77 and 607 were attached the 'Feldherrnhalle' Division; Artillery Battalion II/52 to 13 Panzer-Division; Artillery Battalions I/27, II/818; and III/818 to 15. Infantry Division.

53 HGr Süd Ia/Art, Nr 4274/44 g. Kdos. 1.11.1944. NARA T311/159/7209645.

54 6. Armee Ia/Id, Nr 5747/44 geh. 23.11.1944. NARA T311/159/7210220-7210221.

55 Ibid.

56 The spare parts situation varied from formation to formation. Thus, while 23 Panzer-Division reported 'serious shortages', the 'Feldherrnhalle' division had no problems. See the monthly condition reports submitted by the divisions to Guderian in BAMA, RH10.

57 6.Armee Ia/Id, Nr 5747/44 geh. 23.11.1944. NARA T311/159/7210220-7210221.

58 Ibid.

59 HGr Süd Ia, Nr 181/44 g.K. Chefs. 27.10.1944. NARA T311/159/7209517-7209521.

60 Anlage 2 zu O.B.H. HGr Süd Ia, Nr 181/44 g.K. Chefs. 27.10.1944. NARA T311/159/7209525.

61 These staffs, officially known as *Deutscher-Verbindungsstab zur Armee* (at army level), *Deutscher-Verbindungskommando zum Korps* (at corps level) and *Deutsches-Verbindungskommando zur Division* (at divisional level), had an authorised strength of 50, 16 and 10 men respectively. The auxiliary/liaison staffs operated in accordance with the same order-of-battle as existed in the respective allied armies, to which they were attached. Thus in the case of Hungarian 3 Army, the most senior staff was DVSt 3, to which DVK 14 and DVK 21 were subordinate, which, in turn, controlled six DVK attached to the Magyar divisions (as per 28 October 1944). The full list of the auxiliary staffs is given in Appendix 2.7.

62 HGr Süd Ia, Nr 4206/44 g.K. 28.10.1944. NARA T311/159/7209529-7209530.

63 Eby, op cit, p.42, cit. an interview with József Kiss, 18 June 1989.

64 6.Army, Order No.2125/44, 22.10.1944. TsAMO, fu.500, inv.12462, f.235, pp.8–10. 'Barrier Line A' was to run along the Abony–Jászapáti–Füzesabony [6 Army]–Miskolc–Szerensc–Sátoraljaújhely [8 Army] line. Each of its sectors (apparently, one sector was assigned to one corps) was to be patrolled by 100–200 gendarmes, both mounted and on foot; checkpoints were to be erected at the main crossroads. 'Barrier Line B' was to run along the Dunaföldvár–Jászberény–Gyöngyös–Eger–Miskolc–Kassa (Košice) line. For the time being, it was to be left unoccupied.

65 VII Army Corps (Hung), Operations Department, Order 4537/7 a.k., 21.10.1944, TsAMO, fu.500, inv.12462, f.235, pp.39–40.

66 6.Army, Operations Department, Order No.1599, 26.10.1944. TsAMO, fu.500, inv.12462, f.235, p.63.

67 HGr Süd Ia Nr 4634/44 g.Kdos. 1.12.1944. NARA T311/160/7210895.

68 OKH/GenStdH/Op.Abt. Nr 440 661/g.K. NARA T311/159/7209511-7209513.

69 See the table in the Appendix showing the combat strength of the divisions of the army group at the moment of the arrival of Hitler's directive.

70 Phone conversation between Friessner and Guderian, 27.10.1944, 21:55. KTB Ia HGr Süd, NARA T311/158/7209280.

71 OKH/GenStdH/Op.Abt. Nr 4207/g.K. NARA T311/159/7209514-7209516.

72 Guderian, op cit, p.464.

73 Ibid, pp.373–374.

74 Zakharov, *Osvobozhdenie yugo-vostochnoi i tsentral'noi Evropy voiskami 2-go i 3-go Ukrainskih frontov 1944–1945*, p.290.

75 HGr Süd IIa, Nr 2720/44 geh. 3.10.1944. NARA T311/265/000536.

76 Zakharov, *Osvobozhdenie yugo-vostochnoi i tsentral'noi Evropy voiskami 2-go i 3-go Ukrainskih frontov 1944–1945*, p.291, cit. a captured German document Nr 1729/44.

77 Dr F.-W. Lochmann, et al. (eds), *Combat History of schwere Panzer-Abteilung 503*, Winnipeg, J.J. Fedorowicz Publishing, 2000, p.286.

Chapter 7

1 Zakharov, *Osvobozhdenie yugo-vostochnoi i tsentral'noi Evropy voiskami 2-go i 3-go Ukrainskih frontov 1944–1945*, p.247.

2 War diary of 2nd Ukrainian Front, order No. 00675/op, 23:45, 28.10.1944. TsAMO, fu.240, inv.2779, f.1190, pp.145–146. See also *Sbornik materialov po izucheniu opyta voiny* No. 21, Voenizdat, Moscow, 1946, pp.11–12. (Hereafter cited as SMPIOV No. 21, pp.11–12.)

3 S. Grechko, *Reshenia prinimalis' na zemle*, Voenizdat, Moscow, 1984, p.253.

4 Ibid.

5 23rd Rifle Corps and 4th Guards Mechanised Corps were attached to 46th Army just after midnight on 28/29 october. See the war diary of 2nd Ukrainian Front, orders No. 00678/op (00:20, 29.10.1944) and No. 00676/op (00:30, 29.10.1944) respectively. TsAMO, fu.240, inv.2779, f.1190, pp.149–150.

6 War diary of 37th Rifle Corps, entry for 28.10.1944. TsAMO, fu.37SK, inv.1, f.21, p.60. The mentioned tanks most probably belonged to the 24 Panzer-Division

7 For instance, according to the manual, the immediate objective of a rifle regiment during the first day of the attack was the destruction of the enemy battalion-level defence (depth: 1.5–2km from the jump-off position); the follow-up mission assigned to it was the capture of the enemy artillery positions, thus achieving a penetration of up to 4.5km by the end of Day 1 of the offensive.

8 One of the best sources for the evolution of Soviet tactics during the Second World War is Kolganov's book: (K.S. Kolganov, et al. (eds), *Razvitie taktiki*, Moscow, Voenizdat, 1958).

9 Those overambitious plans included, for instance, the follow-up offensives in the vicinity of Budapest in November and December 1944.

10 Platonov, op cit, pp.599–600.

11 Minasyan, op cit, p.312.

12 Platonov, op cit, p.599.

13 The taking of Lajosmizse was one of the missions of the corps.

14 War diary of 46th Army, entry for 28.10.1944. TsAMO, fu.401, inv.9511, f.438, pp.54–55. The 48th Guards Mortar Regiment was to participate in the initial artillery bombardment first, and only then was it to join 2nd Guards Mechanised Corps with two of its battalions. The third battalion, apparently, was to continue to support 37th Rifle Corps. By the beginning of the battle the regiment had 20 M-8 'Katyusha' rocket launchers (report of the 37th Rifle Corps for October 1944. TsAMO, fu.37SK, inv.1, f.21, p.75). The two regiments of the 9th Anti-Aircraft Artillery Division mentioned in the order were the 981st and the 993rd. The former was equipped with 37mm automatic guns, while the latter with 85mm guns.

15 After-action report of 2nd Guards Mechanised Corps. TsAMO, fu.3426, inv.1, f.36, pp.4–8.

16 Combat report No.0144 of the 4th Guards Mechanised Brigade to the HQ of the 2nd Guards Mechanised Corps, 30.10.1944. TsAMO, fu.3426, inv.1, f.54, p.305.

17 Combat report No.08 of the 37th Guards Tank Brigade to the HQ of the 2nd Guards Mechanised Corps, 23:00, 30.10.1944. TsAMO, fu.3426, inv.1, f.54, p.318.

18 See, for example, the combat history of the 59th Guards Rifle Division, A. Chmelev, '*Proshla s boyami…*' *Karta moldovenească*, Kishinev, 1983, p.106. Most of these reinforcements sent to Shlemin were either freed POWs from the liberated camps in Romania or recruits from Ukraine and Moldavia. The interrogations of Soviet POWs captured by the Germans and Hungarians during the first days of Operation *Budapest* reveal that the 'bayonet strength' of the most of the rifle companies of the 46th Army was between 50 and 70 men, while those of the recently rehabilitated 68th Guards Rifle Division were even stronger at about 80 men each. (See the daily intelligence reports of Armeegruppe Fretter-Pico for 29 October, 1, 4, 5 and 6 November 1944. TsAMO, fu.500, inv.12462, f.236, pp.117, 118, 177, 246, 274, 301, 302). One has to keep in mind that late in the war Soviet divisions rifle companies numbering more than 70 men were scarce. Therefore, at the beginning of the offensive Shlemin's army was quite fresh and strong.

19 SMPIOV No. 21, p.84.

20 Ibid. The 24th Anti-Tank Artillery Brigade was subordinated to the 46th Army barely two hours before the beginning of the offensive at 12:00 MT on 29.10.1944. (War diary of 2nd Ukrainian Front, entry for 29.10.1944, cit. order No. 00677/op, 29.10.1944. TsAMO, fu.240, inv.2779, f.1190, p.152) It was made of two regiments equipped with 76mm ZIS-3 divisional guns and one regiment with 57mm ZIS-2 anti-tank guns.

21 The 991st Self-Propelled Artillery Regiment had 14 SU-76s, the 1505th had 18 SU-76s, while the 1897th was at full strength with 21 SU-76s. See the after-action report of the commander of the Armoured and Mechanised Forces of the 2nd Ukrainian Front. TsAMO, fu.240, inv.2799, f.366, p.7.

22 V. Tolubko and N. Baryshev, *Na yuzhnom flange*, Nauka, Moscow, 1973, pp.335–337.

23 After-action report of 2nd Guards Mechanised Corps. TsAMO, fu.3426, inv.1, f.36, p.26. For a more detailed breakdown see Appendix 3.2.

24 After-action report of 4th Guards Mechanised Corps. TsAMO, fu.3430, inv.1, f.161, p.29. For a more detailed breakdown see Appendix 3.5.

25 D. Dragunsky, *Ot Volgi do Pragi*, Voenizdat, Moscow, 1966, p.186, cit. TsAMO, fu.341, inv.5312, f.864, p.19.

26 S. Davtyan. *Pyataya vozdushnaya*, Voenizdat, Moscow, 1990, p.212, cit. TsAMO, fu.327, inv.4999, f.170, p.22.

27 This is indirectly confirmed in Friessner's memoirs. See Friessner, op cit, p.162.

28 This was, actually, the so-called Regimental Group 'Szücs' (see the next chapter, footnote 7, for more details.). It most probably was tactically subordinate to the regimental group of 10 Infantry Division deployed east of it.

29 The German condition reports used five different categories to evaluate the combat worth of the infantry battalions: 'strong' meaning a battalion with approximately 400 infantrymen fit for combat; 'medium-strong' meaning 300; 'average' meaning 200; 'weak' meaning 100; and 'exhausted' meaning 50. Usually the engineer, reconnaissance and field-training battalions were regarded as infantry too. These reports, however, did not represent the full strength of the units (the so-called 'ration strength'), but only their capacity to fight (the so-called 'bayonet strength').

30 This was actually a regimental group only and this is exactly how it was designated on the German operational maps of the time. During the last week of October the bulk of the division was moving down by train from Budapest to Kecskemét.

31 Often it was designated as 'Reserve Division' as well. As a matter of fact, there were two types of reserve divisions in the *Honvédség*: regular (*tartalék*) and 'accidental' (*pót*). For instance, 8, 12 and 23 Reserve Divisions were 'regular' formations. Their creation was planned beforehand and carried out according to the wartime mobilisation plans. The 'accidental' divisions, like 5 Reserve Division, were established as an *ad hoc* measure when the front reached Hungary. They had no combat value at all.

32 Most probably they belonged to Hungarian Assault Gun Battalion 7, which on 27 October 1944 reported an inventory of 19 StuG III (7 operational). N. Számvéber, *Pánzélosütközet Kecskemét körzetében* in J. Szijj (ed), *Ad Acta: A Hadtörténelmi Levéltár évkönyve 2004*, Budapest, 2005, p.157, cit. BAMA RH 2/5126, Lagekarte Ost, HGr Süd, Panzerlage 27.10.1944.

33 This information is extracted from a hand-drawn map dated 24.10.1944. NARA T311/265/000127. One has to keep in mind, however, that in the last week of October additional Hungarian troops arrived in that area (for instance, the 5 Reserve Division and the rest of 10 Infantry Division). This did not change the situation much.

34 Abrosimov, op cit, p.120. See also the after-action report of 2nd Guards Mechanised Corps. TsAMO, fu.3426, inv.1, f.36, p.4.

35 KTB HGr Süd Ia, 26.10.1944. NARA T311/158/7209261. At that moment the division was stationed in the vicinity of Pécs, in Transdanubia, some 60km to the west of Baja.

36 The Romanian bridgehead was cleared by the morning of 27 October. The Soviet one was attacked simultaneously from the south (by the 24 Panzer-Division) and from the north (by the 4 SS-Police-Panzer-Grenadier-Division of IV Panzer Corps).

37 Phone conversation between Wenck and von Grolman, 25.10.1944, 11:45. KTB Ia HGr Süd, NARA T311/158/7209254. See also the phone conversation between Friessner and Lieutenant-Colonel von dem Planitz (the Chief of Staff of the LVII Panzer Corps), 25.10.1944, 13:20. KTB Ia HGr Süd, NARA T311/158/7209254-7209255. On the next morning the HQ of Army Group South continued to insist the division be pulled out of the battle. After a series of intense phone conversations with the staffs of 3 Army (Hung) and LVII Panzer Corps, at 11:02 BT Friessner gave his approval the 24 Panzer-Division to continue its attempts to push the dangerous Soviet bridgeheads into the Tisza. His main argument was that 'the enemy still hasn't launched an offensive toward Kecskemét.' (KTB HGr Süd Ia, 26.10.1944. NARA T311/158/7209264)

38 KTB HGr Süd Ia, 28.10.1944. NARA T311/158/7209287. Panzer-Grenadier-Regiment 21 was to be relieved on the next day by the arriving forward regiment of the Hungarian 5 Reserve Division. (Report No.860/3 of the Hungarian 3.Army to Armeegruppe Fretter-Pico, 28.10.1944, 21:30. TsAMO, fu.500, inv.12462, f.235, p.76.)

39 The 24 Panzer-Division was formed in November 1941 in East Prussia using 1 Cavalry-Division as its nucleus. The 24th was unique amongst the panzer divisions; because of its cavalry background, it retained unit designation and uniform piping that were characteristic of the former branch of the service. Thus the divisional panzer-grenadier battalions and the field-replacement battalions and their companies were designated as 'detachments' (*Abteilungen*) and 'squadrons' (*Schwadronen*) respectively, instead of the usual 'battalions' (*Bataillonen*) and 'companies' (*Kompanien*). The same applies to the

divisional escort company and the companies of Panzer-Regiment 24 and Panzer-Reconnaissance Battalion 24, which were also designated as squadrons. The uniforms of the personnel of the Panzer-Regiment 24, Panzer-Reconnaissance Battalion 24 and Panzer-Grenadier-Regiments 21 and 26 were piped in golden yellow instead of pink and grass green.

40 Report No.860/3 of the Hungarian 3.Army to Armeegruppe Fretter-Pico, 28.10.1944, 21:30. TsAMO, fu.500, inv.12462, f.235, p.76. Tiszaujfalu was a small settlement just to the south of Alpár. In 1973 they were merged into a single village called Tiszaalpár.

41 Report No.860/3 of the Hungarian 3.Army to Armeegruppe Fretter-Pico, 28.10.1944, 21:30. TsAMO, fu.500, inv.12462, f.235, p.75. Heszlényi substantiated his assessment stating that 'the enemy has pulled out some of his troops from the Kiskunfélegyháza area and now is assembling them west of the Kiskunmajsa–Kiskunhalas area with the probable mission of mounting an attack toward Soltvadkert.' See also the already mentioned hand-drawn map in the files of Army Group South (T311/265/000127).

42 KTB HGr Süd Ia, 28.10.1944. NARA T311/158/7209289.

43 Order No.1606/44 of the 6.Army, 27.10.1944. TsAMO, fu.500, inv.12462, f.235, pp.67–68.

44 Order No.1612/44 of the 6.Army, 28.10.1944. TsAMO, fu.500, inv.12462, f.235, pp.74–75.

45 Ibid. Mezőkövesd is a town in Northern Hungary that lies some 50km southwest of Miskolc.

46 An urgent teletype message No.5202/44 of the 6.Army to the HQ of the 8.Army, 29.10.1944. TsAMO, fu.500, inv.12462, f.235, p.78.

47 Ibid, p.79.

48 Most probably this was 10 Infantry Division, part of which was already deployed ont the frontline in the vicinity of Kiskunhalas.

49 Hiwi (short for *Hilfswilliger* or 'voluntary helper') were volunteers from the occupied territories, mainly of the Soviet Union. They were predominately used for ancillary services: drivers, cooks, security guards, ammunition carriers. On some occasions, however, they were employed in combat as well.

50 NARA T311/265/000128-000129.

51 Ibid.

52 A. Juhász and B. Mihályi, 'Object and event reconstruction (WWII) with GIS' in *ISPRS Technical Commission II Symposium*, Vienna, 12–14 July 2006, p.147.

53 Ibid, p.148.

54 HGr Süd Ia, Nr 4416/44 g.K. 14.11.1944. NARA T311/159/7210009.

55 Armeegruppe 'Wöhler' was organised in a similar way to Armeegruppe Fretter-Pico; it consisted of the Hungarian 1 Army and the German 8 Army.

56 HGr Süd Ia, Nr 4207/44 g.K. 28.10.1944. NARA T311/159/7209514-7209516.

57 Friessner, op cit, p.149. For a detailed summary of the talk between Friessner and General Beregfy, Szálasi's Minister of Defence and Chief of the Hungarian General Sstaff, see Friessner's memo destined for the combat diary of Army Group South. NARA T311/159/7209551-7209552. For the conversation between Friessner and Szálasi see the third page of the same document. (NARA T311/159/7209553.)

58 Friessner, op cit, pp.149–150.

59 NARA T311/159/7209552.

60 Ibid.

61 NARA T311/159/7209553.

62 Friessner, op cit, p.150.

Chapter 8

1 S. Andryushchenko, *Nachinali my na Slavutyche...*, Moscow, Voenizdat, 1979, p.199.

2 Ibid, pp.200–201.

3 Ibid, p.201.

4 Grechko, op cit, p.255.

5 War diary of 2nd Ukrainian Front, entry for 29.10.1944. TsAMO, fu.240, inv.2779, f.1190, p.153.

6 Daily report of the Hungarian 3 Army, 30.10.1944. TsAMO, fu.500, inv.12462, f.236, p.159.

7 SMPIOV No. 21, pp.83–84.

8 After-action report of the Commander of the Armoured and Mechanised Forces of the 2nd Ukrainian Front. TsAMO, fu.240, inv.2799, f.366, p.8.

9 After-action report of the 2nd Guards Mechanised Corps. TsAMO, fu.3426, inv.1, f.36, p.10. See also Abrosimov, op cit, p.124.

10 A. Kanevsky, *Vperedy razvedka shla*, Kiev, Ukraina, 1991.

11 Grechko, op cit, p.255.

12 War diary of 2nd Ukrainian Front, entry for 29.10.1944. TsAMO, fu.240, inv.2779, f.1190, p.152.

13 The Group 'Szücs' (commander: Colonel Szücs) consisted of 7/I and 7/II Reserve (*pót*) Battalions, 20/III Reserve Battalion, 13th Reserve Recon-Battalion, II and III River-Blocking Battalions and two artillery batteries. C. Veress, *Magyarország hadikrónikája 1944–1945, Vol.1*, Militaria, Budapest, 2002, p.376. *Pót* means a unit, which is composed from the very last reserve in the military district. Its fighting power was usually very low. River-blocking units specialised in fighting along rivers; they could help in river crossing, fighting near rivers, and laying or destroying riverside minefields.

14 War diary of 2nd Ukrainian Front, entry for 29.10.1944. TsAMO, fu.240, inv.2779, f.1190, p.152.

15 War diary of 37th Rifle Corps, entry for 29.10.1944. TsAMO, fu.37SK, inv.1, f.21, p.60. The history of the 108th Guards Rifle Division, however, gives a higher figure of 371 POWs (V. Saveliev and N. Popov, *Gvardeiskaya Nikolaevskaya*, Moscow, Voenizdat, 1978, p.116).

16 Ibid.

17 Daily report of Hungarian 3 Army, 30.10.1944. TsAMO, fu.500, inv.12462, f.236, p.159. The tanks mentioned in the report were either SU-76, not T-34, or the claim was inflated (a widespread practice amongst troops on both sides), because a careful examination of the daily reports submitted to 2nd Guards Mechanised Corps by the brigades on 29 and 30 October shows that during their raid to Kecskemét (i.e. until the morning of 30 October) they had sustained no combat losses whatsoever. Moreover, in his article Számvéber (Számvéber, '*Pánzélosütközet Kecskemét körzetében*' p.163) claims that during one of the counter-attacks six StuG III of the Hungarian 7th Assault Gun Battalion, supported by infantry, had ambushed a Soviet armoured unit and destroyed 11 tanks without loss. This claim, however, finds no support in the existing Soviet documents, or the German ones. In various books (German, English/American, Russian) I have seen too many instances when claims had been taken at their face value. I am not in a position to verify or deny most of the kills claimed by both sides so I prefer to provide the information that I have found in the respective documents and sources with a caveat.

18 Ibid.

19 War diary of 37th Rifle Corps, entry for 29.10.1944. TsAMO, fu.37SK, inv.1, f.21, p.60.

20 Shlemin, op cit, p.7.

21 3.Ung. Armee, Nr 881. 29.10.1944. NARA T311/159/7209603-7209604.

22 29/30 October.

23 R. Knebel-Doeberitz, '24th Panzer Division Operations' in D. Glantz (ed), *1986 Art of War Symposium*, p.227.

24 KTB HGr Süd Ia, 29.10.1944. NARA T311/158/7209297.

25 Phone conversation between Gaedcke and von Grolman, 29.10.1944, 20:00. KTB Ia HGr Süd, NARA T311/158/7209301. Even after the war, Friessner continued to insist that the Soviet attacks of 29 October were just reconnaissance missions and that the main Soviet offensive had began on the following day. (Friessner, op cit, p.160.)

26 KTB HGr Süd Ia, 29.10.1944. NARA T311/158/7209301.

27 Knebel-Doeberitz, '24th Panzer Division Operations' in D. Glantz (ed), *1986 Art of War Symposium*, pp.218–219.

28 Ibid, p.227.

29 M. Hastings, *Armageddon*, London, Pan Macmillian, 2005, p.133.

30 Kanevsky, op. cit.

31 Combat report No.0144 of the 4th Guards Mechanised Brigade to HQ of the 2nd Guards Mechanised Corps, 11:00, 30.10.1944. TsAMO, fu.3426, inv.1, f.54, p.305.

32 Combat report No.0223 of the 6th Guards Mechanised Brigade to HQ of the 2nd Guards Mechanised Corps, 30.10.1944. TsAMO, fu.3426, inv.1, f.54, p.309.

33 After-action report of the 2nd Guards Mechanised Corps. TsAMO, fu.3426, inv.1, f.36, p.10.

34 Ibid. In his after action report Sviridov claims that he had not ordered a frontal attack on Kecskemét 'because this would have led to heavy losses'. The situation reports of the 37th Guards Tank Brigade and the 6th Guards Mechanised Brigade, however, clearly testify to the contrary: both formations were under orders to seize the town. See, for instance, combat report No.08 of 37th Guards Tank Brigade to

HQ of 2nd Guards Mechanised Corps, 30.10.1944, 15:00, which says 'the forward detachment has cut the road to Lajosmizse, while the main forces of the brigade are trying to meet the assigned objective: to help the 6th Guards Mechanised Brigade in capturing Kecskemét' (TsAMO, fu.3426, inv.1, f.54, p.318). Sviridov's claim is nothing more than an attempt to cover up his own failure.

35 Számvéber, *Pánzélosütközet Kecskemét körzetében*, p.166.

36 Daily report of Armeegruppe Fretter-Pico, 30.10.1944. TsAMO, fu.500, inv.12462, f.236, p.124.

37 The other units that defended Kecskemét were mostly leftovers of 8 Reserve Division: III Battalion/ Reserve Regiment 24 and an engineer company, as well as 3 Battery/Assault Gun Battalion 7. As we already know, these units were 'intercepted' by Flak-Regiment 133 and press-ganged into defending Kecskemét. (See previous footnote for source.)

38 Phone conversation between Marcks and Schäfer, 30.10.1944, 07:45. KTB Ia HGr Süd, NARA T311/158/7209308.

39 KTB Ia HGr Süd, NARA T311/158/7209308.

40 KTB Ia HGr Süd, NARA T311/158/7209310.

41 Phone conversation between Schäfer and Ia of the Air Fleet 4, 30.10.1944, 09:35. KTB Ia HGr Süd, NARA T-311/158/7209309.

42 KTB Ia HGr Süd, NARA T311/158/7209305.

43 KTB Ia HGr Süd, NARA T311/158/7209309-7209312.

44 KTB Ia HGr Süd, NARA T311/158/7209306.

45 Phone conversation between Wenck and von Grolman, 30.10.1944, 11:35. KTB Ia HGr Süd, NARA T-311/158/7209310.

46 KTB Ia HGr Süd, NARA T311/158/7209306.

47 KTB Ia HGr Süd, NARA T311/158/7209310.

48 Ibid.

49 KTB Ia HGr Süd, NARA T311/158/7209311.

50 Phone conversation between von Grolman and von Greiffenberg, 30.10.1944, 09:55. KTB Ia HGr Süd, NARA T311/158/7209309.

51 In his article Számvéber claims that, alongside the Hungarian tanks, the division also had 27 Pz III tanks. (Számvéber, 'Pánzélosütközet Kecskemét körzetében', p.157.) I, however, found no confirmation of this in the strength reports submitted by the division.

52 War diary of 46th Army, entry for 30.10.1944. TsAMO, fu.401, inv.9511, f.438, p.57.

53 I.N. Shkadin et al. (eds), 'Geroi Sovetskogo Soyuza', Vol.1, Moscow, Voenizdat, 1987, p.810.

54 Daily report of LVII Panzer Corps, 30.10.1944. TsAMO, fu.500, inv.12462, f.236, p.138.

55 Morning report of 3 Army (Hung), 30.10.1944. TsAMO, fu.500, inv.12462, f.236, p.134.

56 Although precise information is lacking, 24 Panzer-Division probably counter-attacked with two battle groups. (The war diary of Army Group South speaks of 'northern' and 'southern' battle groups.) The armoured battle group was most probably the 'southern' one, while Panzer-Grenadier Regiment 21, which arrived in the afternoon, was the 'northern' one. The official history of 24 Panzer-Division says that the armoured battle group consisted of II Battalion/Panzer-Regiment 24, Panzer-Reconnaissance Battalion 24 and I Battalion/Panzer-Grenadier Regiment 26 (F.M. von Senger and Etterlin Jr, *Die 24. Panzer-Division vormals 1. Kavallerie-Division 1939–1945*, Kurt Vowinckel Verlag, Neckargemünd, 1962, p.271). But this information most probably is not complete; judging from earlier accounts, the armoured battle group probably included the Staff of Panzer-Grenadier Regiment 26, the self-propelled I Battalion/Panzer-Artillery Regiment 89 and the armoured company of Panzer-Engineer Battalion 40. The composition of the 'motorised' battle group is not known, but without doubt it was formed around Panzer-Grenadier Regiment 21.

57 War diary of 37th Rifle Corps, entry for 30.10.1944. TsAMO, fu.37SK, inv.1, f.21, p.61.

58 Számvéber, *Pánzélosütközet Kecskemét körzetében*, p.166.

59 War diary of 37th Rifle Corps, entry for 30.10.1944. TsAMO, fu.37SK, inv.1, f.21, p.61. Today Kisfái is a suburb of Kecskemét.

60 TsAMO, fu.3426, inv.1, f.54, p.314.

61 In 1950 Koháry Szent Lőrinc (Koháryszentlőrinc) and Koháry-major (farming settlement) were merged and renamed Nyárlőrinc.

62 War diary of 37th Rifle Corps, entry for 30.10.1944. TsAMO, fu.37SK, inv.1, f.21, p.61.

63 Ibid.

64 Saveliev and Popov, op cit, p.117.

65 Ibid, cit. TsAMO, fu.33, inv.793756, f.27, p.37 (the award recommendation) and TsAMO, fu.1299, inv.1, f.66, pp.66, 71 (the after-action report).

66 War diary of 37th Rifle Corps, entry for 30.10.1944. TsAMO, fu.37SK, inv.1, f.21, p.61.

67 Combat report No.08 of the 37th Guards Tank Brigade to the HQ of the 2nd Guards Mechanised Corps, 30.10.1944. TsAMO, fu.3426, inv.1, f.54, p.318. The order was issued after 15:00.

68 War diary of 37th Rifle Corps, entry for 30.10.1944. TsAMO, fu.37SK, inv.1, f.21, p.61.

69 Ibid. See also Saveliev and Popov, op cit, p.117.

70 Saveliev and Popov, op cit, p.117, cit. TsAMO, fu.1299, inv.1, f.51, pp.149–150.

71 War diary of 37th Rifle Corps, entry for 31.10.1944. TsAMO, fu.37SK, inv.1, f.21, p.62.

72 Combat report No.01 of the 4th Mechanised Tank Brigade to the HQ of the 2nd Guards Mechanised Corps, 30.10.1944. TsAMO, fu.3426, inv.1, f.54, p.307.

73 After-action report of 2nd Guards Mechanised Corps. TsAMO, fu.3426, inv.1, f.36, p.10.

74 Combat report No.08 of 37th Guards Tank Brigade to the HQ of the 2nd Guards Mechanised Corps, 30.10.1944. TsAMO, fu.3426, inv.1, f.54, p.318.

75 Knebel-Doeberitz, op cit, p.228.

76 Combat report No.08 of 37th Guards Tank Brigade to the HQ of the 2nd Guards Mechanised Corps, 30.10.1944. TsAMO, fu.3426, inv.1, f.54, p.318.

77 Phone conversation between Marcks and 5a (5th General Staff Officer) of Army Group South, 30.10.1944, 18:40. KTB Ia HGr Süd, NARA T311/158/7209311. Most probably the northern battle group was the reinforced Panzer-Grenadier Regiment 21 whilst the southern one was the panzer battle group.

78 Combat report No.08 of the 37th Guards Tank Brigade to the HQ of the 2nd Guards Mechanised Corps, 30.10.1944. TsAMO, fu.3426, inv.1, f.54, pp.318–319.

79 Chmelev, op cit, p.107.

80 KTB Ia HGr Süd, NARA T311/158/7209309-7209311. The Soviet archival sources more or less confirm these claims. By 20:00 MT 4th Guards Mechanised Brigade had lost six tanks; by 18:00 MT the 6th Guards Mechanised Brigade reported the loss of six tanks too (four burned-out and two knocked out). By 23:00 MT 37th Guards Tank Brigade had lost five tanks (three burned-out and two knocked out), all of them due to accurate 'enemy artillery fire'; the losses of 30th Guards Tank Regiment were still not reported by midnight. (TsAMO, fu.3426, inv.1, f.54, pp.307, 310, 319.)

81 Daily report of LVII Panzer Corps, 30.10.1944. TsAMO, fu.500, inv.12462, f.236, p.138.

82 KTB Ia HGr Süd, NARA T311/158/7209311. Some of Rudel's claims sound like fairytales. For example, a survey prepared by the staff of the Armoured and Mechanised Forces of the 2nd Ukrainian Front shows that during the Budapest operation (29 October 1944–13 February 1945) only 10 AFVs had been lost due to attacks from the air. (After-action report of the Commander of the Armoured and Mechanised Forces of the 2nd Ukrainian Front. TsAMO, fu.240, inv.2799, f.366, p.118.)

83 Abrosimov, op cit, p.125–126, cit. newspaper *V boi za Rodinu*, 3.11.1944. (The newspaper was the corps' official publication during the war.) The other members of the crew were: N. Suprun (gunner), V. Snegirev (driver) and V. Pervolchansky (loader). It is very difficult to say whether Dolya's tank was a T-34/76 or a T-34/85 simply because many T-34/85s that fought in Hungary were driven by four-man crews instead of the regular five. (The seat of the radio operator was empty and the tank commander acted simultaneously as a radio operator as well.) Strangely enough, Dolya's incredible act of heroism finds confirmation in the German records: the daily report of the LVII Panzer Corps of 30.10.1944 says that '[in Kecskemét] one [enemy] tank crushed one of our heavy batteries' (TsAMO, fu.500, inv.12462, f.236, p.138).

84 Számvéber, *Pánzélosütközet Kecskemét körzetében*, p.165.

85 Phone conversation between Marcks and 5a of Army Group South, 30.10.1944, 18:40. KTB Ia HGr Süd, NARA T311/158/7209311.

86 Phone conversation between von Grolman and Gaedcke, 30.10.1944, 21:20. KTB Ia HGr Süd, NARA T311/158/7209312.

87 War diary of 2nd Ukrainian Front, entry for 30.10.1944. TsAMO, fu.240, inv.2779, f.1190, p.160. The war diary of 46th Army gives slightly different figures: 23 tanks and 2 armoured personnel carriers

knocked out, 6 aircraft shot down and more than 1000 enemy troops taken prisoner (War diary of 46th Army, entry for 30.10.1944. TsAMO, fu.401, inv.9511, f.438, p.58).

88 After-action report of the Commander of the Armoured and Mechanised Forces of the 2nd Ukrainian Front. TsAMO, fu.240, inv.2799, f.366, p.9. Although this criticism was addressed exclusively to Sviridov, there is no doubt that Shlemin had received a heavy bashing too.

89 War diary of 46th Army, entry for 30.10.1944. TsAMO, fu.401, inv.9511, f.438, p.58.

90 After-action report of the Commander of the Armoured and Mechanised Forces of the 2nd Ukrainian Front. TsAMO, fu.240, inv.2799, f.366, p.9.

91 Ibid, p.12.

92 Senger und Etterlin jr., op cit, p 272.

93 Daily report of LVII Panzer Corps, 31.10.1944. TsAMO, fu.500, inv.12462, f.236, p.155.

94 After-action report of the 2nd Guards Mechanised Corps. TsAMO, fu.3426, inv.1, f.77, p.16.

95 R. Stoves, *1. Panzer Division 1935–1945*, Verlag Hans-Henning Podzun, Bad Nauheim, 1961, p.678.

96 G. Schmidt, *Panzer-Artillerie-Regiments 73*, Walther Boetther Verlag, Bremen, 1959, p.180.

97 Morning report of the LVII Panzer Corps, 31.10.1944. TsAMO, fu.500, inv.12462, f.236, p.152.

98 Stoves, op cit, p.677.

99 KTB Ia HGr Süd, NARA T311/158/7209321.

100 Daily report of LVII Panzer Corps, 31.10.1944. TsAMO, fu.500, inv.12462, f.236, p.155.

101 Morning report of Armeegruppe Fretter-Pico, 1.11.1944. TsAMO, fu.500, inv.12462, f.236, p.162.

102 Ibid, p.154.

103 E. Rebentisch (ed), *Zum Kaukasus und zu den Tauern*, Esslingen, Traditionsverband der 23. Panzer-Division, 1963, p.434.

104 KTB Ia HGr Süd, NARA T311/158/7209322.

105 KTB Ia HGr Süd, NARA T311/158/7209315.

106 Daily report of LVII Panzer Corps, 31.10.1944. TsAMO, fu.500, inv.12462, f.236, p.155.

107 After-action report of the 2nd Guards Mechanised Corps. TsAMO, fu.3426, inv.1, f.36, p.12.

108 This was probably the armoured battle group comprising Panzer-Grenadier Regiment 126 and 10 tanks, which had arrived in Nagykőrös earlier that day. See Rebentisch, op cit, p.434.

109 After-action report of the 2nd Guards Mechanised Corps. TsAMO, fu.3426, inv.1, f.36, p.12.

110 Ibid, p.14.

111 Ibid.

112 Számvéber, *Pánzélosütközet Kecskemét körzetében*, pp.170–171.

113 KTB Ia HGr Süd, NARA T311/158/7209317.

114 H.-U. Rudel, *Stuka Pilot*, Ballantine Books, New York, 1967, pp.171–173.

115 Phone conversation between von Grolman and Gaedcke, 31.10.1944, 20:50. KTB Ia HGr Süd, NARA T311/158/7209322.

116 KTB Ia HGr Süd, NARA T311/158/7209319.

117 Phone conversation between von Grolman and Gaedcke, 31.10.1944, 20:50. KTB Ia HGr Süd, NARA T311/158/7209320.

118 War diary of 37th Rifle Corps, entry for 31.10.1944. TsAMO, fu.37SK, inv.1, f.21, pp.62–63. It was the 59th Guards Rifle Division that bore the brunt of the fighting for the town. On that day it lost 41 killed and 115 wounded, as well as 1 howitzer and 8 machine guns. Moreover, another 7 howitzers, 3 45mm anti-tank guns, 1 76mm gun, 4 82mm mortars and 6 heavy machine guns were knocked out or damaged. The 320th Rifle Division had none killed, nor did it report any damaged weapons and equipment.

119 Phone conversation between von Grolman and Gaedcke, 31.10.1944, 20:50. KTB Ia HGr Süd, NARA T311/158/7209320.

120 The combat history of 24 Panzer-Division states that 'Kecskemét was declared a *festen Platz* ['secure place'] on the orders of Hitler and the division was to defend the town until further notice.' (von Senger und Etterlin jr., op cit, p 272) The records of Army Group South, however, keep no information on any such orders or instructions. On the contrary, they leave the impression that Friessner and his staff did not care that much whether Kecskemét would be lost or not.

121 Chmelev, op cit, p.108.

122 von Senger und Etterlin jr., op cit, p 272. Though unsuccessful, the relief attack of 23 Panzer-Division that took place in the evening most probably had largely facilitated the breakout of von

Uslar-Gleichen's battle group, since it managed to divert the covering detachment of 6th Guards Mechanised Brigade that had been left by Sviridov to block the escape route of the defenders of Kecskemét to the north (see above).

123 Daily situation report of 46th Army, 1.11.1944.TsAMO, fu.320.

124 Ibid.

125 Morning report of 3 Army (Hung), 30.10.1944.TsAMO, fu.500, inv.12462, f.236, p.132.

126 Daily report of LVII Panzer Corps, 30.10.1944.TsAMO, fu.500, inv.12462, f.236, p.137.

127 Morning report of LVII Panzer Corps, 31.10.1944.TsAMO, fu.500, inv.12462, f.236, p.152.

128 War diary of 2nd Ukrainian Front, entry for 30.10.1944.TsAMO, fu.240, inv.2779, f.1190, p.156.

129 War diary of 2nd Ukrainian Front, entry for 31.10.1944.TsAMO, fu.240, inv.2779, f.1190, p.165.

130 Daily report of LVII Panzer Corps, 31.10.1944.TsAMO, fu.500, inv.12462, f.236, p.154.

131 Veress, op cit,Vol.1, p.385.

132 HGr Süd, Ia Tgesmeldung, 30.10.1944, NARA T311/158/7209478.

133 War diary of 2nd Ukrainian Front, entry for 31.10.1944.TsAMO, fu.240, inv.2779, f.1190, pp.164–165.

134 KTB Ia HGr Süd, NARA T311/158/7209304.

135 KTB Ia HGr Süd, NARA T311/158/7209321.

136 Ibid.

137 Tolubko and Baryshev, op cit, p.337.

138 Ibid, p.338.

139 The tactical insignia of 13th Guards Mechanised Brigade was a deer, the 14th Guards Mechanised Brigade an elephant, 15th Guards Mechanised Brigade a swallow, 36th Guards Tank Brigade a bear, 352nd Guards Heavy Self-Propelled Regiment a lizard, 62nd Independent Motorcycle Regiment a giraffe. I. Moshchanskii, *1944-y: Ot Korsuni do Belgrada*, Moscow,Veche, 2008, p.160.

140 Andryushchenko, op cit, p.202.

141 Ibid, pp.202–203.

142 War diary of 2nd Ukrainian Front, order No. 00691/op, 19:20, 31.10.1944.TsAMO, fu.240, inv.2779, f.1190, p.163.

143 After-action report of the 4th Guards Mechanised Corps.TsAMO, fu.3430, inv.1, f.161, p.13.

144 Ibid, p.14.

145 Andryushchenko, op cit, p.204.

146 A German intelligence map, 1.11.1944, reproduced in D. Glantz (ed), *1986 Art of War Symposium*, p.137.

147 War diary of 2nd Ukrainian Front, Report to Stalin, No. 00692/op, 23:45, 31.10.1944.TsAMO, fu.240, inv.2779, f.1190, pp.166–168.

148 War diary of 2nd Ukrainian Front, order No. 00693/op, 15:00, 1.11.1944.TsAMO, fu.240, inv.2779, f.1199, pp.6–7.

149 Muzsik was a small place, probably a hamlet, which no longer exists today. It was situated southwest of Alberti.

150 War diary of 46th Army, entry for 1.11.1944.TsAMO, fu.401, inv.9511, f.441, pp.10–11. I have underlined the most important phrases in the directive.

151 24 Panzer-Division was identified on 30 October 1 and 23 Panzer-Divisions on 2 November (i.e. two days after their arrival on the battlefield), 13 Panzer-Division and 22 SS-Cavalry-Division were identified on 3 November, while the 'Feldherrnhalle' only on 4 November.

152 War diary of 2nd Ukrainian Front, entry for 1.11.1944.TsAMO, fu.240, inv.2779, f.1199, p.5.

153 KTB Ia HGr Süd, NARA T311/159/7209698.

154 This information proved to be false.

155 *Obergruppenführer* Hermann Fegelein (30.10.1906–29.4.1945) was Himmler's adjutant and brother-in law to Adolf Hitler through his marriage to Eva Braun's sister, Gretl.

156 Phone conversation between von Grolman and Wenck, 1.11.1944, 10:15; phone conversation between von Grolman and von Buttlar-Brandenfels, 1.11.1944, 10:40 and 12:50; phone conversation between von Grolman and von Buttlar-Brandenfels, 1.11.1944, 10:40 and 12:50, as well as the phone conversation between von Grolman and Ia Op.Abt./GenStdH in the afternoon of 1.11.1944. KTB Ia HGr Süd, NARA T311/159/7209695-7209696.

157 Phone conversation between Ia Op.Abt./GenStdH and 5a HGr Süd, 1.11.1944, 18:10. KTB Ia HGr Süd, NARA T311/159/7209696.

158 KTB Ia HGr Süd, NARA T311/159/7209696.

159 Ibid. The war diary of Army Group South says that the division in question 'probably' was fighting somewhere along the Kecskemét–Izsák road.

160 Morning report of Armeegruppe Fretter-Pico, 1.11.1944. TsAMO, fu.500, inv.12462, f.236, p.162. The attack in question was most probably launched by the 4th Guards Mechanised Brigade.

161 Ibid.

162 War diary of 37th Rifle Corps, entry for 1.11.1944. TsAMO, fu.37SK, inv.1, f.21, p.78.

163 Ibid.

164 Rebentisch, op cit, pp.435–436.

165 Ibid, pp.434–435.

166 Ibid, p.436.

167 Lochmann, op cit, p.287.

168 Daily situation report of 46th Army, 1.11.1944. TsAMO, fu.401.

169 War diary of 37th Rifle Corps, entry for 1.11.1944. TsAMO, fu.37SK, inv.1, f.21, p.78.

170 Order of the Command of Air Fleet 4, 30.10.1944. TsAMO, fu.500, inv.12462, f.236, p.162.

171 War diary of 37th Rifle Corps, entry for 1.11.1944. TsAMO, fu.37SK, inv.1, f.21, p.78.

172 Davtyan, op cit, p.212.

173 Ibid, pp.212–213.

174 Ibid, p.213.

175 Ibid.

176 'Group Sword' was formed in the summer of 1943, just before the battle of Kursk. It was the brainchild of General Podgorny (commander of 3rd Guards Fighter Air Corps), who wanted to have an elite unit of first-class fighter pilots that could be used 'as a fist' to deliver the decisive blow when and where required. Usually it numbered 12 planes. For the complete story of 'Group Sword' see A. Yakimenko, *Prikroi, atakuyu! V atake – Mech*, Eksmo, Moscow, 2005. Yakimenko himself was the commander of that elite group.

177 Phone conversation between von Grolman and Gaedcke, 1.11.1944, 20:05. KTB Ia HGr Süd, NARA T311/159/7209699.

178 After-action report of 2nd Guards Mechanised Corps. TsAMO, fu.3426, inv.1, f.36, p.14.

179 Daily report of LVII Panzer Corps, 1.11.1944. TsAMO, fu.500, inv.12462, f.236, p.183.

180 Schmidt, op cit, p.181.

181 Daily situation report of 46th Army, 1.11.1944, 15:00. TsAMO, fu.401.

182 Daily situation report of 46th Army, 1.11.1944, 20:00. TsAMO, fu.401.

183 Ibid.

184 War diary of 37th Rifle Corps, entry for 1.11.1944. TsAMO, fu.37SK, inv.1, f.21, p.78. See also the daily report of LVII Panzer Corps, 1.11.1944. TsAMO, fu.500, inv.12462, f.236, p.183.

185 Daily report of LVII Panzer Corps, 1.11.1944. TsAMO, fu.500, inv.12462, f.236, p.184.

186 Mizsei Péter and Mizsei Péter-major (cattle farm or farm seettlement) were two different places. Mizsei Péter was situated northeast of Lajosmizse, while Mizsei Péter-major was east of Lajosmizse.

187 Daily report of LVII Panzer Corps, 1.11.1944. TsAMO, fu.500, inv.12462, f.236, pp.183–184.

188 HGr Süd Ia, Nr 4281/44g.K., which is mentioned in KTB Ia HGr Süd, NARA T311/159/7209699.

189 Evening intelligence report of Armeegruppe Fretter-Pico, 1.11.1944. TsAMO, fu.500, inv.12462, f.236, pp.175–176.

190 After-action report of the 4th Guards Mechanised Corps. TsAMO, fu.3430, inv.1, f.161, pp.15–16.

191 Tolubko and Baryshev, op cit, p.341.

Chapter 9

1 Minutes of the conversation between the command of 2nd Ukrainian Front and the Chief of Staff of the Hungarian Armed Forces J. Vörös. TsAMO, fu.240, inv.2761, f.208, pp.45–53. Reproduced in V. Zolotarev, op cit, Vol.14, pp.311–316.

2 Daily situation reports of 46th Army, 1.11.1944. TsAMO, fu.401.

3 46th Army, situation report #949/op, 13:00, 2.11.1944. TsAMO, fu.401.

4 Zakharov, *Budapeshtenskaya Operatsiya*, p.31. Zakharov's article was published at the same time as Malinovsky's work (in the spring of 1965). The passage in question contradicts Malinovsky's 'phone

call story', as well as Zakharov's own statement published six years later (see Chapters 5 and 7). Was Zakharov trying to say that one of the 'correct decisions' was to launch a surprise attack on Budapest?

5 In the German records the foothold in question is called 'the bridgehead at Dunaföldvár', but the correct designation would be 'the bridgehead at Solt', because Dunaföldvár is situated on the western bank of the Danube, while Solt was on the eastern one.

6 HGr Süd Ia, Nr 4281/44 g.Kdos. 1.11.1944. NARA T311/159/7209628-7209629. The idea of launching an attack from the bridgehead at Dunaföldvár (Solt) was abandoned on the morning of 2 November, since any offensive undertaken from there was by then considered 'pointless' by Fretter-Pico.

7 Armeegruppe Fretter-Pico Ia, Nr 5275/44 geh. 1.11.1944. NARA T311/7209654-7209655. As we will see below, by the morning of 2 November the jumping off positions for the attack were shifted to the north and southwest respectively, owing to the fast-changing situation on the battlefield.

8 46th Army situation report #948/op, 08:00, 2.11.1944. TsAMO, fu.401.

9 After-action report of 2nd Guards Mechanised Corps. TsAMO, fu.3426, inv.1, f.36, p.14.

10 KTB Ia HGr Süd, NARA T311/159/7209709.

11 Stoves, op cit, pp.679–680.

12 Daily report of LVII Panzer Corps, 2.11.1944. TsAMO, fu.500, inv.12462, f.236, p.201.

13 Rebentisch, op cit, p.436.

14 Ibid.

15 Daily report of LVII Panzer Corps, 2.11.1944. TsAMO, fu.500, inv.12462, f.236, p.201.

16 Lochmann, op cit, p.287. The Soviet tanks mentioned by von Rosen most probably were deployed in the forest surrounding Klotild-major and thus engaged the northern flank of the armoured group.

17 Daily report of LVII Panzer Corps, 2.11.1944. TsAMO, fu.500, inv.12462, f.236, p.201. On the next day Kirchner claimed that the attack had stopped just 500m east of Lipot-major (see the daily report of LVII Panzer Corps, 3.11.1944. TsAMO, fu.500, inv.12462, f.236, p.227).

18 War diary of 37th Rifle Corps, entry for 2.11.1944. TsAMO, fu.37SK, inv.1, f.21, p.79.

19 Rebentisch, op cit, p.436.

20 Rebentisch, op cit, p.436; W. Schneider, *Tigers in Combat*, Vol.1, J.J. Fedorowicz Publishing, Winnipeg, 1994, p.167.

21 Rebentisch, op cit, p.436.

22 Ibid. Rebentisch claims that two King Tigers were blown up, while Schneider (Schneider, op cit) says that only one such tank was destroyed.

23 KTB Ia HGr Süd, NARA T311/159/7209711.

24 Pliev's group was encircled twice during the Debrecen Operation: during the second week of October in the area south of Debrecen and once again during the last week of the same month in the area north of Nyíregyháza.

25 Friessner, op cit, p.162. Friessner's observation is actually based on the daily report of LVII Panzer Corps from 2 November, which emphasises these conclusions. See TsAMO, fu.500, inv.12462, f.236, p.201.

26 KTB Ia HGr Süd, NARA T311/159/7209712.

27 The battle group was led by Lieutenant-Colonel Joachim-Helmut Wolff, commander of Fusilier Regiment 'Feldherrnhalle'. Judging from a document dated 3 November 1944 (see NARA T311/159/7209685), it most probably consisted of that regiment, but reinforced with the towed anti-tank guns of the divisional anti-tank battalion, which on 2 November had 12 StuG III assault guns and 9 towed 7.5cm heavy anti-tank guns. The wheeled and the tracked elements, as usual, were transferred separately and that is why the assault guns and the other armoured vehicles did not arrive until 3–4 November. For the detailed strength of the division on 2–3 November 1944 see BAMA, RH 10/206, pp.38–40 and the Appendix.

28 Daily report of Armeegruppe Fretter-Pico, 2.11.1944. TsAMO, fu.500, inv.12462, f.236, p.189.

29 46th Army, situation report #043/op, 21:30, 2.11.1944. TsAMO, fu.401.

30 After-action report of 2nd Guards Mechanised Corps. TsAMO, fu.3426, inv.1, f.36, p.14.

31 46th Army, situation report #949/op, 13:00, 2.11.1944. TsAMO, fu.401.

32 After-action report of 2nd Guards Mechanised Corps. TsAMO, fu.3426, inv.1, f.36, p.17.

33 Ibid.

34 46th Army, situation report #043/op, 21:30, 2.11.1944. TsAMO, fu.401.

35 Veress, op cit, Vol. 1, p.402. At that moment Billnitzer's group was most probably made up of Assault Gun Battalions 1, 6, 7, 13 and 24 (see ibid., p.402). The battalions in question did not have enough armoured vehicles and sometimes were issued with towed anti-tank guns or even fought as line infantry. The police battalions belonged to the SS-Police-Regiment 1.

36 This estimate is based on the ration strength reports submitted by various German divisions at the end of October and the beginning of November 1944 (see the summary tables in the Appendix). Since the sum of the figures of the divisions deployed under Breith and Kirchner exceeds 80,000 men and this figure does not include the Hungarian troops engaged in the vicinity of Budapest, as well as the ground forces of the Luftwaffe (like the German and Magyar Flak detachments, for example) and various auxiliary units, such as the German military police and the paramilitary formations of the Arrow Cross, we have every reason to believe that this estimate is not an exaggeration.

37 Daily report of Armeegruppe Fretter-Pico, 1.11.1944. TsAMO, fu.500, inv.12462, f.236, p.166.

38 Daily report of LVII Panzer Corps, 1.11.1944. TsAMO, fu.500, inv.12462, f.236, p.183.

39 After-action report of 4th Guards Mechanised Corps. TsAMO, fu.3430, inv.1, f.161, p.16. The widespread panic and overnight disintegration of the 1 Huszar-Division is also confirmed by Hungarian sources. See Veress, op cit, Vol. 1, pp.405–406.

40 Ibid.

41 A. Escuadra Sanchez, *Feldherrnhalle: Forgotten Elite*, Bradford, Shelf Books, 1996, p.64.

42 Throughout the war the fate of the 4th Guards was linked to that of two other armoured formations: the Soviet 2nd Guards Mechanised Corps and the German 13 Panzer-Division. The troops of both mechanised corps fought literally shoulder to shoulder from the end of December 1942 until March 1944 and then again from the end of October 1944 to the winter of 1945. 13 Panzer-Divison became the most common enemy that the 4th Guards Mechanised Corps faced: from August 1943 until February 1945 it encountered time and again this crack German formation or some of its units.

43 Daily report of Armeegruppe Fretter-Pico, 2.11.1944. TsAMO, fu.500, inv.12462, f.236, p.188.

44 After-action report of the 4th Guards Mechanised Corps. TsAMO, fu.3430, inv.1, f.161, p.16.

45 Ibid.

46 Today Sári no longer exists by this name; between 1947 and 1966 the villages Gyón, Alsódabas, Felsődabas and Sári were gradually merged into a single settlement, the town of Dabas.

47 After-action report of the 4th Guards Mechanised Corps. TsAMO, fu.3430, inv.1, f.161, p.18.

48 KTB Ia HGr Süd, NARA T311/159/7209709-7209711.

49 After-action report of 4th Guards Mechanised Corps. TsAMO, fu.3430, inv.1, f.161, p.16.

50 Veress, op cit, Vol. 1, p.406. The Szálasi-rocket was planned as a domestic alternative of the German *Panzerschreck*, which was an 88mm reusable anti-tank rocket launcher. It was designed and produced by Manfred Weiss Company in Budapest (the serial production started in the summer of 1944). The launcher consisted of two metal tubes (which means that it could fire two rockets simultaneously), approximately 1m long and with a diameter of 100mm. The weight of the rocket's warhead was about 4.2 kg and was capable of penetrating armour up to 300mm thick, so theoretically it could destroy absolutely every tank manufactured at that time. Some of the rocket launchers were mounted on trucks (they fired backwards), but the most common version was mounted either on a tripod or on a cumbersome wheeled mount taken from captured Soviet Maxim and Degtyarev machine guns. Veress states that the Hungarian parachute battalion was reinforced with an 'artillery battalion', 3 batteries strong, with a total of 12 launchers. The use of Szálasi-rockets in that area was additionally confirmed in early 2000 when remnants of two launchers were found in the vicinity of Alsónémedi.

51 After-action report of the 4th Guards Mechanised Corps. TsAMO, fu.3430, inv.1, f.161, p.16.

52 Veress, op cit, Vol. 1, pp.417–418.

53 46th Army, situation report #043/op, 21:30, 2.11.1944. TsAMO, fu.401.

54 KTB Ia HGr Süd, NARA T311/159/7209703.

55 46th Army, situation report # 949/op, 13:00, 2.11.1944. TsAMO, fu.401.

56 Daily report of LVII Panzer Corps, 2.11.1944. TsAMO, fu.500, inv. 12462, f.236, p. 201.

57 46th Army, situation report # 948/op, 8:00, 2.11.1944. TsAMO, fu.401. 58 Saveliev and Popov, op cit, pp.117–118.

59 46th Army, situation report , 15:50, 2.11.1944. TsAMO, fu.401.

60 Daily report of I Air Corps, 2.11.1944. TsAMO, fu.500, inv.12462, f.236, p.229.

61 Ibid, pp.229–300.

62 G. Punka, *Hungarian Aces of World War 2*, Oxford, Osprey Publishing, 2002, p.60.

63 Daily report of I Air Corps, 2.11.1944.TsAMO, fu.500, inv.12462, f.236, p.229. In his report Deichmann especially stresses the fact that 'the enemy anti-aircraft defence is very strong' and the Soviet fighters were constantly present over the battlefield.

64 Punka, op cit, p.60.

65 Davtyan, op cit, pp.213–214, cit. TsAMO, fu.327, inv.4999, f.170, p.55. The war diary of the 2nd Ukrainian Front says that '14 enemy aircraft were destroyed or damaged' during that attack. (War diary of 2nd Ukrainian Front, entry for 2.11.1944. TsAMO, fu.240, inv.2779, f.1199, p.20.) The daily report of the German I Air Corps, however, claims that only three Fw-190 were damaged during the Soviet air raid on the Tápiószentmárton airfield on that day (daily report of I Air Corps, 2.11.1944.TsAMO, fu.500, inv.12462, f.236, p.230).

66 Knebel-Doeberitz, '24th Panzer Division Operations' in Glantz (ed), *1986 Art of War Symposium*, p.227.

67 46th Army, situation report #952/op, 8:00, 3.11.1944.TsAMO, fu.401.

68 After-action report of the 2nd Guards Mechanised Corps.TsAMO, fu.3426, inv.1, f.36, p.17.

69 Kanevsky, op cit. Some Soviet reports (for instance, the situation report of 46th Army from 3 November and the after-action report of 2nd Guards Mechanised Corps) incorrectly claim that Üllő was captured by 15:00 MT on 3 November, that is, only in the afternoon. Kanevsky, however, is right; the town was taken during the night of 2/3 November. This is confirmed not only by the official history of the 2nd Guards Mechanised Corps, but also by the German records.

70 Ibid.

71 In that morning the brigade's left wing captured not only Üllő, but Vecsés also. Even though the documents in my possession do not reveal when exactly this occurred, it is clear that in order to consolidate his forces around Üllő, shortly afterwards Kanevsky decided to pull out from Vecsés, which was abandoned without a fight.

72 Abrosimov, op cit, pp.131–132; Kanevsky, op cit.

73 Daily report of III Panzer Corps, 3.11.1944.TsAMO, fu.500, inv.12462, f.236, p.225.

74 KTB Ia HGr Süd, NARA T311/159/7209720.

75 Lochmann, op cit, p.288.

76 Morning report of Panzer Group 'Breith', 3.11.1944.TsAMO, fu.500, inv.12462, f.236, p.223.

77 Daily report of Armeegruppe Fretter-Pico, 3.11.1944.TsAMO, fu.500, inv.12462, f.236, p.208.

78 Kanevsky, op. cit.; Abrosimov, op cit, p.130.

79 Daily report of Armeegruppe Fretter-Pico, 3.11.1944.TsAMO, fu.500, inv.12462, f.236, pp.210–211. The units of 8 SS-Cavalry-Division, which had arrived during the day and were involved in the attacks on Üllő, were SS-Cavalry Regiment 15 (with four squadrons), SS-Reconnaissance Battalion 8, SS-Engineer Battalion 8 and SS-Anti-Tank Battalion 8. (Daily report of III Panzer Corps, 3.11.1944. TsAMO, fu.500, inv.12462, f.236, pp.210–211) Which units of the 'Feldherrnhalle' Division took part in those attacks, however, is still not known to me.

80 Shkadin, op cit, Vol.1, p.464.

81 Daily report of III Panzer Corps, 3.11.1944.TsAMO, fu.500, inv.12462, f.236, p.225.

82 Abrosimov, op cit, p.129.

83 After-action report of 2nd Guards Mechanised Corps.TsAMO, fu.3426, inv.1, f.36, p.19.

84 Phone conversation between Gaedcke and von Grolman, 3.11.1944, 11:00. KTB Ia HGr Süd, NARA T311/159/7209722.

85 Morning report of Panzer Group 'Breith', 3.11.1944.TsAMO, fu.500, inv.12462, f.236, p.223.

86 F. von Hake, *Das waren wir – Das erlebten wir!* Munich, Traditionsverband e.V. der 13.Panzer-Division, 1971, p.206. The documents of Armeegruppe Fretter-Pico clearly show that all Panther tanks and 5 Pz IV/70 of Panzer-Grenadier Division 'Feldhernhalle' were also subordinate to 13 Panzer-Division and presumably were attached to Gehrig's group. Most probably I Battalion/Panzer-Artillery Regiment 13, which was equipped with Hummel self-propelled howitzers, was attached to Gehrig's group as well. It is worth mentioning that other smaller armoured units – Anti-Tank Companies 1179 and 1257 (which were equipped with Hetzer tank-destroyers) and 4 Company/Anti-Tank Battalion 661 (equipped with Nashorn tank destroyers) – were also placed under 13th Panzer. Whether they supported Gehrig or Schöning, however, is still not clear.

87 Ibid. One could only guess where exactly Schöning's battle group was deployed and how it was used on that day, since, as we already know, Vecsés was taken by the Germans without a fight in late morning. Those Škoda tanks most probably were Hungarian-made Turan tanks.

88 After-action report of the 2nd Guards Mechanised Corps. TsAMO, fu.3426, inv.1, f.36, p.19.

89 Daily report of Armeegruppe Fretter-Pico, 3.11.1944. TsAMO, fu.500, inv.12462, f.236, p.208.

90 Abrosimov, op cit, pp.131–132.

91 Daily report of III Panzer Corps, 3.11.1944. TsAMO, fu.500, inv.12462, f.236, p.225.

92 After-action report of the 4th Guards Mechanised Corps. TsAMO, fu.3430, inv.1, f.161, p.18.

93 SS-Police Regiment 1, which was tactically subordinate to the division since the beginning of the Soviet offensive.

94 After-action report of 4th Guards Mechanised Corps. TsAMO, fu.3430, inv.1, f.161, pp.18, 20.

95 Ibid.

96 46th Army, situation report #952/op, 08:15, 3.11.1944. TsAMO, fu.401.

97 Ibid, situation report #953/op, 13:00; situation report #44/op, 21:30, 3.11.1944, TsAMO, fu.401.

98 The southeastern shoulder of the so-called Gödöllő hills (*Gödöllői-dombság*) runs along the western part of the town. It was along theset hills that the Axis command erected part of the 'Attila' line fortifications, which later managed to contain the Soviet advance on Budapest for almost two months.

99 War diary of 37th Rifle Corps, entry for 3.11.1944. TsAMO, fu.37SK, inv.1, f.21, p.79.

100 Ibid, p.80.

101 46th Army, situation report, 11:00, 3.11.1944. TsAMO, fu.401.

102 War diary of 37th Rifle Corps, entry for 3.11.1944. TsAMO, fu.37SK, inv.1, f.21, pp.79–80.

103 Daily report of Harko 306, 3.11.1944. TsAMO, fu.500, inv.12462, f.236, p.221.

104 Daily report of LVII Panzer Corps, 3.11.1944. TsAMO, fu.500, inv.12462, f.236, p.229.

105 Daily report of Armeegruppe Fretter-Pico, 3.11.1944. TsAMO, fu.500, inv.12462, f.236, pp.211–212; morning report of LVII Panzer Corps, 3.11.1944. TsAMO, fu.500, inv.12462, f.236, p.224.

106 KTB Ia HGr Süd, NARA T311/159/7209722-7209723.

107 Daily report of LVII Panzer Corps, 3.11.1944. TsAMO, fu.500, inv.12462, f.236, p.229.

108 KTB Ia HGr Süd, NARA T311/159/7209721.

109 Morning report of LVII Panzer Corps, 3.11.1944. TsAMO, fu.500, inv.12462, f.236, p.223.

110 KTB Ia HGr Süd, NARA T311/159/7209721.

111 Evening intelligence report of Armeegruppe Fretter-Pico, 3.11.1944. TsAMO, fu.500, inv.12462, f.236, p.219.

112 Daily report of Harko 306, 3.11.1944. TsAMO, fu.500, inv.12462, f.236, p.221.

113 Morning report of LVII Panzer Corps, 3.11.1944. TsAMO, fu.500, inv.12462, f.236, p.224.

114 Ibid.

115 Army situation report #952/op, 08:15, 3.11.1944. TsAMO, fu.401.

116 46th Army situation report, 11:00, 3.11.1944. TsAMO, fu.401.

117 Morning report of LVII Panzer Corps, 3.11.1944. TsAMO, fu.500, inv.12462, f.236, p.224.

118 Ibid.

119 Stoves, op cit, pp.678–679.

120 Morning report of LVII Panzer Corps, 3.11.1944. TsAMO, fu.500, inv.12462, f.236, p.224.

121 Stoves, op cit, p.679.

122 Phone conversation between Gaedcke and von Grolman, 3.11.1944, 11:00. KTB Ia HGr Süd, NARA T311/159/7209721.

123 Schmidt, op cit, p.182.

124 Ibid. It is quite probable that the T-34s in question were actually SU-76 self-propelled guns, or were not destroyed at all – a typical case of incorrect reporting/overclaiming), since there is no evidence that any Soviet T-34-equipped units operated in that area on 3 November.

125 The 'Feldherrnhalle' units were Wehrmacht combat formations that drew their manpower from the SA (*Sturmabteilung*), a notorious Nazi paramilitary organisation that traced its history back to the days of the 1923 Munich Putsch and subsequently played a key role in Hitler's rise to power. The SA men were often called 'brownshirts' after the colour of their uniforms. The 'Feldherrnhalle' units and formations were named after the Feldherrnhalle loggia in Munich where the attempted coup was crushed by the German state police. In 1944–45 many members of the 'Feldherrnhalle' units were young volunteers indoctrinated

in Nazi ideology, who were not only highly motivated but also were very well trained. Panzer-Grenadier Division 'Feldherrnhalle' was the first large SA-combat formation. It was formed in the summer of 1943. Because of the high number of SA members that volunteered for frontline service, on 15 May 1944 the German General Staff decided to create a second SA-division and 13 Panzer-Division was chosen for that purpose. Following that order, throughout the summer and the autumn of the same year the Grenadier-Regiment (mot.) 1030 'Feldherrnhalle' and Panzer-Brigade 110 'Feldherrnhalle' were incorporated into 13th Panzer. The division began to draw most of its replacements from the 'Feldherrnhalle' Training Brigade in Danzig, which gradually transformed it into a SA-formation.

126 Phone conversation between Marcks and 5a, 5th General Staff Officer of Army Group South, 3.11.1944, 11:40. KTB Ia HGr Süd, NARA T311/159/7209722.

127 Phone conversation between Marcks and 5th General Staff Officer of Army Group South, 3.11.1944, 18:40. KTB Ia HGr Süd, NARA T311/159/7209722.

128 Daily report of Armeegruppe Fretter-Pico, 3.11.1944. TsAMO, fu.500, inv.12462, f.236, p.209.

129 Stoves, op cit, p.679.

130 46th Army, situation report #954/op, 20:00, 3.11.1944. TsAMO, fu.401.

131 Phone conversation between Gaedcke and von Grolman, 3.11.1944, 11:00. KTB Ia HGr Süd, NARA T311/159/7209721.

132 Daily report of Armeegruppe Fretter-Pico, 3.11.1944. TsAMO, fu.500, inv.12462, f.236, p.209.

133 Daily report of LVII Panzer Corps, 3.11.1944. TsAMO, fu.500, inv.12462, f.236, p.227.

134 Rebentisch, op cit, p.438.

135 Daily report of Armeegruppe Fretter-Pico, 3.11.1944. TsAMO, fu.500, inv.12462, f.236, p.209.

136 Daily report of LVII Panzer Corps, 3.11.1944. TsAMO, fu.500, inv.12462, f.236, pp.227–228.

137 Ceglédbercel is a village situated some 12km northwest of Cegléd, at the Cegléd–Budapest railway line.

138 Rebentisch, op cit, p.438.

139 Daily report of LVII Panzer Corps, 3.11.1944. TsAMO, fu.500, inv.12462, f.236, p.228.

140 Rebentisch, op cit, p.438.

141 Daily report of LVII Panzer Corps, 3.11.1944. TsAMO, fu.500, inv.12462, f.236, pp.228–229.

142 Csepeli Dunaág (also known as Soroksári Duna) is a tributary – an anabranch – of the Danube. (An anabranch is a section of a river that diverts from the main watercourse and rejoins it downstream.)

143 War diary of 46th Army, entries for 1.11.1944 (pp.10–11) and 3.11.1944 (pp. 14–15). TsAMO, fu.401, inv.9511, f.441.

144 Morning report of LVII Panzer Corps, 4.11.1944. TsAMO, fu.500, inv.12462, f.236, p.250.

145 War diary of 37th Rifle Corps, entry for 4.11.1944. TsAMO, fu.37SK, inv.1, f.21, p.80.

146 Ibid. The division also captured in Cegléd one ammunition dump.

147 Saveliev and Popov, op cit, pp.118–119, cit. TsAMO, fu.1299, inv.7, f.2, p.102.

148 46th Army, situation report #958/op, 20:00, 4.11.1944. TsAMO, fu.401.

149 Daily report of Armeegruppe Fretter-Pico, 4.11.1944. TsAMO, fu.500, inv.12462, f.236, p.234.

150 Ibid, p.235.

151 Colonel Gustav-Adolf von Nostitz-Wallwitz, the commander of the 24.Panzer-Division.

152 P. Gosztony, *Endkampf an der Donau*, Vienna, Verlag Fritz Molden, 1969, pp.84–85, cit. Tömöry J., *A 12. magyar királyi tartalék hadosztály a Duna-Tisza közén 1944 öszén* (manuscript).

153 A. Puskas, *Vengria v gody Vtoroi Mirovoi Voiny*, Nauka, Moscow, 1966, p.459, cit. BMI, V-19430, X, 59.1. The acts of looting committed by the Germans were facilitated by the mass exodus of the civilian population from Cegléd, which took place on 3 November. (For a more detailed description of the situation in the Cegléd area and the total chaos that reigned in and around the town on 3–4 November see Veress, op cit, Vol.1, pp.415, 417 and 418.)

154 At that time Alberti and Irsa were nominally two separate villages, although the wartime maps show them as one big settlement. In 1950 they merged into a single village, Albertirsa, which in 2003 was given a town status.

155 46th Army, situation report 11:30, 4.11.1944. TsAMO, fu.401; War diary of 37th Rifle Corps, entry for 4.11.1944. TsAMO, fu.37SK, inv.1, f.21, p.80. The latter says 'There is a heavy concentration of enemy firepower between Cegléd and Alberti' and that 'tanks, armoured halftracks and self-propelled guns are patrolling on the roads.'

156 46th Army, situation report #958/op, 20:00, 4.11.1944.TsAMO, fu.401.

157 War diary of 37th Rifle Corps, entry for 4.11.1944.TsAMO, fu.37SK, inv.1, f.21, p.81.

158 Apart from the two panzers, 170 Axis troops and 3 machine guns were reportedly 'destroyed', while another 34 were taken prisoner (two of them were members of 23 Panzer-Division).The division itself lost only 7 men killed and 30 wounded, while 4 of its 76mm guns were knocked out.War diary of 37th Rifle Corps, entry for 4.11.1944.TsAMO, fu.37SK, inv.1, f.21, p.81.

159 46th Army, situation report #957/op, 13:00, 4.11.1944.TsAMO, fu.401.

160 Daily report of LVII Panzer Corps, 4.11.1944.TsAMO, fu.500, inv.12462, f.236, pp.250–251.

161 Ibid, p.251.

162 Rebentisch, op cit, p.438.

163 Morning report of LVII Panzer Corps, 4.11.1944.TsAMO, fu.500, inv.12462, f.236, p.249.

164 Stoves, op cit, p.681.According to the aforementioned report of Kirchner's HQ, the group was to be made of 'all operational tanks and self-propelled guns', which were to be supported by 'a self-propelled artillery battalion'. Since by then most of the armoured units of 1st Panzer had very few vehicles in running condition, it makes no sense to designate them as 'regiments', 'battalions' and 'companies'.

165 Daily report of LVII Panzer Corps, 4.11.1944.TsAMO, fu.500, inv.12462, f.236, p.251; Daily report of Armeegruppe Fretter-Pico, 4.11.1944.TsAMO, fu.500, inv.12462, f.236, p.233.

166 46th Army, situation report #045/op, 21:30, 4.11.1944.TsAMO, fu.401. I have not been able to find out when exactly Nyáregyháza was captured by the Soviets; the Soviet and German documents in my possession do not mention a time. Most probably this happened either at midday on 4 November, or in the afternoon of the same day, when the 109th Guards Rifle Division was advancing on a broad front through that area, because on the next day the German reports speak of the 'recapture' of the town.

167 Morning report of III Panzer Corps, 4.11.1944.TsAMO, fu.500, inv.12462, f.236, p.249; Daily report of III Panzer Corps, 4.11.1944.TsAMO, fu.500, inv.12462, f.236, p.254.

168 Daily report of III Panzer Corps, 4.11.1944.TsAMO, fu.500, inv.12462, f.236, p.254.

169 46th Army, situation report 11:30, 4.11.1944.TsAMO, fu.401.This battle group was definitely formed by the 'Feldherrnhalle' Division, which was responsible for the defence of the Üllő–Monor sector.

170 Ibid.

171 Daily report of III Panzer Corps, 4.11.1944.TsAMO, fu.500, inv.12462, f.236, p.254.

172 Ibid.

173 Evening intelligence report of Armeegruppe Fretter-Pico, 4.11.1944.TsAMO, fu.500, inv.12462, f.236, p.241.

174 46th Army, situation report #959/op, 06:00, 5.11.1944.TsAMO, fu.401.

175 As it was already mentioned above (and as we will see below), the battle groups of the German divisions appeared on the battlefield in order of their arrival and when situation was critical this very often led to their dispersed employment.Thus on 4 November the units of Panzer-Grenadier Division 'Feldherrnhalle' were engaged in three different sectors (Monor, Üllő and Vecsés), while the 8 SS-Cavalry-Division was split into two combat teams deployed at Üllő and Vecsés respectively.

176 Phone conversation between Marcks and 5th General Staff Officer of Army Group South, 4.11.1944, 18:40. KTB Ia HGr Süd, NARA T311/159/7209732; Daily report of Armeegruppe Fretter-Pico, 4.11.1944.TsAMO, fu.500, inv.12462, f.236, p.233; Daily report of III Panzer Corps, 4.11.1944. TsAMO, fu.500, inv.12462, f.236, p.254.

177 Evening intelligence report of Armeegruppe Fretter-Pico, 4.11.1944.TsAMO, fu.500, inv.12462, f.236, p.244.The German assessment was totally wrong here.Whilst in the evening of 4 November Malinovsky did indeed order both mechanised corps to be pulled out of the battle, his intention was not to throw them in combat in the vicinity of Vecsés, but to give them a break to replenish and recuperate. (See the next chapter for more details.)

178 Daily report of III Panzer Corps, 4.11.1944.TsAMO, fu.500, inv.12462, f.236, p.254.

179 Daily report of Armeegruppe Fretter-Pico, 4.11.1944.TsAMO, fu.500, inv.12462, f.236, p.233.

180 Shkadin, op cit,Vol.1, p.838.

181 TsAMO, fu.33, inv.793756, f.46, pp.191–192.

182 As we shall see, shortly after midnight the 4th Guards Mechanised Corps also attacked Gyál. Throughout the day both Soviet corps attempted to take the settlement, storming it from

southwest/west (the 4th Guards Mechanised Corps and the 200th Guards Rifle Regiment) and southeast/east (the 2nd Guards Mechanised Corps and the 265th Guards Rifle Regiment). German documents say that 'early in the morning the enemy began an attack from its foothold on both sides of Gyál.' (Daily report of Armeegruppe Fretter-Pico, 4.11.1944. TsAMO, fu.500, inv.12462, f.236, p.232) A look at the situation maps from those days shows Gyál as a tiny Axis peninsula in a vast Soviet sea.

183 After-action report of 2nd Guards Mechanised Corps. TsAMO, fu.3426, inv.1, f.77, p.21.

184 Daily report of III Panzer Corps, 4.11.1944. TsAMO, fu.500, inv.12462, f.236, p.253. (At that time Felsőhalom was a western suburb of Vecsés.)

185 Ibid.

186 Like Felsőhalom, Andrássy (Andrássy-telep) was a southwestern suburb of Vecsés, which today is a district of the town.

187 Daily report of III Panzer Corps, 4.11.1944. TsAMO, fu.500, inv.12462, f.236, p.254; Daily report of Armeegruppe Fretter-Pico, 4.11.1944. TsAMO, fu.500, inv.12462, f.236, p.232. The armoured battle group that launched the attack in question was most probably Major Gehrig's.

188 After-action report of 2nd Guards Mechanised Corps. TsAMO, fu.3426, inv.1, f.77, p.21.

189 After-action report of 2nd Guards Mechanised Corps. TsAMO, fu.3426, inv.1, f.77, pp.21, 23; morning report of III Panzer Corps, 4.11.1944. TsAMO, fu.500, inv.12462, f.236, p.249.

190 46th Army situation report #957/op, 13:00, 4.11.1944. TsAMO, fu.401.

191 Daily report of III Panzer Corps, 4.11.1944. TsAMO, fu.500, inv.12462, f.236, p.253.

192 46th Army situation report #958/op, 20:00, 4.11.1944. TsAMO, fu.401.

193 After-action report of 2nd Guards Mechanised Corps. TsAMO, fu.3426, inv.1, f.77, p.21.

194 After-action report of 4th Guards Mechanised Corps. TsAMO, fu.3430, inv.1, f.161, p.22.

195 Veress, op cit, Vol.1, p.407.

196 After-action report of 4th Guards Mechanised Corps. TsAMO, fu.3430, inv.1, f.161, p.22.

197 Ibid, p.20.

198 Kossuth-Ferenc was the western suburb of Pestszentimre and was situated just to the west of the Kecskemét–Budapest railway line. (Pestszentimre was lying to the east of it.) Today both settlements are part of the XVIII district of Budapest.

199 After-action report of 4th Guards Mechanised Corps. TsAMO, fu.3430, inv.1, f.161, pp.22, 24.

200 Ibid, pp.20–22.

201 KTB Ia HGr Süd, NARA T311/159/7209733.

202 G.F. Eber, *Pinball Games*, Bloomington, Trafford, 2010, p.171.

203 KTB Ia HGr Süd, NARA T311/159/7209733.

Chapter 10

1 Shtemenko, *The Last Six Months*, pp.262–263.

2 Stavka directive #220256. TsAMO, fu.148a, inv.3763, f.167, p. 93, reproduced in Zolotarev, op cit, Vol.16 (5–4), pp.165–166.

3 War diary of 2nd Ukrainian Front, order No. 00698/op, 17:00, 4.11.1944. TsAMO, fu.240, inv.2779, f.1199, pp.24–25.

4 Shtemenko, *The Last Six Months*, p.264.

5 War diary of 2nd Ukrainian Front, order No. 00701/op, 24:00, 4.11.1944. TsAMO, fu.240, inv.2779, f.1199, pp.25–26. The missions of 40th, 27th and 53rd Armies mentioned here did not differ much from those discussed in Chapter 8.

6 Bénye is a village halfway between Monor and Pánd.

7 War diary of 46th Army, entry for 4.11.1944. TsAMO, fu.401, inv.9511, f.441, p.17.

8 Phone conversation between Marcks and von Grolman; phone conversation between Gaedcke and von Grolman, 3.11.1944, 20:10. KTB Ia HGr Süd, NARA T311/159/7209722–7209723.

9 Ibid.

10 OKH/GenStdH/Op.Abt. (Ia) Nr 440673/44 Gkdos, Chefs., 4.11.1944. NARA T311/159/7209842–7209843.

11 Phone conversation between von Grolman and von Bonin, 4.11.1944, 10:15. KTB Ia HGr Süd, NARA T311/159/7209731.

12 Phone conversation between von Bonin and 5a of Army Group South, 4.11.1944, 10:45. KTB Ia HGr Süd, NARA T311/159/7209731.

13 Phone conversation between von Grolman and Gaedcke, 4.11.1944, 11:05. KTB Ia HGr Süd, NARA T311/159/7209731.

14 Phone conversation between Marks and 5a of Army Group South, 4.11.1944, 18:45. KTB Ia HGr Süd, NARA T311/159/7209731.

15 Phone conversation between von Bonin and Schäfer, 4.11.1944, 18:15. KTB Ia HGr Süd, NARA T311/159/7209731.

16 Daily report of LVII Panzer Corps, 5.11.1944. TsAMO, fu.500, inv.12462, f.236, p.280.

17 Morning situation report of Armeegruppe Fretter-Pico, 5.11.1944. TsAMO, fu.500, inv.12462, f.236, pp.257–258.

18 Daily situation report of LVII Panzer Corps, 5.11.1944. TsAMO, fu.500, inv.12462, f.236, p.280.

19 46th Army situation report #046/op, 21:30, 5.11.1944. TsAMO, fu.401. The report just says that 'by 18:00 some individual enemy tanks reached the northern limits of Alsóódabas and opened fire at the motorway.' 18:00 Moscow Time would mean 16:00 CET.

20 46th Army situation report #962/op, 20:00, 5.11.1944. TsAMO, fu.401.

21 War diary of 2nd Ukrainian Front, order No. 00708/op, 20:00, 5.11.1944. TsAMO, fu.240, inv.2779, f.1199, pp.31–32.

22 Daily situation report of III Panzer Corps, 5.11.1944. TsAMO, fu.500, inv.12462, f.236, pp.281, 283.

23 After-action report of 4th Guards Mechanised Corps. TsAMO, fu.3430, inv.1, f.161, p.24.

24 Morning report of Armeegruppe Fretter-Pico, 6.11.1944. TsAMO, fu.500, inv.12462, f.236, p.288.

25 After-action report of 4th Guards Mechanised Corps. TsAMO, fu.3430, inv.1, f.161, p.24.

26 46th Army situation report #964/op, 08:00, 6.11.1944. TsAMO, fu.401.

27 Morning report of Armeegruppe Fretter-Pico, 6.11.1944. TsAMO, fu.500, inv.12462, f.236, p.288.

28 Daily situation report of LVII Panzer Corps, 6.11.1944. TsAMO, fu.500, inv.12462, f.236, p.307.

29 After-action report of the 4th Guards Mechanised Corps. TsAMO, fu.3430, inv.1, f.161, pp.25, 27.

30 Anti-Tank Companies 1179 and 1257, 4.Company/Anti-Tank Battalion 661. Most probably, the operational Panthers of Panzer-Grenadier Division 'Feldherrnhalle' were also placed under 13th Panzer.

31 Daily situation report of III Panzer Corps, 6.11.1944. TsAMO, fu.500, inv.12462, f.236, p.309.

32 Ibid. Kegel-major, Csévi-major and Máté-tanya were small farms situated several kilometres south and southeast of Vasad. Today Csévi-major (on same wartime maps it is called Pusztacsév) exists as a small settlement called Csévharaszt; the rest no longer exist.

33 The five Panthers of the 23.Panzer-Division were definitely part of the group, too. Whether any other armored units were incorporated into Bradel's armored group is not known to me.

34 Daily situation report of III Panzer Corps, 6.11.1944. TsAMO, fu.500, inv.12462, f.236, p.310.

35 Rebentisch, op cit, p.440.

36 Shkadin, op cit, Vol.1, p.254.

Chapter 11

1 Midday situation report, 6 November 1944. Conference transcription. Reproduced in Heiber and Glantz, op. cit., p. 507.

2 Abt. Fremde Heere Ost (I), Nr. 4012/44 g. Kdos., 10.11.1944. NARA T78/646/000171.

3 Ibid. NARA T78/646/000172.

4 Ibid. NARA T78/646/000175-000176.

5 Ibid. NARA T78/646/000176-000177.

6 Operationsabteilung I/S, Nr. 11794/44 g. K., 10.11.1944. NARA T78/646/000185.

7 The figures given here by me are based not on the so-called 'author's estimates', but on primary sources (Axis documents) available in various archives. After many years of research, I have every reason to insist that these are the most correct figures pertaining to the strength of the garrison of 'Fortress Budapest'. The fact that during the siege a considerable number of locals were recruited (actually press-ganged) into the ranks of *Honvédség* remains totally overlooked by historians writing about the war in Hungary or the Eastern Front as a whole. Their number will remain forever unknown, but there are indications that up 30,000 additional men were put into service, thus bringing the number of Axis troops involved to about 130,000. I intend to discuss the subject in greater detail in a future book.

BIBLIOGRAPHY

Archives

Bundesarchiv-Militärarchiv, Freiburg: RH 2, RH 10, N528
Imperial War Museum, London: AL 1501, MI 14/270
National Archives, Washington DC: Microfilmed records series T78, T175, T311
Tsentral'nyi Arkhiv Ministerstva Oborony (Central Archive of the Ministry of Defence of the Russian
    Federation), Podolsk: funds 33, 240, 243, 244, 327, 401, 500, 3426, 3430, 37SK

Articles

Elvedi, I., 'Debretsenskaya operatsia i Sovetsko-Vengerskie peregovory o peremirii' *Voenno-Istoricheskii
    Zhurnal*, 1973, No 9
Gosztony, Peter, 'Fortress Budapest' *Hungarian Quarterly* No. 151, Autumn 1998
Gosztony, Peter, 'Der Kampf um Budapest 1944/45' *Wehrwissenschaftliche Rundschau* 1963, Nos. 10–12;
    1964, Nos. 1–3
Gundelach, Karl, 'Der allierte Luftkrieg gegen die deutsche Flugtribstoffversorgung' *Wehrwissenschaftliche
    Rundschau* 1963, No. 12
Ivanov, S. 'K 40-letiu Budapeshtenskoi Operatsii' *Voenno-Istoricheskii Zhurnal* 1984, No. 11
Macartney, C.A., 'Ungarns Weg aus dem Zweiten Weltkrieg' *Vierteiljahrhefte für Zeitgeschichte* 1966/1
Malashenko, Yevgeny, 'Wartime strategic direction of Soviet Armed Forces: Historical Lessons' *Military
    Thought* July 2003
Márai, Sándor, 'Journal' *Hungarian Quarterly* No. 171, Autumn 2003
Shlemin, Ivan, 'Osvobozhdenie *Vengrii' Voennyi Vestnik* 1964, No. 12
Shtemenko, S. 'Kak planirovalas poslednyaya kampania po razgromu gitlerovskoi Germanii' *Voenno-
    Istoricheskii Zhurnal* 1965, No. 5
Shumilov, Mikhail, 'Budapeshtenskaya operatsiya' *Voennyi Vestnik* 1969, No. 12
Srágli, L., 'American Capital and the Hungarian Oil Industry' *Hungarian Quarterly* No. 162, Summer 2001

Books

Abrosimov, Gleb, et al, (eds), *Gvardeiskii Nikolaevsko-Budapeshtenskii* (Moscow: Voenizdat, 1976)
Andryushchenko, Sergei, *Nachinali my na Slavutyche* (Moscow: Voenizdat, 1979)
Axworthy, Mark, et al, *Third Axis Fourth Ally* (London: Arms and Armour Press, 1995)
Baross, Gabor, *Hungary and Hitler* (Los Angeles: University of Southern California, 1964)
Bayer, Hanns, *Die Kavallerie der Waffen-SS* (Heidelberg: Selbstverlag, 1980)
Bialer, Seweryn (ed), *Stalin and his Generals* (Boulder and London: Westview Press, 1984)

Biryukov, Nikolai, *Tanki – frontu!* (Smolensk: Rusich, 2005)

Bouchery, Jean, *The British Soldier* (Paris: Histoire and Collections, 1999)

Braham, Randolph, *The Politics of Genocide* Vols. 1 and 2 (New York: Columbia University Press, 1981)

Bykov, Mikhail (ed), *Sovetskie asy 1941–1945* (Moscow: Yauza-Eksmo, 2008)

Chmelev A., *Proshla s boyami…* (Karta moldovenească: Kishinev, 1983)

Churchill, Winston, *The Second World War* Vol. 4 (London: Cassel and Co, 1954)

Davtyan, S.M., *Pyataya vozdushnaya* (Moscow: Voenizdat, 1990)

Drabkin, Artem (ed), *Ya dralsya s Panzerwaffe* (Moscow: Yauza-Eksmo, 2007)

Dragunsky, David A. (ed), *Ot Volgi do Pragi* (Moscow: Voenizdat, 1966)

Duffy, Christopher, *Red Storm on the Reich* (New York: Da Capo Press, 1993)

Eber, George F., *Pinball Games* (Bloomington: Trafford, 2010)

Eby, Cecil D., *Hungary at War* (University Park: The Pennsylvania State University Press, 1998)

Ehrman, John, *Grand Strategy* Vols. 5 and 6 (London: Her Majesty's Stationery Office, 1956)

Erickson, John, *The Road to Berlin* (London: Weidenfeld and Nicolson, 1983)

Escuadra Sanchez, Alfonso, *Feldherrnhalle: Forgotten Elite* (Bradford: Shelf Books, 1996)

Fenyo, Mario, *Hitler, Horthy and Hungary* (New Haven: Yale University Press, 1972)

Friessner, Hans, *Verratene Schlachten* (Hamburg: Holsten Verlag, 1956)

Gaedcke, Heinz, *Translation of the Taped Conversation with General Heinz Gaedcke, 13 April 1979* (Columbus: Battele, 1979)

Glantz, David M. (ed), *1986 Art of War Symposium: From the Vistula to the Oder: Soviet Offensive Operations, October 1944 – February 1945* (Carlisle: US Army War College, 1986)

Glantz, David M. and House, Jonathan, *When Titans Clashed* (Lawrence: University Press of Kansas, 1995)

Golubovich, V., *Marshal R.Y. Malinovsky* (Moscow: Voenizdat, 1983)

Gorbunov, Mikhail, *Soldat, polkovodets* (Moscow: Izdatelstvo politicheskoi literatury, 1972)

Gorkov, Yuri, *Kreml. Stavka. Genshtab* (Tver, 1995)

Gorodetsky, Gabriel, *Rokovoi samoobman* (Moscow: Rosspen, 2001)

Gosztony, Peter, *Endkampf an der Donau* (Vienna: Verlag Fritz Molden, 1969)

Grechko, Stepan, *Reshenia prinimalis' na zemle* (Moscow: Voenizdat, 1984)

Grigorenko, Petro, *Memoirs* (New York: W.W. Norton and Company, 1982)

Guderian, Heinz, *Panzer Leader* (London: Macdonald Futura, 1980)

Hajdu, Janos and Tóth, Bela, *The 'Volksbund' in Hungary* (Budapest: Pannonia Press, 1962)

Hake, Friedrich von, *Das waren wir – Das erlebten wir!* (Munich: Traditionsverband e.V. der 13. Panzer-Division, 1971)

Handler, Andrew, *A Man for All Connections* (Westport: Praeger, 1996)

Hastings, Max, *Armageddon* (London: Pan Macmillian, 2005)

Hilberg, Raul, *The Destruction of the European Jews* Vol. 2 (New York: Holmes and Meier, 1985)

Hillgruber, Andreas, *Hitler, König Carol and Antonescu* (Wiesbaden: Franz Steiner Verlag, 1954)

Hoensch, Jorg, *A History of Modern Hungary 1867–1994* (London: Pearson, 1996)

Horthy, Miklós, *Memoirs* (Safety Harbor: Simon Publications, 2000)

Irving, David, *Hitler's War and The War Path* (London: Focal Point Publications, 2002)

Jentz, Thomas (ed), *Panzertruppen,* Vol. 2 (Atglen: Schiffer Publishing, 1996)

Kanevsky, Alexander, *Vperedy razvedka shla* (Kiev: Ukraina, 1991)

Kiselev, A. (ed), *Polkovodtsy i voenachal'niki Velikoi Otechestvenoi* Vol. 1 (Moscow: Molodaya gvardia, 1971)

Khrushchev, Nikita, *Vremia. Liudi. Vlast* Vol. 1 (Moscow: Moskovskie Novosti, 1999)

Khrushchev, Nikita, *Memoirs of Nikita Khrushchev* Vol. 1 (State College: Penn State Press, 2004)

Knebel-Doeberitz, Rudolf von, *24th Panzer Division Operations* in Glantz, David M. (ed), *1986 Art of War Symposium*

Kolganov, K.S. et al. (eds), *Razvitie taktiki* (Moscow: Voenizdat, 1958)

Komjathy, Anthony Tihamer, *A Thousand Years of the Hungarian Art of War* (Toronto: Rakoczi Foundation, 1982)

Konev, Ivan (ed), *Za osvobozhdenie Chehoslovakii* (Moscow: Voenizdat, 1965)

Kursietis, Andris J., *The Hungarian Army and its Leadership in World War II* (Bayside: Axis Europa Books, 1996)

Lakatos, Géza, *As I Saw It* (Englewood: Universe Publishing Company, 1993)

Landwehr, Richard, *Budapest: The Stalingrad of the Waffen-SS* (Brookings: Siegrunen, 2001)

Lochmann, Dr Franz-Wilhelm, et al. (eds), *Combat History of Schwere Panzer-Abteilung 503* (Winnipeg: J.J. Fedorowicz Publishing, 2000)

Macartney, C.A., *Hungary: A Short History* (Edinburgh: University Press, 1962)

Macartney, C.A., *October Fifteenth* Vol.2 (Edinburgh: University Press, 1957)

Malakhov, M.M., *Osvobozhdenie Vengrii i Vostochnoi Avstrii* (Moscow: Voenizdat, 1965)

Malinovsky, Rodion, et al. (eds), *Budapest – Vena – Praga* (Moscow: Nauka, 1965)

McTaggart, Pat and Zwack, Peter B., *'Budapest 45'* in *Hitler's Army* (Conshohocken: Combined Publishing, 2000)

Minasyan, M., *Osvobozhdenie narodov Yougovostochnoi Evropy* (Moscow: Voenizdat, 1967)

Moshchansky, Ilya, *1944-y: Ot Korsuni do Belgrada* (Moscow: Veche, 2008)

Nagy-Talavera, Nicholas, *The Green Shirts and the Others* (Stanford: Hoover Institution Press, 1970)

Niehorster, Leo W.G., *The Royal Hungarian Army 1920–1945* Vol.1 (Bayside: Axis Europa Books, 1998)

Pierik, Perry, *Hungary 1944– 1945: The Forgotten Tragedy* (Nieuwegein: Aspekt, 1998)

Pintér, István and Szabó, László, *Criminals at Large* (Budapest: Pannonia Press, 1961)

Pliev, Issa, *Dorogami Voiny* (Moscow: Kniga, 1985)

Pogrebnoi, Alexei, *Lavinoi stali i ognya* (Moscow: Voenizdat, 1989)

Polcz, Alaine, *One Woman in the War: Hungary 1944–1945* (Budapest: Central European University Press, 2002)

Portugalsky, R. et al., *Marshal S.K. Timoshenko* (Moscow: Pobeda, 1994)

Punka, György. *Hungarian Aces of World War 2* (Oxford: Osprey Publishing, 2002)

Puskas, Andrei, *Vengria v gody Vtoroi Mirovoi Voiny* (Moscow: Nauka, 1966)

Radzievsky A.I. et al. (eds), *Armeiskie operatsii* (Moscow: Voenizdat, 1977)

Rebentisch, Ernst (ed), *Zum Kaukasus und zu den Tauern.* (Esslingen: Traditionsverband der 23. Panzer-Division, 1963)

Richardson, S., *The Secret History of the World War II* (New York: Richardson and Sterman, 1986)

Rudel, Hans-Ulrich, *Stuka Pilot* (New York: Ballantine Books, 1967)

Rzhevsky, O., *Stalin i Churchill* (Moscow: Nauka, 2004)

Samsonov, A.M. (ed), *Osvobozhdenie Vengrii ot Fashizma* (Moscow: Nauka, 1965)

Saveliev, Vasily and Popov, Nikolai, *Gvardeiskaya Nikolaevskaya* (Moscow: Voenizdat, 1978)

Schmidt, Gerhard, *Panzer-Artillerie-Regiments 73* (Walther Boetther Verlag: Bremen, 1959)

Schneider, Wolfgang, *Tigers in Combat,* Vol.1 (Winnipeg: J.J. Fedorowicz Publishing, 1994)

Seaton, Albert, *The Russo-German War 1941–45* (Novato: Presidio Press, 1993)

Senger und Etterlin, F.M. von, jr., *Die 24. Panzer-Division vormals 1. Kavallerie-Division 1939–1945* (Neckargemünd: Kurt Vowinckel Verlag, 1962)

Sharp, Charles C., *Soviet Order of Battle World War II* Vols.1–12 (West Chester: George F. Nafziger, 1995–1998)

Shmakov, V. (ed), *Vyshli na front 'Katiushi'* (Moscow: Moskovskii rabochii, 1982)

Shtemenko, Sergei, *Generalnyi Shtab v gody voiny* Vols.1 and 2 (Moscow: Voenizdat, 1989)

Shtemenko, Sergei, *The Last Six Months* (Garden City: Doubleday, 1977)

Shtemenko, Sergei, *The Soviet General Staff at War* Vol.2 (Moscow: Progress Publishers, 1986)

Shtempel, Mikhail, *Ot Astrahani do Veny* (Moscow: Nauka, 1983)

Sokolov, Boris, *Neizvestnyi Zhukov: portret bez retushi* (Minsk: Rodiola-plus, 2000)

Stoves, Rolf, *Comments on German Counterattacks in Hungary* in Glantz, David M. (ed), *1986 Art of War Symposium*

Stoves, Rolf, *1. Panzer Division 1935–1945* (Bad Nauheim: Verlag Hans-Henning Podzun, 1961)

Számvéber, Norbert, *Pánzélosütközet Kecskemét körzetében* in Szijj, Jolán (ed), *Ad Acta: A Hadtörténelmi Levéltár évkönyve 2004* (Budapest, 2005)

Számvéber, Norbert, *Páncélosok a Tiszántúlon* (Paktum Nyomdaipari Társaság: Budapest, 2002)

Szép, Ernõ, *The Smell of Humans* (Budapest: Central European University Press, 1994)

Tolubko, V.F. and Baryshev N.I., *Na yuzhnom flange* (Moscow: Nauka, 1973)

Trevor-Roper, Hugh, *Hitler's Table Talk, 1941–1944* (New York: Enigma Books, 2000)

Tronev, I.P., *Frontovye dorogi 66-go gvardeiskogo* in Shmakov, V. (ed), *Vyshli na front 'Katiushi'*

Ufimtsev, V.S. et al. (eds), *109-ya strelkovaya, a poprostu pehotnaya…* (Omsk: Omich, 1995)

Ungváry, Krisztián, *Battle for Budapest* (London: I.B.Tauris, 2003)

Veress, Csaba, *Magyarország hadikrónikája 1944–1945* Vol.1 (Militaria: Budapest, 2002)

Veress, Laura-Louise, *Clear the Line* (Cleveland: Prospero Publications, 1995)

Webster, Charles and Frankland, Noble (eds), *The Strategic Bomber Offensive against Germany* Vol.4 (London: Her Majesty's Stationery Office, 1961)

Wilmot, Chester, *The Struggle for Europe* (Ware: Wordsworth, 1997)

Yakimenko, A., *Prikroi, atakuyu! V atake – Metch* (Moscow: Yauza-Eksmo, 2005)

Zakharov, Matvei, *Budapeshtenskaya operatsiya* in Samsonov, A.M. (ed), *Osvobozhdenie Vengrii ot Fashizma*)

Zakharov, Matvei, *Marshal Sovetskogo Soyuza Rodion Malinovsky* in Kiselev, A. (ed), *Polkovodtsy i voenachal'niki Velikoi Otechestvenoi*

Zakharov, Matvei. *Osvobozhdenie yugo-vostochnoi i tsentral'noi Evropy voiskami 2-go i 3-go Ukrainskih frontov 1944–1945* (Moscow: Nauka, 1970)

Ziemke, Earl F., *Stalingrad to Berlin: The German Defeat in the East* (Washington DC: Office of the Chief of Military History, United States Army, 1968)

____ *Istoria na Vtorata Svetovna Voina 1939– 1945* Vols.9 and 10 (Sofia: Voenno izdatelstvo, 1979–1981)

____ *Istoria Velikoi Otechestvenoi Voiny Sovetskogo Soiuza 1941–1945* Vol.4 (Moscow: Voenizdat, 1963)

____ *Velikaya Otechestvennaya Voina 1941–1945* Vol.3 (Moscow: Nauka, 1999)

Published Document Anthologies

Esti, Béla (ed), *The Liberation of Hungary 1944–1945* (Budapest: Korvina, 1975)

Gryler A.N. et al. (eds), *Boevoi sostav Sovetskoi Armii* Vol.4 (Moscow: Voenizdat, 1988)

Heiber, Helmut and Glantz, David (eds), *Hitler and His Generals* (New York: Enigma Books, 2003)

Mehner, Kurt (ed), *Die Geheimen Tagesberichte der deutschen* Wehrmachtführung im Zweite Weltkrieg 1939– 1945 Vol.11 (Osnabrück: Biblio Verlag, 1985)

Patrushev N. et al. (eds), *Organy gosudarstvennoi bezopasnosti SSSR v Velikoi Otechestvenoi Voine* Vol.5/2 (Moscow: Kuchkovo pole, 2007)

Schramm, Pecy, et al. (eds), *Kriegstagebuch des Oberkommandos der* Wehrmacht Vol.4/1 (Munich: Bernard and Graefe, 1961)

Shkadin I.N. et al. (eds), *Geroi Sovetskogo Soyuza* Vols.1 and 2 (Moscow: Voenizdat, 1987 – 1988)

Zhilin P. et al. (eds), *Osvoboditelnaya missia Sovetskih vooruzhennyh sil v Evrope vo Vtoroi Mirovoi Voine* (Moscow: Voenizdat, 1985)

Zolotarev V. et al. (eds), *Velikaia Otechestvennaia Voina* Vols.13(2–2), 13(2–3), 14, 15(4–5), 15(4–10), 16(5–4), 21(10) and 23(12–4) (Moscow: Terra, 1995–2001)

Soviet General Staff Studies

Platonov S.P. et al. (eds), *Operatsii Sovetskih vooruzhennyh sil* Vol.3 (Moscow: Voenizdat, 1958)

Sbornik materialov po izucheniu opyta voiny No 21. Budapeshtenskaia operatsia (Moscow: Voenizdat, 1946)

Sbornik materialov po izucheniu opyta voiny No 23 (Moscow: Voenizdat, 1947)

PLACES INDEX